Equivalents

MISCELLANEOUS
Fruit is fresh unless otherwise st[...]
and frozen juice are the standar[...]
Canned pitted tart red cherries [...]
unless otherwise stated

1 orange=about 8 tablespoons juice
1 lemon=about 3 tablespoons juice
Grated rind 1 orange=about 1 tablespoon
Grated rind 1 lemon=1½-2 teaspoons
1 pound nuts=about 2 cups nut meats
¼ pound chopped nuts=1 cup (scant)
1 pound seedless raisins=about 3 cups
1 square chocolate=1 ounce
1 square chocolate=3 tablespoons
   cocoa+1 tablespoon butter

Temperatures

ALL TEMPERATURES IN THIS BOOK ARE FAHRENHEIT
Preheat the oven to the desired temperature for
baking. Set the refrigerator at the coldest point to
freeze desserts. Candy thermometer temperatures
for confections and frostings can be found at the
beginning of Chapter 11, page 242

180°=simmering point
212°=boiling point of water at sea level
75°-85°=lukewarm
110°-115°=warm (used in yeast recipes)

OVENS
200°-250°=very slow
300°=slow
325°=moderately slow
350°=moderate
375°=moderately hot
400°=hot
450°-500°=very hot
Over 500°=extremely hot

LADIES' HOME JOURNAL
DESSERT COOKBOOK

Ladies' Home Journal
DESSERT COOKBOOK

Edited by Carol Truax

Doubleday & Company, Inc., Garden City, New York

1964

Plate 1 (Frontispiece). Delicious Fruits. PEARS WITH RASP-BERRY SAUCE (Pears Christine), CHERRY SHERBET gar-nished with Raspberries, MACEDOINE OF FRESH FRUITS served in a Spanish melon, and FRENCH FRUIT TARTS.

FIRST EDITION

LIBRARY OF CONGRESS CATALOG CARD NUMBER 64-16206

CONTENTS

LIST OF COLOR PLATES

INTRODUCTION

by Carol Truax

For over eight decades women have chosen their favorite desserts from the *Ladies' Home Journal*. The American mother, the American housewife, the American hostess, and the American cook have wanted to keep these mouth-watering recipes. Here are over 1000 of them, dedicated to the proposition that not only should one never underestimate the power of a woman but also never underestimate the pleasure of a sweet.

Our mood when we leave the table depends to a large extent upon what we had for dessert. Desserts spell love and devotion. Meat and potatoes are taken for granted; desserts are for fun!

The dessert is the last course, a proper end, not something to be added haphazardly, but a very real part of any well-planned meal. There's a fitting end for every repast. This may be anything from an unadorned apple to an elaborate Zuppa Inglese. A light dessert after a heavy meal is indicated, but equally good and perhaps less usual is a light main course with an ending that is a conversation piece.

Surprising as it may seem, a number of desserts have far fewer calories than the dishes which have preceded them. Many desserts have fewer than 200 calories a serving—the same as a single broiled lamb chop, a small helping of roast chicken, a cup of cream soup, or a single hard roll with a pat of butter. For the benefit of weight-watchers, sauces and whipped creams should be served on the side. The dessert should be a major consideration in planning a sensibly balanced luncheon or dinner.

There are times for sweets that do not end a meal: teacakes or coffeecake at tea time or at the bridge table; "Come for dessert and coffee" parties; plates of sugared doughnuts, warm from the kettle, or dainty lace cookies to nibble with a cool drink, day or night. Desserts are not always at dessert time!

Do not scorn aids such as pie, cake, cooky, and pudding mixes. Many cooks feel much more confident of achieving a heavenly angel-food cake from a mix than by starting from scratch. Short cuts to good eating are wonderful if you are sure it is *good* eating. Take the trouble to personalize these useful products. For example, try using rum for part of the moisture in the pie crust mix for an apple pie or a little grated Cheddar cheese in a crust for mince pie. In a chocolate pudding a teaspoon of instant coffee and a few nuts will add your personal touch. Puddings can be glorified by sauces; use your ingenuity to find a taste and texture contrast, secure in the knowledge that the basic pudding is sound and easy to make.

The *Ladies' Home Journal Dessert Cookbook* contains countless cakes and cookies, plentiful pies and pastry, seventy-seven sauces, fifty frostings, and fabulous fruits. Make the dessert of your choice and try to make it a memorable one, but *do make a dessert*. Remember, a festive dessert is what makes the meal festive.

LADIES' HOME JOURNAL
DESSERT COOKBOOK

KEY TO USE OF RECIPES

The *asterisk* (*) following items in recipes (such as Pastry for 9-Inch 2-Crust Pie* or Zabaglione Sauce*) indicates that the recipe is in this book (consult index) and the method of preparation is described.

TEMPERATURES are Fahrenheit
Preheat oven to desired temperature for baking
Set refrigerator dial at coldest point to freeze desserts

MEASUREMENTS are level
Sift flour before measuring
Sift confectioners' sugar after measuring
Measure brown sugar firmly packed
Pinch or dash is less than ⅛ teaspoon

FRUIT is fresh unless otherwise stated
Wash all berries gently. Wash strawberries before you hull them to avoid loss of juice.
Wash whole fruit whether it is to be peeled or not
Frozen fruit packages and frozen juice cans are the standard small size
Canned pitted tart red cherries are water-packed unless otherwise stated

SOUR CREAM and buttermilk are the commercial variety

CHOCOLATE is baking chocolate unless otherwise stated

GLYCERINE, oil of peppermint, and rose water are available at drug stores

CHAPTER ONE

Captivating Cakes

Cakes do honor to your guests and show devotion to the family. Cakes dress up a holiday. Imagine a birthday or wedding without birthday cake or wedding cake!

There is only one rule to follow when making a cake, and that is to *follow the rule*. You must not improvise with cake recipes as you may with sauces for ice cream or with combinations of fruits. You must be as exact as an alchemist mixing a love potion.

In mixing cake batter, if the directions call for adding sifted dry ingredients alternately with liquids, always begin and end with the dry ingredients. The pans used in baking layer cakes are usually round and are often lined on the bottom with waxed paper. Sheet cakes are baked in square or rectangular pans 2 inches deep; they should be lined on the bottom with waxed paper only if the cake is to be turned out. A loaf-cake pan is usually $9 \times 5 \times 2\frac{3}{4}$ inches. Cakes should be baked in the middle of a preheated oven, the pans arranged so they do not crowd each other. Heat should circulate freely around each pan. Test cakes for doneness at the minimum baking time given in recipes. Open the door just enough to test. Do not open the oven door before that. Touch the cake lightly with your finger; if the cake springs back to the touch, leaving no imprint, it is done. Another test is to insert a tester or toothpick into the center of the cake; if it comes out clean, the cake is done. Cakes tend to pull slightly away from the edge of the pan when done.

Frostings make the cake. In the frosting chapter you will find a list of basic cakes and suggestions for mouth-watering frostings and fillings appropriate to the cakes.

Would you both eat your cake and have your cake?
John Heywood, *Proverbs*

WHITE CAKE
(Basic)

> 2¼ cups flour
> 1½ cups sugar
> 3¼ teaspoons baking powder
> 1 teaspoon salt
> ½ cup hydrogenated vegetable shortening
> 1 cup milk
> 4 egg whites
> 1 teaspoon vanilla

Sift the flour, sugar, baking powder, and salt together in a large bowl. Add the shortening and milk. Beat until dampened and then 1½ minutes at low speed on an electric mixer or 250 strokes by hand. Add the egg whites and vanilla. Continue beating for another 1½ minutes with the mixer or 250 strokes by hand. Pour the batter into 2 greased and floured 9-inch cake pans. Bake in a 350° oven for 25–30 minutes, until cake shrinks slightly from sides of pan, is golden on top, and springs back when lightly touched in the center. Remove from oven and cool 5 minutes in pans before turning out on cake racks. Cover with cloth until cooled. Pineapple Orange Frosting* is recommended. Serves 8–10.

DELICATE WHITE LAYER CAKE

> 1 cup butter
> 2 cups sugar
> 2 teaspoons vanilla
> 1 teaspoon almond flavoring
> 3 cups cake flour
> 1 tablespoon baking powder
> ½ teaspoon salt
> 1 cup milk
> 6 egg whites

Cream the butter and gradually add the sugar. Cream until light and fluffy. Add vanilla and almond flavoring. Sift the flour with the baking powder and salt 3 times. Add alternately with the milk to the creamed mixture, ending with flour. Beat until smooth. Beat the egg whites until a soft peak forms and gently fold into the batter. Line the bottoms of two greased 9-inch cake pans with waxed paper. Pour the batter into the pans and bake in a 375° oven for 30–35 minutes. Turn out on rack, remove paper, and cool before frosting. Serves 8–10.

*See *Key to Use of Recipes,* page 6.

LADY BALTIMORE CAKE

Use a Delicate White Layer Cake* with Lady Baltimore Filling and Frosting.* Bake the cake in 3 cake pans, greased and lined on the bottom with waxed paper, for 20–25 minutes.

TWO-EGG LAYER CAKE

> ½ cup butter
> 1 cup sugar
> 2 eggs
> 1 teaspoon vanilla
> 1¾ cups cake flour
> ½ teaspoon salt
> 2½ teaspoons baking powder
> ½ cup milk

Cream the butter and gradually add the sugar. Cream until light and fluffy. Add the well-beaten eggs and vanilla and mix well. Sift the flour with salt and baking powder. Add to the first mixture alternately with the milk. Divide the batter between two 8-inch cake pans lined on the bottom with waxed paper. Bake in a 375° oven for 20–25 minutes. Turn out on racks, remove paper, and cool before frosting. Serves 8.

CHIFFON CAKE

> 2¼ cups cake flour
> 1½ cups sugar
> 1 tablespoon baking powder
> 1 teaspoon salt
> ½ cup cooking oil
> 5 egg yolks
> 2 teaspoons grated lemon or orange rind
> 2 teaspoons vanilla
> 1 cup (8–10) egg whites
> ½ teaspoon cream of tartar

Sift the flour, sugar, baking powder, and salt together into a bowl. Make a well in the center and add in this order: the oil, egg yolks, ¾ cup cold water, lemon rind, and vanilla. Beat until batter is satin-smooth. In a large bowl beat the egg whites until slightly foamy, add the cream of tartar, and beat until a stiff peak forms. Pour the egg-yolk mixture gradually over the surface of the egg whites, gently folding it in as you pour. Continue to fold until completely blended. Pour into an ungreased 10-inch tube pan and bake in a 325° oven for 1 hour and 10 minutes, until top springs back to the touch. Cool cake in pan, upside down, 1–2 hours, until the cake is completely cold. To remove cake from the pan, loosen from sides and center tube with a spatula, invert, and hit edge of pan sharply on table. Serves 10–12.

GOLD LOAF CAKE

½ cup butter
1 cup sugar
1 teaspoon vanilla
1½ teaspoons grated orange rind
4 egg yolks
1¾ cups cake flour
½ teaspoon salt
1½ teaspoons baking powder
½ cup milk

Cream the butter with the sugar until light and fluffy. Add the vanilla, orange rind, and egg yolks which have been beaten until thick. Sift the cake flour, salt, and baking powder together. Add to creamed mixture alternately with the milk, ending with flour, and beating well after each addition. Pour into a greased and floured 9×5×2¾-inch loaf pan. Bake in 350° oven for 1 hour. Turn out and cool on rack. Serves 8.

WHIPPED-CREAM CAKE

1½ cups heavy cream
3 eggs
2¼ cups cake flour
1½ cups sugar
2 teaspoons baking powder
½ teaspoon salt
1½ teaspoons vanilla

Whip the cream until stiff. Beat the eggs until thick and lemon-colored and fold into the cream. Sift the flour, sugar, baking powder, and salt together. Fold very gently into the cream mixture and blend in the vanilla. Pour into two 8-inch cake pans lined on the bottom with waxed paper. Bake in a 325° oven for 30 minutes, until cake pulls away from sides of the pan. Turn out of pan, remove paper, and cool before frosting. Serves 8–10.

GENOISE

4 eggs
1 teaspoon vanilla
⅔ cup sugar
¾ cup flour
6 tablespoons melted butter

In a 3-quart double boiler beat the eggs, vanilla, and sugar together until frothy. Set over a pan of *barely* simmering water (the water must never bubble) and continue to beat until the mixture thickens to the consistency of mayonnaise, becomes light-colored, and triples in bulk; this will take about 10 minutes with an electric beater. Remove from heat. Place over a pan of cold water and continue to beat at low speed until the mixture is cool. Gradually fold in the flour alternately with the cooled melted butter; continue folding until well mixed. Pour into a 9×9×2-inch pan lined with waxed paper. Bake in a 350° oven for 25–30 minutes, until cake pulls away from sides of pan slightly and top springs back to a light touch. Cool in pan on a rack for 5 minutes before turning out. Peel off waxed paper. You may also bake the mixture in two layer-cake pans or a 15½×10½×1-inch jelly-roll pan; bake in a 350° oven for 15–20 minutes and test as above. The cake from the 9-inch square pan is good for cutting into shapes for petits fours. Genoise is often used as a foundation for special anniversary or birthday cakes.

ORANGE SPONGECAKE

8 eggs
1⅓ cups sugar
¼ cup orange juice
1 tablespoon grated orange rind
¼ teaspoon salt
1 teaspoon cream of tartar
1¼ cups cake flour

Beat the egg yolks until very thick and lemon-colored, gradually adding ⅔ cup sugar. Add the orange juice and grated rind and continue to beat until the mixture is again very thick and light. Sprinkle the salt and cream of tartar over the egg whites and beat until foamy. Gradually add the remaining sugar, beating until very soft mounds form; the whites should flow gently when the bowl is tipped. Fold the yolk mixture into the whites. Sift ¼ of the flour over the surface and gently fold it in. Repeat with the remaining flour mixture, a part at a time. Pour into an ungreased 10-inch tube pan and bake in a 300° oven for 1 hour and 10 minutes, until cake springs back to the touch. Cool cake in pan, upside down. Then loosen from sides and center tube with a knife and gently remove cake. Frost or cover with whipped cream if you wish. Serves 10–12.

IMPERIAL SPONGECAKE

1 cup cake flour
¾ teaspoon cream of tartar
1¼ cups sugar
6 eggs
¼ teaspoon salt
1 teaspoon vanilla or orange flavoring

Sift the cake flour and cream of tartar together 4 times. Mix the sugar with ½ cup water and boil until syrup reaches hard-ball stage (250°). Beat the egg whites with salt until a soft peak forms. Pour hot syrup over egg whites in a fine stream, beating as you pour. Beat until cool. Beat the egg yolks until very thick and fold into mixture. Fold in the sifted dry ingredients. Add vanilla or orange flavoring. Pour into an ungreased 10-inch tube pan. Bake in a 325° oven for 1 hour. Invert cake to cool before removing carefully from pan. Serves 10–12.

VICTORIA SPONGE   (Plate 35)

1 cup butter
1 teaspoon vanilla
1 cup sugar
2 cups flour
2 teaspoons baking powder
4 eggs
½ cup raspberry preserves
Confectioners' sugar

Cream the butter and vanilla. Gradually add the sugar and continue creaming until very light and fluffy. Sift the flour and baking powder together. Add alternately with the well-beaten eggs. Spoon into 2 greased and floured 9-inch cake pans. Bake in a 350° oven for 20–25 minutes. Cool for a few minutes in the pans, then remove to racks. Just before serving, spread one layer with the raspberry preserves. Top with the second layer and sprinkle with confectioners' sugar. Serves 8–10.

SPONGE LAYER CAKE

1 cup milk
11 egg yolks
2 cups sugar
2¼ cups cake flour
2 teaspoons baking powder
⅛ teaspoon salt
1½ teaspoons vanilla
½ cup melted butter

Eggnog Sauce* or other filling
Frosting or whipped cream
Flaked coconut (optional)

Scald the milk. Beat the egg yolks until very thick and lemon-colored. Add the sugar slowly, beating well after each addition. Sift the cake flour, baking powder, and salt together. Add the dry ingredients alternately with the scalded milk and vanilla. Fold in the melted butter and mix just enough to make smooth. Pour into two 9-inch cake pans lined on the bottom with waxed paper. Bake in a 350° oven for 30–35 minutes. Cool in pans 10 minutes before turning out. Remove paper and cool. Fill with Eggnog Sauce or other filling of your choice. Frost the cake with your favorite frosting, Boiled* or Seven-Minute,* or with whipped cream, and sprinkle with coconut if you wish. Serves 8–10.

LEMON SPONGECAKE

6 eggs
3 tablespoons lemon juice
1 tablespoon grated lemon rind
¼ teaspoon salt
1¼ cups superfine sugar
½ teaspoon cream of tartar
1¼ cups cake flour

Beat the egg yolks with the lemon juice, lemon rind, and salt. Gradually add ½ cup sugar and continue to beat until very thick and lemon-colored. Beat the egg whites until frothy. Add the cream of tartar and continue to beat, adding ½ cup sugar a tablespoonful at a time. When the meringue is stiff and glossy, gently fold in the yolk mixture. Sift the flour with the remaining sugar and carefully fold into the egg mixture. Turn into an ungreased 10-inch tube pan. Bake in a 325° oven for about 55 minutes, until the cake springs back to the touch. Invert cake to cool before removing from pan. Serves 10–12.

POUNDCAKE I

2¼ cups cake flour
½ teaspoon baking powder
¼ teaspoon salt
1 teaspoon nutmeg (optional)
1 cup butter
1 cup sugar
2 tablespoons lemon juice
5 eggs
2 tablespoons brandy (optional)

Sift together 3 times the flour, baking powder, salt, and the nutmeg if you wish. Cream the butter and sugar until light and fluffy. Add the lemon juice and egg yolks which have been beaten until very thick. Add the brandy if you wish. Fold in the egg whites, beaten until a soft peak forms, and then the dry ingredients. Pour into a greased and floured 9×5×2¾-inch loaf pan. Bake in a 325° oven for about 1 hour. Serves 10–12.

POUNDCAKE II   (Plate 3)

3½ cups flour
1 tablespoon baking powder
¼ teaspoon salt
1 cup butter
2 cups sugar
4 eggs
1 cup milk
1 teaspoon vanilla

Sift the flour, baking powder, and salt together. Cream the butter and sugar together until light and fluffy. Add the eggs one at a time, beating well after each addition. Add the milk and dry ingredients alternately, beating well; then add the vanilla. Pour the batter into two 9×5×2¾-inch loaf pans which have been well greased and dusted with flour. Bake in a 325° oven for 1 hour and 20–25 minutes, until cakes have pulled away from sides of the pans and are golden brown. Remove from oven, cool 5 minutes, and then turn out on racks to cool. You may decorate if you wish with strips of angelica held in place with warm corn syrup; then dust lightly with confectioners' sugar. Serves 18–20.

CHOCOLATE POUNDCAKE

3 ounces unsweetened chocolate
2¾ cups cake flour
½ teaspoon baking soda
1½ teaspoons salt
¾ teaspoon cream of tartar
1¾ cups sugar
1 cup butter
⅔ cup milk
1 teaspoon vanilla
3 eggs plus 1 egg yolk

Melt the chocolate and cool slightly. Sift the flour, soda, salt, cream of tartar, and sugar together. Cream the butter just until softened. Sift in the dry ingredients. Add the milk and

vanilla all at once and beat for 2 minutes. Add the eggs and chocolate and beat about 1 minute longer, scraping the bowl and spoon often. Pour into a 9-inch tube pan lined on the bottom with waxed paper. Bake in a 350° oven for 60–70 minutes. Loosen sides of cake with a spatula, turn out of pan, remove paper, and cool. Serves 12.

LEMON-BUTTER POUNDCAKE

2 (1 lb. 1 oz.) packages poundcake mix
2½ teaspoons grated lemon rind
¼ cup butter
⅔ cup sugar
2 tablespoons lemon juice

Prepare both packages of cake mix according to package directions; stir in 1 teaspoon lemon rind. Spoon into a lightly greased and floured 10-inch tube pan and bake in a 325° oven for 1¼–1½ hours. While the cake is baking, melt the butter in a small saucepan. Add remaining ingredients with 2 tablespoons water and cook until all sugar is dissolved, about 5 minutes. Remove from heat. When cake is done, remove from oven and set on a rack. Pour the lemon glaze evenly over the cake in the pan. Let the cake cool completely before removing from the pan. Serves 12–14.

ANGEL-FOOD CAKE

1½ cups sugar
1 cup plus 3 tablespoons cake flour
¼ teaspoon salt
1¼ teaspoons cream of tartar
1½ cups egg whites
1¼ teaspoons vanilla
½ teaspoon almond flavoring

Sift the sugar and flour together twice. Sprinkle the salt and cream of tartar over the egg whites and beat or whip until very soft mounds form; the whites should flow gently when the bowl is tipped. (Not overbeating the egg whites is the secret of making this cake.) Sift about ¼ of the flour mixture over the surface of the whites and gently fold it in. Repeat with remaining flour mixture a portion at a time. Fold in vanilla and almond flavoring. Pour into an ungreased 10-inch tube pan and bake in a 300° oven for 1 hour and 5 minutes, until the cake springs back to the touch. Cool cake in pan, upside down, 1–2 hours. Then loosen from sides and center tube with a knife and gently remove cake. Serves 10–12.

SPICED ANGEL-FOOD CAKE

Add ½ teaspoon nutmeg, 1 teaspoon cinnamon, and ⅛ teaspoon cloves to the flour before sifting, and proceed as for Angel-Food Cake.*

NUT ANGEL-FOOD CAKE

Add 1 cup finely chopped walnuts or black walnuts, ½ cup chopped toasted almonds, or ¾ cup finely chopped mixed nuts to the Angel-Food Cake* batter just before putting it into the pan for baking.

CHOCOLATE ANGEL-FOOD CAKE

Substitute ¼ cup cocoa for ¼ cup of the flour in Angel-Food Cake.* Then sift the combined flour and cocoa 5 times. Proceed as for Angel-Food Cake.

MARBLE ANGEL-FOOD CAKE

Make the batter for Angel-Food Cake* as usual. Divide in half. Fold 2 tablespoons cocoa into half of the batter. Alternate the batters in the tube pan and bake as usual.

LEMON ANGEL LAYER CAKE   (Plate 3)

1 (10-inch) Angel-Food Cake*

LEMON FILLING
½ cup sugar
2 tablespoons butter
Pinch salt
1 tablespoon grated lemon rind
3 egg yolks
2 tablespoons lemon juice

LEMON BUTTER FROSTING
¼ cup butter
1¾ cups confectioners' sugar
1 egg white
1½ teaspoons grated lemon rind
2 tablespoons milk

Cut the cake into three layers of equal thickness, using a very sharp knife.

Lemon Filling. Blend all of the ingredients together in a double boiler. Cook, uncovered, over simmering water until thickened, stirring from time to time. Cool and spread between the layers of the cake.

Lemon Butter Frosting. Cream butter; add 1 cup sugar gradually. Add egg white and beat until light. Then add remaining sugar, lemon rind, and milk if needed to make proper spreading consistency. Frost top and sides of cake. Serves 12.

ORANGE ANGEL CAKE

1 (10-inch) Angel-Food Cake*
1 cup orange juice
3 cups sour cream
6 tablespoons confectioners' sugar
¼ cup Cointreau
2 tablespoons grated orange rind

Slice the cake in half. Pour ½ cup orange juice over the cut side of each layer, pricking the cake with a fork so that all the juice will be absorbed. Set aside. Mix the sour cream with confectioners' sugar, Cointreau, and grated orange rind, reserving about 1 teaspoon of rind. Spread about ⅓ of this mixture over the bottom layer of cake. Cover with the top layer and spread the remaining cream mixture over the top and sides. Sprinkle the remaining orange rind over all. Chill 3–4 hours before serving. Serves 10–12.

EASY PEPPERMINT ANGEL CAKE

1 package angel-food cake mix
1 package fluffy white frosting mix
½ cup crushed peppermint candy

Bake the cake in a 10-inch tube pan, following package directions. Cool as directed and remove from pan. Place on cake plate. Prepare the frosting, following package directions. Frost the top and sides of cake and sprinkle with the candy. Serves 10–12.

TWICE-FROSTED ANGEL CAKE

1 (10-inch) Angel-Food Cake*
2 tablespoons instant coffee
2 cups heavy cream
Seven-Minute Frosting*
1 teaspoon vanilla
Yellow food coloring (optional)

Split the cake twice, making 3 layers. Add the instant coffee to the cream and beat until stiff. Use no sugar. Spread the cream on 2 bottom layers and put the 3 layers together; then frost the top and sides with cream. Chill overnight. Add vanilla to the frosting and add a few drops of yellow food coloring if you wish. Frost top and sides of cake; be careful not to work the cream into the frosting. If you wish to decorate the cake, save about ½ cup of frosting without yellow coloring. Put frosting into pastry bag and make scattered flowers or dots on the top and sides of the cake. Serves 10–12.

DAFFODIL CAKE

1 package angel-food cake mix
½ teaspoon lemon flavoring
6 egg yolks
*Seven-Minute Frosting**

Prepare the angel-food cake batter according to package directions and add the lemon flavoring. Divide the batter in half. Meanwhile, beat the egg yolks until very thick and lemon-colored. Carefully fold them into half of the cake batter, a little at a time. Pour the yellow batter into an ungreased 10-inch tube pan and top with the remaining white batter. Bake according to package directions. Invert until cool. Then loosen and remove cake. Frost with a Seven-Minute Frosting. Serves 10–12.

BASIC DEVIL'S-FOOD CAKE

1½ cups sugar
1½ cups milk
2 eggs plus 1 egg yolk
2½ ounces unsweetened chocolate
½ cup butter
2 cups cake flour
½ teaspoon salt
1½ teaspoons baking soda
1 teaspoon vanilla

Combine ½ cup sugar, ½ cup milk, 1 egg yolk, and chocolate in a double boiler. Cook, stirring occasionally, until mixture is smooth and slightly thickened. Remove from heat and cool. Cream the butter with remaining sugar until light and fluffy. Add the 2 eggs, well beaten, and mix thoroughly. Sift the flour and salt together and add to mixture alternately with remaining milk. Dissolve the soda in 1 tablespoon hot water and add to batter. Flavor with vanilla. Last, blend in the cooled chocolate mixture. Pour into two 9-inch cake pans lined

on the bottom with waxed paper. Bake in a 350° oven for ½ hour. Turn out of pans and pull off paper. Cool and frost. Serves 8–10.

DEVIL'S-FOOD CAKE

⅔ cup cocoa
2½ cups flour
1 teaspoon baking soda
1½ teaspoons baking powder
¼ teaspoon salt
½ cup butter
2 cups sugar
3 eggs
1 teaspoon vanilla
1 cup sour milk or buttermilk

Dissolve the cocoa in ½ cup boiling water and cool. Sift the flour, soda, baking powder, and salt together. Cream the butter with the sugar. Add the egg yolks, vanilla, and the cocoa mixture and beat well. Add the dry ingredients alternately with the milk. Beat the egg whites until a soft peak forms, and stir into the batter. Pour into two 9-inch cake pans lined on the bottom with waxed paper. Bake in a 375° oven for ½ hour. Turn out of pans onto racks, remove paper, and cool. Frost with your favorite frosting. Serves 8–10.

SOUR-CREAM DEVIL'S-FOOD CAKE

3 eggs
1¼ cups sugar
1 teaspoon vanilla
1¼ cups cake flour
¾ teaspoon salt
1 teaspoon baking soda
1 cup sour cream
2 ounces unsweetened chocolate

Beat the egg yolks until thick and lemon-colored. Add ½ cup sugar gradually, beating until very thick. Add the vanilla and mix well. Sift the flour, salt, and soda together. Add the dry ingredients slowly to the egg mixture, alternately with sour cream and melted chocolate. Beat until smooth. Beat egg whites until foamy and add remaining sugar by spoonfuls, beating after each addition until sugar is dissolved. Fold this lightly but thoroughly into the batter. Pour into two 8-inch cake pans lined on the bottom with waxed paper. Bake in a 375° oven for ½ hour. Remove from pans, pull off paper; cool before frosting. Serves 8.

BUTTERMILK DEVIL'S-FOOD CAKE

2 cups cake flour
½ cup cocoa
1 teaspoon baking soda
½ teaspoon salt
¾ cup butter
1 teaspoon vanilla
1½ cups sugar
2 eggs
½ cup buttermilk

Sift the flour, cocoa, soda, and salt together. Cream the butter with vanilla and sugar until light and fluffy. Add the well-beaten eggs; beat until blended. Add the sifted dry ingredients alternately with buttermilk, beating well after each addition. Now pour in ½ cup boiling water and beat until smooth. Divide between two 8-inch cake pans lined on the bottom with waxed paper. Bake in a 350° oven for 35 minutes. Turn out on racks and remove paper. Cool before frosting. Serves 8.

SOUR-MILK DEVIL'S-FOOD CAKE

½ cup butter
4 ounces unsweetened chocolate
2 cups sugar
2 eggs
2 cups flour
1 teaspoon salt
2 teaspoons baking powder
½ teaspoon baking soda
2 teaspoons vanilla
½ cup sour milk or buttermilk

Heat the butter, 1 cup water, and chocolate in a double boiler until chocolate is melted. Add the sugar, mix well, and cool by putting top part of double boiler in a pan of cold water. When mixture is cool, add the eggs and beat thoroughly with a rotary beater. Sift the flour, salt, baking powder, and baking soda together. Add to chocolate mixture and beat hard with a spoon until very smooth. Add vanilla and sour milk or buttermilk. Beat smooth again. Pour mixture into two 9-inch cake pans lined with waxed paper. Bake in 350° oven for 30–35 minutes. Cool in pans a few minutes before loosening cakes and turning out on racks. Remove waxed paper and cool. Put layers together with Pecan Filling* and frost with Sea Foam Frosting,* or use your favorite filling and frosting. Serves 8–10.

CHOCOLATE-CHIP CAKE

½ cup butter
1⅓ cups sugar
¾ teaspoon vanilla
¼ teaspoon almond flavoring
2¼ cups flour
½ teaspoon salt
1 tablespoon baking powder
1 cup milk
3 egg whites
1½ ounces unsweetened chocolate

Cream the butter and 1 cup sugar until light and fluffy. Add the vanilla and almond flavoring. Sift the flour, salt, and baking powder together. Add alternately to the creamed mixture with the milk. Beat the egg whites until a soft peak forms and add the remaining sugar a tablespoon at a time, beating well after each addition. Fold into the batter. Shave the chocolate and fold in last. Pour into two 9-inch cake pans lined on the bottom with waxed paper. Bake in a 375° oven for 20–25 minutes. Turn out, remove paper, and cool before frosting. Serves 8–10.

CHOCOLATE SQUARE—ALL BLACK
(Plate 3)

3 cups flour
1½ teaspoons salt
¾ cup shortening
2½ cups sugar
3 eggs
¾ cup cocoa mixed with 1½ cups hot strong coffee
1½ teaspoons vanilla
1½ teaspoons baking soda
*Chocolate Butter Cream Frosting**

Sift the flour with salt. Cream the shortening until light; then add sugar gradually, beating all the while until mixture is fluffy. Beat in the eggs one at a time, then the cocoa-coffee mixture. Add vanilla and then fold in the flour. Dissolve the soda in ¾ cup boiling water and mix into the batter. Pour into two 9×9×2-inch pans lined on the bottom with waxed paper. Bake in a 350° oven for about 50 minutes, until cake springs back to the touch. Let cool slightly, then turn out on a rack. Remove paper and cool. Frost the cake with Chocolate Butter Cream Frosting or other chocolate frosting. Garnish with grated coconut if you wish. Serves 12.

MOCHA CAKE

½ cup very hot extra-strong coffee
2 ounces unsweetened chocolate
½ cup butter
2 cups brown sugar
2 eggs
2 cups flour
1 teaspoon baking soda
½ teaspoon salt
½ cup sour milk or buttermilk
1 teaspoon vanilla

Heat the coffee and chocolate until the chocolate has melted. Cool. Cream the butter and sugar until light and fluffy. Add the eggs one at a time, beating well after each addition. Sift the flour, soda, and salt together. Add to the sugar mixture alternately with the sour milk or buttermilk, beginning and ending with dry ingredients. Then add the chocolate mixture and vanilla. Mix well and pour into an 8×8×2-inch pan lined on the bottom with waxed paper. Bake for about 1 hour in a 325° oven. Turn out of pan and pull off paper. Cool before frosting. Good with a chocolate or mocha frosting. Serves 6–8.

SWEET-CHOCOLATE CAKE

¼ pound sweet baking chocolate
1 cup butter
2 cups sugar
4 eggs
1 teaspoon vanilla
½ teaspoon salt
1 teaspoon baking soda
2½ cups cake flour
1 cup buttermilk

Melt the chocolate with ½ cup water over hot water. Cream the butter and sugar until light and fluffy. Add the egg yolks one at a time, beating well after each addition. Add the cooled chocolate and vanilla. Sift the salt, soda, and flour together. Add alternately with the buttermilk, beating after each addition. Beat until batter is smooth. Beat the egg whites until a very stiff peak forms. Fold into the batter. Pour into three 9-inch cake pans lined on the bottom with waxed paper. Bake in a 350° oven 30–40 minutes. Remove from pans, pull off waxed paper, and cool before frosting. Serves 12–14.

CHOCOLATE FUDGE CAKE

4 ounces unsweetened chocolate
½ cup butter
2 cups sugar
2 eggs
2¼ cups cake flour
1 tablespoon baking powder
¼ teaspoon salt
1½ cups milk
1 teaspoon vanilla

Melt the chocolate and let cool. Cream the butter and gradually add the sugar, beating until light and fluffy. Add the well-beaten egg yolks and the chocolate. Mix well. Sift the flour, baking powder, and salt together and add alternately with the milk. Beat well after each addition. Add the vanilla. Fold in the stiffly beaten egg whites. Pour into two 9-inch cake pans lined on the bottom with waxed paper. Bake in a 350° oven for ½ hour. Turn out on racks, remove paper, and cool. Especially good with a coffee or mocha frosting. Serves 8–10.

CHOCOLATE RIBBON CAKE

2½ cups flour
1 tablespoon baking powder
1 teaspoon salt
⅔ cup butter
1⅔ cups sugar
¼ teaspoon almond flavoring
3 eggs
1¼ cups skim milk
⅛ teaspoon baking soda
3 tablespoons cocoa

Sift the flour, baking powder, and salt together twice. Cream the butter and sugar until light and fluffy. Add the almond flavoring and the eggs one at a time, beating after each addition. Add the flour mixture a little at a time alternately with the milk, beating after each addition and ending with flour. Line the bottoms of two 9-inch cake pans with waxed paper. Spoon exactly half the batter into one cake pan. Add soda mixed with 1 teaspoon water and the cocoa to remaining batter. Spoon into the second pan. Bake in a 350° oven for 30–35 minutes, until tops spring back to the touch. Cool 5 minutes; then turn out on racks and remove paper. Cool thoroughly. If you wish to make 4 layers, split the cake layers in half, using a sharp knife. Alternate the colors and put together with frosting. Serves 8–10.

CUTTING CAKES

To cut cake, use a serrated knife or a sharp pointed knife with a thin blade. Insert the point of the knife, then slice with a gentle sawing motion, keeping the point down and the handle up. If the knife is sticky, wipe it after each piece is cut; if the frosting is very sticky, dip the knife into hot water. A layer cake is usually cut into pie-shaped pieces.

To cut a large layer cake, first cut an inner circle halfway to the center, then cut wedge-shaped pieces from the outer circle. When this is all cut, make pie-shaped pieces of the smaller cake, cutting as you would any layer cake. For daintier small pieces from a large layer cake, cut the cake first in quarters and then slice each quarter in parallel slices. The pieces closest to the middle will be larger and may be cut in half.

A sheet cake may be cut in half or thirds lengthwise and then in rectangular, square, or diamond-shaped pieces with parallel or diagonal cross cuts.

A loaf cake is usually sliced. The slices may be cut in half.

To cut a tiered wedding cake, cut vertically around and through the bottom tier at the base of the center tier. Cut slices of cake and then cut vertically around and through the center tier at the base of the top tier. Cut slices of cake and serve. Go back to the bottom tier and cut slices again. Next, remove the top tier of the cake and cut into wedge-shaped pieces. (Sometimes this tier is frozen and saved for the first wedding anniversary celebration.) At this point it is usually easier to remove each round of cake to a plate before cutting.

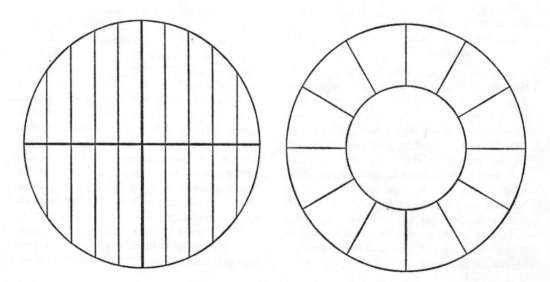

MARBLE CAKE

2½ cups cake flour
1½ teaspoons baking powder
¾ teaspoon baking soda
1 teaspoon salt
1⅔ cups plus 1 tablespoon sugar
¾ cup butter
¾ cup buttermilk
1 teaspoon vanilla
3 eggs
1 ounce unsweetened chocolate

Sift the flour, baking powder, ½ teaspoon soda, salt, and 1⅔ cups sugar together. Stir the butter just enough to soften. Add the flour mixture, buttermilk, and vanilla and mix until the flour is dampened. Then beat 2 minutes on low speed of electric mixer (300 strokes by hand). Add the eggs and beat 1 minute longer. Combine 2 tablespoons hot water, remaining soda and sugar, and the melted chocolate. Remove ¼ of the batter to a separate bowl; to this add the chocolate mixture. Put large spoonfuls of these batters alternately into two 9-inch cake pans greased and lined on the bottom with waxed paper. Then with a table knife cut through the batter once in a zigzag pattern to distribute color a bit. Bake in a 350° oven for 35 minutes. Turn out on racks; remove paper; cool before frosting. Serves 8–10.

WALNUT APPLESAUCE CAKE

½ cup shortening
1 cup sugar
1 egg
1 teaspoon cinnamon
½ teaspoon cloves
¼ teaspoon nutmeg
1 teaspoon vanilla
2 cups flour
½ teaspoon salt
1 teaspoon baking soda
1 teaspoon baking powder
¾ cup chopped raisins
1 cup chopped walnuts
1 cup thick sweetened applesauce

Cream the shortening and sugar until light and fluffy. Add the egg; then beat well. Add the spices and vanilla. Sift 1¾ cups flour with the salt, soda, and baking powder. Mix the raisins and walnuts with the remaining flour. Add the sifted dry ingredients to the spiced mixture alternately with the applesauce. Beat

until smooth. Stir in the floured nuts and raisins. Pour batter into a greased 8×8×2-inch pan. Bake in a 350° oven for 45 minutes. Turn out and cool on rack. Serves 6.

APPLESAUCE CAKE I

½ cup butter
1 cup sugar
1½ cups applesauce
2¾ cups flour
1 teaspoon baking soda
¼ teaspoon salt
1 cup raisins
½ cup chopped nuts (optional)

Cream the butter and sugar together. Add the applesauce; a flavorful applesauce improves the cake. Sift 2½ cups flour with the soda and salt. Stir into batter. Toss the raisins and nuts with remaining flour and add last. Mix well and pour into a greased and floured 8×8×2-inch pan. Bake in a 325° oven for 50 minutes. Turn out of the pan onto a cake rack to cool. Dust with confectioners' sugar if you wish. Serves 6–8.

APPLESAUCE CAKE II   (Plate 3)

3 cups flour
2 teaspoons cinnamon
½ teaspoon cloves
½ teaspoon allspice
2 teaspoons baking soda
2 cups raisins
1 cup chopped walnuts or pecans
½ cup butter
2 cups sugar
2 cups applesauce
Candied orange peel (garnish)

Sift 2½ cups flour, the spices, and soda together. Toss raisins and nuts with remaining flour. Cream the butter and sugar together until light and fluffy. Add applesauce and blend. Stir in the flour mixture gradually, beating until smooth after each addition. Add raisins and nuts and mix well. Grease and flour a 2-quart mold or pan. Fill about ⅔ full. Bake in a 350° oven for 1¼ hours. Cool 5 minutes; then turn out of pan onto a cake rack to cool. Garnish if you wish with small pieces of candied orange peel brushed with corn syrup. Serves 12–14.

APPLESAUCE GRAHAM-CRACKER CAKE

¼ cup butter
½ cup sugar
1 teaspoon grated lemon rind
2 egg yolks
½ cup chopped nuts
1 cup raisins
2½ teaspoons baking powder
½ teaspoon nutmeg
1 teaspoon cinnamon
½ teaspoon salt
1¾ cups graham-cracker crumbs
1 cup applesauce

Cream the butter with the sugar and lemon rind until fluffy. Add the well-beaten egg yolks, then the nuts and raisins. Stir the baking powder, nutmeg, cinnamon, and salt into the cracker crumbs. Blend thoroughly and add alternately with the applesauce to the creamed mixture. Beat until well mixed. Bake in a greased 8×8×2-inch pan in a 350° oven for 50–60 minutes. Serves 6–8.

DUTCH APPLE CAKE

1½ cups flour
½ teaspoon salt
2 teaspoons baking powder
¼ cup butter
⅓ cup milk
1 egg
6 large tart apples

SPICED TOPPING
¼ cup soft butter
½ cup sugar
¼ teaspoon nutmeg
¼ teaspoon cinnamon

Sift the flour, salt, and baking powder together. Cut in the butter until the mixture resembles coarse corn meal. Add the milk to the beaten egg and stir into the flour mixture. The dough will be quite stiff. Pat it evenly over the bottom of a 15½×10½×1-inch pan. Pare, quarter, and slice the apples. Set the slices, overlapping each other, in rows and press into the dough. Bake in a 425° oven for 25 minutes.

Spiced Topping. Cream the butter with the sugar and spices.

Remove the cake from the oven and spread the topping over the apples. Reduce oven heat to 350° and bake 20 minutes more. This cake will not rise very much; it is more a cake which is called a flan in America. Serve warm. Serves 12.

BANANA CAKE

½ cup butter
1½ cups sugar
2 eggs
2¼ cups cake flour
½ teaspoon baking powder
¾ teaspoon baking soda
½ teaspoon salt
1 cup mashed bananas
1 teaspoon vanilla
¼ cup sour milk
2 bananas
1 cup whipped cream
Confectioners' sugar

Cream the butter, add the sugar gradually, and beat until creamy. Beat in the eggs one at a time. Sift the dry ingredients together. To the cup of lightly mashed bananas, add the vanilla and sour milk. Add the dry ingredients and banana mixture alternately to the first mixture. Beat after each addition until smooth. Pour into two 9-inch cake pans lined on the bottom with waxed paper and bake in a 350° oven for ½ hour. Turn out on racks, remove paper, and cool. Slice the bananas and place between layers with the whipped cream. Sprinkle the top of the cake with confectioners' sugar. Serves 8–10.

BLACKBERRY LOAF

1 (1 lb.) can blackberries
½ cup butter
1 cup sugar
1 egg
1⅔ cups flour
1 teaspoon baking powder
¼ teaspoon cinnamon
Pinch salt

Drain the liquid from the blackberries, setting aside ¼ cup. Rub the blackberries through a sieve to remove the seeds. You should have 1 cup of purée. Add the reserved liquid to the purée. Cream the butter, gradually adding the sugar, until light and fluffy. Add the egg and beat again. Sift the flour, baking powder, cinnamon, and salt together. Add to the creamed mixture alternately with the black-berry purée, beating after each addition until well blended. Pour into a greased and floured 9×5×2¾-inch loaf pan. Bake in a 350° oven 50–60 minutes. Cool in pan 5 minutes, then turn out on a rack to cool. Frost with Lemon Butter Cream Frosting,* if you wish. Serves 6–8.

SOUTHERN COCONUT CAKE (*Plate 6*)

2 (1 lb. 4 oz.) packages white cake mix
1 cup grated coconut
1 teaspoon almond flavoring
Lemon Butter Filling*
Fluffy White Frosting*
1 (4 oz.) can shredded coconut

Prepare the 2 packages of cake mix according to package directions, adding ½ cup coconut and ½ teaspoon almond flavoring to each batter. Bake in four 9-inch cake pans according to package directions. Freeze one layer for later use. Put the remaining 3 layers together with the Lemon Butter Filling. Frost with Fluffy White Frosting and sprinkle the entire cake with the coconut. Serves 10–12.

GRAPEFRUIT CAKE

1½ cups sugar
1 tablespoon grated grapefruit rind
½ teaspoon grated lemon rind
¾ cup butter
3 eggs
3 cups cake flour
¾ teaspoon salt
3½ teaspoons baking powder
¼ teaspoon baking soda
½ cup grapefruit juice
Fluffy Grapefruit Cheese Frosting*

Cream the sugar, grated rinds, and butter until very light and fluffy. Add eggs one at a time, beating well after each addition. Sift the flour, salt, baking powder, and soda together. Divide dry ingredients into 4 parts. Mix grapefruit juice with ½ cup water. Add ¼ of the dry ingredients with ⅓ of the liquid to the creamed mixture and mix just enough to blend. Repeat twice; finally mix in the last of the dry ingredients. Divide the batter between two 9-inch cake pans lined on the bottom with waxed paper. Bake in a 375° oven for about ½ hour,

until cake is browned and pulls away from sides of pans. Turn out on racks, remove paper, and cool. Good with Fluffy Grapefruit Cheese Frosting. Serves 8–10.

HARLEQUIN CAKE

1 package coconut cake mix
1 package fluffy white frosting mix
Currant jelly and apricot preserves

Bake the cake, following package directions for two 9-inch layers. Prepare frosting according to directions. Spread frosting smoothly between layers and over the top and sides of the cake, reserving ¾ cup for decorating. Place this frosting in a pastry bag with a small plain tip. Pipe lines both ways across the top to form squares and also pipe decorative edgings. Fill every other square with softened jelly and apricot preserves. Serves 8–10.

BUTTERFLY CAKE (*Plate 13*)

1 (1 lb. 3½ oz.) package orange cake mix
1 (13.8 oz.) package lemon creamy-type frosting mix
Lime and orange candy slices (garnish)

Line the bottoms of a 9-inch spring-form pan and a 9-inch layer pan with waxed paper. Grease and flour the sides. Prepare the cake mix according to package directions. Place 1⅓ cups batter in the layer pan and the remaining batter in the spring-form pan. Bake in a 350° oven 10–15 minutes for the layer pan and about 35 minutes for the spring-form pan. The thin layer will pull away from sides of pan when done; the large cake should be tested with a cake tester. Cool 5 minutes before removing from pans; finish cooling on racks. Prepare the frosting mix according to package directions. Place the large layer on serving plate. Cut the thin layer in half. To form "wings," secure the halves to the base at a 45° angle with frosting and pack the frosting under the "wings" to support them. Use a decorating tube and star tip to decorate the edges of the "wings" and the cake. Garnish with the candy slices if you wish. To start to serve, cut into wedge-shaped pieces, avoiding the "wings." Serves 8–10.

DATE CAKE

1½ cups flour
1 teaspoon baking powder
½ teaspoon salt
1 cup chopped pitted dates
1 teaspoon baking soda
⅓ cup softened butter
1 cup sugar
1 egg
1 teaspoon vanilla
½ cup chopped walnuts

Sift the flour, baking powder, and salt together. Pour 1 cup boiling water over the dates and soda. Allow to stand while mixing the cake batter. Cream the butter with sugar until very smooth and creamy. Add the egg and vanilla and beat well. Mix the dry ingredients with the creamed mixture until well blended. Stir in the walnuts and the date mixture. Pour into a greased and floured 13×9×2-inch pan. Bake in a 375° oven for 35 minutes. Remove from pan and cool. Frost if desired. Serves 15.

DATE NUT CAKE   (Plate 10)

½ pound candied cherries
1 pound pitted dates
½ pound candied pineapple slices
1 pound shelled pecan halves
1 cup flour
2 teaspoons baking powder
1 cup sugar
Pinch salt
6 eggs
1½ teaspoons vanilla
2 tablespoons port wine

Cut the cherries and dates in half and the pineapple in quarters. Put into a large mixing bowl and add the nuts. Sift the flour, baking powder, sugar, and salt together. Add to fruit mixture and mix well. Beat the eggs slightly and add the vanilla and wine. Pour over the dry ingredients and mix well. Grease a 9×5×2¾-inch loaf pan and line with brown paper. Grease the paper. Pack the batter into the pan, pressing down well in the corners. Bake in a 300° oven for 2–2½ hours, until done when tested with cake tester. Cool the cake slightly before removing from pan. When cake is cool, remove paper and wrap cake in cheesecloth moistened with additional port wine or brandy; then wrap in foil and store in a cool place several days before serving. Serves 12–14.

EIGHT-MINUTE HONEY MERINGUE CAKE

1 (12 oz.) poundcake
¼ cup honey
½ cup flaked coconut
⅓ cup applesauce
2 egg whites
3 tablespoons sugar

Cut a thin slice from the top of the cake to level it off. Place the cake on a baking sheet. Spread with honey, then sprinkle with coconut, and spoon applesauce over the coconut. Preheat broiler. Beat the egg whites until frothy. Add the sugar a tablespoon at a time, beating constantly. When mixture holds stiff peaks, spread generously on top of the cake. Broil until top is golden. Serve at once. Serves 6–8.

INDIANA PICNIC CAKE

½ cup butter
1½ cups light brown sugar
2 eggs
2½ cups flour
1 tablespoon baking powder
½ teaspoon salt
1 cup milk
1 teaspoon vanilla

MARSHMALLOW TOPPING
10 large marshmallows
½ cup light brown sugar
½ cup pecans

Cream the butter with sugar until light and fluffy. Add the eggs one at a time and beat well. Sift the flour, baking powder, and salt together. Stir the dry ingredients into the creamed mixture alternately with a mixture of the milk and vanilla. Beat smooth after each addition. Grease and flour the bottom of a 9×9×2-inch pan. Pour in the batter.

Marshmallow Topping. Cut the marshmallows in half and arrange cut side down on top of the batter. Mix the brown sugar with the pecans, chopped coarse. Sprinkle over top.

Bake in a 350° oven for 50 minutes. It will shrink slightly from the sides of the pan. Cool in the pan before cutting. Serves 8.

COOKTIP

If storing egg yolks in the refrigerator, cover them with cold water.

Plate 2. STRAWBERRY TORTE with swirls of pink whipped cream topped with berries.

CAKE
SALE!

Where the best cooks in America
become famous and help raise fund
for charities the year 'round

$2.50
Mrs Patricia Morse

$2.00
Enid Harlow

3.50
Mrs Holly Allen

Plate 3. Cake Sale—left to right: LEMON ANGEL LAYER CAKE, JAPANESE FRUIT CAKE, APPLESAUCE CAKE,

$1.50
Gwen Simpson

5.00
Miss E. Gill

CHOCOLATE SQUARE—ALL BLACK, POUNDCAKE, OLD-FASHIONED JELLY ROLL, BURNT-SUGAR CAKE.

Plate 4. GOLD AND WHITE WEDDING CAKE decorated simply but effectively.

ORANGE MAPLE CAKE

½ cup butter
½ cup sugar
½ cup maple syrup
2 teaspoons grated orange rind
1 teaspoon vanilla
2 eggs
1¾ cups cake flour
½ teaspoon salt
2½ teaspoons baking powder
¼ cup orange juice
½ cup chopped walnuts
Maple Frosting*

Cream the butter and sugar until light and fluffy. Add the maple syrup a little at a time while beating, then the orange rind and vanilla. Cream well again. Add the eggs one at a time and beat well. Sift the flour, salt, and baking powder together and add alternately with the orange juice, beating well after each addition. Stir in the nuts. Pour into two 8-inch cake pans lined on the bottom with waxed paper. Bake in a 375° oven for 25–30 minutes. Remove from pans, pull off paper, and cool on racks. Frost with Maple Frosting. Serves 8.

ORANGE LAYER CAKE

⅔ cup milk
2 tablespoons butter
4 eggs
2 cups sugar
½ teaspoon salt
½ teaspoon orange flavoring
2 cups cake flour
2 teaspoons baking powder
⅓ cup frozen orange-juice concentrate

Scald the milk, stir in the butter, and cool. Beat the eggs until thick and lemon-colored, gradually add the sugar, and beat until light and fluffy. Then add the salt and orange flavoring. Pour in the cooled milk mixture and beat again. Sift the cake flour and baking powder together. Add alternately to batter with the thawed orange-juice concentrate, ending with dry ingredients. Beat thoroughly. Divide the batter among three 8-inch cake pans lined on the bottom with waxed paper. Bake in a 350° oven for 25–30 minutes. Turn out on racks and remove paper. Cool before frosting. A chocolate, orange, or lemon frosting is suggested. Serves 10–12.

GLAZED ORANGE CAKE (Plate 5)

3 cups cake flour
1 tablespoon baking powder
Pinch salt
1 cup butter
2 cups sugar
½ teaspoon vanilla
2 tablespoons grated orange rind
5 eggs
¾ cup milk

ORANGE GLAZE
¼ cup butter
⅔ cup sugar
⅓ cup orange juice

Sift the cake flour, baking powder, and salt together twice. Cream the butter and sugar until light and fluffy. Add vanilla and orange rind. Add eggs one at a time, beating well after each addition. Add the flour mixture alternately with the milk, ending with the flour. Beat well after each addition. Spoon into a floured, buttered 10-inch tube pan and bake in a 350° oven for about 1 hour, until cake springs back to the touch. Cool in pan on rack for only 2 minutes and glaze immediately.

Orange Glaze. Make the glaze so that it is ready when the cake is baked; this glaze is used on a hot cake. Heat all of the ingredients in a saucepan until the sugar is dissolved.

Pour evenly over cake in pan while cake is still hot. Allow cake to cool thoroughly in the pan before removing. Serves 14–16.

ALMOND CAKE

3 eggs
½ teaspoon almond flavoring
½ cup sugar
Pinch salt
1⅓ cups finely chopped almonds
Whipped cream or ice cream (optional)

Beat the egg yolks with almond flavoring until thick and lemon-colored. Add sugar gradually, beating until thick. Beat the egg whites with salt until a soft peak forms. Fold into yolks alternately with almonds. Pour into an 8-inch cake pan lined on the bottom with waxed paper. Bake in a 350° oven for 35–40 minutes. Turn out on rack, remove paper, and cool. Especially good served with whipped cream and/or ice cream on top. Serves 4.

ORANGE RUM CAKE

⅔ cup butter
1 teaspoon salt
1 tablespoon grated orange rind
1½ cups sugar
3 eggs
2½ cups cake flour
1 tablespoon baking powder
¼ cup rum
¼ cup orange juice
2 tablespoons lemon juice
Orange Filling*
Orange Seven-Minute Frosting* or Boiled
 Frosting*

Cream the butter, salt, and orange rind. Add sugar gradually and beat until fluffy. Add the eggs one at a time, beating thoroughly after each addition. Sift the flour and baking powder together. Combine the rum with orange juice, lemon juice, and enough water to make 1 cup. Add the dry ingredients to creamed mixture alternately with the liquid and beat smooth. Pour batter into two 9-inch cake pans lined on the bottom with waxed paper. Bake in a 375° oven for 25–30 minutes. Remove from pan, pull off paper, and cool. Put the layers together with Orange Filling and frost with Orange Seven-Minute or Boiled Frosting. Serves 8–10.

BLACK-WALNUT CAKE

1 cup butter
2 cups sugar
4 eggs
3 cups flour
½ teaspoon salt
2 teaspoons baking powder
1 cup milk
2 teaspoons vanilla
1 cup chopped black walnuts, butternuts, or
 walnuts

Cream the butter with 1 cup sugar until light and fluffy. Beat the egg yolks, gradually adding the remaining sugar, until very thick. Add the beaten yolks to the butter mixture. Sift the flour, salt, and baking powder together. Add to butter-egg mixture alternately with milk. Add vanilla and fold in the egg whites, beaten until a soft peak forms. Add the chopped nuts and pour the batter into two 9-inch cake pans lined on the bottom with waxed paper. Bake in a 350° oven for 35–40 minutes. Remove from pans, pull off paper, and cool on racks. Good with Maple Frosting* or Caramel Butter Frosting.* Serves 10–12.

RAISIN PECAN CAKE   *(Plate 36)*

1 pound butter
1 pound light brown sugar
6 eggs
4 cups flour
1 teaspoon baking powder
1 tablespoon nutmeg
¼ cup brandy
1 pound seedless raisins
3 cups chopped pecans

Cream the butter and sugar together. Add the eggs one at a time, beating well after each addition. Sift the flour, baking powder, and nutmeg together. Add gradually and beat until well blended. Stir in the brandy. Fold in the raisins and pecans. Pour into a greased and floured 10-inch tube pan. Bake in a 300° oven for about 1 hour and 40 minutes. Cool slightly in the pan before removing to a rack to cool completely. Wrap and store for at least a week. You may decorate with a frosting made of 1 cup confectioners' sugar and enough light cream to make a spreading consistency and garnish with candied cherries and citron if you wish. Serves 12–14.

PRUNE CAKE

¾ pound prunes
¾ cup butter
1 cup sugar
3 eggs
2 cups cake flour
1½ teaspoons cinnamon
1 teaspoon baking soda
½ teaspoon salt
¼ teaspoon allspice
¼ teaspoon nutmeg
⅓ cup sour milk or buttermilk
½ cup chopped nuts (optional)

Cover the prunes with boiling water and let stand 30 minutes. Drain well, remove pits, and chop the prunes. You will need 1 cup. Cream the butter and sugar until light and fluffy. Add the eggs one at a time, beating well after each addition. Sift the flour, cinnamon, soda, salt, allspice, and nutmeg together. Add to the creamed mixture alternately with the sour milk or buttermilk, beating well after each addition. Stir in the chopped prunes, and nuts if you wish. Pour into a greased and floured 8×8×2-inch pan and bake in a 350° oven for 1 hour and 25 minutes. Turn out and cool. Serves 8.

POPPY-SEED CAKE

⅔ cup poppy seeds
1 cup milk
⅔ cup butter
1½ cups sugar
2 cups flour
2½ teaspoons baking powder
½ teaspoon salt
1 teaspoon vanilla
4 egg whites
Lemon Custard Filling*
Confectioners' sugar

Soak the poppy seeds in ¾ cup milk for 2 hours. Cream the butter, gradually adding the sugar, until light and fluffy. Sift the flour, baking powder, and salt together. Stir the remaining milk and the vanilla into the poppy-seed mixture. Add the dry ingredients in 3 parts alternately with the poppy-seed milk to the batter, beating after each addition only until blended. Beat the egg whites until a soft peak forms and fold into the batter. Turn into two 9-inch cake pans lined on the bottom with waxed paper. Bake in a 375° oven for 25 minutes. Remove from pans, pull off paper, and cool on racks. Fill with Lemon Custard Filling and sift confectioners' sugar over the top. Serves 10–12.

STRAWBERRY ALMOND CAKE

1 (1 lb. 4 oz.) package white cake mix
¼ teaspoon almond flavoring
3 tablespoons softened butter
½ cup shaved blanched almonds
1 tablespoon flour
1 (12 oz.) jar strawberry jam
1 teaspoon lemon juice

Prepare the cake mix according to package directions. Stir in the almond flavoring. Spread softened butter generously on the insides of a heavy 11-cup mold. Coat the bottom and sides of the mold with the almonds. Lightly sprinkle the flour over the almonds. Pour the cake batter slowly into the mold. Bake in a 350° oven for about 1 hour, until the cake pulls away from the sides of the pan. Cool on a rack for 10–15 minutes before removing from the pan. Heat the jam with lemon juice just enough to soften. Rub through a sieve. Brush the jam over the entire surface of the cake. Let cake cool approximately 1 hour before slicing. Serves 8–10.

WHITE LOAF CAKE WITH STRAWBERRY CREAM

STRAWBERRY CREAM

3 pints strawberries
1½ cups sugar
3 cups milk
4½ tablespoons cornstarch
3 cups confectioners' sugar
1½ cups heavy cream

WHITE LOAF CAKE

2½ cups flour
1 tablespoon baking powder
½ teaspoon salt
½ cup butter
1⅓ cups sugar
1 teaspoon vanilla
1 cup milk
4 egg whites

Strawberry Cream. Hull the berries and cut them in half. Mix with the sugar. Let them stand at room temperature for 2 hours, stirring occasionally. Heat 2½ cups milk. Stir the cornstarch into remaining ½ cup and add to the hot milk. Cook and stir until smooth and thickened. Chill. Beat smooth. Add confectioners' sugar a little at a time, beating after each addition. Fold in the cream, whipped. Then fold in the berries and syrup. Chill.

White Loaf Cake. Sift the flour, baking powder, and salt together twice. Cream the butter and sugar until light and fluffy. Add vanilla. Then add alternately the dry ingredients and milk, beating well after each addition. Beat the egg whites until a soft peak forms and fold into the batter. Divide between two greased and floured 9×5×2¾-inch loaf pans. Bake in a 350° oven for 35–40 minutes. Turn out on racks to cool. Serve slices of warm cake with the strawberry cream. Serves 20.

RASPBERRY RUM CAKE

Poundcake*
⅓–½ cup rum
3 packages frozen raspberries
Rum Custard Sauce*

Pierce the top of the cake in several places with a fork. Sprinkle with the rum and let it stand for at least ½ hour. Serve with thawed berries and Rum Custard Sauce. Serves 8–10.

STRAWBERRY DREAM CAKE

1 (1 lb. 4 oz.) package white cake mix
1 package strawberry-flavored gelatin
2 tablespoons flour
4 eggs
½ package frozen sliced strawberries
¾ cup cooking oil
Strawberry Frosting*

Mix the cake mix, gelatin, flour, eggs, and ½ cup water together. Beat at medium speed for 2 minutes on mixer. Add the thawed strawberries (including syrup) to batter and beat 1 more minute on mixer. Add the oil and beat 1 more minute. Divide batter evenly into two greased and floured 8-inch square or 9-inch round cake pans. Bake in a 350° oven for 35–40 minutes. Cool on racks about 10 minutes, then remove from pan. When completely cool, fill and frost with Strawberry Frosting. Serves 8–10.

STRAWBERRY TOWER LAYER CAKE

6 eggs
3–3½ cups sugar
¼ teaspoon salt
1½ teaspoons almond flavoring
1½ cups cake flour
¾ cup very finely chopped blanched almonds
½ cup dry sherry
2 quarts strawberries
2 cups heavy cream
¼ cup confectioners' sugar

Beat the eggs, 1½ cups sugar, and salt together until very thick. Add 1 teaspoon almond flavoring and mix well. Sift the cake flour twice and fold into the egg-sugar mixture a little at a time alternately with the almonds, ending with flour. Divide the batter between two 9-inch cake pans lined on the bottom with waxed paper. Bake in a 350° oven for 30–35 minutes. Turn out on racks, remove paper, and cool. Split each cake layer in half and pierce all over with a fork. Sprinkle each layer with 2 tablespoons sherry. Wrap each in foil and refrigerate overnight. Hull the strawberries. Sprinkle 1 pint strawberries with 1 cup sugar and crush them. Cover, and let stand 1 hour. Reserve a few whole berries for garnish. Slice remaining berries into a bowl and sprinkle with ½–1 cup sugar; the amount of sugar will depend on sweetness of berries. Cover and let stand 1 hour. Rub the crushed strawberries through a sieve. Spoon the purée over two of the cake layers. Whip the cream, confectioners' sugar, and remaining almond flavoring until thick and shiny. Place one of the plain cake layers on a cake plate and cover with half the drained sliced strawberries. Add a cake layer topped with strawberry purée. Spread with about 1 cup whipped cream. Repeat. Refrigerate until serving time. Finish by frosting the cake all over with whipped cream. Decorate the top with strawberries. Serves 14–16.

BISCUIT SHORTCAKE

2 cups flour
¾ teaspoon salt
1 tablespoon baking powder
1½ teaspoons sugar
5 tablespoons shortening
¾ cup milk

Sift the flour, salt, baking powder, and sugar together. Cut in the shortening thoroughly until the mixture resembles coarse corn meal. Add the milk all at once. Stir together quickly until the milk is blended. The dough should be light and soft. Turn out on a lightly floured board. Dip your hands in flour and knead dough lightly and briefly—not more than half a minute. Roll the dough into 1 large circle about 1½ inches thick, or make 2 layers about ¾ inch thick. Place on a greased baking sheet and bake in a 450° oven for 10–12 minutes, until an even light brown. This shortcake is appropriate for use with any berries, fresh or frozen, or with sliced peaches. Serves 8.

OLD-FASHIONED STRAWBERRY SHORTCAKE

3 pints strawberries
¾ cup sugar
Biscuit Shortcake*
Soft butter
2 cups heavy cream

Hull and crush or slice the strawberries. (Save a few whole berries for the top of the cake if you wish.) Mix with the sugar and let stand in a warm place to draw out the juice. Make the biscuit shortcake. If you bake the cake in one layer, split and butter the layers while warm. Butter adds to the flavor of the shortcake. You may invert the top crust if you wish. Put half of the berries between the layers and the other half on top. Whip the cream slightly unless you have really thick cream, in which case by all means serve it plain. Serve with some of the cream over the shortcake and pass the rest. Serves 8.

RASPBERRY SHORTCAKE

Proceed as for Old-Fashioned Strawberry Shortcake.* Substitute raspberries for the strawberries. The raspberries may be left whole between the layers instead of crushing them.

PEACH SHORTCAKE

Use 3 pounds of peaches, sliced and sugared, and proceed as for for Old-Fashioned Strawberry Shortcake.*

STRAWBERRY SCONE SHORTCAKE

3 pints strawberries
½ cup plus 1 tablespoon sugar
2 cups flour
1 tablespoon baking powder
½ teaspoon salt
¼ cup shortening
⅓ cup light cream
2 eggs
Butter
Heavy cream

Hull and slice the strawberries, crush slightly, and sweeten to taste with about ½ cup sugar. Let the berries stand at room temperature for a couple of hours to draw out the juice, then chill them. Sift the flour, baking powder, salt, and 1 tablespoon sugar together. Cut in the shortening. Add the light cream mixed with the well-beaten eggs. Stir quickly just until dough holds together. Knead for half a minute on a lightly floured board. Shape into a circle about ½ inch thick and 8 inches in diameter. Place on a lightly greased baking sheet and bake in a 425° oven for 15 minutes, until golden brown. Split while hot, spread generously with butter, and keep hot until ready to serve. Fill and top with the strawberries. Serve with cream. Serves 8.

MERINGUE STRAWBERRY SHORT-CAKES (Low Calorie)

4 egg whites
⅛ teaspoon salt
⅓ teaspoon cream of tartar
1 cup superfine sugar
¾ teaspoon vanilla
6 cups sliced hulled strawberries
¼ teaspoon granulated noncaloric sweetener

TOPPING
1 cup liquefied nonfat dry milk
½ teaspoon vanilla
1 teaspoon liquid noncaloric sweetener

Beat the egg whites until frothy. Add salt and cream of tartar and continue beating until a soft peak begins to form. Gradually add sugar a tablespoonful at a time, beating well after each addition. Add vanilla and continue to beat until sugar is dissolved. Draw twelve 3-inch circles and twelve 2-inch circles on ungreased brown paper cut to fit baking sheets. Fill circles with meringue to make disks—use pastry tube or back of a spoon. Bake in a 250° oven for about ½ hour. Remove carefully from paper and allow to cool. If meringues stick to paper, place a damp cloth under the paper for a minute. Sprinkle the berries with granulated sweetener and chill.

Topping. Freeze the milk until mushy. Turn into chilled bowl and whip until thick. Flavor with vanilla and add liquid sweetener.

Place 1 large meringue disk on each serving plate, top each with ⅓ cup berries, place smaller disk over berries, and top with a spoonful of berries. Place a generous fluff of whipped milk topping on each. Serves 12.

BUTTER PECAN SAUCE CAKE

1¾ cups light brown sugar
2 tablespoons maple syrup
2 tablespoons butter
1 (13½ oz.) package butter pecan cake mix
½ cup coarsely chopped pecans

Prepare the sauce first. Mix together 2 cups water, sugar, syrup, and butter. Bring to a fast boil. Remove from heat and let cool completely. Prepare the cake mix according to package directions. Pour into a greased 8×8×2-inch pan. Slowly pour the sauce over the batter. Sprinkle with nuts. Bake in a 350° oven for 40–45 minutes. Serve warm, spooning the sauce over each piece. Serves 6–8.

QUICK SPICECAKE

1½ cups flour
1 cup sugar
½ teaspoon salt
1 teaspoon baking soda
½ teaspoon allspice
¼ teaspoon cloves
¾ teaspoon cinnamon
¼ teaspoon nutmeg
½ cup hydrogenated vegetable shortening
1 egg
1 cup sour milk or buttermilk
½ cup raisins (optional)

Sift the dry ingredients together into a mixing bowl. Add the shortening, egg, and sour milk or buttermilk. Beat until smooth. Pour into a greased and floured 8×8×2-inch pan and bake in a 350° oven for 40–50 minutes. If you like raisins in your spicecake, reserve 2 tablespoons of the flour and mix with the raisins. Stir in the floured raisins last. Serves 6.

LEMON SPICECAKE

⅓ cup butter
¾ cup sugar
1 egg
1½ cups flour
½ teaspoon salt
¼ teaspoon nutmeg
¼ teaspoon cinnamon
¼ teaspoon ginger
2 teaspoons baking powder
¼ cup lemon juice
½ cup raisins
1 teaspoon grated lemon rind
¼ cup finely chopped walnuts

TOPPING

2 tablespoons soft butter
½ cup light brown sugar
¼ teaspoon nutmeg
¼ teaspoon cinnamon
¼ teaspoon ginger
⅛ teaspoon salt
2 tablespoons flour
¼ cup chopped walnuts (optional)

Cream the butter and sugar together until light and fluffy. Add the egg and beat until light. Sift all but 2 tablespoons of the flour with the salt, spices, and baking powder. Add to the creamed mixture alternately with lemon juice mixed with ¼ cup water, ending with the dry ingredients. Dredge the raisins very lightly with remaining flour and add to mixture. Add lemon rind and walnuts. Pour batter into a greased and lightly floured 8×8×2-inch pan.

Topping. Toss the butter, brown sugar, spices, salt, and flour with a fork.

Sprinkle the topping mixture over the cake batter. Sprinkle the walnuts as a last layer if you wish. Bake in a 350° oven for 50 minutes. Cool on a rack. Do not turn out of the pan. Serves 6–8.

MERINGUE-TOPPED SPICECAKE

¾ cup butter
2 cups brown sugar
1 teaspoon vanilla
2 eggs
2½ cups cake flour
1 teaspoon baking soda
1 teaspoon baking powder
½ teaspoon cloves
¼ teaspoon nutmeg
1 teaspoon cinnamon
1⅛ teaspoons salt
1¼ cups sour milk or buttermilk
¼ cup sugar
⅓ cup chopped nuts

Cream the butter and brown sugar until light and fluffy. Add the vanilla. Add the egg yolks one at a time, beating well. Sift the flour, soda, baking powder, cloves, nutmeg, cinnamon, and 1 teaspoon salt together. Add alternately to the creamed mixture with the sour milk or buttermilk. Beat until smooth. Pour into a well-greased and floured 13×9×2-inch pan. Beat the egg whites with remaining salt and add the sugar gradually as for a soft meringue. Spread this over the batter and sprinkle with nuts. Bake in a 350° oven for 1¼ hours. Serves 15.

COOKTIPS

To keep cake fresh, put half an apple in the cake box.

When adding dry ingredients alternately with liquid to a creamed mixture, add the dry ingredients in 4 equal parts and liquid in 3, beginning and ending with the dry.

GINGERBREAD

½ cup butter
½ cup sugar
1 egg
1 cup molasses
2½ cups cake flour
1½ teaspoons baking soda
½ teaspoon salt
1 teaspoon ginger
1 teaspoon cinnamon
½ teaspoon cloves

Cream the butter with the sugar until light and fluffy. Add the well-beaten egg and then the molasses. Beat well. Sift the flour, soda, salt, and spices together and add to the creamed mixture, beating until smooth. Add 1 cup hot water and beat again until thoroughly blended. Pour into a well-greased and floured 9×9×2-inch pan and bake in a 350° oven for 45 minutes. Serve warm if you wish. Good with whipped cream, Custard Sauce,* or Foamy Eggnog Sauce.* Serves 8.

MAPLE-SYRUP GINGERBREAD

2 eggs
1 cup maple syrup
½ cup light brown sugar
1 cup sour cream
½ cup melted hydrogenated vegetable
    shortening
2½ cups flour
1 teaspoon baking soda
1 teaspoon baking powder
¾ teaspoon salt
1 tablespoon ginger
2 teaspoons cinnamon
½ teaspoon cloves
¼ teaspoon nutmeg
¼ cup chopped candied orange peel

Beat the eggs. Add the maple syrup, sugar, cream, and melted shortening. Stir until blended. Sift the flour, soda, baking powder, salt, and spices together; stir into the liquids and beat until smooth. Add the candied orange peel and pour into a 9×9×2-inch pan lined on the bottom with waxed paper. Bake in a 350° oven for 35 minutes; turn off the heat and let gingerbread stand in oven 5 minutes more. The gingerbread should be firm to the touch. Especially good served warm with cold applesauce and whipped cream. Serves 8.

MOCHA GINGERBREAD

2 cups flour
2 teaspoons baking powder
½ teaspoon baking soda
½ teaspoon salt
½ cup sugar
1½ teaspoons ginger
¼ teaspoon cloves
½ teaspoon cinnamon
¼ teaspoon allspice
1 tablespoon instant coffee
1–2 ounces semisweet chocolate
½ cup hydrogenated vegetable shortening
⅓ cup dark molasses
2 eggs

Sift the dry ingredients together and add the chocolate which has been grated. Pour ¾ cup hot water over shortening and stir until shortening melts. Mix in the molasses. Then add eggs and blend thoroughly. Quickly stir in the dry ingredients and pour into a 7×11×1½-inch pan lined on the bottom with waxed paper. Bake in a 350° oven for about 45 minutes. Allow to cool a few minutes before turning out of pan. Serve warm. Serves 6–8.

WHITE GINGERBREAD

2 cups flour
1 cup sugar
½ cup butter
1 teaspoon cinnamon
½ teaspoon ginger
¼ teaspoon mace
¼ teaspoon salt
½ teaspoon baking soda
½ teaspoon baking powder
1 egg
½ cup buttermilk

Rub the flour, sugar, and butter together until mixture resembles corn meal. Add ½ teaspoon cinnamon and toss. Set aside 1 cup of this crumbly mixture. To the rest add the ginger, mace, salt, soda, baking powder, and the remaining cinnamon. Toss; then add egg and buttermilk. Beat smooth. Sprinkle ½ cup of the reserved crumbly mixture in the bottom of an 8×8×2-inch pan and spread the batter over it. Sprinkle the remaining crumbly mixture evenly over the top. Bake in a 350° oven for 35–40 minutes. Serves 6–8.

MOLASSES GINGER CAKE   (Plate 7)

    2½ cups flour
    1 teaspoon baking soda
    1½ teaspoons ginger
    ½ teaspoon salt
    ¾ cup currants or raisins
    1 egg
    1 cup dark molasses
    1 cup buttermilk or sour milk
    ¼ cup melted butter

Sift the dry ingredients together; add currants or raisins and toss to coat. Add the well-beaten egg, molasses, and milk. Stir until blended. Pour in the butter and mix well. Turn the batter into a greased and floured 9×5×2¾-inch loaf pan. Bake in a 325° oven for about 1 hour and 10 minutes. Let stand 5 minutes before turning out of pan. Cool. Good with Butter Cream Frosting.* Serves 8.

LAFAYETTE GINGER CAKE

    1 cup dark molasses
    ½ cup butter
    ½ cup brown sugar
    ½ cup milk
    ½ cup strong coffee
    3 cups flour
    2 tablespoons powdered ginger
    1 teaspoon cinnamon
    1 teaspoon mace
    1 teaspoon nutmeg
    1 teaspoon cream of tartar
    3 eggs
    1 teaspoon baking soda
    ½ cup orange juice
    Grated rind 1 orange
    ½ cup finely chopped crystallized ginger

Heat the molasses, butter, sugar, milk, and coffee until sugar is dissolved. Sift the flour, spices, and cream of tartar together. Beat the eggs until extremely thick. Fold the dry ingredients into the molasses mixture alternately with the eggs. Add the soda to the last addition of flour. Next add the orange juice and rind. Mix and pour into a 13×9×2-inch pan lined on the bottom with waxed paper. Sprinkle with crystallized ginger and bake in a 350° oven for about 40 minutes. This cake may be served hot or cold, with or without a frosting. Try it with Strawberry Cheese Frosting.* Serves 12.

PLANTATION DESSERT CAKE

    2 cups flour
    ¾ cup sugar
    ½ teaspoon cinnamon
    ⅛ teaspoon ginger
    ⅛ teaspoon cloves
    6 tablespoons butter
    ¾ cup molasses
    1½ teaspoons baking soda
    Lemon Sauce* (optional)
    Whipped cream cheese (optional)

Sift the flour, sugar, cinnamon, ginger, and cloves together. Cut in the butter until mixture resembles coarse corn meal. Put about ⅓ of this crumb mixture on the bottom of a greased 8×8×2-inch pan and pat out evenly. Combine the molasses and baking soda with ¾ cup hot water. Pour half the liquid over the crumbs. Sprinkle with remaining crumbs and then drizzle the remaining liquid over the top to give a marbled effect. Bake in a 350° oven for 25–30 minutes. Cut into 6 pieces and serve warm with Lemon Sauce topped with whipped cream cheese if you wish. Serves 6.

CHERRY CHEESECAKE

    1½ recipes Crumb Crust*
    2 (8 oz.) packages cream cheese
    1 cup light cream
    1 cup sugar
    2 tablespoons flour
    ¼ teaspoon salt
    3 eggs
    1 teaspoon vanilla
    ¾ teaspoon grated lemon rind

CHERRY TOPPING
    1 (1 lb.) can pitted tart red cherries
    1 tablespoon cornstarch
    ⅓ cup sugar
    ⅛ teaspoon grated lemon rind

Butter a 9-inch spring-form pan generously and pat the crumb crust on the bottom and up the sides of the pan. Chill. Soften the cream cheese and blend in the cream; add the sugar which has been mixed with the flour and salt. Beat the egg yolks until thick and light, fold in carefully, and flavor with vanilla and lemon rind. Beat the egg whites to soft peaks and fold in. Pour into the crust. Bake in a 325° oven for 1 hour and then leave in oven another hour with heat off. Cool thoroughly.

Cherry Topping. Drain the cherries, reserving the liquid. Mix the cornstarch with ¾ cup cherry liquid, add the sugar and lemon rind, and cook 15 minutes over low heat, stirring constantly. Add the cherries and cool slightly.

Pour the topping on the cooled cake, spreading to ½ inch from the edge. Serves 8–10.

CHEESECAKE I

1½ recipes Crumb Crust*
2 (8 oz.) packages cream cheese
1 tablespoon vanilla
6 tablespoons sugar
¼ cup flour
¼ teaspoon salt
4 eggs
1 tablespoon lemon juice
1 cup heavy cream

Press the crust into a 9-inch spring-form pan, covering the bottom and sides. Cream the cheese with the vanilla and 2 tablespoons sugar. Add the flour and salt and continue creaming until light and fluffy. Add the well-beaten egg yolks and beat until smooth. Add the lemon juice and cream. Mix well again. Beat the egg whites until very foamy and add the remaining sugar gradually, beating constantly. Fold into the cheese mixture and pour into the cake pan. Bake in a 325° oven for 1½ hours; turn off heat and let cake stand in the oven ½ hour before removing. Serves 8–10.

CHEESECAKE II

Crumb Crust*
2 (8 oz.) packages cream cheese
2 eggs
⅔ cup plus 2 tablespoons sugar
2 teaspoons vanilla
1 cup sour cream

Press the crumb crust into the bottom and up the sides of a 9-inch slip-bottom pan. Chill. Cream the cheese until soft and smooth. Blend in the eggs, ⅔ cup sugar, and 1 teaspoon vanilla. Pour into crust and bake in a 375° oven for 20 minutes. Remove from oven and let stand 15 minutes. Meanwhile, combine the sour cream with the remaining sugar and vanilla. Carefully spread this over the baked filling. Return pie to a 425° oven and bake 10 minutes more. Cool; then chill overnight. Serve small pieces. Serves 8–10.

CHEESECAKE III

Crumb Crust*
8 ounces cottage cheese
2 (3 oz.) packages cream cheese
¾ cup sugar
2 eggs
1 teaspoon vanilla
½ cup sour cream

Press the crumb crust into the bottom and up the sides of a 9-inch pie plate. Sieve the cottage cheese and blend with the cream cheese and ½ cup sugar. Add to the beaten eggs and mix well. Stir in ½ teaspoon vanilla. Fill the crust with the cheese mixture and bake in a 350° oven for 25 minutes. Cover with a mixture of the sour cream and remaining sugar and vanilla. Return to oven for 10–15 minutes. Cool. Serves 8.

ICEBOX CHEESECAKE
(Low Calorie)

2 envelopes unflavored gelatin
½ cup sugar
½ teaspoon granulated noncaloric sweetener
⅛ teaspoon salt
2 eggs
1 cup skim milk
2 teaspoons grated lemon rind
1 pound dry cottage cheese
1 cup yoghurt
1 teaspoon vanilla
½ cup nonfat dry milk powder
2 tablespoons lemon juice
2 tablespoons graham-cracker crumbs
Dash ground mace

Mix the gelatin, ¼ cup sugar, sweetener, and salt in a double boiler. Add the egg yolks and skim milk. Stir just to mix. Cook about 5 minutes, until the gelatin is dissolved, stirring constantly. Remove from heat and add lemon rind. Cool to room temperature. Rub the cottage cheese through a sieve; stir in the yoghurt and vanilla. Fold into the gelatin mixture and chill. Beat the dry milk with ½ cup ice water with a rotary beater until thickened. Add lemon juice and continue to beat until consistency of whipped cream. Fold this into the cheese mixture. Beat the egg whites until frothy; gradually add the remaining sugar and continue to beat until thick shiny peaks form. Fold this into the cheese mixture and chill slightly. Turn into a 9-inch slip-bottom pan. Sprinkle top with the crumbs mixed with mace. Chill for about 2 hours, until firm. Serves 12.

DUNDEE CAKE   (Plate 35)

¾ cup butter
¾ cup sugar
3 eggs
2¼ cups flour
1 teaspoon baking powder
½ teaspoon salt
½ cup milk
1 teaspoon vanilla
Grated rind 1 orange
¼ cup chopped blanched almonds
1½ cups currants
1 cup raisins
6–8 blanched almonds (garnish)

Cream the butter with the sugar until soft and fluffy. Add the eggs one at a time, beating well after each addition. Sift the flour with the baking powder and salt. (Set aside 2 tablespoons to sprinkle over the raisins and currants.) Add the flour alternately with the milk to the creamed mixture. Mix lightly by hand after each addition. Mix in the vanilla, orange rind, chopped almonds, and the currants and raisins which have been tossed in the remaining flour. Spoon into a greased and floured 9×5×2¾-inch loaf pan. Decorate the top with split blanched almonds. Bake in a 325° oven for 1¼ hours, until done. Cool in the pan about 10 minutes before removing to a rack. Serves 12.

BURNT-SUGAR CAKE   (Plate 3)

1½ cups sugar
3 cups cake flour
1 tablespoon baking powder
¾ teaspoon salt
¾ cup butter
3 eggs
1 cup milk
1 teaspoon vanilla

BURNT-SUGAR CREAM FROSTING
½ cup butter
1 egg yolk
1 pound confectioners' sugar
2 tablespoons burnt-sugar syrup
2 tablespoons light cream

Melt and stir ½ cup sugar in a small heavy skillet. When dark in color and smooth, add ⅓ cup boiling water slowly and stir until dissolved. Cool the burnt-sugar syrup. Sift the flour, baking powder, and salt together. Cream the butter, add remaining sugar gradually, and beat until light and fluffy. Add egg yolks one at

a time, beating after each addition. Add 3 tablespoons burnt-sugar syrup and blend. Add flour mixture alternately with milk, beginning and ending with flour. Beat until smooth after each addition. Add vanilla. Beat the egg whites until a soft peak forms and fold into the batter. Turn into two 9-inch cake pans lined on the bottom with waxed paper. Bake in a 375° oven for 25–30 minutes. Turn out of the pans, remove paper, and cool.

Burnt-Sugar Cream Frosting. Cream the butter, add egg yolk, and continue beating. Add sugar gradually and the burnt-sugar syrup; then add the cream and beat until frosting is smooth, light, and of spreading consistency.

Frost the cake. Boil down the remaining burnt-sugar syrup until it spins a thread, cool almost to room temperature, and spoon it in patterns over the top of the frosting. Garnish with walnuts if you wish. Serves 8–10.

CHERRY UPSIDE-DOWN CAKE

2 (1 lb.) cans pitted tart red cherries
3 tablespoons butter
½ cup sugar
1½ teaspoons light corn syrup

BATTER
¼ cup butter
½ cup sugar
1 egg
1 cup cake flour
1 teaspoon baking powder
¼ teaspoon salt
6 tablespoons milk
¼ teaspoon almond flavoring
¼ teaspoon vanilla

SAUCE
1½ tablespoons cornstarch
6 tablespoons sugar

Drain the cherries thoroughly and save the liquid. Melt the butter in an 8×8×2-inch pan. Add the sugar and corn syrup and stir over low heat until sugar is dissolved and mixture is golden brown. Cool and top with cherries. Chill while you prepare the cake.

Batter. Cream the butter and sugar until light, add the egg, and beat until fluffy. Sift the cake flour with baking powder and salt. Add alternately with the milk. Add the flavorings and beat until smooth. Pour over the cherries. Bake in a 350° oven for 50–60 minutes, until the cake springs back lightly to the touch. Cool 15 minutes in the pan and turn out upside down on a platter.

Sauce. Mix the cornstarch with the sugar, add the cherry liquid, and cook, stirring constantly, for 10 minutes. Pour over the cake. Serve warm. Serves 6–8.

UPSIDE-DOWN PEACH GINGERBREAD

2 (1 lb. 4 oz.) cans sliced cling peaches
1 cup butter
1 cup dark brown sugar
2 tablespoons light corn syrup
Maraschino cherry halves
Pecan halves
½ cup chopped pecans
2 cups flour
1½ teaspoons ginger
1 teaspoon nutmeg
1 teaspoon baking soda
½ teaspoon salt
½ cup molasses
1 cup sugar
2 eggs
1 teaspoon grated lemon rind
1 cup heavy cream
2–3 tablespoons finely chopped crystallized
   ginger (optional)

Drain the peaches as dry as possible on paper toweling. Melt ½ cup butter in a heavy 10-inch skillet with an ovenproof handle. Add the brown sugar and corn syrup. Stir over medium heat until blended. Cool. Now arrange the peach slices in a circular pattern on top, covering as much of the sugar as possible. Fill in any spaces with well-drained maraschino cherries and with pecan halves. Sprinkle with the chopped nuts. Sift the flour, ginger, nutmeg, soda, and salt together twice. In a separate bowl mix the molasses and ½ cup boiling water. Cream remaining butter with the sugar until light and fluffy. Add the eggs one at a time, beating well after each addition. Flavor with grated lemon rind. Add the dry ingredients alternately with the molasses, ending with the flour. Pour into the skillet and spread evenly. Bake in a 350° oven for about 1½ hours. Let cool a little in the pan. Loosen the sides with a spatula and turn out onto a platter. Serve hot or cold with the cream, whipped. Add the crystallized ginger to the whipped cream if you wish. Serves 8–10.

PINEAPPLE UPSIDE-DOWN SCONE CAKE

1 (13 oz.) package scone mix
3 tablespoons butter
1 (1 lb. 4 oz.) can pineapple slices
8 maraschino cherries
½ cup chopped walnuts
1 cup light brown sugar
Whipped cream (garnish)

Prepare the scone mix according to package directions. Divide the dough into 8 equal parts. Form into balls and flatten them so they are about ½ inch thick. Spread 2 tablespoons melted butter on the bottom of a 15½ × 10½ × 1-inch jelly-roll pan. Drain syrup from the pineapple and set aside. Arrange 8 slices of pineapple in the pan. Place a maraschino cherry in the center of each and sprinkle with nuts. Cover each pineapple slice with a scone round, patting it evenly so it covers the pineapple. Measure 1 cup of the reserved syrup into a saucepan. Add the sugar and remaining butter. Bring to a boil and cook for 5 minutes. Cool. Spoon the syrup mixture over and around the cakes in the pan. Bake in a 450° oven for 20 minutes, until golden, basting the cakes occasionally with the syrup. Serve warm, pineapple side up, with whipped cream. Serves 8.

UPSIDE-DOWN MOCHA CAKE

1¼ cups sugar
1 cup flour
⅛ teaspoon salt
2 teaspoons baking powder
1 ounce unsweetened chocolate
2 tablespoons butter
½ cup milk
1 teaspoon vanilla
½ cup dark brown sugar
¼ cup cocoa
1 cup cold double-strength coffee

Sift ¾ cup sugar, the flour, salt, and baking powder together. Melt the chocolate and butter together over hot water. Blend in the milk and vanilla; mix well. Stir into the dry ingredients. Pour into a greased 8 × 8 × 2-inch pan. Combine the brown sugar, remaining granulated sugar, and the cocoa. Sprinkle over the batter. Pour the coffee over the top. Bake in a 350° oven for 40 minutes. Turn out upside down, allowing the sauce to drip down over the cake. Serve warm or cold. Serves 6–8.

PINEAPPLE UPSIDE-DOWN CAKE

3 tablespoons butter
1 cup dark brown sugar
Pineapple slices
Apricot halves
Maraschino cherries

BATTER

½ cup butter
1½ teaspoons grated orange rind
1 cup sugar
2 eggs
1½ cups cake flour
2 teaspoons baking powder
¼ teaspoon salt
½ cup orange juice
Whipped cream (garnish)

Melt the butter in a 10-inch iron skillet or one that has an ovenproof handle. Add the brown sugar. Heat slowly until the sugar and butter blend and begin to bubble. Arrange half slices of pineapple around the edge and a whole slice in the center. In between lay apricot halves cut side up. Put maraschino cherries here and there. Chill.

Batter. Cream the butter and grated orange rind. Add the sugar gradually and continue creaming until light and fluffy. Add the well-beaten eggs. Sift the flour, baking powder, and salt together and add alternately with the orange juice, beating after each addition until smooth.

Pour the batter over the fruit. Bake in a 350° oven for 50–60 minutes, until it springs back lightly to the touch. Turn out upside down. Serve warm or cold. Garnish with whipped cream. Serves 8.

BOSTON CREAM PIE

1 egg
½ cup sugar
1½ tablespoons melted shortening
½ cup plus 2 tablespoons flour
1 teaspoon baking powder
Pinch salt
6 tablespoons milk
Dash lemon juice

FILLING

1 cup heavy cream
3 tablespoons flour
6 tablespoons sugar
Pinch salt

1 egg
¼ teaspoon lemon juice
¼ teaspoon vanilla
Confectioners' sugar or Chocolate Glaze*

Beat the egg until light and add the sugar gradually. When well blended, add the melted shortening. Sift the flour, baking powder, and salt together. Add alternately with the milk. Flavor with lemon. Pour batter into an 8-inch cake pan lined on the bottom with waxed paper. Bake in a 375° oven for 20–25 minutes. Remove from pan and pull off paper. Cool. Split into 2 layers.

Filling. Scald the cream. Mix the flour with the sugar and salt. Beat the egg well and add the cream. Blend this into the dry ingredients and cook in a double boiler, stirring constantly, until thick and smooth. Cool and flavor with lemon, and vanilla.

Put the layers of cake together with the filling. Sift a little confectioners' sugar over the top, or top with Chocolate Glaze. Although this is traditionally called pie, it is actually a cake. Serves 6–8.

WASHINGTON CREAM PIE

Make the cake as for Boston Cream Pie* and fill with jam or jelly, omitting the custard filling. Sprinkle the top with confectioners' sugar.

PLAIN CAKE ROLL

4 eggs
¾ teaspoon baking powder
¼ teaspoon salt
¾ cup sugar
1 teaspoon vanilla
¾ cup cake flour
Confectioners' sugar

Beat the eggs with baking powder and salt in a bowl and set over (not in) hot water. Beat until foamy. Then begin adding the sugar gradually and continue beating until mixture becomes thick and lemon-colored. Remove bowl from over the hot water and add vanilla. Fold in the cake flour. Grease a 15½ × 10½ × 1-inch jelly-roll pan, line the bottom with waxed paper, and grease again. Spread the batter evenly in the pan. Bake in a 400° oven for 12–13 minutes, until it springs back to the touch. Turn out upside down on a cloth dusted with confectioners' sugar. Pull the paper off carefully, trim off edges, and roll up in the cloth. Cool. Unroll to fill. Serves 8.

CHOCOLATE ROLL

2 ounces unsweetened chocolate
4 eggs
¾ cup plus 2 tablespoons sugar
½ cup flour
½ teaspoon baking powder
¼ teaspoon baking soda
1 teaspoon vanilla
Confectioners' sugar
Sweetened Whipped Cream*

Melt the chocolate and let cool. Beat the eggs well, gradually add ¾ cup sugar, and continue beating until thick and light. Sift the flour with the baking powder and fold into the eggs. Fold in the melted chocolate, remaining sugar, 3 tablespoons cold water, soda, and vanilla. Grease a 15½ × 10½ × 1-inch pan, line with waxed paper, and grease again. Spread the mixture evenly in the pan and bake in a 350° oven for 25–30 minutes. Remove from pan, dust with confectioners' sugar, and turn out on a towel sprinkled with confectioners' sugar. Remove paper. Roll up immediately in the towel and leave until cool. Unroll, spread with almond-flavored Sweetened Whipped Cream and roll up immediately. Serves 6–8.

COCOA ROLL WITH MOUSSE FILLING

MOUSSE FILLING
1½ cups semisweet chocolate bits
⅓ cup sugar
2 teaspoons vanilla
5 eggs

COCOA ROLL
6 tablespoons cake flour
6 tablespoons cocoa
¼ teaspoon salt
¾ teaspoon baking powder
4 eggs
¾ cup sugar
1 teaspoon vanilla
Confectioners' sugar

Mousse Filling. Melt the chocolate with the sugar and ¼ cup water in a double boiler. Stir until smooth. Remove from heat, cool, and add the vanilla and egg yolks, beaten until

thick. Add the stiffly beaten egg whites and beat with rotary beater just to incorporate all the whites. Refrigerate for 3–4 hours, until of spreading consistency.

Cocoa Roll. Sift the flour, cocoa, salt, and baking powder together 3 times. Beat the egg whites until they form a soft peak, and beat in the sugar 1 tablespoon at a time. Beat the egg yolks until thick, add vanilla, and fold in the egg whites. Next, fold in the dry ingredients. Grease a 15½ × 10½ × 1-inch pan and line on the bottom with greased waxed paper. Spread the batter evenly and bake in a 400° oven for 13 minutes. Turn out on a towel sprinkled with confectioners' sugar. Remove paper. Quickly cut off crisp edges, roll up in the towel, and cool.

Unroll, spread generously with the filling, and roll up again. Chill several hours or overnight. This roll freezes well. Serves 8.

NUT ROLL

6 eggs
¾ cup sugar
Pinch salt
1 teaspoon baking powder
1½ cups finely ground walnuts, pecans, or almonds
Confectioners' sugar

MAPLE FILLING
¾ cup maple syrup
2 egg whites

Beat the egg yolks until thick and lemon-colored and add the sugar gradually. Then add the salt, baking powder, ground nuts, and the egg whites which have been beaten until a soft peak forms. Mix well. Grease a 15½ × 10½ × 1-inch pan, line the bottom with waxed paper, and grease again. Spread the mixture in the pan and bake in a 350° oven for 15 minutes, until golden brown. Turn out on a towel that has been dusted with confectioners' sugar. Carefully peel the waxed paper from the bottom of the cake and cut off crisp edges. Roll it up in the towel to cool.

Maple Filling. Cook the maple syrup until it is thick enough to spin a thread (238°). Beat the egg whites until a soft peak forms. Gradually pour in the hot syrup, continuing to beat until filling is very thick and glossy.

Unroll the cake, spread with the filling, and roll up like a jelly roll. Serves 8–10.

OLD-FASHIONED JELLY ROLL (*Plate 3*)

1 cup cake flour
¼ teaspoon salt
¾ teaspoon baking powder
5 eggs
1 teaspoon grated lemon rind
2 tablespoons lemon juice
1 cup sugar
1 cup red currant jelly

SUGAR GLAZE

1 tablespoon lemon juice
2 teaspoons light cream
¾ cup confectioners' sugar
Few drops cooking oil

Sift the flour, salt, and baking powder together. Beat the egg yolks until thick and lemon-colored. Stir in lemon rind and juice and beat well. Gradually add sugar, beating until very thick. Beat the egg whites until a soft peak forms. Add the flour to the yolk mixture alternately with egg whites in three additions, folding in gently and thoroughly. Spread evenly in a 15½ × 10½ × 1-inch pan that has been lightly greased, lined on the bottom with waxed paper, and greased again. Bake in a 400° oven for 12–14 minutes, until it springs back to the touch. Turn cake out onto a cloth that has been dusted with confectioners' sugar. Quickly remove paper and trim crisp edges. Roll up in towel and cool. Put jelly in a bowl and break it up with a fork. Unroll cake and evenly spread with jelly. Roll up again and place seam side down on a serving plate. You may serve sprinkled with confectioners' sugar or with glaze.

Sugar Glaze. Stir the lemon juice and cream into sugar, add oil, and beat until smooth. Spoon over the cake roll. Decorate if you wish. Serves 8.

ANGEL RASPBERRY ROLL
(Low Calorie)

1 package angel-food cake mix
1 package dessert topping mix
1 pint raspberries
2 tablespoons confectioners' sugar (garnish)

Make the cake according to package directions; spread half in a 15½ × 10½ × 1-inch pan. Bake and cool. (Bake the rest in a loaf pan for another dessert.) Remove cooled cake from pan and roll up in a towel which has been dusted with confectioners' sugar. Pre-

pare the dessert topping mix according to package directions. Beat in ½ cup berries as you whip. Unroll cake and spread with filling, reserving ½ cup for garnish. Roll as a jelly roll. Wrap well in foil and store in refrigerator for an hour before serving. Arrange on a serving plate, sift sugar over the top, and garnish platter with fluffs of remaining filling and berries. Serves 12 (100 calories per serving).

BABAS AU RHUM

1 package active dry or compressed yeast
3 eggs
¼ teaspoon salt
1½ cups plus 1 tablespoon flour
5 teaspoons sugar
6 tablespoons melted butter

SYRUP

½ cup sugar
½ cup apricot juice or 1 cup water
1 teaspoon lemon juice
½–¾ cup rum

Soften the yeast in ½ cup warm water (110°–115°). Beat 2 eggs until very light, add salt, and stir into the yeast liquid. Put the flour into a bowl, make a well in the center, and pour in the egg mixture. Beat thoroughly with a spoon until smooth. Beat the other egg until very light and mix into the dough. Cover the bowl and let the dough rise for 1 hour in a warm place. When it has risen, beat in the sugar and slightly cooled melted butter. Cover and let rise another hour. Butter 8 individual custard cups and fill each ⅓ full. Bake 15–20 minutes in a 400° oven. The babas should be golden brown. Loosen with a spatula and turn out.

Syrup. Combine the sugar and apricot juice or water in a saucepan and simmer for 10 minutes. Remove from heat and add lemon juice and ½ cup rum.

Invert the babas and pour the syrup over them. Let them stand several hours, basting with the syrup several times before serving. However, if you wish to serve them flambé, warm them and pour an additional ¼ cup warmed rum over them and ignite. Serves 8.

SAVARIN
(Baba au Rhum Ring)

Proceed as for Babas au Rhum,* baking in a ring mold in a 375° oven for 25–30 minutes until golden brown. Serves 8.

FROSTED APRICOT BABA RING

1 (1 lb. 2½ oz.) package yellow cake mix
½ cup toasted flaked coconut
½ teaspoon vanilla
1 (1 lb. 13 oz.) can peeled apricot halves
¼ cup sugar
2 tablespoons rum or rum flavoring
2 tablespoons lemon juice
3 pints vanilla ice cream and/or lemon
  sherbet (optional)
Coconut (garnish)

Prepare the cake mix according to package directions. Stir in the toasted coconut and vanilla. Pour into a well-greased and floured 3-quart ring mold. Bake in a 350° oven for 40–50 minutes, until cake is golden and springs back to the touch. Cool on a rack for 15 minutes before removing from the mold. While the cake is baking, drain the syrup from the apricots. Measure ¾ cup apricot syrup into a saucepan; add the sugar, rum or rum flavoring, and lemon juice. Bring to a boil and cook for 5 minutes. Cool slightly and spoon over the cake. Purée the apricots in a blender or food mill. Spread over the top and sides of the cake. Fill the center of ring with balls of vanilla ice cream and/or lemon sherbet if you wish. Sprinkle with coconut. Serves 10.

CHILLED MOCHA TORTE

1 (10-inch) Angel-Food Cake*
2 ounces unsweetened chocolate
6 tablespoons very strong coffee
1 cup butter
1½ cups confectioners' sugar
Pinch salt
1 teaspoon vanilla
2 eggs
Sweetened Whipped Cream* (garnish)

This dessert must be made the day before it is to be served. Slice the cake into 6 layers. Melt the chocolate with the coffee and stir until smooth. Cool. Cream the butter and sugar together thoroughly. Add salt, vanilla, and the egg yolks. Beat thoroughly and add the chocolate. Fold in the egg whites beaten until a soft peak forms. Spread mixture between the layers of the cake. Chill overnight. Garnish or frost with Sweetened Whipped Cream if you wish. Serves 8–10.

FRUITED ORANGE CREAM LADY-FINGER CAKE

1½ cups raisins
2 envelopes unflavored gelatin
1 cup sugar
¼ teaspoon salt
1 cup frozen orange-juice concentrate
2 cups heavy cream
⅔ cup mixed candied fruits
½ cup coarsely chopped walnuts
18–20 ladyfingers

Cover the raisins with boiling water and let stand for 10 minutes. Drain thoroughly. Soften the gelatin in ½ cup cold water; add 1 cup boiling water and stir until dissolved. Add the sugar, salt, and the orange-juice concentrate. Mix thoroughly and chill until syrupy. Fold the cream, whipped, into the orange mixture with raisins, fruits, and nuts. Line an 8-inch spring-form mold on bottom and sides with split ladyfingers. Pour in the fruit mixture and chill until firm, preferably overnight. Unmold and serve. Serves 8–10.

CHOCOLATE MOUSSE CAKE (Plate 8)

18–20 ladyfingers
1 pound 2 ounces sweet baking chocolate
¼ cup confectioners' sugar
5 eggs plus 2 egg yolks
1½ teaspoons vanilla
Sweetened Whipped Cream*
1 ounce unsweetened chocolate (garnish)

Split the ladyfingers and arrange a layer on the bottom of a 9×5×3-inch pan which has been lined with waxed paper. Trim the ladyfingers if necessary to fill the area completely. Break up the chocolate and melt it with 3 tablespoons water in a double boiler. Remove from heat and stir in the confectioners' sugar, egg yolks, and vanilla. Beat smooth; cool. Beat the egg whites until a soft peak forms and blend into chocolate mixture. Spread half of this over the layer of ladyfingers. Make another layer of ladyfingers and top with the rest of the chocolate. Arrange remaining ladyfingers on top, cover with foil or Saran, and refrigerate overnight. Turn out of pan, peel off waxed paper, frost with Sweetened Whipped Cream, and garnish with chocolate curls. Serves 8–10.

CHOCOLATE ICEBOX CAKE

2 (6 oz.) packages semisweet chocolate bits
7 eggs
1 teaspoon vanilla
18 ladyfingers or spongecake strips
1 cup heavy cream
Chocolate shavings (garnish)

Melt the chocolate with 4½ tablespoons hot water in a double boiler. Add the well-beaten egg yolks and cook, stirring constantly, about 7 minutes, until thickened. Remove from heat, add vanilla; cool. Line a 1½–2-quart glass loaf pan with waxed paper. Use 2 wide strips of paper, laying one lengthwise, the other crosswise, leaving enough paper to cover the top from both ends and sides. Beat the egg whites until a soft peak forms and fold carefully into the chocolate mixture. Pour into the paper-lined pan. Layer the top with ladyfingers or spongecake strips cut to fit. Fold the paper over. Refrigerate several hours. When ready to serve, cut away the top paper and turn out on a platter. Remove the rest of the paper and frost with the cream, whipped. Garnish with chocolate shavings. Serves 8.

CHOCOLATE GRAHAM ICEBOX CAKE

⅓ cup sugar
¼ cup cocoa
1 cup heavy cream
½ teaspoon vanilla
16 graham crackers

Mix the sugar and cocoa. Whip the cream until slightly thickened; then add cocoa mixture gradually while beating. Add vanilla and beat until stiff. Spread the graham crackers with whipped cream, placing one in front of the other on a platter. Press gently together. Spread remaining cream over top and down the sides. Chill at least 4 hours, preferably overnight. To serve, slice diagonally. Serves 6.

GINGER ICEBOX CAKE

2 cups heavy cream
5 tablespoons dark molasses
½ pound ginger wafers

Whip the cream and mix with molasses. Reserve ¾ cup molasses cream for the frosting. Spread the ginger wafers with the remaining mixture and stack in a long roll on a platter or long pan. Frost the roll completely with the reserved molasses cream. Chill at least 6 hours or overnight. Slice diagonally to serve. Serves 8.

CHILLED ORANGE CAKE

1 envelope unflavored gelatin
1 cup sugar
Pinch salt
1 cup orange juice
3 tablespoons lemon juice
3 egg whites
1 dozen ladyfingers or 1 spongecake
Orange sections (garnish)
Shredded coconut (garnish)

Soften the gelatin in ¼ cup cold water; add ½ cup boiling water, the sugar, and salt, and stir until dissolved. Add the orange and lemon juices. Mix well and chill until syrupy. Beat until foamy and fold in the stiffly beaten egg whites. Pour into a 1½-quart mold which has been lined with split ladyfingers or strips of spongecake. Chill at least 6 hours or overnight. Unmold and garnish with orange sections and coconut if you wish. Serves 6.

CHILLED PINEAPPLE CAKE

1 (9-inch) white layer cake
PINEAPPLE FILLING
3 eggs
6 tablespoons sugar
1 (1 lb. 4 oz.) can crushed pineapple
¾ cup butter
1 cup superfine sugar
Pinch salt
1 tablespoon lemon juice
Sweetened Whipped Cream* (garnish)
Canned or crystallized pineapple (garnish)
Coconut (garnish)

Use your favorite 2-layer cake recipe or mix, but bake in three 9-inch pans instead of two, decreasing the baking time about 10 minutes.

Pineapple Filling. Beat the egg yolks until thick; add the sugar gradually while beating. Drain the pineapple and add 3 tablespoons of the syrup to the egg mixture. Cook for about 10 minutes in a double boiler, stirring constantly. Cool. Cream the butter with the superfine sugar until light. Add the cooled custard and beat well. Beat the egg whites and salt until a soft peak forms and fold into the custard. Fold in the pineapple and lemon juice.

Split the cake layers to make 6 very thin layers. Put together with the filling; use some on top if you wish. Chill overnight. If you have left the top plain, cover with almond-flavored Sweetened Whipped Cream before serving. If you wish, garnish with pieces of pineapple and/or grated coconut. Serves 12.

FOUR-LAYER CHOCOLATE TORTE

10 ounces semisweet chocolate
1¼ cups butter
12 eggs
3 cups confectioners' sugar
1½ cups cake flour

CHOCOLATE CREAM FROSTING
6 ounces unsweetened chocolate
½ cup butter
6 cups confectioners' sugar
1 cup heavy cream
2 teaspoons vanilla
2–3 tablespoons semisweet chocolate curls (garnish)

Melt the semisweet chocolate and butter in a double boiler. Cool and reserve. Beat 6 eggs until lemon-colored and thick. Gradually add 1½ cups sugar and continue beating 5–10 minutes, until sugar is dissolved. Sift the cake flour 3 times; fold ¾ cup into egg-sugar mixture. Add exactly half the cooled chocolate mixture to the batter a little at a time, mixing well after each addition. Divide the batter between two 9-inch cake pans lined with waxed paper. Bake in a 350° oven for about 25 minutes, until the tops spring back to the touch. Cool in pans 1–2 minutes, turn out on racks, and remove paper. Cool thoroughly. Use the remaining ingredients to prepare and bake 2 more cake layers in exactly the same way.

Chocolate Cream Frosting. Melt the chocolate in a double boiler. Cool. Cream the butter until light and fluffy. Add the sugar a little at a time, alternating with the cream and melted chocolate, beating well after each addition. Beat until sugar dissolves. Add vanilla and mix well.

Put the layers of cake together with about 1 cup frosting between layers (3 cups in all). Use remaining frosting to cover the top and sides of cake. Decorate the top with chocolate curls. Serves 14–16.

EASY COFFEE TORTE

1 (10-inch) Angel-Food Cake*
1 tablespoon instant coffee
1 (7½ oz.) jar marshmallow cream
¾ cup heavy cream
½ teaspoon vanilla
Shaved chocolate and/or toasted chopped almonds (garnish)

Split the cake into 4 layers. Dissolve the instant coffee in 1 teaspoon hot water. Blend into the marshmallow cream. Fold in the cream, whipped and flavored with vanilla. Spread on layers and top of the cake. Sprinkle with chocolate and/or almonds. Chill thoroughly. Serves 10–12.

STRAWBERRY TORTE   (*Plate 2*)

1 package white cake mix
2 eggs plus 2 egg whites
1½ teaspoons almond flavoring
¼ teaspoon cream of tartar
1 cup sugar
½ teaspoon nutmeg
1 quart strawberries
2 cups heavy cream
Red food coloring (optional)

Mix the cake according to package directions, but use 2 egg yolks in place of the egg whites and add 1 teaspoon almond flavoring. Divide the batter evenly among three 9-inch cake pans which have been lined on the bottom with waxed paper. Refrigerate. Beat the egg whites with the cream of tartar until frothy. Add the sugar 2 tablespoons at a time, beating well after each addition. Continue beating until all sugar is dissolved and a very stiff meringue is formed. Fold in the nutmeg and spread the meringue evenly over the tops of the pans of batter. Bake in a 325° oven for 40 minutes. While the cake is baking, cut the hulled berries in half and sugar lightly. Cool the cake slightly, loosen edges, and turn out of pans. Remove paper and cool completely. Whip the cream with the remaining almond flavoring and with a few drops of red food coloring if you wish. Spread a little of the whipped cream on the top of a layer, add a few berries, then place the next layer on top. Repeat. When the third layer is in place, frost the sides of the cake with the rest of the whipped cream and make a crown effect on top with small spoonfuls of cream. Mound the remaining berries in the center. Serves 12.

DATE NUT TORTE

1 cup sugar
2 tablespoons flour
1 teaspoon baking powder
2 eggs
1 cup coarsely chopped walnuts
1½ cups cut-up pitted dates
1 teaspoon cinnamon
Whipped cream (optional)

Sift ¾ cup sugar, the flour, and baking powder together. Beat the eggs until light and fluffy. Add the dry ingredients and mix well. Fold in the nuts and dates. Pour into a well-greased and floured 8-inch spring-form pan. Sprinkle with a mixture of the remaining sugar and the cinnamon. Bake in a 300° oven for 30–40 minutes, until golden brown. Serve warm with almond- or rum-flavored whipped cream if you wish. Serves 6–8.

MERINGUE NUT TORTE

1½ cups crushed saltines
2 cups chopped pecans
2 teaspoons baking powder
6 egg whites
2 cups sugar
2 tablespoons rum or 2 teaspoons almond
    flavoring
Sweetened Whipped Cream* (optional)

Mix the crumbs with the nuts and baking powder. Beat the egg whites until a peak forms and add the sugar a tablespoon at a time, continuing to beat until stiff and glossy. Add the rum or almond flavoring. Fold in the cracker-crumb mixture. Spread into 2 greased and floured 9-inch slip-bottom cake pans. Mound the mixture up in the middle slightly. Bake 40 minutes in a 325° oven. Remove from pans and cool on a rack. Put the layers together with the Sweetened Whipped Cream. Serves 6–8.

WALNUT TORTE

3 cups finely chopped walnuts
1 cup commercial toasted bread crumbs
¼ teaspoon salt
9 eggs
1½ cups sugar
¾ cup orange juice
1½ teaspoons grated orange rind
2 cups heavy cream
¼ cup confectioners' sugar
1 (12 oz.) jar raspberry jam or jelly
Fresh or frozen raspberries (garnish)

Mix the walnuts with bread crumbs and salt. Beat the egg yolks until very thick and lemon-colored, gradually adding 1 cup and 2 tablespoons sugar while continuing to beat. Blend in the orange juice and rind. Beat the egg whites until a meringue is formed, gradually adding the remaining sugar a tablespoon at a time, beating well after each addition. Fold the nut-crumb mixture into the yolk mixture alternately with the meringue, ending with meringue. Divide into 2 greased 9-inch round cake pans lined on the bottom with waxed paper. Bake in a 325° oven for 30–35 minutes. Turn out on racks, remove paper, and cool. Whip the cream with the confectioners' sugar. If you use jam, put it through a sieve to remove seeds; if jelly, break it up with a fork. Put the layers together with whipped cream and jam or jelly. Spread the top with whipped cream and top with jam or jelly. Decorate with more whipped cream and with raspberries if you wish. This may be put together some hours ahead of time. Serves 12.

SANDTORTE

1 cup butter
1 cup sugar
2 teaspoons grated lemon rind
6 eggs
2 tablespoons rum or 1½ tablespoons lemon
    juice
1 cup flour
1 cup cornstarch
2 teaspoons baking powder
½ teaspoon salt

Cream the butter thoroughly and add the sugar and lemon rind gradually while beating. Beat in the egg yolks one at a time and add the rum or lemon juice. Sift the flour, cornstarch, baking powder, and salt together. Beat the dry ingredients into the creamed mixture. This cake needs a great deal of beating. Fold in the egg whites which have been whipped until a soft peak forms. Pour at once into a well-greased 9-inch spring-form or tube pan and bake in a 350° oven for 45 minutes. Serve with flavored whipped cream if you like. Serves 8–10.

DOBOSCHTORTE
(Many-Layer Cake)

8 eggs
1 cup sugar
1 teaspoon vanilla
¼ teaspoon salt
1 cup cake flour
Sweet butter
2 recipes Chocolate Frosting*
Chopped toasted filberts (optional)

Beat the egg yolks until thick and light; add ½ cup sugar while beating and flavor with vanilla and salt. Beat the egg whites until a soft peak forms, gradually adding ¼ cup sugar. Gently fold the yolks into the whites. Sift part of the flour over the eggs and fold in gently; repeat with remaining flour. Generously butter the bottom of four 8-inch cake pans and divide half the batter among them. Bake in a 325° oven for about 15 minutes, until light golden. Remove from pan and cool. Repeat with remaining batter. Cool layers for several hours. Spread 7 of the layers with Chocolate Frosting and top with the plain one. Make a caramel by boiling the remaining sugar with ¼ cup water. Stir constantly until sugar dissolves and liquid is brown and smooth. Quickly spread the caramel over the top of the torte and score with a heated knife into V-shaped serving portions. If you like, spread the Chocolate Frosting on the sides also and sprinkle thickly with chopped nuts. Let stand several hours before serving. Serves 8–10.

LINZERTORTE

1½ cups butter
1 cup confectioners' sugar
1 egg
2¾ cups flour
1½ cups ground filberts
Pinch salt
½ teaspoon cinnamon
2 cups raspberry jam
2 teaspoons lemon juice
Confectioners' sugar (garnish)

Cream the butter with the sugar until light and fluffy. Add the egg and beat well. Fold in the flour alternately with a mixture of the ground filberts, salt, and cinnamon. Chill the dough. Roll it out ¼ inch thick. Cover the bottom and make a rim about 1 inch up the sides of a 9-inch spring-form pan. Mix 1½ cups jam and lemon juice and spread over the bottom. Roll out the remaining dough, cut it into ½-inch strips, and form a lattice over the jam. Bake in a 375° oven for 40 minutes. Cool, remove from pan, and fill the squares formed by the lattice with the remaining jam. Sprinkle with confectioners' sugar. Serves 10.

PISCHINGERTORTE

6 Oblaten (Carlsbader)
1½ cups sugar
12 ounces semisweet chocolate
½ cup ground filberts
1 tablespoon butter

Oblaten are large round wafers and are available in specialty food departments. Heat the sugar with ¾ cup water in a saucepan. When it comes to a boil, add 8 ounces chocolate and stir until melted. Add the nuts. Cool slightly and spread on the Oblaten layers, stacking them on top of each other like a layer cake. Melt the remaining chocolate with butter and pour it over the top and sides of the cake. Work fast, as chocolate sets quickly. Chill. Serves 8.

SACHERTORTE

5 ounces unsweetened chocolate
⅔ cup butter
1 cup sugar
6 eggs
1 cup flour
1 (12 oz.) jar apricot jam or jelly
2–3 tablespoons apricot brandy or water
Chocolate Frosting*
Sweetened Whipped Cream* (optional)

Finely grate the chocolate. Cream the butter and sugar until light and fluffy. Add the egg yolks alternately with the flour, beating after each addition. Blend in the grated chocolate. Beat the egg whites until a soft peak forms and fold gently into the batter. Turn into an 8-inch spring-form pan which has been greased only on the bottom and bake in a 325° oven for about 1 hour. Cool. Remove from pan and let stand overnight. Melt the apricot jam or jelly and cool slightly. Thin with the brandy or water. Spread generously over the top and sides of the torte and frost with Chocolate Frosting. In Vienna this moist, rich torte is served with Sweetened Whipped Cream. Serves 8.

VIENNA TORTE

This cake is very rich; ideal for large parties or teas. It may be completely prepared and kept as much as a week before you plan to serve it.

> 12 eggs
> 1 cup sugar
> 1 teaspoon vanilla
> 1½ cups flour
> 2 teaspoons baking powder

MOCHA FILLING
> 4 ounces sweet baking chocolate
> ½ cup strong coffee
> 1½ cups confectioners' sugar
> 2 cups sweet butter

CHOCOLATE FROSTING
> 5 ounces unsweetened chocolate
> 1 pound confectioners' sugar
> 2 eggs
> ⅔ cup butter
> 2 teaspoons vanilla

Beat the egg yolks until light. Add the sugar and continue beating until very light-colored and thick. Add 6 tablespoons water and the vanilla. Sift the flour with the baking powder and add to the egg mixture. Beat the egg whites until a stiff peak forms. Carefully fold them into the batter. Divide the batter evenly among four 15½ × 10½ × 1-inch jelly-roll pans generously greased with sweet butter. You may refrigerate part of the batter while baking 1 or 2 layers at a time. The batter should barely cover the bottom of the pans, as thin layers are important. Bake in a 375° oven for 15 minutes. Turn the layers out and cool on wire racks. Cut each cake in half crosswise so you have 8 layers. Cover with a towel while you prepare the filling and frosting.

Mocha Filling. Break the chocolate into pieces. Cook with the coffee and ½ cup confectioners' sugar until it reaches 220° on a candy thermometer. Cool. Meanwhile, cream the butter and remaining sugar until fluffy. Mix in the chocolate mixture and chill until spreading consistency. Assemble the cake with filling divided equally among the layers.

Chocolate Frosting. Melt the chocolate in a mixing bowl over hot water. Beat in the sugar and 6 tablespoons water with a rotary beater. Add the remaining ingredients and beat well. The mixture will be thin at this point. Place the bowl in ice water and beat until the right consistency to spread.

Frost the top and sides of the cake, making swirls with the back of a spoon. Refrigerate the cake overnight for ease in slicing. Cut the cake into 1-inch slices, then each piece in half. Serves 20.

SCHAUMTORTE

> 8 egg whites
> ¼ teaspoon salt
> ½ teaspoon cream of tartar
> 2 cups superfine sugar
> ¾ teaspoon vanilla
> 1 quart strawberries or raspberries
> ⅓–½ cup sugar
> ½ cup finely chopped toasted filberts or almonds
> 4 cups Sweetened Whipped Cream*

Beat the egg whites with the salt and cream of tartar until a peak forms. Add the sugar a tablespoonful at a time, beating well after each addition. Add vanilla and continue to beat until smooth and glossy and sugar is completely dissolved. Draw three 9-inch circles on heavy brown paper. Carefully fill in one with a layer of meringue, and pipe a border around the edge with a pastry tube. Fill in the other two circles with meringue, using either a pastry tube or back of a spoon. Bake on baking sheets in a 225° oven for about 45 minutes, until the meringue is cream-colored. You may have to change the position of the meringues in the oven to insure even baking. Pull off the paper and return meringues to a slightly warm oven (about 200°) for 1–2 hours. Reserve a few perfect berries. If you are using large strawberries, slice them. Sprinkle them with sugar. Fold the nuts into 3 cups of the Sweetened Whipped Cream and spread on the two plain meringue disks. Cover with berries. Put the layers together and top with the bordered one. Decorate with the remaining Sweetened Whipped Cream and garnish with the reserved whole berries. This should be served at once. Serves 12–14

COOKTIPS

Add a little salt to flour before mixing with a liquid to prevent lumping.

Grease and dust pans with cocoa when baking chocolate cupcakes.

Plate 5. GLAZED ORANGE CAKE glistening with orange glaze.

Plate 6. SOUTHERN COCONUT CAKE with a lemon butter filling.

Plate 7. MOLASSES GINGER CAKE with white frosting decorated with jelly beans.

Plate 8. CHOCOLATE MOUSSE CAKE decorated with whipped cream and chocolate curls.

Plate 9. WHITE FRUITCAKE AMANDINE is covered with crunchy, sugary AMANDINE TOPPING.

COCONUT CRUNCH TORTE

4 egg whites
¼ teaspoon salt
1 cup sugar
1 teaspoon vanilla
1 cup graham-cracker crumbs
½ cup flaked coconut
½ cup chopped pecans
1 pint butter pecan ice cream (optional)

Beat the egg whites with the salt until frothy. Add sugar gradually and continue to beat until whites stand in soft peaks. Add vanilla. Fold in cracker crumbs, coconut, and pecans. Spread in a buttered 9-inch cake pan. Bake in a 350° oven for ½ hour. Cool, cut in wedges, and serve with ice cream if you wish. Serves 6.

ZUPPA INGLESE
(A Rich Italian Cake)

9 egg yolks
⅔ cup sugar
½ cup orange juice
½ cup Marsala or sweet sherry
1½ teaspoons unflavored gelatin
5 seedless oranges
1 (10-inch) Spongecake* or Angel-Food
  Cake*
½ cup chopped nuts
3–4 tablespoons finely chopped candied
  orange peel
2 cups heavy cream
Bing cherries (garnish)

Beat the egg yolks, adding the sugar gradually, until very thick and light. Add the orange juice, wine, and gelatin which has been softened in 2 tablespoons water. Mix well and pour into a double boiler. Cook over simmering water, beating constantly with a rotary beater until custard is thick and doubled in bulk, about 8 or 9 minutes. Immediately set the pan of sauce in cold water to chill. Peel the oranges with a sharp knife and cut into sections, avoiding all connecting membranes. Split the cake into 3 layers. Lift the large layer of cake onto the center of a cake plate. Spread ⅓ of the cold zabaglione (the custard) on the cake layer, arrange ⅓ of the orange sections on it, and sprinkle with nuts and about 1 tablespoon of the candied orange peel. Put the second layer of cake on top of this and repeat the routine with zabaglione, oranges, nuts, and peel. Put on top layer of cake and heap the remaining za-baglione on it. If some of the zabaglione comes out between the layers, smooth it onto the sides of the cake. Refrigerate overnight. Frost the sides of the cake with the cream, whipped; mound the rest on top. Sprinkle the center with bits of candied orange peel and make a border around the outer rim of the top with orange sections. Decorate the platter with mounds of orange sections and pitted Bing cherries stuffed with candied orange peel if you wish. Serves 12–14.

EASY ZUPPA INGLESE

1 package vanilla pudding mix
1 cup milk
1 cup Nesselrode sauce
3 (8–9 inch) layers bakery spongecake
Sweetened Whipped Cream*

Cook the vanilla pudding mix, using the milk. Add the Nesselrode sauce. Split the cake layers and put them together with the filling. Chill. Top with the Sweetened Whipped Cream. Serves 8–10.

GRAHAM-CRACKER CAKE

½ cup flour
2 teaspoons baking powder
¼ teaspoon salt
½ cup butter
1 cup sugar
1 teaspoon vanilla
3 eggs
1¾ cups graham-cracker crumbs
¾ cup milk
½ cup chopped nuts

Sift the flour, baking powder, and salt together. Cream the butter and sugar together. Add the vanilla. Beat the egg yolks until light and thick and add. Mix thoroughly. Stir in part of the cracker crumbs and part of the milk. Then add the rest of the crumbs and beat thoroughly. Add the remaining milk alternately with the flour, beginning and ending with flour. Beat until smooth. Stir in the nuts. Fold in the stiffly beaten egg whites. Pour into two 9-inch cake pans lined on the bottom with waxed paper. Bake in a 375° oven for 25–30 minutes. Remove from pan, pull off paper, and cool. Good with Seven-Minute* or other frosting. Serves 8.

FRUITCAKE

¼ *pound candied lemon peel*
¼ *pound candied orange peel*
¼ *pound citron*
1½ *pounds mixed candied fruit*
½ *pound white raisins*
6 *tablespoons pineapple juice*
1 *cup toasted filberts*
½ *cup blanched almonds split lengthwise*
⅔ *cup pecans*
2 *cups plus 2 tablespoons flour*
1 *cup butter*
½ *cup sugar*
½ *cup honey*
5 *eggs*
1 *teaspoon salt*
1 *teaspoon baking powder*
1 *teaspoon allspice*
1 *teaspoon cloves*
Candied cherries (*garnish*)
Blanched almonds (*garnish*)
Brandy or sherry (*optional*)

Cut the lemon peel, orange peel, citron, and candied fruit into small pieces and combine with the raisins. Let stand overnight in pineapple juice. Mix the filberts (skins rub off easily after toasting), almonds, and pecans. Toss the nuts with 2 tablespoons flour. Mix with the fruit. Cream the butter and sugar until fluffy. Add the honey gradually. Then add the eggs one at a time, beating well after each addition. Cream well. Sift the remaining 2 cups of flour, the salt, baking powder, allspice, and cloves together. Add to batter and beat until smooth. If using a mixer, remove beater and add fruits and nuts by hand. Mix thoroughly. Line two 9×5×2¾-inch pans with two thicknesses of buttered brown paper; pour the batter into the pans. Decorate with candied cherries and blanched almonds. Bake in a 275° oven for 3½–4 hours. Put a pan of hot water on bottom of oven to keep cake from drying out. Bake at least 3 weeks in advance. Wrap cakes in cheesecloth dampened with sherry or brandy, if you like, and then wrap in foil. Serves about 40.

REFRIGERATOR FRUITCAKE

½ *pound pitted dates*
½ *pound figs*
¾ *pound marshmallows*
1 *cup chopped walnuts*
¼ *teaspoon salt*
1 *tablespoon grated orange rind*
1 (3 *oz.*) *package candied cherries or mixed fruit peel*
2 *cups graham-cracker or vanilla-wafer crumbs*
1 *cup heavy cream*

Snip the dates, figs, and marshmallows into small pieces with scissors dipped in confectioners' sugar. Add the nuts, salt, orange rind, and cherries or fruit peel. Mix in 1½ cups crumbs. Whip the cream and blend into the mixture. Line a 9-inch spring-form pan with waxed paper. Shape the mixture into a round cake and coat with the remaining crumbs. Press firmly into cake pan, cover with waxed paper, and chill overnight. Turn out and pull off paper. Good served with whipped cream or Custard Sauce.* Serves 12.

WHITE FRUITCAKE AMANDINE

(*Plate 9*)

3½ *cups cake flour*
2 *teaspoons baking powder*
1 *teaspoon salt*
1 *cup butter*
1½ *cups sugar*
⅓ *cup quartered candied cherries*
1 *cup slivered citron*
1 *cup toasted slivered blanched almonds*
1½ *cups finely chopped flaked coconut*
½ *cup milk*
1 *tablespoon almond flavoring*
4 *teaspoons vanilla*
10 *egg whites*
Kirsch or brandy (*optional*)
*Amandine Topping**

Sift the flour, baking powder, and salt together. Cream the butter. Add the sugar gradually and continue beating until light and fluffy. Sprinkle ¼ of the flour mixture over the cut fruits and nuts. Work it around them until they are evenly coated and each piece is separate. Then add the remaining flour alternately with the milk to the butter-sugar mixture. Mix well. Add the floured fruits and nuts and the flavorings. Stir thoroughly. Beat the egg whites until they hold soft peaks. Stir them quickly and thoroughly into the batter. Divide the batter between two 9×5×2¾-inch loaf pans lined with oiled brown paper. Bake in a 300° oven for 1 hour and 35–40 minutes; keep a pan of water on the bottom rack of the oven during baking. Remove the cakes from the oven and allow them to stand about 5 minutes before removing from pans. Pull off the brown paper and cool. Wrap in heavy foil and store in a cool place for several days to bring out the delicate almond flavoring. If you wish, wring out cheesecloth in kirsch or brandy and wrap around the cakes before using the foil. Two days before serving, top with crunchy Amandine Topping. Serves 16–20.

JAPANESE FRUITCAKE (*Plate 3*)

3 cups plus 2 tablespoons flour
1 tablespoon baking powder
1 cup butter
2 cups sugar
5 eggs
1 cup milk
1 teaspoon vanilla
1 cup currants
1 cup raisins
1 teaspoon nutmeg
1 teaspoon cinnamon
½ teaspoon cloves
1 teaspoon cocoa

ORANGE COCONUT FILLING
¼ cup cornstarch
1 cup sugar
2 cups orange juice
Juice 1 lemon
Grated rind 1 orange
½ cup raisins
2 (3⅓ oz.) cans flaked coconut
2 tablespoons butter

GLAZE
3 cups confectioners' sugar
2 tablespoons lemon juice
Few drops cooking oil

Sift 3 cups flour with the baking powder. Cream the butter and sugar until light. Add the egg yolks and beat well. Add flour and milk alternately. Flavor with vanilla. Fold in the egg whites, beaten until a soft peak forms. Line two 9-inch cake pans on the bottom with waxed paper. Pour ⅔ of the batter into one pan. Toss currants and raisins with a mixture of 2 tablespoons flour, the spices, and cocoa. Stir into the remaining batter and pour into the second pan. Bake in a 375° oven for about 45 minutes. Turn out onto racks, remove paper, and cool.

Orange Coconut Filling. Mix the cornstarch and sugar; add the fruit juices and blend well. Add orange rind and raisins and cook, stirring constantly, for 5–7 minutes, until mixture thickens. Remove from heat and add the coconut and butter. Cool.

Split the cake layers in half. Place a fruit-spice layer, cut side up, on a plate and spread with ⅓ of the filling. Cover with a plain layer, cut side down, and spread with more filling. Repeat.

Glaze. Mix all the ingredients with 2 tablespoons and 1 teaspoon water. Drop spoonfuls of glaze over the top of the cake, letting it run unevenly down the sides. Serves 10–12.

INEXPENSIVE FRUITCAKE

1 pound fat salt pork
1 cup molasses
2 cups brown sugar
1 tablespoon vanilla
¼ cup cold strong coffee
1 pound raisins
1 pound currants
2 cups finely chopped nuts
7 cups flour
2 teaspoons cloves
2 teaspoons cinnamon
½ teaspoon nutmeg
½ teaspoon ginger
½ teaspoon salt
½ teaspoon baking soda
2 tablespoons baking powder
¼ cup brandy

Grind the salt pork fine and cover with 2 cups boiling water. Cool. Stir in the molasses and sugar. Add the vanilla and coffee. Dredge the raisins, currants, and nuts with 1 cup flour and set aside in a bowl. Sift the remaining 6 cups flour with the spices, salt, soda, and baking powder. When the liquid mixture is fairly cool, sift in the dry ingredients and beat until smooth. Add the fruit and nuts and mix well. Pour into a deep 10-inch tube pan lined on bottom and sides with 2 thicknesses of greased brown paper. Bake a total of 2½ hours. Start with a 275° oven for the first ½ hour, increase heat to 300° for the next ½ hour, and then end with a 325° oven for 1½ hours. Put a pan of hot water in the oven to keep the cake moist. Cool the cake on a rack. Sprinkle with brandy. Wrap in foil and store several days before serving. Serves 25.

GOLD AND WHITE WEDDING CAKE
(Plate 4)

Basic recipe for one mixing
½ cup butter
½ cup shortening
2 cups sugar
4 eggs (room temperature)
1 teaspoon vanilla
1 teaspoon lemon flavoring
½ teaspoon almond flavoring
3 cups flour
1 tablespoon baking powder
1 cup milk (room temperature)

PINEAPPLE COCONUT FILLING
3 (1 lb. 4 oz.) cans or 7½ cups crushed pineapple
2¼ cups sugar
¾ cup lemon juice
¾ cup cornstarch
1½ cups coconut milk or water
3 cups grated fresh coconut or 3 (3½ oz.) cans or packages flaked coconut

FROSTING
Basic recipe for one mixing
1 cup white vegetable shortening
2 pounds confectioners' sugar
½ cup milk
Juice 1–2 lemons

SUGAR BELLS
2½ pounds superfine sugar
1 egg white
Cornstarch

You will need the following equipment: one 16-inch cake pan 2 inches deep; one 13-inch, one 10-inch, and one 7-inch cake pan each 2½-inches deep; one 20-inch circle of plywood about ⅜ inch thick; heavy aluminum foil and waxed paper; eight 12-inch circular paper doilies; 1 large Lazy Susan—to make frosting and decorating easier; white pasteboard cake dividers cut to measure—one 13 inches, one 10 inches, and one 7 inches in diameter; one 3¼-inch, one 2-inch, and one 1¼-inch plastic bell mold; 2½-inch cooky cutter; 4 yards narrow white satin ribbon; sprays of artificial lily of the valley if you wish; decorating tips—rose, star, and leaf.

Step-by-step directions.

1. Three to four days before the wedding day, start baking cakes. You will need 10 mixings of the basic cake recipe given here to make a four-tiered wedding cake. This makes eight layers—two 16-inch, two 13-inch, two 10-inch, and two 7-inch layers. As each layer is baked and cooled, wrap securely in aluminum foil and keep in a cool place.

2. Two days before the wedding, make sugar bells and decorative roses of white frosting, using a No. 124 rose tip. Form each on a piece of waxed paper. Bells and roses should dry 4–6 hours or overnight.

3. The day before the wedding, cover the plywood with foil. Put this on a Lazy Susan if you have one. Arrange doilies on foil so that they extend gracefully over edge of circle, taping them to center of board. Cover outer edge of doilies with triangles of waxed paper—the points of the triangles should be just under the edge of the cake when it is in place. They will protect the doilies while the cake is being frosted and can be easily pulled out after decorating is completed.

To assemble the cake: Place one 16-inch cake layer on prepared board. Spread with pineapple coconut filling. Cover with second 16-inch layer, bottom side up. Frost top lightly to seal crumbs. Place one 13-inch cake layer on a 13-inch divider. Spread layer with filling. Now place cake and divider on top of 16-inch tier, taking care to center it. Cover with second 13-inch layer, bottom side up. Frost top lightly. Repeat until all layers are in place. Then frost the cake. Starting from the top, lightly frost sides of each tier to seal crumbs. Let dry 1–2 hours. Then frost the entire cake (starting from the top as before), making the surface as smooth as possible. Let dry at least 2–3 hours before decorating.

To decorate: First, decorate the sugar bells with a narrow edge of frosting. Put aside to dry. When decorating the cake, begin at the top. Connect each tier to the one below with a decorative design. Mark semicircles with cooky cutter; use decorative tip to outline. Complete decorating as you wish. Pull out waxed-paper triangles from over the doilies. Make a large design around base of cake to "seal" it to board. Arrange bells and roses on cake. Secure with white frosting. Add lily-of-the-valley sprays and white satin ribbon bows if you wish.

Cake. Line the bottom of each cake pan with waxed paper. Cream the butter, shortening, and sugar until light and fluffy. Add the eggs one at a time, beating after each addition. Add flavorings. Sift flour with baking powder and add to creamed mixture a little at a time alternately with the milk, beginning and ending with flour. Half fill the cake pans with batter. This makes a very high cake. The pans can be filled ⅓–½ full if you prefer more shallow tiers. The basic recipe will make about 7 cups batter. To half fill the pans, you will need about 14 cups batter (2 mixings) for the 16-inch pan, 10 cups batter for the 13-inch pan, 6½ cups batter for the 10-inch pan, and 3 cups batter for the 7-inch pan. When you require 2 mixings to fill a pan, turn first mixing into prepared pan or a bowl and refrigerate while you mix the second batch. Bake 16-inch and 13-inch cakes in a 325° oven, about 1¼ hours for the 16-inch cake and about 1 hour and 5 minutes for the 13-inch, until tops spring back to the touch. Bake 10-inch and 7-inch cakes in a 350° oven, about 50 minutes for the 10-inch and 45 minutes for the 7-inch. Remove from oven and cool in pans on racks for 10 minutes. Loosen edges of cakes and invert on racks. (An oven rack can be used for the largest cakes, or tie 2 cake racks together.) Peel off waxed paper. Cool thoroughly before wrapping in foil. Remember, you need to bake 2 *cakes* of each size to make a tier.

Pineapple Coconut Filling. Heat pineapple, sugar, and lemon juice in a large saucepan. Mix cornstarch and coconut milk or water. Add to pineapple mixture. Cook and stir until clear and thickened. Remove from heat and stir in coconut. Let stand until cold. This amount (12 cups) is sufficient for spreading between layers of the 4-tier cake.

Frosting. Beat the shortening until light and fluffy. Add sugar and milk alternately, beating after each addition. Add lemon juice and beat until mixture is very smooth. Keep covered with a damp cloth to prevent drying.

For Decorative Uses (roses, sugar-bell trim, and tip decoration): Make 1 mixing of the basic frosting recipe, but reduce milk to 1–2 tablespoons to make frosting firm enough to hold shape of decorations.

Sugar Bells. Mix sugar and egg white. Rub between palms of hands until egg white is distributed evenly throughout sugar. Dust inside of each mold with cornstarch. Fill molds with sugar, packing mixture down very firmly. Level off the surface. Invert mold on waxed paper. Carefully remove mold. Allow sugar molds to dry at room temperature for 1–2 hours, depending on size. Do not allow to dry until solid throughout. Hollow out the bells by carefully scraping the moist sugar from inside, leaving a shell ⅛–¼ inch thick. Use a small spoon or knife or the handle of a spoon for the smallest bells. Sugar removed from inside can be used to fill other molds. Allow to dry overnight at room temperature. Serves about 100–125.

ORANGE ALMOND WEDDING CAKE

7½ cups cake flour
5 teaspoons baking powder
1¼ teaspoons salt
2½ cups butter
5 cups sugar
10 eggs plus 5 yolks
2½ teaspoons orange flavoring
5 tablespoons grated orange rind
2½ cups milk

ALMOND FILLING
2 recipes Butter Cream Frosting*
2 cups very finely chopped blanched almonds
5 tablespoons light cream
2 recipes Butter Cream Frosting*

Sift the flour, baking powder, and salt together twice. Cream the butter and sugar together until light and fluffy. Add the egg yolks one at a time, beating well after each addition. Add the orange flavoring and rind. Add the dry ingredients alternately with the milk a little at a time while beating. Beat the egg whites until a soft peak forms and fold into the batter. Grease the bottom and sides of one 14-inch, one 10-inch, and one 7-inch cake pan (2½ inches deep). Half fill the pans with batter. Cover largest pan and refrigerate until the other 2 cakes are baked. Bake in a 300° oven for about 1 hour and 20 minutes, until cake tester comes out clean. Turn out on a rack. Cool thoroughly and cut in half horizontally. Bake the large cake in the same way, allowing about 1 hour and 30 minutes. Have ready 2 racks big enough to hold this cake. Cut layer in half when cool.

Almond Filling. Make the Butter Cream Frosting with almond flavoring. Mix in the almonds and cream.

Spread the cut surfaces of the cakes with the filling and put back together. Assemble the layers with filling between them. Frost and decorate the top and sides of the cake with almond-flavored Butter Cream Frosting. Serves about 35–40.

DARK FRUIT WEDDING CAKE

1½ pounds citron
¾ pound candied orange peel
¾ pound candied lemon peel
6 ounces crystallized ginger
¾ pound candied cherries
¾ pound shelled pecans
3 pounds seedless raisins
1½ pounds currants
1½ pounds seeded raisins
Grated rind 6 lemons
1½ cups orange marmalade
1½ teaspoons vanilla
1½ teaspoons lemon flavoring
¾ cup plus 1½ tablespoons lemon juice
¾ cup orange juice
6 cups flour
1½ teaspoons salt
1½ teaspoons baking powder
1 tablespoon cinnamon
1½ teaspoons nutmeg
¾ teaspoon mace
¾ teaspoon cloves
¾ teaspoon allspice
1½ pounds butter
3 cups sugar
18 eggs

FROSTING

3 pounds almond paste
About 4 egg whites
3 recipes Royal Ornamental Frosting*

Cut the citron, candied orange and lemon peel, and ginger into small slivers; cut the cherries into quarters and chop the pecans fine. Put into a large bowl. Add the seedless raisins, currants, and seeded raisins. Mix well. Add the lemon rind, orange marmalade, vanilla, and lemon flavoring. Pour the lemon and orange juices over the fruit and mix again. Cover the bowl and let stand overnight in a moderately warm place—by morning the fruit should have absorbed all the liquid. Line the bottom and sides of one 13-inch, one 10-inch, and one 7-inch cake pan (2½ inches deep) with a double thickness of oiled brown paper.

Sift the flour, salt, baking powder, and spices together 3 times. Cream the butter with the sugar until light and fluffy. Add the eggs one at a time, beating well after each addition. Add dry ingredients gradually, beating after each addition. Add fruit. Use a spoon to mix. Fill cake pans to within ½ inch of the top. Cover largest pan with foil and refrigerate until the other 2 cakes are baked. Bake on the middle rack in a 250° oven for 4½–5 hours. Place a pan of water on bottom rack to prevent the cakes from drying out. If the surface of the cakes browns too quickly, cover with foil. When cakes are baked, remove and cool for 5 minutes in the pan. Loosen paper from sides with a spatula. Turn out onto wire rack. Peel off paper and turn cakes right side up. Cover loosely with a clean cloth and cool overnight. Bake the large cake in exactly the same way, allowing 5½–6 hours. Have ready 2 racks big enough to hold this layer. If you like, wrap cakes in cheesecloth soaked in brandy. Cover, airtight, with several thicknesses of foil. Keep these cakes for at least 2 weeks before frosting. Add more brandy if you wish.

Frosting. First, turn all three cakes upside down. Fill in any holes with small pieces of almond paste.

For the small cake: Roll a ¼-pound piece of paste into a circle ⅛ inch thick; cut it to fit the top of the cake exactly. Brush top and sides of the cake with a little beaten egg white. Place the circular piece of paste on top and roll on the cake very lightly. Roll a 5-ounce piece into a strip 2½ inches wide and about 23 inches long. Trim the edges evenly. Place the strip around the small cake, making sure the ends just meet, not overlap. Make the edges as smooth and sharp as possible.

Repeat these methods for the top and sides of the other 2 cakes. You may put the side on the large cake in 2 pieces, but the joints must be smooth.

Buy disks or plates to fit your cakes exactly, also supporting posts and separating columns if you wish. Supporting posts must be placed in the cakes before they are frosted with Royal Ornamental Frosting.

Frost the outside of each cake as smoothly as possible with Royal Ornamental Frosting. Dry overnight. The next day assemble the cakes. Fit the disks into the supporting posts. Decorate with additional Royal Ornamental Frosting (practice on a cake pan first), or buy decorations from your local confectioner. Serves about 100.

DARK FRUITCAKE (Plate 10)

Use ⅓ recipe for Dark Fruit Wedding Cake* and bake in a 10-inch round pan 2½ inches deep.

ENGLISH CHRISTMAS CAKE

1¾ cups coarsely chopped candied cherries
1¾ cups coarsely chopped candied pineapple
1 pound white raisins
3 cups broken pecans
6 tablespoons brandy
1 cup butter
2¼ cups sugar
6 eggs
4 cups flour
1½ teaspoons salt
1 teaspoon nutmeg
*Marzipan Frosting**
Marzipan candy fruits (garnish)

Mix the fruits, nuts, and ¼ cup brandy together and let stand, stirring once or twice. Meanwhile, cream the butter, add the sugar, and beat until light and fluffy. Beat in the eggs, one at a time. Sift the flour with the remaining dry ingredients, then divide in half. Stir half into the egg mixture with the remaining brandy. Stir the other half into the fruits and nuts. When they are well coated, mix them into the batter. Pour it into a foil-lined 10-inch tube pan and bake for 3¾ hours in a 275° oven. Place a pan of water on the bottom of the oven to keep the cake moist. Cool the cake for 5 minutes, remove from pan, and then cool completely. Wrap in brandy-soaked cheesecloth and then in foil. Store for several weeks; however, this cake cuts very well after only 2 days. Frost the cake with Marzipan Frosting. Decorate with marzipan candy fruits if you wish. Serves 14–16.

COOKTIP

Pies, cookies, cakes—in fact, almost all baked products—freeze well. If you're lucky enough to have a freezer, bake extras for future feasting. Wrap tightly in foil and label.

Cupcakes

Cupcakes may be made from cake-batter recipes. Bake in greased muffin pans or use paper muffin cups. Bake these cupcakes about 25 minutes in a 350° oven. Test as for cake: when they spring back to the touch and pull away from the side of the pan, they are done.

CUPCAKES

½ cup butter
1 cup sugar
2 eggs
1 teaspoon vanilla
1¾ cups flour
½ teaspoon salt
2 teaspoons baking powder
½ cup milk

Cream the butter. Gradually add the sugar and beat until light and fluffy. Add the eggs one at a time, beating well after each addition. Mix in the vanilla. Sift the flour, salt, and baking powder together. Add to the first mixture alternately with the milk. Fill well-greased muffin pans or paper baking cups ⅓ full. If using paper cups, place them on a baking sheet or in muffin pans before baking. Bake in a 350° oven for about 25 minutes. Cool on racks. Yield: about 2 dozen.

ORANGE GINGERBREAD CUPCAKES

½ cup butter
1 tablespoon grated orange rind
1 cup sugar
1 cup dark molasses
2 eggs
2½ cups flour
1 teaspoon ginger
½ teaspoon cinnamon
½ teaspoon cloves
½ teaspoon salt
1 teaspoon baking soda

ORANGE ALMOND TOPPING
2 teaspoons melted butter
⅓ cup sugar
1 tablespoon grated orange rind
⅓ cup chopped toasted almonds

Cream the butter with the orange rind. Gradually add the sugar and molasses and continue to beat until light and fluffy. Add the eggs one at a time, beating well after each addition. Sift the flour, spices, salt, and soda together. Add slowly to the creamed mixture and beat until smooth. Quickly mix in ½ cup boiling water. Line muffin cups with paper liners and fill ⅔ full with batter. Bake in a 350° oven for 15 minutes. Meanwhile, mix the ingredients together for the topping. Quickly sprinkle over the cupcakes and return to oven immediately. Bake an additional 5–10 minutes, until done. Remove from muffin pans and cool on racks. Yield: about 2 dozen cupcakes.

COCONUT ORANGE CUPCAKES

½ cup butter
2 teaspoons grated orange rind
1 cup sugar
3 egg yolks
2 cups cake flour
1 tablespoon baking powder
¼ teaspoon salt
¾ cup milk
*Boiled Frosting**
Flaked coconut

Cream the butter and orange rind with the sugar until light. Beat the egg yolks until very thick and add to the creamed mixture. Beat well. Sift the flour, baking powder, and salt together. Add to the creamed mixture alternately with the milk, beating after each addition until smooth. Fill greased and floured small cupcake pans or muffin tins ½ full with batter. Bake in a 375° oven for about 13 minutes for the small cupcakes and 20 minutes for the muffin size. Turn out and cool on a rack. Frost the tops and sides of the cakes with the Boiled Frosting and sprinkle with flaked coconut. Yield: about 16 muffin-size cakes or 48 small ones.

ORANGE-FILLED CUPCAKES

*8 Cupcakes**
ORANGE FILLING
½ cup skim milk
2 tablespoons sugar
½ teaspoon unflavored gelatin
¾ teaspoon grated orange rind
⅛ teaspoon orange flavoring
Yellow food coloring
Confectioners' sugar

Orange Filling. Heat the milk, sugar, and gelatin together, stirring until gelatin is dissolved. Cool 10 minutes and mix in the orange rind, orange flavoring, and a few drops of yellow coloring. Chill until mixture is thick and syrupy. Beat until fluffy. Chill again until firm and whip once more. Chill.

Meanwhile, cut round wedges from the top of each cupcake. Fill each cake with about 1 heaping teaspoon of the thickened orange mixture. Replace top and sprinkle lightly with confectioners' sugar. Yield: 8 cupcakes.

ORANGE CREAM CUPCAKES

*1 recipe Orange Layer Cake**
FILLING
3 tablespoons honey
1 teaspoon grated orange rind
½ cup heavy cream
Confectioners' sugar (garnish)

Grease and flour regular cupcake pans and fill ⅔ full with the batter, or use very small cupcake pans and fill only ½ full. Bake in a 375° oven for about 20 minutes, or 15 minutes for the very small ones.

Filling. Meanwhile, make the filling by stirring the honey and rind into the cream, whipped.

When the cakes are cool, cut out the centers with a sharp pointed knife and fill. Replace the tops and sprinkle with confectioners' sugar. Yield: about 18 regular or 4–5 dozen small cupcakes.

ICE CREAM CUPCAKES

*6 Cupcakes**
1 pint ice cream
3 egg whites
½ cup honey

Scoop the centers from the cupcakes and fill with the ice cream of your choice. Beat the egg whites with honey, added gradually, until stiff. Cover tops with the honey meringue, piling it high over the ice cream. Brown quickly in a preheated 425° oven. Serve immediately. Serves 6.

LEMON CAKE SQUARES

6 tablespoons butter
1⅔ cups sugar
2 eggs
1½ cups flour
1½ teaspoons baking powder
¼ teaspoon salt
½ cup milk
Grated rind 1 lemon
Juice 1 lemon

Cream the butter with 1 cup sugar. Add and mix in this order: the beaten eggs, flour, baking powder, salt, milk, and lemon rind. Pour batter into a greased 13×9×2-inch baking pan and bake in a 350° oven for 25 minutes. Meanwhile, mix the remaining sugar with the lemon juice. Spoon the lemon-sugar mixture over the hot cake and bake 5 minutes more. Cut while still warm into 1-inch squares. Yield: about 115 tea-size squares.

TEACAKES FOR A PARTY   (*Plate 35*)

1 package white cake mix

FROSTING

½ cup butter
1 egg
1 teaspoon vanilla
¼ teaspoon salt
1 (1 lb.) package confectioners' sugar
3–4 tablespoons heavy cream
Chopped blanched pistachio nuts (garnish)
Food coloring (optional)

Bake the batter in tiny muffin pans 1¾ inches in diameter. The package of mix will make 6–7 dozen tiny cupcakes.

Frosting. Cream the butter until light and fluffy. Add the egg, vanilla, and salt. Beat until well blended. Gradually add the sugar. Soften to spreading consistency with cream. Frost the tops of the cakes. Sprinkle with nuts. If you wish to decorate the cakes, stiffen a small amount of frosting with more confectioners' sugar. Tint with a few drops of food coloring and press through pastry tube onto tops of cakes. Yield: 6–7 dozen cupcakes.

SIMNEL CAKE
(Almond Teacake)

2 cups sugar
1½ cups butter
6 eggs
4½ cups flour
1 teaspoon salt
¾ pound raisins
¾ cup mixed candied fruits
1 teaspoon vanilla

ALMOND TOPPING AND FILLING

½ pound almond paste
1½ cups sugar
2 egg whites

Cream the sugar and butter until light and fluffy. Add the eggs one at a time, beating well after each addition. Sift the flour and salt together and add to the batter. Stir in the raisins, fruits, and vanilla and mix well. Spread half the batter in a 9×9×2-inch pan which has been lined with buttered brown paper or with foil. Blend the almond paste, sugar, and egg whites together and spread half the mixture over the cake batter. Cover with remaining batter and bake in a 275° oven for 2½ hours. Remove from oven, spread with the rest of the almond mixture, and bake 30 minutes longer, until very lightly browned. This cake keeps well in a tin for 3–4 weeks and is best sliced thin. Slice ⅜ inch thick and cut into 2-inch pieces. Yield: about 100 pieces.

PRALINE PARTY CAKE

1 package yellow cake mix
½ cup butter
1 pound light brown sugar
2 tablespoons flour
2 eggs
1 teaspoon vanilla
1½ cups coarsely chopped pecans

Prepare the mix according to package directions. Pour the batter into two greased and floured 13×9×2-inch pans. Bake in a 350° oven for about ½ hour, until done. Remove from oven. Melt the butter in a skillet. Mix the sugar, flour, and beaten eggs. Add to the butter and bring to a boil. Lower heat and cook for 3 minutes. Remove from heat and stir in the vanilla and nuts. Spread evenly over the surface of the cooled cakes. Return cakes to oven and bake at 400° for 8 minutes to "set" the frosting. Cool. Cut into 1½-inch strips. Yield: 60 bite-size pieces.

HONEY CREAM TEACAKES

1 (11½ oz.) package orange cake mix
1 cup heavy cream
1 teaspoon grated orange rind
1 teaspoon grated lemon rind
6 tablespoons honey
Confectioners' sugar

Prepare the cake according to package directions. Grease and flour very small cupcake pans, 1¾×¾-inch. Fill them ½ full. Bake for 15 minutes in a 375° oven. Let them cool briefly in the pans before removing. Cover with a towel to keep moist. Whip the cream until thick and glossy. Stir in the rinds and honey. Cut out the centers of each cake with a sharp pointed knife. Fill, mounding slightly, with some of the honey cream. Replace the tops and sprinkle with sugar. Yield: 4 dozen small cakes.

ANGEL COCOROONS

About 1 cup soft butter
3 (3½ oz.) cans flaked coconut
1 package angel-food cake mix

Spread 1 teaspoon soft butter evenly on the bottom and sides in each of 4 dozen muffin cups. Press a generous layer of coconut on the bottom and sides of each muffin cup. Prepare the angel-food cake mix according to package directions. Fill the muffin cups ¾ full. Bake in a 375° oven for 15–20 minutes, until the tops of the cakes spring back to the touch. Cool slightly. Loosen the cakes from the cups and lift out onto a cake rack to finish cooling. Yield: 4 dozen.

PECAN TEACAKES

2 eggs
1 cup light brown sugar
1 teaspoon vanilla
½ cup cake flour
¼ teaspoon salt
½ teaspoon baking powder
1 cup finely chopped pecans

Beat the egg yolks until light and fluffy. Gradually add the sugar, beating after each addition. Add vanilla. Sift the flour, salt, and baking powder together. Reserve 1 tablespoon to mix with the nuts and mix the rest into the egg mixture. Stir in the nuts. Fold in the egg whites which have been beaten until a soft peak forms. Fill greased very small cupcake pans ⅔ full. Bake in a 375° oven for 12–15 minutes. Yield: about 30 cupcakes.

HOT LEMON TEACAKE

½ cup plus 2 tablespoons butter
½ cup plus 2 teaspoons sugar
2 eggs
Grated rind 1 lemon
¾ cup flour
1 teaspoon baking powder
¼ teaspoon salt
1 teaspoon lemon juice
Confectioners' sugar

Cream ½ cup butter, gradually add ½ cup sugar, and beat until light and fluffy. Add the beaten egg yolks and lemon rind and beat well. Sift the flour, baking powder, and salt together and add to mixture. When smooth, fold in the egg whites, beaten stiff. Spread in an 8-inch cake pan lined on the bottom with waxed paper. Bake for 25 minutes in a 375° oven. Turn out, remove paper, split in half, and put halves together with remaining butter creamed with remaining sugar and lemon juice. Dust with confectioners' sugar and serve hot. Serves 4.

PETITS FOURS

½ cup butter
1 cup sugar
1 egg plus 5 egg yolks
1¾ cups cake flour
2½ teaspoons baking powder
¼ teaspoon salt
½ cup milk
½ teaspoon vanilla
Petits-Fours Frosting*

Cream the butter and sugar, adding the sugar a little at a time. When smooth and creamy, add the egg and yolks beaten together until very thick. Sift the flour, baking powder, and salt together. Add alternately to the first mixture with the milk. Flavor with vanilla and turn into a greased and floured 13×9×2-inch pan. Bake in a 350° oven for 25–30 minutes. Turn out and cool on a rack. Trim crust from top of cake, but leave bottom crust on; cut the cake into quite small circles, squares, diamonds, and rectangles. Frost with Petits-Fours Frosting. Dip each petit four quickly into warm frosting by holding upside down with a fork, covering top and sides. Insert the fork at such an angle that the cake will not fall off. Then place right side up on a rack to dry. When the frosting is set, trim off excess around the base. Decorate with Butter Cream Frosting,* silver dragées, or candied violets. Yield: about 4 dozen petits fours.

Little Jack Horner sat in the corner,
Eating a Christmas pie;
He put in his thumb, and pulled out a plum,
And said, "What a good boy am I!"

Anonymous, *Little Jack Horner*

Magic of Mixes

Every mix is a bagful of tricks. By following instructions on the package, you will have a foolproof dessert. However, what makes the magic is what happens when you use these mixes as an ingredient or add your personal touch. A boxed cake can become a baba ring or a chocolate mousse; a chiffon mix can be transformed into a glistening mold or a cranberry cream. It's a great convenience to be able to bake successfully in a hurry.

CAKE-MIX VARIATIONS

WHITE CAKE MIX

(1 lb. 4 oz.) package

MAPLE NUT CAKE

Add a few drops of maple flavoring to the batter; pour into pans and sprinkle tops with ½ cup minced nuts.

LEMON COCONUT CAKE

Add ¼ teaspoon lemon flavoring or 1 teaspoon grated lemon rind and ½ cup finely chopped or flaked coconut to the batter.

SPICY NUT CAKE

Add 1 teaspoon cinnamon, ½ teaspoon nutmeg, and ¼ teaspoon cloves to the dry mix. Add ¼ cup minced nuts to the batter.

CHOCOLATE-FLECK CAKE

Fold 1 or 2 ounces grated unsweetened chocolate into the batter.

CHERRY ALMOND CAKE

Add ½ cup minced blanched almonds and 8 minced well-drained maraschino cherries to the batter.

DATE CAKE

Add 1 teaspoon grated lemon rind and ½ cup finely chopped, pitted dates to the batter.

COFFEE-FLAVORED CAKE

Add 4 teaspoons instant coffee to the dry cake mix.

PEANUT CAKE

Add ¾ cup finely chopped salted peanuts to the batter.

CINNAMON CAKE

Add ¾ teaspoon cinnamon to the dry mix.

COCONUT CAKE

Add ½–¾ cup finely chopped or flaked coconut to the batter.

ORANGE CAKE

Add 1 teaspoon grated orange rind to the batter.

PEPPERMINT CAKE

Fold ⅓ cup finely crushed peppermint-stick candy into the batter.

YELLOW CAKE MIX

(1 lb. 2½ oz.) package

LEMON YELLOW CAKE

Add 2 teaspoons grated lemon rind to the batter.

CHOCOLATE-FLECK YELLOW CAKE

Fold 1 or 2 ounces grated unsweetened chocolate into the batter.

SPICE CAKE

Add 1 teaspoon cinnamon, ½ teaspoon nutmeg, and ¼ teaspoon cloves to the dry mix.

ORANGE COCONUT CAKE

Add 1 tablespoon grated orange rind and ½ cup finely chopped or flaked coconut to the batter.

COFFEE CAKE

Add 4 teaspoons instant coffee to the dry mix.

COCONUT YELLOW CAKE

Add ½ cup finely chopped or flaked coconut to the batter.

ANGEL-FOOD CAKE MIX

(15 oz.) package

ALMOND ANGEL-FOOD CAKE

Fold ½ cup very finely chopped blanched almonds into the batter.

PINEAPPLE ALMOND ANGEL CAKE

Fold ⅓ cup minced blanched almonds and ⅓ cup finely diced preserved pineapple into the batter.

CHERRY ANGEL-FOOD CAKE

Use 2 tablespoons maraschino cherry juice as part of the liquid called for in the package directions. Fold ⅓ cup chopped, thoroughly drained maraschino cherries into the batter.

CHOCOLATE-FLECK ANGEL-FOOD CAKE

Fold 1 or 2 ounces grated unsweetened chocolate into the batter; *or* alternate layers of grated chocolate and batter, beginning and ending with batter, and cut through batter with a spatula.

COCONUT ANGEL-FOOD CAKE

Fold ¾ cup finely chopped flaked coconut into the batter.

COFFEE ANGEL-FOOD CAKE

Stir 1 tablespoon instant coffee into the liquid called for in the package directions.

SPICY ANGEL-FOOD CAKE

Add 1 teaspoon cinnamon, ¼ teaspoon nutmeg, and ⅛ teaspoon cloves to the dry mix.

CHOCOLATE MARBLE ANGEL CAKE

Fold 2 tablespoons cocoa into half of the batter. Alternate chocolate and plain batter by spoonfuls. Cut through with a spatula.

DEVIL'S-FOOD CAKE MIX

(1 lb. 3 oz.) package

CHOCOLATE-FLECK DEVIL'S-FOOD CAKE

Fold 1 or 2 ounces of grated unsweetened chocolate into the batter.

COCONUT DEVIL'S-FOOD CAKE

Add ½–¾ cup finely chopped or flaked coconut to the batter.

ORANGE COCONUT DEVIL'S-FOOD CAKE

Add 1 tablespoon grated orange rind and ½–¾ cup finely chopped or flaked coconut to the batter.

COFFEE SPICE DEVIL'S-FOOD CAKE

Add 4 teaspoons instant coffee, ½ teaspoon cinnamon, ¼ teaspoon allspice, and ¼ teaspoon nutmeg to the dry mix.

NUT DEVIL'S-FOOD CAKE

Add ½ cup minced nuts to the batter.

PEPPERMINT DEVIL'S-FOOD CAKE

Add a few drops peppermint flavoring to the batter.

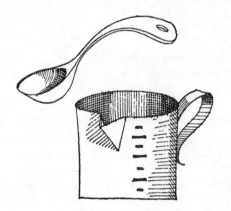

CHAPTER TWO

Countless Cookies

Where there's a child there should be a cooky jar. If you remember your enjoyment of cookies in childhood, you will want to have a cooky supply to be proud of.

Cookies are for variety. There are small crisp ones to accompany ice cream or fruit desserts and richer ones like brownies or filled cookies as a complete dessert. Cookies also for between-meal snacks, cookies for lunch boxes, for trips, for picnics, for gifts to children or neighbors, for Christmas presents, cookies on hand for expected and unexpected guests, cookies for everything.

Often one's first cooking experience was in the cooky world, since cookies are almost as easy to make as they are to eat. A successful kitchen adventure can inspire the younger generation to try other dessert recipes; this in time leads to further cooking experiments. Happy hours condition the young to regard cooking as a pleasure rather than a chore. Many a young housewife owes some of the success of her marriage to this enjoyment.

Cookies give you a chance to use your artistic imagination. Many cookies are a base on which to paint a picture with glaze or frosting or to build a sculpture with nuts, fruits, or candy. Designs can be appropriate to the season or to the occasion. Make Santas or gingerbread men or red and green cookies at Christmas time. For weddings, everything is all white, decorated perhaps with scrolls or flowers made with ornamental frosting. Try putting names on cookies to be used as place cards for a children's party. Think up ideas; really, it's fun.

ALMOND COOKIES I

½ cup butter
1 cup light brown sugar
1 egg
1 cup flour
Pinch cream of tartar
¼ teaspoon salt
½ cup (about 4 oz.) coarsely chopped
toasted blanched almonds

Cut the butter into pieces in a mixing bowl. Add sugar to the butter and cream together very thoroughly until light and fluffy. Add the well-beaten egg. Sift the flour with cream of tartar and salt. Add to the mixture and then add the nuts and beat well. Drop the dough by ½ teaspoonfuls onto greased baking sheets. Don't put them too close together. Bake in a 325° oven until a light brown. Yield: about 4 dozen cookies.

ALMOND COOKIES II

1 cup butter
1 cup sugar
1 egg
3 tablespoons almond flavoring
3 cups flour
1½ teaspoons baking soda
¼ cup light corn syrup
1 cup blanched almonds

Cream the butter and sugar until light and fluffy. Add the beaten egg and almond flavoring and continue beating. Slowly stir in the flour, soda, and corn syrup; mix until smooth. Form the dough into 1-inch balls and place on baking sheets. Flatten each ball into a thick cooky with the bottom of a tumbler, and place an almond in the center of each. Bake in a 375° oven for 15–20 minutes, until golden brown. Yield: about 4 dozen cookies.

ALMOND WAFERS

⅓ cup blanched almonds
¼ cup sugar
2 teaspoons flour
1 tablespoon milk
¼ cup melted butter

Grind the almonds fine and mix with the sugar, flour, milk, and butter. Stir well and drop by teaspoonfuls about 4 inches apart onto floured, well-greased baking sheets. Bake in a 350° oven for 8–10 minutes, until golden brown. Let cool slightly and remove carefully with a spatula. If you want them curved, place them over a rolling pin while still warm to shape. Yield: about 25 thin lacy cookies.

ALMOND NUGGETS

½ cup butter
2 hard-cooked egg yolks
¼ cup sugar
1 cup flour
3 tablespoons finely chopped or ground
almonds
½ teaspoon almond flavoring
Superfine sugar (garnish)

Cream the butter. Rub the egg yolks through a sieve and add to the butter with the sugar. Beat until light and fluffy. Stir in the flour, almonds, and then the almond flavoring. Mix well. Chill. Form into small balls about ¾ inch in diameter. Place on baking sheets and press each ball with a fork. Bake in a 375° oven for about 10 minutes. Sprinkle with superfine sugar while still hot. Yield: about 3 dozen cookies.

APPLESAUCE COOKIES

1 cup dark brown sugar
¼ cup sugar
¾ cup butter
1 egg
⅔ cup applesauce
3 cups flour
2 teaspoons cinnamon
2 teaspoons ginger
1 teaspoon allspice
½ teaspoon cloves
½ teaspoon salt
½ teaspoon baking soda
1 cup raisins
1 cup chopped pecans
1 teaspoon vanilla

Cream the sugars with the butter. Beat in the egg, then the applesauce. Sift the flour, spices, salt, and soda together. Lightly coat the raisins and pecans with some of the spiced flour. Mix the remaining flour into the batter, add vanilla, and fold in the floured raisins and nuts. Drop batter by teaspoonfuls several inches apart onto greased baking sheets and bake for 12–15 minutes in a 375° oven. Yield: 4–5 dozen cookies.

APRICOT BUTTONS

⅓ cup dried apricots
⅔ cup sugar
½ cup butter
1 egg
½ teaspoon vanilla
1 cup flour
½ teaspoon salt
½ cup chopped nuts

Rinse the apricots with cold water. Put into a saucepan, cover with water, and cook until very tender. Rub through a coarse sieve. Add ⅓ cup sugar and cook slowly until thick, stirring constantly. Cool. Cream the butter with remaining sugar thoroughly. Stir in the egg yolk and vanilla. Sift the flour and salt together and mix into the creamed mixture. Shape into 3 dozen small balls. Dip the balls in unbeaten egg white, then roll in chopped nuts. Place 2 inches apart on lightly greased baking sheets. Make a deep dent in the center of each ball. Bake in a 300° oven for ½ hour. Remove with spatula to racks to cool. While cookies are still warm fill centers with the cooled apricot mixture. Store between layers of waxed paper in a container with a tight lid. Yield: 3 dozen cookies.

APRICOT BRAZIL-NUT COOKIES

(Plate 11)

¾ cup butter
½ cup sugar
1 egg
1½ teaspoons vanilla
2 cups flour
⅛ teaspoon salt
¾ cup finely chopped Brazil nuts
Apricot jam
Brazil-nut slices (garnish)
Candied cherries (optional)

Cream the butter and sugar together. Add the egg and vanilla and continue to cream until fluffy. Blend in the flour and salt. Add the chopped nuts and mix well. Shape into ¾-inch balls. Place about 2 inches apart on ungreased baking sheets. Flatten each with the bottom of a glass which has been dipped in flour. Make an indentation in the center of each cooky. Bake in a 375° oven for about 4 minutes. Remove from oven and press center again. Fill with a little apricot jam and return to oven for 4–6 minutes, until edges are slightly golden. Remove to racks to cool. Decorate each cooky with 3 slices of nuts, arranged spoke fashion, and add pieces of cherry if you wish. Brazil nuts slice easily if they are boiled for a few minutes and sliced while warm. Yield: about 5 dozen cookies.

APRICOT JAM SQUARES

½ cup shortening
½ cup sugar
1 egg
½ teaspoon lemon flavoring
1½ cups flour
1½ teaspoons baking powder
½ teaspoon salt
½ teaspoon cinnamon
¼ teaspoon cloves
2 tablespoons milk
¾ cup apricot jam

Cream the shortening. Add the sugar gradually, beating until light and fluffy. Add the well-beaten egg and lemon flavoring and mix well. Sift the dry ingredients together. Stir the milk into the creamed mixture and add the sifted dry ingredients. Spread ½ of the batter in a greased 9×9×2-inch pan, spread the apricot jam over the batter, and cover with the remaining batter. Bake in a 400° oven for 25 minutes. Cool and cut into squares. Yield: about 20 squares.

APPLE HERMIT COOKIES

½ cup butter
1 cup dark brown sugar
2 eggs
1 cup chopped, pitted dates
1 cup chopped, cored peeled apple
½ cup rolled oats
½ cup chopped walnuts
1¾ cups flour
½ teaspoon cinnamon
½ teaspoon baking powder
¼ teaspoon salt

Cream the butter with the sugar. Add the eggs and beat well. Stir in the dates, apple, rolled oats, and walnuts. Add the flour which has been sifted with the cinnamon, baking powder, and salt. Mix well and drop by spoonfuls onto baking sheets. Bake in a 350° oven for 15 minutes. Yield: 4–5 dozen cookies.

ENGLISH MATRIMONIALS   (*Plate 35*)

1½ cups flour
1 cup brown sugar
1¼ cups rolled oats
¾ cup butter
¾ cup raspberry jam

Mix the flour, sugar, and rolled oats together. Work in the butter until the mixture is crumbly. Press half evenly into the bottom of a greased 8×8×2-inch pan.

Spread with the jam. Press the remaining mixture over the jam, covering it completely. Bake in a 325° oven 40–45 minutes, until golden. Cool and cut into squares. Yield: about 1½ dozen small squares.

BROWNIES

1 cup flour
¾ teaspoon baking powder
¼ teaspoon salt
3 ounces unsweetened chocolate
½ cup butter
1½ cups sugar
3 eggs
¾ cup coarsely chopped pecans
1 teaspoon vanilla

Sift the flour, baking powder, and salt together. Melt the chocolate and butter in a double boiler. Stir the sugar gradually into the beaten eggs and add to the melted chocolate and butter mixture. Blend in the flour and then add the pecans and vanilla. Bake in a greased 9×9×2-inch pan in a 350° oven for 30–40 minutes. Cool on a rack. Then cut into rectangular pieces. Yield: about 3 dozen brownies.

DOUBLE-DECKER BROWNIES

¾ cup butter
1½ cups sugar
3 eggs
1 teaspoon vanilla
1 cup chopped pecans
1¼ cups flour
¾ teaspoon baking powder
1 teaspoon salt
1½ tablespoons instant coffee
2 ounces unsweetened chocolate

Cream the butter, add sugar gradually, and beat until light and fluffy. Beat in the eggs; then add the vanilla and nuts. Sift the flour, baking powder, and salt together and add to mixture. Divide in half. Add coffee to one half and spread into a greased 8×8×2-inch pan. Add melted chocolate to the other half and spread carefully over the first layer. Bake in a 350° oven for 45 minutes. Cool in pan, turn out, and then cut into 2-inch squares. Yield: 16 brownies.

FUDGE NUT BROWNIES

2 ounces unsweetened chocolate
¼ cup butter
1 cup sugar
½ cup flour
1 egg
1 tablespoon milk
1 teaspoon vanilla
Pinch salt
½ cup coarsely chopped nuts

Melt the chocolate and butter in a double boiler. Remove from heat and cool slightly. Add the rest of the ingredients all at one time and mix well. Pour into an 8×8×2-inch pan lined on the bottom with waxed paper. Bake in a 325° oven for about ½ hour. Remove from oven, let stand a few minutes, and then turn out of pan and pull off waxed paper. Cool and cut into serving pieces. These brownies will be very chewy. Yield: 16–20 brownies.

SAUCEPAN BROWNIES

⅓ cup butter
2 ounces unsweetened chocolate
1 cup sugar
2 eggs
½ teaspoon vanilla
¾ cup flour
¼ teaspoon salt
½ cup chopped pecans

Melt the butter and chocolate in a saucepan over low heat, stirring frequently. Remove from heat and stir in, in this order: sugar, eggs, vanilla, flour, salt, and nuts. Pour the batter into a greased 8×8×2-inch pan and bake in a 375° oven for 25–30 minutes, until brownies are firm and begin to pull away from the sides of the pan. Cool and cut into 2-inch squares. These are the chewy variety. Yield: 16 brownies.

WALNUT BROWNIES (Plate 11)

1/3 cup butter
2 ounces unsweetened chocolate
1 cup sugar
2 eggs
1/2 teaspoon vanilla
3/4 cup flour
1/4 teaspoon salt
1/2 cup broken walnuts
Fudge Frosting* (optional)

Melt the butter and chocolate in a double boiler. Remove from heat and cool slightly. Add the sugar, beaten eggs, vanilla, flour, salt, and walnuts. Mix well. Pour into an 8×8×2-inch pan lined with waxed paper and bake in a 375° oven for 25–30 minutes. Remove from oven and cool in pan a few minutes before turning out on a rack to cool. Frost if you wish with Fudge Frosting or serve plain. Yield: 20 brownies.

BUTTERSCOTCH BROWNIES

1/4 cup butter
1 cup dark brown sugar
1 egg
1 teaspoon vanilla
1/2 cup flour
1/2 teaspoon salt
1 teaspoon baking powder
1/2 cup finely chopped nut meats

Melt the butter and stir the sugar into it until dissolved. Cool slightly and beat in the egg and vanilla. Sift the flour with salt and baking powder and add to mixture. When blended, add the nuts and pour into a greased 8×8×2-inch pan. Bake in a 350° oven for 1/2 hour. Cut into 1×2-inch bars. Yield: 32 brownies.

SNOW-CAPPED BROWNIES

1/2 cup butter
3/4 cup sugar
2 eggs
2 ounces unsweetened chocolate
1/3 cup flour
1/8 teaspoon salt
Pinch baking soda
3/4 cup chopped walnuts
1/2 teaspoon vanilla

MERINGUE

1 egg white
1/2 cup sugar
1/2 teaspoon vanilla

Cream the butter with sugar and then add the eggs and beat until fluffy. Melt the chocolate and stir it in. Add the flour, salt, and soda; mix well. Blend in nuts and vanilla. Spread in greased and floured 8×8×2-inch pan.

Meringue. Beat the egg white until stiff. Add the sugar a tablespoon at a time, beating after each addition. Continue to beat until meringue is stiff and glossy. Add vanilla.

Spread the meringue over the brownie batter. Draw the tip of a knife through the meringue and batter lengthwise and crosswise. Bake in a 325° oven for 50–60 minutes, until brownies test done. Yield: 16 brownies.

BROWN-SUGAR PECAN CRISPS

1 cup butter
2 1/2 cups brown sugar
2 eggs
2 1/2 cups flour
1/2 teaspoon baking soda
1/2 teaspoon salt
1 teaspoon vanilla
1 1/2 cups coarsely chopped pecans

Cream the butter and sugar until very light and fluffy. Beat in the slightly beaten eggs. Sift the dry ingredients together and mix into the butter mixture. Finally, stir in the vanilla and pecans. Drop by teaspoonfuls onto lightly greased baking sheets. Bake in a 350° oven for 12–15 minutes. Yield: 8–9 dozen cookies.

CHINESE CHEWS

1/2 cup butter
1 cup brown sugar
2 eggs
1/2 cup chopped mixed nuts
1/4 cup cut-up dates
1 tablespoon chopped raisins
1 tablespoon flaked coconut
3/4 cup flour

Cream the butter and sugar until light and fluffy. Add the eggs, nuts, dates, raisins, and coconut. Mix well. Add the flour and beat until blended. Bake in an 8×8×2-inch pan, lined with waxed paper, in a 350° oven for 40 minutes. While still warm, cut into 2-inch squares. Yield: 16 squares.

BROWN-SUGAR PEANUT BARS

2 cups flour
2 teaspoons baking powder
1 teaspoon baking soda
½ teaspoon salt
½ cup butter
½ cup sugar
1½ cups dark brown sugar
2 eggs
1 teaspoon vanilla
1 (6 oz.) package semisweet chocolate bits
½ cup salted peanuts

Sift the flour, baking powder, soda, and salt together. Cream the butter, gradually adding sugar and ½ cup brown sugar. Next, add the well-beaten egg yolks and vanilla. Add the dry ingredients alternately with 3 tablespoons cold water. This makes a very stiff dough. Press dough into two greased and floured 8×8×2-inch pans or a 9×13×2-inch pan. Sprinkle with chocolate bits, pressing them gently into the dough. Slowly add remaining brown sugar to beaten egg whites and continue to beat until stiff, like a meringue. Spread this over the chocolate and top with the peanuts, chopped fine. Bake in a 325° oven for 30–35 minutes. Cut into bars while still warm. Yield: about 3 dozen bars.

LEMON BUTTER DAISIES   (*Plate 11*)

2 cups butter
1 cup sugar
2 eggs
1 tablespoon plus 1 teaspoon grated lemon rind
5 cups flour
1 teaspoon baking powder
2 tablespoons lemon juice
Colored sugar (garnish)
Almond halves (garnish)

Cream the butter and add the sugar gradually. Continue beating until light and fluffy. Add the slightly beaten egg yolks and the lemon rind. Sift the flour with baking powder and stir in. Add the lemon juice and mix well. Chill the dough for several hours. Roll out ¼ inch thick and cut with a 1½-inch cooky cutter. Brush each cooky with egg white. Sprinkle with colored sugar and decorate with almond halves. Bake in a 350° oven for about 10 minutes, until the cookies begin to turn golden. Yield: 5 dozen cookies.

CARAWAY-SEED BUTTER COOKIES

1 cup butter
½ cup sugar
2 cups flour
½ teaspoon salt
1 teaspoon vanilla
Caraway seed

Cream the butter with the sugar. Gradually add the flour and salt. Then add the vanilla and mix well. Form into a roll 1¼ inches in diameter, wrap in waxed paper, and chill at least overnight. Slice the dough fairly thin, place on baking sheets, and sprinkle with caraway seed. Bake in a 350° oven for 15 minutes, until edges are slightly browned. Yield: 10 dozen cookies.

RAINBOW BUTTER CRISPS

2 cups flour
½ cup sugar
¼ teaspoon salt
2 teaspoons instant coffee
1 cup butter
Colored sugar or multicolored candy sprinkles

Sift the flour, sugar, salt, and coffee together. Cut in the butter until very well blended. Press the dough together with your hands. Chill. When ready to bake, pinch off small amounts of dough and shape into small balls. Roll them in colored sugar or candy sprinkles. Arrange on baking sheets. Bake in a 300° oven for 20 minutes. Let cool about 5 minutes before removing from the sheets. Cool on racks. Yield: about 3 dozen cookies.

BUTTERSCOTCH JEWEL BARS (*Plate 11*)

½ cup butter
1 cup dark brown sugar
3 eggs
2 cups flour
¼ teaspoon salt
¼ teaspoon nutmeg
3 tablespoons milk
1½ cups skinned filbert halves
¾ cup diced candied pineapple
¾ cup candied red cherries cut in halves
½ cup raisins
1 teaspoon vanilla
1 tablespoon brandy
¼ cup sugar

Cream the butter and brown sugar and then add 1 egg. Sift the flour, salt, and nutmeg together. Add alternately with the milk to the butter mixture and blend well. Spread in a buttered 15½×10½×1-inch pan. Bake in a 350° oven for 10 minutes. Meanwhile, mix the nuts, fruits, vanilla, and brandy. Beat the remaining eggs slightly and stir in the sugar. Add to the fruit mixture and spread over the hot layer. Bake in a 350° oven for another 20 minutes. While still warm, cut into 5 lengthwise strips about 2 inches wide, then cut into bars about 1½ inches long. Yield: 50 bars.

CHOCOLATE DROP COOKIES

½ cup butter
1 cup dark brown sugar
1 egg
1½ cups flour
¼ teaspoon baking powder
¼ teaspoon baking soda
¼ teaspoon salt
½ cup sour milk or buttermilk
1½ teaspoons vanilla
2 ounces unsweetened chocolate
½ cup chopped walnuts (optional)

Cream the butter with the sugar. Add the egg and beat until light and fluffy. Sift the flour, baking powder, soda, and salt together. Add to the creamed mixture alternately with sour milk or buttermilk. Stir in the vanilla and melted chocolate; add nuts if you wish. Drop by tablespoonfuls on greased baking sheets, spreading each cooky slightly with a spatula. Bake in a 350° oven for 12 minutes. Yield: about 1½ dozen cookies.

CHOCOLATE NUT COOKIES

2 ounces unsweetened chocolate
¼ cup butter
½ cup sugar
1 egg
1 cup flour
¼ teaspoon baking soda
¼ teaspoon salt
5 tablespoons milk
½ cup finely chopped walnuts or pecans
2 teaspoons vanilla

Melt the chocolate and butter in a double boiler; add sugar and stir until smooth. Remove from heat and add the slightly beaten egg. Sift the dry ingredients together and add alternately with the milk, stirring well after each addition. Add the nuts and flavor with vanilla. Drop by level teaspoonfuls about 1½ inches apart onto greased baking sheets. Bake in a 375° oven for 5–6 minutes. Remove from sheets at once and cool on racks. Yield: about 5 dozen cookies.

CHOCOLATE CRISPIES

2 ounces unsweetened chocolate
½ cup butter
1 cup sugar
½ cup flour
¼ teaspoon salt
2 eggs
1 teaspoon vanilla
½ cup finely chopped walnuts or pecans

Melt the chocolate and butter in a double boiler. Remove from heat and add the sugar, flour, and salt. Stir and add the well-beaten eggs. Flavor with vanilla and beat again. Spread with a spatula on a greased baking sheet, having the mixture spread *extremely* thin. Sprinkle thickly with nuts. Bake in a 400° oven for 10 minutes. Cut into squares or shapes while warm, working fast. Yield: about 30 cookies.

CHOCOLATE NUT CRISPS

½ cup butter
1 cup sugar
2 eggs
1½ teaspoons vanilla
3 ounces unsweetened chocolate
1 cup flour
¾ teaspoon salt
½ teaspoon baking powder
1½ cups chopped walnuts
1–1½ cups walnut halves

Cream the butter with the sugar until light and fluffy. Beat in the eggs, vanilla, and the melted and slightly cooled chocolate. Sift the flour, salt, and baking powder. Add to mixture and mix well. Stir in the chopped nuts. Drop dough by teaspoonfuls onto baking sheets and top each with a walnut half. Bake in a 350° oven for 10–12 minutes. Yield: about 4½ dozen cookies.

MILK-CHOCOLATE BALLS

ALMOND FILLING

½ cup ground blanched almonds
1 egg white
½ teaspoon almond flavoring

4 ounces milk chocolate
2 tablespoons milk
¾ cup butter
¼ cup sugar
1 teaspoon vanilla
2 cups flour
½ teaspoon salt
Confectioners' sugar

Almond Filling. Blend the almonds, egg white, 1 tablespoon water, and the almond flavoring into a paste. Set aside while preparing the dough.

Melt the chocolate with the milk over hot water. Cream the butter with the sugar until fluffy. Add vanilla and melted chocolate mixture. Sift the flour and salt together and gradually add to the dough, mixing thoroughly. Form into balls, using a rounded teaspoonful of dough for each.

Make a hole in the center of each ball with the end of a spoon and fill with about ¼ teaspoon of the almond filling. Gently seal the hole with a bit of dough and place the ball, hole side down, on a baking sheet. Bake in a 350° oven for 10–12 minutes. Roll in confectioners' sugar while still hot; cool on racks. Yield: about 3 dozen balls.

SWISS CHOCOLATE COOKIES

½ pound unblanched almonds
1 cup sugar
1½ teaspoons cocoa
1¼ teaspoons cinnamon
Dash cloves
1½ ounces unsweetened chocolate
2 egg whites

Grind the almonds and mix with the sugar, cocoa, cinnamon, and cloves. Add the melted chocolate, slightly cooled, and the egg whites. Mix just to moisten. Sprinkle board with a little sugar and, working with a small portion of dough at a time, roll to ⅛-inch thickness. Cut out with cooky cutter and place on greased baking sheets. Let stand a few hours to dry. Bake in a 300° oven for 15 minutes. Yield: about 3 dozen cookies.

CHOCOLATE CHEESE DROP COOKIES

½ cup butter
½ cup shortening
1 (3 oz.) package cream cheese
1½ cups sugar
1 egg
½ teaspoon salt
2 tablespoons milk
1 teaspoon vanilla
2 ounces unsweetened chocolate
2¼ cups flour
1½ teaspoons baking powder
½ cup chopped pecans or walnuts

Cream the butter, shortening, cream cheese, and sugar together. Add the egg, salt, milk, and vanilla. Mix well. Stir in the melted chocolate. Sift the flour with baking powder and add to the batter a little at a time, mixing well. Stir in the nuts. Drop by teaspoonfuls onto greased baking sheets. Bake in a 350° oven for 15 minutes. Yield: about 6 dozen cookies.

CHOCOLATE-FILLED COOKIES

2 cups flour
½ teaspoon baking powder
1 teaspoon salt
¾ cup butter
½ cup sugar
1 egg
1 cup very finely chopped nuts
1 teaspoon vanilla

CHOCOLATE FILLING

2 ounces unsweetened chocolate
1½ tablespoons butter
2 cups confectioners' sugar
2 tablespoons milk
Pinch salt

Sift the flour, baking powder, and salt together. Cream the butter, add the sugar and egg, and beat until well mixed and fluffy. Add the nuts, then the flour mixture, and flavor with vanilla. Stir until well mixed. Divide dough in half and shape into bars about 1 inch in diameter. Roll in waxed paper and chill. Slice the dough thin, place on baking sheets, and bake in a 350° oven for 8–10 minutes.

Chocolate Filling. Melt the chocolate and butter together. Add the confectioners' sugar, milk, and salt. Mix well and chill until thickened.

Spread the filling between cookies. Yield: about 4 dozen cookies.

Plate 10. A window display of candy and cake: Jars filled with ROYAL BRITTLE and SABLES. The tiered dish holds CHOCOLATE FUDGE and FRUITED MERINGUE KISSES. A DARK FRUITCAKE is on the high pedestal. POPCORN BALLS in the center next to a BUTTERSCOTCH BUBBLE LOAF. In the foreground from the left: SPICED CANDY ROLL, STUFFED DATES, TURKISH PASTE, and a DATE NUT CAKE.

Plate 11. Assorted cookies—from the top: WALNUT BROWNIES, LEMON BUTTER DAISIES, HONEY POPCORN BALLS, SABLES, APRICOT BRAZIL-NUT COOKIES, SPICY FRUIT NUT JUMBLES, and BUTTERSCOTCH JEWEL BARS.

TOLL HOUSE COOKIES

1 cup plus 2 tablespoons flour
½ teaspoon baking soda
½ teaspoon salt
½ cup butter
6 tablespoons sugar
6 tablespoons brown sugar
½ teaspoon vanilla
1 egg
1 (6 oz.) package semisweet chocolate bits
⅔ cup coarsely chopped nuts

Sift the flour, soda, and salt together. Cream the butter with the sugars. Add vanilla and beat in the egg. Add the flour mixture and mix well. Stir in the chocolate pieces and nuts. Drop by teaspoonfuls onto greased baking sheets. Bake in a 375° oven for 10–12 minutes, until brown around the edges. Yield: about 4 dozen.

CHOCOLATE-CHIP SQUARES

¼ cup butter
1 cup dark brown sugar
1 egg
½ teaspoon vanilla
1 cup flour
1 teaspoon baking powder
¼ teaspoon salt
1 cup semisweet chocolate bits
¾ cup chopped walnuts

Melt the butter. While it is still hot, add the sugar, egg, and vanilla. Beat until the mixture is fluffy. Sift the flour, baking powder, and salt together and stir into the first mixture. Mix in the chocolate bits and nuts. Spread evenly in a greased 8×8×2-inch pan. Bake in a 350° oven for ½ hour. Cut into 2-inch squares. These cookies should be chewy. Yield: 16 squares.

CHOCOLATE MINT WAFERS

2 cups flour
1 teaspoon baking powder
½ teaspoon baking soda
½ teaspoon salt
¾ cup cocoa
⅔ cup butter
1 cup sugar
1 egg
¼ cup milk

MINT FILLING

⅛ teaspoon salt
2 cups confectioners' sugar
3 tablespoons light cream
¼ teaspoon mint flavoring

Sift the flour, baking powder, soda, salt, and cocoa together. Cream the butter with sugar until light and fluffy. Add the well-beaten egg and beat again. Add the dry ingredients alternately with the milk. Mix thoroughly. Chill the dough until it can be handled. Form into rolls 1 inch in diameter, wrap each in waxed paper, and chill overnight. Cut into ⅛-inch slices. Bake on baking sheets in a 350° oven for 10–12 minutes. Cool.

Mint Filling. Add the salt to the sugar. Gradually add the cream, stirring until smooth. Add the mint flavoring.

Put the cookies together with the filling. Yield: about 4 dozen wafers.

LEMON-FROSTED COCONUT BARS

½ cup butter
1½ cups brown sugar
1¼ cups flour
2 eggs
1 teaspoon vanilla
1 teaspoon baking powder
½ teaspoon salt
1 cup flaked coconut
¾ cup finely chopped blanched almonds

LEMON FROSTING

2 cups confectioners' sugar
¼ cup half-and-half or light cream
Grated rind 1 lemon
2 teaspoons lemon juice

Cream the butter and ½ cup brown sugar until light and fluffy. Add 1 cup flour and mix well. Press mixture evenly over the bottom of a 13×9×2-inch pan. Bake in a 350° oven for 10 minutes. Beat the eggs, vanilla, and remaining brown sugar until frothy. Sift remaining flour, the baking powder, and salt together. Fold into egg mixture; add coconut and almonds. Mix well. Spread evenly over mixture in pan and bake for 20 minutes more. Cool in the pan.

Lemon Frosting. Mix the confectioners' sugar and cream. Add lemon rind and juice. Heat and stir over simmering water until smooth and shiny. Cool a little and pour over coconut mixture. When cold, cut into rectangular pieces. Yield: about 2 dozen bars.

CINNAMON COOKIES

1 cup butter
1 cup sugar
1 teaspoon vanilla
2 egg yolks
2¼ cups flour
2 teaspoons cinnamon
½ teaspoon salt

TOPPING

1 egg white
⅓ cup sugar
1½ teaspoons cinnamon

Cream the butter and sugar together. Add the vanilla and egg yolks and blend well. Sift the dry ingredients together and add to the creamed mixture. Chill. Roll dough out thin and cut with a cooky cutter. Brush the top of each cooky with egg white and sprinkle with a mixture of sugar and cinnamon. Bake on baking sheets in a 375° oven for 8–10 minutes. Yield: about 5 dozen cookies.

CINNAMON SQUARES

1 cup butter
1⅓ cups dark brown sugar
2 cups flour
2 teaspoons cinnamon
¼ teaspoon salt
¼ teaspoon nutmeg
¼ teaspoon baking powder

Cream the butter with the sugar until light and fluffy. Sift the remaining ingredients together. Add to butter mixture and mix well. Pat into an 8×8×2-inch pan and prick with a fork. Bake in a 375° oven for ½ hour, until browned. Cool and cut into squares. Yield: about 2½ dozen cookies.

COCONUT PECAN SQUARES

½ cup butter
½ cup dark brown sugar
1 cup plus 2 tablespoons flour
2 eggs
1 cup light brown sugar
Pinch salt
1 cup coarsely chopped pecans
½ cup flaked coconut
1 teaspoon vanilla
Confectioners' sugar

Cream the butter with the dark brown sugar. Add 1 cup flour and mix well. Press into a greased 8×8×2-inch pan, spreading the batter evenly into the corners. Bake in a 350° oven for 20 minutes. Meanwhile, beat the eggs until frothy. Gradually add the light brown sugar and salt, beating until thick. Add the pecans and the coconut which has been tossed with the remaining flour. Flavor with vanilla. Mix well. Spread over the baked crust and bake in a 350° oven for 20 minutes, until well browned. When cool, sprinkle with confectioners' sugar and cut into 1-inch squares. Yield: 64 squares.

DATE SQUARES

1 pound pitted dates
1 cup chopped nuts
3 eggs
¾ cup sugar
1 teaspoon vanilla
5 tablespoons flour
2 teaspoons baking powder
⅛ teaspoon salt
¼ teaspoon cinnamon
¼ teaspoon cloves

Cut the dates into small pieces and mix with the chopped nuts. Beat the eggs with the sugar and add the vanilla. Sift the dry ingredients together. Dredge the dates and nuts with the flour mixture, separating the pieces well. Stir in the egg mixture. Pour into a greased 8×8×2-inch pan. Bake in a 350° oven for ½ hour. When cool, cut into 2-inch squares. Yield: 16 squares.

UNBAKED DATE WALNUT BARS

1½ cups graham-cracker crumbs
2 tablespoons sugar
½ teaspoon cinnamon
¼ teaspoon salt
1 teaspoon vanilla
¼ cup soft butter

FILLING

2 cups finely cut pitted dates
2 tablespoons sugar
2 tablespoons lemon juice
1 cup chopped walnuts

Mix the graham-cracker crumbs with the sugar, cinnamon, and salt. Add the vanilla and work in the butter with the back of a spoon. Press ¾ of this mixture into a well-buttered

8×8×2-inch pan, covering bottom and sides. Chill while making the filling.

Filling. Put the date pieces in a saucepan with the sugar and lemon juice and cook for 3–4 minutes over low heat. Remove from heat and cool. Add ¾ cup walnuts and pat the mixture onto the graham-cracker base. Cover with the rest of the crumb mixture and press down firmly onto the filling. Sprinkle the remaining walnuts over the top. Chill for at least 4 hours. Cut into 1½×2-inch bars. Yield: 20 bars.

CREAM-CHEESE DATE COOKIES

1 cup butter
1 (8 oz.) package cream cheese
2 cups flour
½ teaspoon salt
1 pound pitted dates
Confectioners' sugar

Cream the butter and cheese together. Blend in the flour and salt. Chill well. Roll out to about ⅛-inch thickness on a lightly floured board. Cut into 1½×3-inch pieces. Place a date on each and roll up. Arrange cookies folded side down on baking sheets. Bake in a 375° oven for 12–15 minutes, until lightly golden. Sprinkle with confectioners' sugar. Yield: about 5 dozen cookies.

DATE PIN WHEELS

½ pound pitted dates
¼ cup sugar
1 teaspoon lemon juice
½ cup butter
1½ cups dark brown sugar
1 egg
2 cups flour
¼ teaspoon salt
½ teaspoon baking soda

Cut the dates into pieces and cook with the sugar, lemon juice, and ⅓ cup water for 5 minutes. Cool. For the dough, cream together the butter, brown sugar, and egg. Add the flour which has been sifted with the salt and soda. Chill the dough thoroughly to roll. The chilling of the dough is most important. Roll to ¼-inch thickness in 2 rectangles of about 9×10 inches on a floured board. Spread the date filling on the dough not quite to the edges, roll up like a jelly roll, cut in half, wrap each piece in waxed paper, and chill overnight. The rolls will be about 1½ inches in diameter. Cut slices ¼ inch thick and bake on greased baking sheets in a 350° oven for about 8 minutes. The dough can be frozen. Yield: about 100 cookies.

SPICY FRUIT NUT JUMBLES (*Plate 11*)

½ cup butter
1 cup light brown sugar
1 egg
1¾ cups flour
½ teaspoon baking soda
½ teaspoon salt
⅓ cup sour cream
¾ cup chopped pitted dates
1 cup chopped candied fruit (cherries, pineapple)
¾ cup chopped walnuts
1 teaspoon rum flavoring

Cream the butter and sugar together until light. Add the beaten egg. Sift the flour, soda, and salt together. Add alternately to the butter mixture with the sour cream. Add the fruit, nuts, and rum flavoring and mix well. Drop by teaspoonfuls onto greased baking sheets. Bake in a 400° oven for 10–12 minutes. Transfer to racks to cool. Frost while still warm if you wish; Plain Cooky Frosting* is recommended. Yield: about 5 dozen cookies.

CRISP GINGER COOKIES

4 cups flour
½ cup sugar
½ teaspoon baking soda
½ teaspoon salt
2½–3 teaspoons ginger
1 teaspoon cinnamon
2 cups butter
1¼ cups warm dark molasses

Sift the dry ingredients together. Cut in the butter until the mixture is the consistency of crumbs. Then stir in the warm—not hot—molasses and mix quickly. Cover and chill thoroughly. When quite stiff, divide the dough in half and shape into rolls about 1½ inches in diameter. Wrap well in waxed paper or foil and keep in the refrigerator until needed, or freeze. Slice thin and bake in a 350° oven for about 10 minutes. This dough keeps well; bake cookies as you need them. Yield: 6 dozen very thin cookies.

FLORENTINES

⅔ cup mixed candied fruits and peels
⅓ cup glacéed cherries
¼ cup finely chopped white raisins
⅓ cup finely chopped almonds
¼ cup butter
¼ cup sugar
1 tablespoon light corn syrup
1 teaspoon lemon juice
½ cup flour
1 (6 oz.) package semisweet chocolate bits

Chop the fruits and cherries fine and mix them with the raisins and almonds. Heat the butter, sugar, corn syrup, and lemon juice in a saucepan. Toss the fruit in the flour and stir into the mixture in the saucepan. Drop by teaspoonfuls onto greased baking sheets, leaving plenty of room in between. Flatten them slightly with the bottom of a wet glass. Bake in a 350° oven for 8–10 minutes. They are done when a deep golden brown with crisp, lacy edges. Let them stand a minute, lift from the sheets with a spatula, and invert on racks to cool. Frost the flat side with the chocolate which has been melted over hot water. These cookies may be stored in a cool place for several weeks. Yield: 4 dozen cookies.

ORANGE FLORENTINES

½ cup heavy cream
3 tablespoons sugar
¼ cup shaved blanched almonds
¼ pound finely slivered candied orange peel
Pinch salt
¼ cup flour
Orange* or Lemon Glaze*

Stir the cream and sugar together until the sugar dissolves and the mixture is slightly thickened. Add the almonds, fruit, salt, and flour. Mix well. Drop a little of the mixture from the tip of a teaspoon onto greased and floured baking sheets. Spread each slightly with the back of a spoon. Bake in a 350° oven for about 10–12 minutes. Remove from sheets and cool. Frost the *bottoms* with Orange or Lemon Glaze. Yield: about 2 dozen cookies.

FRUIT AND WALNUT ROLLS

¾ cup flour
1 cup sugar
1 teaspoon baking powder
¼ teaspoon salt
3 eggs
1 cup chopped pitted dates
1 cup chopped walnuts
Superfine sugar

Sift the dry ingredients together; then stir in the eggs, dates, and walnuts. Pour into a greased 8×8×2-inch pan. Bake in a 325° oven for about 40 minutes, until the top springs back to the touch. Cool 10–15 minutes in the pan. Then, while still warm, cut into bars and immediately coat with superfine sugar, shaping them into rolls as you do this. Yield: about 5 dozen cookies.

BRANDY SNAPS   *(Plate 35)*

¼ cup light corn syrup
¼ cup molasses
½ cup butter
1 cup flour
⅔ cup sugar
1 teaspoon ginger
Sweetened Whipped Cream*
Brandy

Heat the corn syrup and molasses to boiling point. Stir in the butter and remove from heat. Sift the dry ingredients together and add gradually to molasses mixture, mixing well. Drop half teaspoonfuls about 3 inches apart onto a greased baking sheet. These cookies spread considerably during baking. Bake in a 300° oven for 10–12 minutes. Remove from sheet one at a time and roll over the handle of a wooden spoon. Slip off carefully. Just before serving, fill with Sweetened Whipped Cream flavored with a little brandy. Yield: about 1½ dozen cookies.

GINGER CUTOUTS

2 cups flour
1 teaspoon baking soda
1 cup shortening (not butter)
¾ cup sugar
1 tablespoon dark corn syrup
1½ teaspoons ginger
1 teaspoon cinnamon

Sift the flour with baking soda. Cream the shortening (when made with anything but shortening, this cooky is too delicate to handle and decorate) and sugar together until light. Mix in the syrup, ginger, and cinnamon. Blend in the flour thoroughly. Wrap the dough in foil or Saran and chill overnight. Roll a bit of dough at a time to ⅛-inch thickness on a well-floured board. Cut into small shapes, place on baking sheets, and bake in a 350° oven for 10–12 minutes, until firm. Cool slightly before removing from baking sheets. Decorate as desired. Yield: about 3 dozen cookies.

DROPPED GINGER COOKIES

1¼ cups butter
⅓ cup dark brown sugar
1½ cups molasses
1 egg
5 cups flour
2 teaspoons ginger
1½ teaspoons cinnamon
1½ teaspoons allspice
4 teaspoons baking soda
½ teaspoon salt

Cream the butter and sugar together thoroughly. Add the molasses and the well-beaten egg. Beat well. Sift 2 cups flour with the spices and stir into the creamed mixture. Add ½ cup boiling water and 1 more cup flour. Mix and chill for ½ hour. Sift the remaining flour with the soda and salt. Mix into the batter and chill at least 1 hour or as long as overnight. If chilled for a long time, soften at room temperature before dropping by tablespoonfuls several inches apart onto greased baking sheets. Bake in a 350° oven for 8–10 minutes. Cool and store in a covered container. Yield: 5 dozen cookies.

GINGERBREAD MEN

¾ cup light molasses
¾ cup butter
4 cups flour
1 teaspoon baking powder
1 teaspoon salt
½ teaspoon baking soda
2 teaspoons ginger
¾ cup dark brown sugar
1 egg
Raisins or currants (optional)
Basic Glaze* (optional)
Assorted food coloring, candy sprinkles or colored sugar (optional)

Heat molasses slowly in a large saucepan. Remove from heat and add butter. Stir until butter is melted and set aside to cool. Sift flour, baking powder, salt, soda, and ginger together. Add the brown sugar and stir into the molasses mixture. Add the slightly beaten egg and blend well. Chill 1–2 hours, until dough is stiff enough to handle easily. Roll out ⅛–¼ inch thick on a lightly floured board. Cut out in the shape of men (make your own pattern with stiff paper or use any cutter you wish). Arrange on lightly greased baking sheets and bake in a 350° oven for 12–15 minutes, until lightly browned. Cool on racks. If you like, make faces and trimmings with raisins or currants before the cookies are baked, or bake plain and spread a few at a time with a very thin layer of Basic Glaze and decorate immediately with candy sprinkles or colored sugar. Or let the glaze dry thoroughly and paint on a design with food coloring. Yield: about 2 dozen.

HUNGARIAN NUT STICKS

1 cup butter
½ cup sugar
1 egg
2¼ cups flour
¼ teaspoon salt
½ teaspoon vanilla

PECAN TOPPING
2¼ cups finely chopped pecans
1 cup sugar
1½ teaspoons cinnamon
½ cup egg whites

Cream the butter and sugar thoroughly. Add the egg and beat well. Sift the flour and salt together and add a part at a time, mixing well. Flavor with vanilla. Spread evenly in a 15½ ×10½ ×1-inch pan. Bake in a 350° oven for 15 minutes.

Pecan Topping. Mix the pecans, sugar, cinnamon, and egg whites in a heavy saucepan. Cook over low heat, stirring constantly, until the sugar dissolves. Increase the heat and stir until the mixture thickens and comes away from the sides of the pan; do not overcook.

Spread the topping evenly over the partially baked cooky dough; this should cover the entire surface. Bake 15 minutes more. Cool slightly before cutting into strips. Yield: about 4 dozen sticks.

HONEY FRUIT COOKIES

½ cup butter
½ cup sugar
½ cup honey
½ teaspoon salt
1 egg
½ teaspoon vanilla
2⅓ cups flour
½ teaspoon baking soda
½ teaspoon baking powder
1 cup chopped mixed candied fruit
½ cup chopped nuts

Cream the butter with the sugar, honey, and salt. Add the egg and vanilla and beat well. Sift the flour, soda, and baking powder together and add. Blend in the candied fruit and chopped nuts. Drop by rounded teaspoonfuls onto baking sheets. Bake in a 350° oven for 12–15 minutes. Yield: about 5 dozen cookies.

HUNGARIAN COOKIES

3 cups flour
¾ teaspoon cinnamon
¾ teaspoon cocoa
1½ cups sweet butter
1½ cups confectioners' sugar
1 teaspoon lemon rind
1½ teaspoons lemon juice
2 cups ground filberts
Raspberry or strawberry jam
1 pound semisweet dipping chocolate
Blanched almond halves or slivers (garnish)

Sift the flour, cinnamon, and cocoa together. Cream the butter with sugar, lemon rind, and juice. Stir in the filberts. Mix in the dry ingredients, about ⅓ at a time. Chill dough for ½ hour. Working with ½ of the dough at a time, roll out on a lightly floured board to about ⅓-inch thickness. Cut with a 2-inch round cutter. Bake on greased baking sheets in a 325° oven for 12 minutes. Cool. Put pairs together sandwich fashion with about 1 tablespoon jam. Melt chocolate over simmering water in a double boiler, stirring constantly until completely melted. Attach candy thermometer and keep stirring chocolate, using a circular motion, until thermometer registers 130°. Remove top of double boiler from water. Pour off hot water and replace with cold. Place chocolate over cold water and stir constantly to cool all chocolate evenly. Continue stirring until chocolate has cooled to 83°, the right consistency for dipping. Dip top of each cooky pair in the chocolate and then top with an almond half or a few slivers. Place cookies on wire racks for chocolate to harden, about 3 hours. Yield: about 2 dozen cookies.

LEMON BARS

½ cup butter
½ cup confectioners' sugar
2 egg yolks
1 cup flour
2 teaspoons grated lemon rind

LEMON NUT MERINGUE

2 egg whites
½ cup sugar
1 tablespoon lemon juice
½ cup chopped nuts

Cream the butter with confectioners' sugar. Add the egg yolks and beat until light. Stir in the flour and lemon rind. Mix until smooth and spread evenly on the bottom of a 13×9×2-inch pan. Bake in a 350° oven for 10 minutes.

Lemon Nut Meringue. Beat the egg whites stiff, gradually adding the sugar. Beat in the lemon juice and fold in the nuts.

Spread the meringue over the baked mixture and bake 25 minutes longer. Cool slightly and cut into 1×3-inch bars. Yield: 39 bars.

MACAROONS

½ cup sugar
½ cup confectioners' sugar
1 cup almond paste
¼ teaspoon salt
1 teaspoon vanilla
2 egg whites

Mix the sugars; then blend into the almond paste. Add the salt and vanilla. Add the egg whites one at a time, beating thoroughly. Drop by teaspoonfuls onto ungreased brown paper on baking sheets. Bake in a 325° oven about 20 minutes, until a light beige. Cool. Wet the underside of the paper by placing on a damp cloth; the cookies will then peel off easily. Place immediately in a tightly covered container so they will remain chewy. Yield: 4 dozen small macaroons.

ORANGE MACAROONS

Proceed as for Macaroons.* Stir in 2½ teaspoons grated orange rind after adding the egg whites.

FILBERT MACAROONS

2 egg whites
⅛ teaspoon salt
1 cup confectioners' sugar
1 ounce unsweetened chocolate
1 cup finely ground filberts
½ teaspoon cinnamon
¼ teaspoon vanilla
¼ teaspoon grated lemon rind (optional)

Beat egg whites with salt until they stand in peaks. Mix the sugar, finely ground chocolate, nuts, and cinnamon together. Fold in the egg whites and add vanilla and, if you wish, the lemon rind. When evenly mixed, drop by teaspoonfuls onto foil-covered baking sheets. Bake in 300° oven for about 20 minutes. Cool slightly and remove from foil. Yield: about 1½ dozen.

FRUITED MERINGUE KISSES (*Plate 10*)

3 egg whites
⅛ teaspoon salt
1 cup sugar
½ teaspoon vanilla
¾ cup diced candied fruit

Beat the egg whites and salt until frothy. Add the sugar a tablespoon at a time, beating until the meringue will stand in a stiff peak and the sugar is dissolved. Fold in the vanilla and the fruit. Drop by spoonfuls onto greased baking sheets. Bake in a 275° oven for about 1 hour, until cream-colored. Yield: about 3 dozen.

MERINGUE COCONUT COOKIES

1 cup butter
1⅔ cups sugar
4 eggs
3 cups sifted flour
1 teaspoon baking powder
½ teaspoon salt
2 teaspoons grated lemon rind
Flaked coconut (garnish)

Cream the butter with 1 cup sugar until light and fluffy. Add 2 eggs and 2 egg yolks,

blending well. Sift the flour, baking powder, and salt together. Add gradually to the creamed mixture. Blend in the grated lemon rind. Chill the dough about 2 hours before using. Roll out small amounts at a time. Cut with a small cooky cutter and place on baking sheets. Make a meringue by beating the remaining egg whites with the rest of the sugar. Top each cooky with a small spoonful of meringue and a sprinkling of coconut. Bake for 10–12 minutes in a 350° oven. Yield: about 10 dozen cookies.

MERINGUE KISSES
(Low Calorie)

1 egg white
Pinch salt
⅓ cup superfine sugar
¼ teaspoon vanilla
½ teaspoon cocoa or instant coffee (optional)

Beat the egg white with salt until very frothy. Add the sugar gradually, a tablespoon at a time. Beat until the meringue stands in a stiff peak and the sugar is dissolved. Fold in the vanilla, and the cocoa or coffee if you wish. Shape with a pastry bag or tube into 24 small spiral cones, or drop from a teaspoon, onto well-greased baking sheets. Bake in a 250° oven for about 45 minutes, until dry but not browned. Yield: about 2 dozen meringues (about 12 calories each).

BONBON MERINGUES

1¼ cups raisins or pitted dates
1 cup pecans or walnuts
1 teaspoon vanilla
2 egg whites
⅛ teaspoon salt
⅔ cup superfine sugar

Grind the fruit and nuts together. Then add ½ teaspoon vanilla. Form into little balls, using about ½ teaspoonful for each. Beat the egg whites with salt until foamy. Gradually add the sugar and continue beating until a stiff meringue forms and all the sugar is dissolved. Fold in the remaining vanilla. Using 2 spoons, roll the fruit-nut balls in the meringue, coating well. As you place each on a greased baking sheet, swirl the top. Bake in a 250° oven about ½ hour, until the meringue is slightly golden on the tips. Remove at once to racks to cool. Yield: about 4 dozen cookies.

PECAN MERINGUES

1 egg white
1 cup dark brown sugar
1 tablespoon flour
⅛ teaspoon salt
1 cup chopped pecans

Beat the egg white stiff. Mix the sugar, flour, and salt. Carefully fold into the egg white. Fold in the pecans. Drop by teaspoonfuls onto greased baking sheets. Bake in a 300° oven for 15 minutes. Cool a little before removing from baking sheets. Yield: 2 dozen.

LEBKUCHEN

3 eggs
1 pound dark brown sugar
2½ cups flour
1 teaspoon cloves
1 teaspoon cinnamon
1 teaspoon allspice
½ teaspoon baking soda
1 cup mixed candied fruit
½ cup chopped nuts
2 cups confectioners' sugar
2½–3 tablespoons lemon or orange juice

Beat the eggs until thick, gradually adding the brown sugar. Sift the flour with the spices and soda and blend in. Add the fruit and nuts and mix well. Spread in a greased 15½ × 10½ ×1-inch pan. Bake in a 375° oven for 20 minutes. Turn out of pan and cool on a rack. Cut into bars, about ½ ×3 inches, and glaze with a thin frosting made of the confectioners' sugar and lemon or orange juice. Yield: about 100 bars.

HOT MINCEMEAT COOKIES

½ cup butter
1 cup sugar
1 egg
3 cups flour
2 teaspoons baking powder
⅛ teaspoon salt
¼ cup milk
1½ teaspoons lemon juice
½ teaspoon grated lemon rind
2 tablespoons brandy
1 cup mincemeat

Cream the butter with the sugar until fluffy. Add the egg and beat well. Sift the flour with baking powder and salt and add to the egg mixture alternately with the milk and lemon juice. Stir in the lemon rind and 1 tablespoon brandy. Turn the dough out on waxed paper and chill for several hours. Working with a small amount at a time, roll the dough quite thin and cut with a 2-inch round cutter. With a ½-inch cutter remove a small circle of dough from the center of half the circles. Stir the remaining brandy into the mincemeat and put about ½ teaspoon of the mixture in the center of the whole circles; top with the cut-out rings. Press edges together firmly. Bake in a 375° oven for about 12 minutes, until bottoms are golden. These may be stored in an airtight container. Warm the cookies before serving. Yield: 5 dozen cookies.

MOLASSES BARS

⅓ cup shortening
⅓ cup superfine sugar
1 egg
⅓ cup dark molasses
⅛ teaspoon salt
⅛ teaspoon baking soda
1 cup minus 2 tablespoons flour
1 teaspoon vanilla
1 cup broken nut meats
Superfine sugar (garnish)

Cream the shortening and add the sugar gradually. Beat until light and creamy. Beat in the egg, molasses, salt, and soda. Add the flour gradually and the vanilla. When smooth, fold in the nut meats. Bake in a greased 8 × 8×2-inch pan in a 375° oven for 15 minutes. Cut into 1×2-inch bars while still warm. Roll in additional superfine sugar. Yield: 32 bars.

MOLASSES COOKIES

1 cup butter
1 cup sugar
2 eggs
1 cup molasses
1 teaspoon ginger
1 teaspoon cinnamon
3½ cups flour
2 teaspoons baking soda
1 teaspoon salt

Cream the butter and sugar together. Add the eggs, molasses, ginger, and cinnamon. Sift the flour with soda and salt. Add to the creamed mixture alternately with ½ cup cold water. Drop by large spoonfuls onto greased baking sheets and bake 8–10 minutes in a 375° oven. This batter can be patted on a floured board to ½-inch thickness, cut with a cooky cutter, and transferred to baking sheets with a spatula. Rolled cookies may be made by adding a little more flour to the batter and chilling the dough before rolling. Don't roll too thin. Yield: about 6 dozen.

ROLLED MOLASSES WAFERS

½ cup molasses
½ cup butter
1 cup flour
⅔ cup sugar
1 teaspoon ginger

Heat the molasses to boiling and add the butter. Stir until well blended. Add the flour, sugar, and ginger. Drop by level teaspoonfuls 4 inches apart onto greased baking sheets. Bake in a 350° oven for about 10 minutes, until they darken a bit and are bubbly. Remove from oven and cool slightly on the baking sheets until they can be loosened with a spatula without sticking. It is important not to let them cool too long as they will become too crisp to roll. As you remove the warm cookies, roll each over the handle of a wooden spoon or any round stick. Cool on racks. Yield: 5–6 dozen cookies.

OATMEAL COOKIES

½ cup butter
½ cup dark brown sugar
1 egg
1 cup flour
¼ teaspoon baking soda
½ teaspoon baking powder
¼ teaspoon salt
½ teaspoon cinnamon
¼ teaspoon nutmeg
Pinch cloves
6 tablespoons milk
1 cup quick-cooking rolled oats
½ cup raisins

Cream the butter with the sugar. Add the well-beaten egg and beat until fluffy. Sift the flour with the soda, baking powder, salt, and the spices. Add alternately to the creamed mixture with the milk. Stir in the oats and raisins. Drop by tablespoonfuls several inches apart on baking sheets and bake in a 375° oven for 10–12 minutes. Yield: about 3 dozen.

OATMEAL LACE COOKIES

½ cup flour
Pinch salt
¼ teaspoon baking powder
½ cup sugar
½ cup rolled oats
2 tablespoons heavy cream
2 tablespoons light corn syrup
⅓ cup melted butter
1 tablespoon vanilla

Sift the flour, salt, baking powder, and sugar together. Add the oats, cream, corn syrup, butter, and vanilla. Mix together until well blended. Using a ¼-teaspoon measuring spoon, drop 4 inches apart onto baking sheets. Bake in a 375° oven 6–8 minutes, until lightly browned. Let stand only a few seconds before removing from baking sheets. Yield: 6 dozen 2-inch cookies.

OATMEAL DATE BARS

DATE NUT FILLING
1 pound pitted dates
1 cup sugar
1 cup chopped walnuts

DOUGH
1 cup butter
1 cup brown sugar
2½ cups quick-cooking rolled oats
2½ cups flour
¾ teaspoon salt
1 teaspoon baking soda

Date Nut Filling. Cut the dates into small pieces. Mix them with the sugar and ½ cup hot water. Cook over low heat until just thick, stirring constantly. Add the nuts and cool.

Dough. Cream the butter with the sugar until light and fluffy. Add the rolled oats. Sift the flour and salt together. Dissolve the soda in ½ cup hot water. Add the sifted flour to the mixture alternately with the liquid. Mix well. Chill dough until firm enough to roll.

Roll out dough to about ⅛-inch thickness on a floured board. Spread the filling over half the dough. With a wide spatula turn the other half of the dough over the top of the date filling, sandwich fashion. Pat smooth and cut into squares or bars. Bake on greased baking sheets in a 350° oven for 15–20 minutes. Yield: about 40 bars.

LACY OATMEAL WAFERS

*3–4 tablespoons finely chopped blanched
  almonds*
½ cup brown sugar
1½ teaspoons baking powder
½ cup butter
*1 cup plus 2 tablespoons quick-cooking
  rolled oats*
2 tablespoons heavy cream

Mix the almonds with the sugar and baking powder. Cream the butter until light and fluffy, then stir in the rolled oats. Add the almond mixture and stir thoroughly. Mix in the cream and chill for about 1 hour. Drop level ½ teaspoons of the batter 3 inches apart on baking sheets. Bake in a 400° oven for 7–8 minutes, until lightly browned on the edges. Watch closely, as they brown quickly. (During the baking, keep the unused batter chilled so it remains stiff.) Cool a little before removing from sheets. Transfer wafers to racks and cool thoroughly before storing in an airtight container. Yield: 6–7 dozen cookies.

OATMEAL NUT COOKIES

¾ cup soft butter
1 cup dark brown sugar
½ cup sugar
1 egg
1 teaspoon vanilla
1 cup flour
1 teaspoon salt
½ teaspoon baking soda
3 cups rolled oats
1 cup chopped walnuts or filberts

Mix the butter thoroughly with the sugar, egg, vanilla, and ¼ cup water. Sift the flour, salt, and soda together and add to the shortening mixture. Mix well. Stir in the rolled oats and nuts. Drop by teaspoonfuls onto greased baking sheets. Bake in a 350° oven for 12–15 minutes. Yield: about 6 dozen cookies.

ORANGE COOKIES

½ cup butter
1 cup sugar
1 egg
Grated rind 1 orange
¼ teaspoon baking soda
½ cup sour cream
1 teaspoon orange juice

2½ cups flour
¼ teaspoon salt
1 teaspoon baking powder
Sugar (topping)

Cream the butter with sugar until light and fluffy. Add the egg, beaten until light and thick, and the orange rind. Dissolve the soda in sour cream and add the orange juice. Sift the flour, salt, and baking powder together. Add the dry ingredients alternately with the sour-cream mixture to the creamed butter. Beat thoroughly until smooth. Drop by teaspoonfuls 1½ inches apart onto greased baking sheets. Sprinkle with sugar and bake 12 minutes in a 375° oven. Yield: 6 dozen small cookies.

ORANGE ICEBOX COOKIES

1 cup butter
½ cup sugar
½ cup light brown sugar
1 egg
3 cups flour
½ teaspoon salt
¼ teaspoon baking soda
Grated rind 1 orange
2 tablespoons orange juice
1 teaspoon vanilla
½ cup chopped toasted blanched almonds

Cream the butter and both sugars together. Beat in the egg. Sift the flour, salt, and soda together and blend into the egg mixture. Mix in the orange rind and juice, vanilla, and nuts. Chill dough until stiff enough to shape into rolls. Make the rolls about 1½–2 inches in diameter and 8–10 inches long. Wrap each in foil. Chill well, or freeze if you like. To bake, slice cookies ⅛ inch thick. Place on baking sheets and bake in a 375° oven for 12–15 minutes. Yield: about 5 dozen cookies.

ORANGE STICKS

½ cup butter
1 cup sugar
1 egg
Grated rind 1 orange
3 cups flour
1½ teaspoons baking powder
⅓ cup orange juice
6 ounces semisweet chocolate
¾ cup chopped walnuts

Cream the butter with the sugar. Add the beaten egg and grated orange rind. Sift the flour and baking powder together and add alternately with the orange juice to the butter and sugar. Mix well. Chill for several hours. Pack the dough into a cooky press fitted with a rosette tip and press out on greased baking sheets to make 1×3-inch strips. Bake in a 350° oven for 10–12 minutes. Cool. Dip each end of the cookies into chocolate which has been melted over hot water. Sprinkle with chopped walnuts. Yield: 4 dozen sticks.

PECAN BARS

1 cup plus 2 tablespoons flour
½ cup butter
2 eggs
1½ cups brown sugar
½ cup flaked coconut
1 cup chopped pecans
½ teaspoon baking powder
½ teaspoon salt
1 teaspoon vanilla
1½ cups confectioners' sugar
1½–2 tablespoons lemon juice

Combine 1 cup flour with the butter and work with a spoon until well blended. Spread this mixture in a 13×9×2-inch pan. Bake in a 350° oven for 12 minutes. Beat the eggs and gradually add the brown sugar, beating well. Add the coconut and pecans. Add remaining flour which has been sifted with the baking powder and salt. Flavor with vanilla. Spread over dough and bake again in a 350° oven for 25 minutes. Thin the confectioners' sugar with lemon juice to spreading consistency and spread over the cake when cool. Cut into bars about 1×2 inches. Yield: about 4 dozen.

PRUNE BARS

1 cup dried prunes
3 eggs
½ cup sugar
½ cup dark brown or maple sugar
1 tablespoon grated orange rind
1 cup flour
1 teaspoon baking powder
¼ teaspoon salt
½–1 cup chopped nuts

Soak the prunes in cold water for 3 hours or so. Remove pits and cut prunes into small pieces. Beat the egg yolks until thick and lemon-colored. Add the sugars a little at a time, beating after each addition; then add the orange rind. Sift the flour with the baking powder and salt. Beat the egg whites until a soft peak forms. Add part of the sifted flour to the egg-yolk mixture; then fold in the prunes and chopped nuts. Fold in some of the egg whites, then the rest of the dry ingredients, and the remaining egg whites last. Spread into a greased 11×7×1½-inch pan. Bake in a 350° oven for about ½ hour, until it springs back lightly to the touch. Cool and cut into bars of about 1×3 inches. Yield: 20 bars.

RAISIN-FILLED COOKIES

1 cup butter
2 cups sugar
2 eggs
2 teaspoons vanilla
6 cups flour
1 teaspoon baking soda
1 teaspoon baking powder
2 teaspoons salt
⅔ cup sour milk or buttermilk

RAISIN FILLING
3 cups raisins
1½ cups sugar
3 tablespoons flour

Cream the butter with the sugar. Add the well-beaten eggs and vanilla. Sift the dry ingredients together. Add alternately to creamed mixture with milk. Mix well. Cover and chill overnight.
Raisin Filling. Grind the raisins. Mix with 1½ cups water and the sugar and flour. Stir and simmer until thickened. Cool.

Roll out the cooky dough a portion at a time on a floured board or cloth. Cut with a 3-inch round cutter. Put a spoonful of filling in the center of one circle, moisten edges with a little water, top with another circle, and press the edges firmly together with a fork. Bake in a 375° oven for 17–20 minutes. Cool. Yield: about 2½–3 dozen cookies.

ROLLED HONEY WAFERS

Substitute honey for the molasses and ½ teaspoon each of almond and orange flavorings for the ginger. Proceed as for Rolled Molasses Wafers.*

SABLES   (Plates 10 and 11)

2 cups flour
½ cup superfine sugar
3 hard-cooked egg yolks
1 cup butter
3 tablespoons grated orange rind
Pinch salt

Put the flour and sugar in a bowl with the egg yolks which have been rubbed through a sieve. Add butter, orange rind, and salt. Blend with a fork or pastry blender. Knead slightly and divide the dough into 4 parts. Chill for about 3 hours. Keeping the unused dough chilled, roll out a portion at a time ⅛ inch thick on floured board and cut with a cooky cutter about 1¾ inches in diameter. Bake on ungreased baking sheets in a 400° oven for 7–8 minutes. Let cool on sheets for a few minutes before removing to racks to cool. (You may use a fancy cooky cutter and sprinkle with sugar candies.) Yield: about 6 dozen thin cookies.

ALMOND SABLES

Omit the grated orange rind in the recipe for Sables* and flavor with 2 teaspoons almond flavoring, or add ¼ cup very finely ground blanched almonds and 1 teaspoon almond flavoring with the egg yolks.

SWEDISH COOKY TARTLETS

1 cup butter
1 cup sugar
1 egg
½ teaspoon almond flavoring
½ teaspoon grated lemon rind
3 cups flour
Pinch salt
Filling

Cream the butter with the sugar until light and fluffy. Add the egg and beat well. Stir in the almond flavoring and lemon rind. Add flour and salt and mix well. Chill thoroughly. When ready to use, pinch off small balls of dough and place in center of miniature fluted tart pans. Press dough with thumb over bottom and sides, spreading as thin as possible. Place on baking sheets and bake in a 350° oven for 12–14 minutes, until lightly browned. Cool slightly. Invert pans and tap lightly. Use point of a knife gently to work edges of pastry away from sides of pans. Fill with preserved loganberries, raspberries, lingonberries, or a chopped cranberry mixture, or any fairly tart-flavored filling. Yield: about 75 tiny tartlets.

MINIATURE SWEDISH ALMOND TARTS

1½ cups butter
1 cup sugar
1 egg
1 teaspoon almond flavoring
½ teaspoon vanilla
3 cups flour
2½ cups minced almonds
Candied fruit and/or nuts (garnish)

Cream the butter and sugar until fluffy. Beat in the egg and flavorings. Work in the flour and almonds. Chill dough until firm. Pinch off about a tablespoonful at a time and press into fluted tart pans or tins 1¾ inches across and ¾ inch deep. Place on baking sheets and bake in a 300° oven for 25–30 minutes, until faintly golden on outside and chewy and moist inside. Cool slightly and slip tarts from the tins, using a toothpick. Decorate if you wish with candied fruits and/or nuts before baking. These may be made in slightly larger tart pans and baked a few minutes longer. Yield: about 5½ dozen tarts.

OLD-FASHIONED
SOUR-CREAM COOKIES

¼ cup butter
1½ cups sugar
2 eggs
2½ cups flour
¼ teaspoon salt
1 teaspoon baking soda
1 cup sour cream
1 teaspoon nutmeg
Seeded raisins (optional)

Cream the butter with sugar until light and fluffy. Add the well-beaten eggs and beat mixture until well blended and light. Sift the flour with salt and baking soda. Add to creamed mixture alternately with the sour cream. Add the nutmeg and mix well. Drop by tablespoonfuls onto baking sheets, allowing several inches between the cookies. Place a large, soft seeded raisin in the center of each if you wish. Bake in a 375° oven for 12–15 minutes. Yield: 2 dozen cookies.

SCOTCH SHORTBREAD

1 cup butter
½ cup sugar
2½ cups flour
Pinch salt

Cream the butter and sugar together until light and fluffy. Add the flour sifted with salt and mix well. Press evenly into an 8×8×2-inch pan and prick with a fork. Bake in a 325° oven for 35–40 minutes, until pale golden. Cool slightly in the pan; then cut into squares. Yield: about 2 dozen squares.

SCOTCH CARAWAY SQUARES

4 cups flour
½ cup sugar
2 teaspoons caraway seed
1½ cups butter

Mix the flour, sugar, and caraway seed. Work in the butter with fingertips until well blended. Press lightly into two 8×8×2-inch pans. Prick with a fork. Mark into squares. Bake in a 325° oven about 45 minutes, until golden. Yield: 4–5 dozen cookies.

QUICK SHERRIED SNOWBALLS

2 tablespoons cocoa
1 cup confectioners' sugar
⅓ cup sherry
3 tablespoons light corn syrup
1 (12 oz.) package crushed vanilla wafers
1 cup broken walnuts

Sift the cocoa and confectioners' sugar together. Stir in the sherry and corn syrup. Add the vanilla wafers and walnuts. Roll the mixture into small balls and dust with additional confectioners' sugar. Yield: about 40 cookies.

SPRITZ COOKIES

1 cup butter
⅔ cup sugar
Pinch salt
3 egg yolks
2 teaspoons vanilla
2 cups flour

Cream the butter with the sugar and salt until fluffy. Add the egg yolks and vanilla and beat well. Work in the flour until a smooth dough is formed. Chill for ½ hour. Force through a cooky press, forming various shapes, onto cold baking sheets. Bake 7–10 minutes in a 400° oven, until set but not browned. Yield: about 6 dozen cookies.

STAGE PLANKS

2 tablespoons butter
½ cup light brown sugar
½ cup dark molasses
1 teaspoon lemon flavoring
⅓ cup buttermilk
3 cups flour
½ teaspoon salt
½ teaspoon ginger
½ teaspoon cinnamon
½ teaspoon cloves
½ teaspoon baking soda

Cream the butter with the sugar and molasses. Add the lemon flavoring to the buttermilk. Sift the flour, salt, spices, and soda together. Add alternately with the buttermilk to the creamed mixture. Blend together well. Chill for several hours. Turn out onto a floured board and roll ¼ inch thick. Cut into 1½ × 2-inch strips. Place on greased baking sheets and bake in a 350° oven for 10–12 minutes. Yield: 3 dozen cookies.

STRAWBERRY JAM BARS

1½ cups flour
½ cup sugar
½ teaspoon baking powder
½ teaspoon salt
½ teaspoon cinnamon
½ cup butter
1 egg
¼ cup milk
½ teaspoon almond flavoring
1 cup strawberry jam
⅓ cup confectioners' sugar

Sift the flour, sugar, baking powder, salt, and cinnamon together. Cut the butter into the dry ingredients until mixture has the texture of corn meal. Add egg, milk, and almond flavoring and mix well. Spread part of the batter into a greased 7×11×1½-inch pan, spread the jam evenly over this, and drop remaining batter by spoonfuls evenly on top. Bake in a 400° oven for ½ hour. Cool in pan. Cut into bars and sprinkle with confectioners' sugar. Yield: about 28 bars.

ROLLED SUGAR COOKIES

½ cup butter
1 cup sugar
1 egg
1 tablespoon heavy cream
1 teaspoon vanilla
2 cups flour
½ teaspoon salt
1 teaspoon baking powder
Sugar (topping)

Cream the butter with the sugar until light; add the slightly beaten egg, cream, and vanilla. Sift the flour, salt, and baking powder together. Add to the creamed mixture and mix thoroughly. Chill overnight. Roll out a small amount at a time *very, very* thin on a lightly floured board. Cut with a scalloped or round 1½-inch cooky cutter, place on greased baking sheets, and sprinkle lightly with sugar. Bake in a 350° oven for 5 minutes. Yield: about 12 dozen small cookies.

SUGAR CUTOUTS

3½ cups flour
1 teaspoon baking powder
½ teaspoon salt
1 cup shortening (not butter)
1½ cups sugar
2 eggs
1½ teaspoons vanilla

Sift the flour with baking powder and salt. Cream the shortening with the sugar until light; stir in the well-beaten eggs and vanilla. Work flour into mixture. Wrap dough in foil or Saran and chill until firm. Roll a bit of dough at a time to ⅛-inch thickness on a floured board. Cut into desired shapes and bake in a 400° oven for 5–8 minutes, until firm and golden at the edges. Cool slightly before removing to racks. Decorate if desired. Yield: about 6 dozen cookies.

VANILLA BALLS

VANILLA SUGAR
2 teaspoons vanilla
¾ cup confectioners' sugar

VANILLA BALLS
¾ cup butter
¼ cup heavy cream
1 teaspoon vanilla
1¾ cups flour

6 tablespoons superfine sugar
1 cup chopped walnuts or pecans

Vanilla Sugar. Add the vanilla to confectioners' sugar. Mix well and rub through a sieve. Prepare before baking cookies so it will have time to dry.

Vanilla Balls. Cream the butter. Beat in the cream and vanilla. Sift the flour and superfine sugar together. Add this gradually to the creamed mixture. Mix in the chopped nuts. Chill. Pinch off pieces of dough and roll into small balls. Place 2 inches apart on greased baking sheets. Bake in a 325° oven for 20 minutes. Take from baking sheets and roll in vanilla sugar. Yield: 3½ dozen cookies.

WALNUT REFRIGERATOR COOKIES

1 cup butter
2 cups light brown sugar
2 eggs
3 cups flour
3½ teaspoons baking powder
½ teaspoon salt
1 cup finely chopped walnuts
1 teaspoon vanilla

Cream the butter with the sugar until light and fluffy. Add the well-beaten eggs and beat until light again. Sift the flour, baking powder, and salt together and work this thoroughly into the creamed mixture. Stir in the walnuts and vanilla. Shape into long rolls 1½ inches in diameter, wrap in waxed paper, and chill at least overnight. Slice the dough as thin as possible and bake on greased baking sheets in a 375° oven for about 8 minutes. Yield: 8–10 dozen cookies.

HONEY-DIPPED WALNUT COOKIES

1 cup butter
½ cup cooking oil
2 eggs
4 cups flour
2 teaspoons baking powder
1 teaspoon salt
½ cup orange juice
1¾ cups chopped walnuts
¼ cup sugar
1 cup honey

Cream the butter and oil until light. Add the eggs one at a time and beat until smooth. Sift the flour, baking powder, and salt together.

Add alternately with orange juice, beginning and ending with dry ingredients. Mix in ¾ cup chopped walnuts. Pinch off pieces of dough the size of a small walnut and roll into balls. Place on greased baking sheets and make a slight depression in the center of each with the end of your finger. Bake in a 300° oven for 45 minutes, until lightly browned. Cool on racks. Simmer the sugar and ¼ cup water for 10 minutes in a small saucepan. Add the honey and heat until just boiling. Using a spoon, dip the cookies into hot sauce, place on a platter or waxed paper, and sprinkle with chopped walnuts. Yield: about 6 dozen cookies.

WHOOPEE PIES

½ cup butter
1 cup sugar
1 egg yolk
2 cups flour
½ teaspoon baking soda
½ teaspoon baking powder
½ teaspoon salt
¼ cup cocoa
½ cup buttermilk or sour milk

VANILLA FILLING
1 egg white
1 teaspoon vanilla
½ cup butter
2 tablespoons flour
2 tablespoons heavy cream
1 cup plus 1 tablespoon confectioners' sugar

Cream the butter and sugar until light and fluffy. Beat in the egg yolk. Sift the flour, soda, baking powder, salt, and cocoa together. Add to creamed mixture alternately with the milk. Drop by teaspoonfuls onto greased baking sheets. Bake in a 375° oven for 10 minutes. Cool on racks.

Vanilla Filling. Combine egg white, vanilla, butter, flour, cream, and 1 tablespoon confectioners' sugar. Beat with rotary beater until very smooth. Beat in remaining confectioners' sugar and continue to beat for about 5 minutes. Chill for about ½ hour before using.

When cookies are cooled, put 2 cookies together sandwich fashion, with the filling in the center. Yield: 2½–3 dozen cookies.

WALNUT DATE BARS

1 cup sifted flour
½ teaspoon baking soda
½ teaspoon cinnamon
¼ teaspoon nutmeg
¼ teaspoon salt
⅓ cup butter
¾ cup brown sugar
1 egg
1 tablespoon grated orange rind
2 tablespoons orange juice
½ cup cut-up dates
1 cup chopped walnuts
½ recipe Orange Butter Cream Frosting*

Sift the flour, soda, spices, and salt together. Cream the butter and sugar until light and fluffy. Add the egg, orange rind and juice and beat well. Stir in the dry ingredients, blending until smooth. Add the dates and ¾ cup walnuts. Turn into a greased and floured 11×7×1½-inch pan. Bake in a 350° oven for 25–30 minutes. Cool a few minutes in the pan, turn out, and cool thoroughly on a rack. Spread the top with Orange Butter Cream Frosting and sprinkle with the remaining walnuts. Cut into 1×2½-inch bars. Yield: about 30 bars.

SUGAR-COATED WALNUT CRESCENTS

1½ cups butter
About 1¼ cups confectioners' sugar
1 egg yolk
1 cup finely chopped walnuts
3¼ cups flour

Cream the butter until light and fluffy. Mix in 2 tablespoons confectioners' sugar and the egg yolk and beat until smooth. Stir in the walnuts. Gradually mix in the flour. Pinch off small pieces of dough and form into crescent or finger shapes. Place on baking sheets and bake in a 275° oven for 40–45 minutes, until delicately browned. Let cool slightly on sheets. Spread a layer of sifted confectioners' sugar in a shallow pan and arrange cookies carefully on sugar. Sift additional sugar generously over the cookies and let stand until cool. Store in tightly covered containers. Handle cookies gently, as they are so rich they crumble easily. Yield: about 3 dozen cookies.

Cakes and Appropriate Frostings

Angel-Food	Light glaze or frosting or often none
Apple	Spiced Topping
Black-Walnut	Burnt-Sugar
Chocolate	Mocha, Chocolate, or any white frosting
Coffeecakes	Glaze
Cupcakes	Chocolate, Strawberry, or any frosting
Devil's-Food	Chocolate, Peppermint-Candy, Coffee, Caramel
Gingerbread	Whipped Cream, Custard Sauce
Mocha	Chocolate
Poundcake	None or glaze
Spicecake	Caramel, Sea Foam
Spongecake	Confectioners' sugar or light glaze or frosting
Tortes	Whipped Cream
Marble	Chocolate, Marshmallow Cream
Orange	Orange, Lemon, or Lime
White	Vanilla, Chocolate, Mocha, Grapefruit, Burnt-Sugar, Lady Baltimore—almost any
Yellow	Chocolate, Orange or Lemon or Lime Butter Cream, Caramel, Maple, Coconut

What are little girls made of?
Sugar and spice, and everything nice;
That's what little girls are made of.
                              Anonymous,
                    What Are Little Boys Made Of?

CHAPTER THREE

Festive Frostings

METHOD OF FROSTING AND DECORATING CAKES

Frosting and filling cakes add glamour as well as flavor. Frosting also protects the cake by keeping it moist.

Choose a frosting to complement your cake: a buttery frosting on a simple cake, a light 7-minute type on a rich cake, and perhaps no frosting at all on some cakes, such as angel-food, sponge-, or poundcakes. Be sure to consider the flavor in relation to the cake as well as its appearance and consistency.

There are four basic frostings; the rest are all variations. 1. Uncooked butter frosting, made with confectioners' sugar and butter, is the easiest and most frequently used. 2. Seven-minute frosting, a short-cut cooked one, is made in a double boiler while beating steadily. 3. Cooked frosting is the fondant type, such as light fudge. 4. Boiled frosting, the hardest to make, is delicious and lavish-looking. This fluffy frosting is made by beating a boiled syrup slowly and carefully into beaten egg whites.

Cover the cake with a cloth while it is cooling. Brush off any crumbs before frosting. For a really good-looking job, it pays to spread the cake first with a thin layer of frosting which is allowed to cool and form an even base to build on. Spread the frosting over the edge and down the sides with a spatula and then pile the rest on top and spread. You can make a smooth or rough surface or swirl designs with a spatula, spoon, or fork.

For a decorative effect you may tint the frosting with a few drops of food coloring. A pastry bag with an appropriate tip works beautifully for writing on cakes and making rosettes or other decorations. There is a limitless variety of edible decorations to choose from: whole, halved, or chopped nuts; fresh, glazed, or preserved fruits; plain, toasted, tinted, or flavored coconut. Jelly or chocolate may be melted to use for designs and names, initials, or dates. Candies that are fun to decorate with include: jelly beans, little silver balls, sprinkles, colorful hard candies, tinted mints, angelica, and candied citrus fruit peel. Use your imagination; you don't need to be an artist in order to design, build, and decorate a cake.

Note

Frosting in the following recipes means both frosting and filling; the quantity is enough to put between layers and to cover the top and sides of a 9-inch cake.   (about 2 cups)

Filling is spread only between layers of a cake.   (about ¾ cup)

Topping is spread over the top and sometimes down the sides of a cake.   (1–2 cups)

Glaze is used over the top and partly down the sides of a cake.   (about 1 cup)

SEVEN-MINUTE FROSTING

2 egg whites
1½ cups sugar
Pinch salt
¼ teaspoon cream of tartar
2 teaspoons light corn syrup
1 teaspoon vanilla

Put the egg whites, sugar, salt, cream of tartar, ⅓ cup water, and corn syrup in a double boiler. Beat with a rotary beater for 1 minute, or until thoroughly mixed. Place over boiling water and beat constantly for 7 minutes, or until frosting will stand in stiff peaks, stirring frosting up from bottom and sides of the pan occasionally. Remove from heat and place over cold water or pour into a bowl. Add the vanilla and beat 1 minute longer, or until thick enough to spread. Yield: frosting for a 2-layer cake.

COCONUT SEVEN-MINUTE FROSTING

Frost cake with Seven-Minute Frosting* and sprinkle with 1½ cups grated coconut or 1 (3½ oz.) can flaked coconut while the frosting is still soft.

LEMON SEVEN-MINUTE FROSTING

Proceed as for Seven-Minute Frosting,* using only 3 tablespoons water. Omit the vanilla and add 2 tablespoons lemon juice and ¼ teaspoon grated lemon rind.

CHOCOLATE-MARBLE SEVEN-MINUTE FROSTING

Add 2 ounces unsweetened chocolate which has been melted and cooled slightly, to Seven-Minute Frosting* just before spreading. For the marbled effect, fold the chocolate in a little at a time.

ORANGE SEVEN-MINUTE FROSTING

Proceed as for Seven-Minute Frosting.* Substitute ¼ cup orange juice for the water. Omit vanilla and add 1 tablespoon lemon juice and ½ teaspoon grated orange rind.

CHERRY SEVEN-MINUTE FROSTING

Proceed as for Seven-Minute Frosting,* using ¼ cup water. Omit the vanilla and add 3 tablespoons maraschino cherry juice and 1 teaspoon grated lemon rind.

PEPPERMINT SEVEN-MINUTE FROSTING

Proceed as for Seven-Minute Frosting.* Omit the vanilla and add ¼ teaspoon peppermint flavoring. Tint with food coloring if you wish and sprinkle with crushed peppermint candy.

BUTTER CREAM FROSTING

½ cup butter
⅛ teaspoon salt
1 teaspoon vanilla or almond flavoring
1 pound confectioners' sugar
5–6 tablespoons cream or 1 egg

Cream the butter until light and fluffy. Add the salt, vanilla or almond flavoring, and half the sugar. Beat until smooth. Blend in part of the cream. Add the remaining sugar, beating until smooth. Add the remaining cream a little at a time until of the right consistency to spread. You may use the beaten egg instead of the cream. Yield: frosting for a 2-layer cake.

LEMON BUTTER CREAM FROSTING

Substitute 1 teaspoon grated lemon rind for the flavoring in the recipe for Butter Cream Frosting.*

ORANGE BUTTER CREAM FROSTING

Use recipe for Butter Cream Frosting,* substituting 1–2 teaspoons grated orange rind for flavoring, part orange juice for the cream.

BURNT-SUGAR BUTTER FROSTING

6 tablespoons butter
1 pound confectioners' sugar
1/3 cup Burnt-Sugar Syrup*
Pinch salt
1/2 teaspoon vanilla
Light cream

Cream the butter. Gradually add the sugar alternately with the syrup. Finally add the salt and vanilla. If the frosting seems a bit dry, add a little light cream to soften to spreading consistency. Yield: frosting for a 2-layer cake.

CARAMEL BUTTER FROSTING

1/4 cup sugar
6 tablespoons butter
Pinch salt
1/2 teaspoon vanilla
1 pound confectioners' sugar

Heat the sugar over low heat in a small heavy pan until golden brown in color, stirring constantly. As the color deepens, the flavor becomes stronger. Remove from heat. Add 1/3 cup boiling water and stir until the sugar is dissolved. Cool. Cream the butter; add salt and vanilla. Then add the confectioners' sugar and the caramelized liquid alternately, a small amount at a time, mixing well after each addition. Yield: frosting for a 2-layer cake.

CHOCOLATE BUTTER CREAM FROSTING

6 ounces unsweetened chocolate
1 pound confectioners' sugar
2 eggs
1/4 cup soft butter
1 teaspoon vanilla

Melt the chocolate over simmering water. Remove from heat and mix in the sugar and 1/3 cup hot water. Add the eggs and then beat in the butter a tablespoon at a time. Add the vanilla. Chill in refrigerator for about 1/2 hour and then beat vigorously until thick enough to spread. Yield: frosting for a 2-layer cake.

SEA FOAM FROSTING

3/4 cup brown sugar
3/4 cup sugar
Pinch cream of tartar
3 egg whites
1 teaspoon vanilla

Mix together the sugars and add the cream of tartar and 1/3 cup hot water. Cover and bring slowly to simmering stage. Uncover and cook until the syrup reaches hard-ball stage (250°–255°). Remove from heat. Beat egg whites until a soft peak forms. When the syrup has stopped bubbling, pour it over the egg whites in a fine stream, beating all the while. Flavor with vanilla. Continue to beat until mixture holds its shape. It will be very fluffy. Yield: frosting for 2-layer cake.

BOILED FROSTING

1 1/2 cups sugar
3 egg whites
Pinch cream of tartar
Pinch salt
1 teaspoon vanilla or 1/2 teaspoon vanilla and
  1/2 teaspoon almond flavoring

Mix the sugar and 1/2 cup water in a heavy saucepan. Stir, cover, and bring slowly to a boil. Remove cover and cook to soft-ball stage (238°). Remove from heat and pour gradually, beating constantly, over the egg whites which have been beaten until a soft peak forms. Add the cream of tartar, salt, and vanilla with or without almond flavoring. Beat until mixture is very glossy, stands up in peaks, and will not run. Yield: frosting for a 2-layer cake.

FLUFFY WHITE FROSTING

2/3 cup sugar
3 tablespoons light corn syrup
2 egg whites
1 teaspoon vanilla

Combine the sugar, corn syrup, and 3 tablespoons water in a heavy saucepan. Cover and bring to a boil. Uncover and continue cooking to the firm-ball stage (244°). Just before the syrup is ready, beat the egg whites until a stiff peak forms. Pour the syrup in a thin steady stream into the beaten egg whites, beating constantly until the frosting is stiff and glossy. Blend in the vanilla. Yield: frosting for a 2-layer cake.

CHOCOLATE FROSTING

6 ounces unsweetened chocolate
3 egg yolks
2¼ cups sugar
¾ cup milk
1½ tablespoons butter
Pinch salt
2 teaspoons vanilla

Melt the chocolate. Beat the egg yolks until thick; add sugar, milk, and butter; cook in a heavy saucepan over very low heat, stirring constantly. (Watch and stir—don't let it stick!) Bring to a boil for 1 minute. Remove from heat and stir in the melted chocolate, salt, and vanilla. Beat until mixture will spread nicely. This has a gloss, stays soft, and doesn't run. Yield: frosting for a 3-layer cake.

FUDGE FROSTING

2 ounces unsweetened chocolate
¾ cup milk
2 cups sugar
Pinch salt
2 teaspoons corn syrup
2 tablespoons butter
1 teaspoon vanilla

Break up the chocolate and add to the milk in a saucepan over low heat. Cook, stirring constantly, until the mixture is smooth and blended. Add the sugar, salt, and corn syrup. Stir until the sugar dissolves and mixture boils. Continue to boil, stirring occasionally, until it reaches the thread stage (232°). Remove from heat. Add butter and vanilla and cool to luke-warm without stirring. Beat until thick enough to spread. Frost the cake immediately. Yield: frosting for a 2-layer cake.

CREAMY CHOCOLATE FROSTING

¼ cup cocoa
1½ tablespoons butter
½ cup milk
1½ cups sugar
2 egg yolks
1 teaspoon vanilla

Combine and heat the cocoa, ½ tablespoon butter, and milk in a heavy saucepan. Beat until smooth. Add the sugar to the well-beaten egg yolks and stir into the chocolate mixture. Cook about 10 minutes, until thick, stirring frequently. Remove from heat; add remaining butter and the vanilla. Allow to cool without stirring until lukewarm; then beat with a spoon until just thick enough to spread on cake. Yield: frosting for a 2-layer cake.

CHOCOLATE MARSHMALLOW TOPPING

18 large marshmallows
2 ounces unsweetened chocolate
1 egg
1 teaspoon butter
½ teaspoon vanilla
Pinch salt

Cut the marshmallows in quarters and put half of them into a double boiler with the other ingredients. Cook and stir over barely simmering water for a few minutes until the marshmallows are melted and ingredients are combined. Fold in the rest of the marshmallows and spread on top of the cake. Yield: topping for a layer cake.

CHOCOLATE CREAM-CHEESE FROSTING

2 (3 oz.) packages cream cheese
6 tablespoons milk or cream
1 pound confectioners' sugar
4 ounces unsweetened chocolate
Pinch salt
2 teaspoons vanilla

Soften the cream cheese with milk or cream. Blend until smooth. Add the confectioners' sugar ½ cup at a time, blending after each addition. Melt the chocolate, cool slightly, and add to the creamed mixture with the salt. Flavor with vanilla. Beat all together until smooth and well blended. This frosting will keep several days in the refrigerator if covered tightly. Yield: frosting for a 3-layer cake.

EASY CHOCOLATE FILLING OR FROSTING

1 (6 oz.) package semisweet chocolate bits
1 cup heavy cream

Mix the chocolate and cream and cook over low heat, stirring constantly, until chocolate is melted. Remove from heat and cool for ½ hour. Beat with a wooden spoon for a few minutes until bubbles appear. Chill for about 24 hours. This can be used as a filling for pastry or cake. If you wish to use as a frosting, let stand at room temperature until of spreading consistency. Yield: filling or topping for a 9-inch cake.

MOCHA BUTTER FROSTING

½ cup butter
¼ cup cocoa
1 egg
2 teaspoons instant coffee
½ teaspoon vanilla
¼ teaspoon salt
1 pound confectioners' sugar

Soften the butter in a bowl. Add the cocoa, egg, coffee, vanilla, and salt. Beat until the coffee and cocoa have dissolved. Add the confectioners' sugar a little at a time, beating well after each addition. The frosting should be moderately stiff. Yield: frosting for a 2-layer cake.

MOCHA TOPPING

3 cups confectioners' sugar
⅛ teaspoon salt
4½ tablespoons cocoa
4½ tablespoons very soft butter
4½ tablespoons strong coffee
¾ teaspoon vanilla
¼ cup broken walnuts (optional)

Put all of the ingredients except the walnuts into a mixing bowl. Stir until well blended. If too soft to spread, chill slightly. Use on brownies or cake. Top if you wish with walnuts. Yield: 1½ cups.

RICH COFFEE FROSTING

6 tablespoons butter
⅛ teaspoon salt
1 tablespoon instant coffee
½ teaspoon vanilla
1 pound confectioners' sugar
1 egg white
½ tablespoon light cream

Cream the butter. Add the salt, coffee, and vanilla. Gradually blend in about 1 cup of the sugar. Add the egg white and beat until smooth. Then add the remaining sugar alternately with the cream, beating well after each addition until smooth and the mixture is of a good consistency for spreading. Yield: frosting for a 2-layer cake.

COFFEE FROSTING

3 cups confectioners' sugar
½ cup butter
Pinch salt
1 teaspoon vanilla
¼ cup strong coffee

Mix the sugar, butter, salt, vanilla, and coffee. Particularly good on spongecake. Yield: frosting for a 2-layer cake.

MAPLE FROSTING

1 cup maple syrup
2 egg whites
Pinch salt
1 teaspoon vanilla

Cook the syrup in a heavy saucepan until it reaches the firm-ball stage (244°). Beat the egg whites with the salt until a soft peak forms. Add the hot syrup very slowly in a thin stream and continue beating until the frosting holds stiff glossy peaks. Blend in the vanilla. Frost cake at once. Yield: frosting for a 2-layer cake.

MARZIPAN FROSTING FOR FRUITCAKE

2 (8 oz.) cans almond paste
2 egg whites
⅛ teaspoon cream of tartar
1¾ cups confectioners' sugar

Knead the almond paste until soft. Sprinkle a board with confectioners' sugar and roll about ⅔ of the paste into a long strip about ⅛ inch thick. Measure your cake and cut this strip to fit the sides. Brush the sides of the cake with 1 slightly beaten egg white and shape the strip of almond paste to the sides. Brush the seam where it joins with egg white. Work the remaining paste into a ball and roll it to fit the top of the cake. Use the bottom of your 10-inch tube pan as a pattern. Brush the top of the cake with egg white, fit the almond-paste circle in place, and brush the seams with egg white. Beat the remaining egg white with the cream of tartar until frothy. Gradually add the sugar, beating well, until very thick. Frost the cake smoothly and allow to dry overnight. Yield: frosting for a 10-inch tube cake.

MINT FROSTING

1 egg white
Pinch salt
½ cup mint jelly

Beat the egg white until frothy, add the salt, and continue beating until a soft peak forms. Add half the jelly and beat with a rotary beater until a soft peak forms. Add the rest of the jelly and beat until frosting stands in stiff peaks. This should be a pale green color and have a mild mint flavor. Frost the cake just before serving. Yield: frosting for the top of a layer cake.

PEPPERMINT-CANDY FROSTING

2 egg whites
½ cup light corn syrup
1 cup confectioners' sugar
Pinch salt
1 teaspoon vanilla
½ cup crushed after-dinner mints

Mix the egg whites with the corn syrup and sugar. Add the salt and vanilla. Beat the mixture with an electric mixer or rotary beater until the frosting stands in stiff peaks. Fold in the peppermints. This frosting is especially good on Devil's-Food Cake.* Yield: frosting for a 2-layer cake.

AMANDINE TOPPING   (*Plate 9*)

4 cups sugar
1⅓ cups light corn syrup
Pinch salt
2 cups toasted shaved blanched almonds

Put the sugar, 2 cups water, corn syrup, and salt in a heavy 2-quart saucepan. Bring slowly to a boil, stirring frequently. Continue boiling, but not stirring, until the syrup reaches the light-crack stage (270°). While the syrup is boiling, wipe any crystals from the sides of the pan with a wet pastry brush. Remove pan from the heat immediately and place over simmering water to keep hot. Working with two forks, drop some nuts into the hot syrup and then arrange them as desired. Add only a few nuts at a time to the syrup so that it will not cool down. If the syrup loses its shine, add more corn syrup and increase the heat under the water. This topping cuts best if the cake is decorated two days before using. Yield: topping for 2 fruitcakes or poundcakes.

COCONUT PECAN FROSTING

1 cup evaporated milk
1 cup sugar
3 egg yolks
½ cup butter
1 teaspoon vanilla
1 (3½ oz.) can flaked coconut
1 cup chopped pecans

Mix the milk, sugar, egg yolks, butter, and vanilla together in a saucepan. Cook over medium heat, stirring constantly, for 12 minutes, until the mixture thickens. Remove from heat. Add the coconut and pecans. Beat until cool and of spreading consistency. This is too heavy to cover the sides of cake. Spread between the layers and on top of the cake only. Yield: frosting for a 3-layer cake.

PECAN FILLING

1 teaspoon cornstarch
⅓ cup sugar
2 tablespoons butter
3 egg yolks
⅔ cup milk
Pinch salt
½ teaspoon vanilla
1 cup chopped pecans

Mix the cornstarch with the sugar, and cream together with the butter. Add the well-beaten egg yolks and milk. Pour into a double boiler and cook, stirring constantly, until mixture thickens. Add the salt and vanilla. Cool. Add the pecans. Yield: filling for a layer cake.

LADY BALTIMORE FILLING AND FROSTING

3 cups sugar
Pinch salt
3 egg whites
½ teaspoon vanilla
1 cup chopped nuts
½ cup raisins
½ cup chopped figs or crystallized fruits

Bring 1 cup water, the sugar, and salt slowly to a boil and continue to boil to hard-ball stage (250°). Add gradually to the egg whites which have been beaten until a stiff peak forms. Beat constantly until almost ready to spread; add vanilla. Add the nuts and fruits to ⅓ of the frosting and spread between the layers. Spread remaining frosting on top and sides of the cake. Yield: enough for a 3-layer cake.

FLUFFY GRAPEFRUIT CHEESE FROSTING

1 (8 oz.) package cream cheese
1 tablespoon softened butter
4 teaspoons grated grapefruit rind
1 teaspoon grated lemon rind
1 teaspoon grated orange rind
¼ teaspoon vanilla
6–6½ cups confectioners' sugar
Sections from 2 grapefruit (garnish)
Sections from 2 oranges (garnish)

Soften the cheese and cream it with the butter, rinds, and vanilla until light. Beat in the sugar a little at a time until fluffy and of good spreading consistency. Put together layers of cake with a thin layer of frosting, then frost sides and top of cake. Garnish with sections of grapefruit and orange if you wish. Yield: frosting for a 2-layer cake.

CRUMB TOPPING
(Streusel)

½ cup flour
¼ cup butter
¼ cup brown sugar
1 teaspoon cinnamon (optional)

Blend the flour, butter, and sugar until they make crumbs. Add the cinnamon if you wish. If used as a topping for coffeecake or pie, sprinkle over the top before baking. Yield: enough for a 9-inch cake or pie.

NUT STREUSEL

½ cup sugar or ¾ cup brown sugar
2 tablespoons flour
2 tablespoons butter
½ cup minced almonds or walnuts
1 teaspoon cinnamon

Mix the ingredients together until crumbly. Use as a topping, or topping and filling, for coffeecake. Use before baking. Yield: enough for filling and topping a coffee ring or 9-inch square cake.

LEMON FILLING

½ cup butter
⅔ cup sugar
6 eggs
1 can frozen lemonade concentrate

Melt the butter in a double boiler. Add the sugar and mix well. Pour in the well-beaten eggs, stirring constantly. Add the lemonade concentrate and cook the mixture, stirring constantly, until it thickens and is smooth and glossy. This filling may be stored in the refrigerator for several days. Yield: filling for a 3-layer cake, 9-inch pie, or 8 tarts.

LEMON BUTTER FILLING (Plate 6)

¼ cup butter
1 cup sugar
3 eggs
Juice 1½ lemons
Grated rind 1 lemon

Melt the butter in a double boiler. Add the sugar and mix well. Stir in the beaten eggs, lemon juice, and rind. Cook, stirring constantly, about 20 minutes, until smooth, glossy, and very thick. Chill for several hours. Yield: filling for a 3-layer cake.

LEMON CUSTARD FILLING

1½ teaspoons cornstarch
⅓ cup sugar
⅔ cup milk
3 egg yolks
2 tablespoons soft butter
Pinch salt
1 teaspoon grated lemon rind
½ teaspoon vanilla

Mix the cornstarch, sugar, and milk together. Add the well-beaten egg yolks and the butter. Cook in a double boiler, stirring constantly, until the mixture thickens. Add the salt, lemon rind, and vanilla. Cool, beating occasionally. Yield: filling for a 2-layer cake.

LIME FROSTING

6 tablespoons butter
¼ teaspoon salt
1 pound confectioners' sugar
1 egg white
1 teaspoon vanilla
2½ teaspoons grated lime rind
2 tablespoons lime juice

Cream the butter until soft. Add the salt and part of the sugar gradually, blending well. Add the egg white, vanilla, and lime rind. Add the remaining sugar alternately with the lime juice until of a good consistency to spread, beating after each addition until smooth. Yield: frosting for a 2-layer cake.

LIME FRUIT FILLING

To ½ cup of Lime Frosting* add 2 table-spoons each: chopped white raisins, pecans, green candied cherries, and candied pineapple. Spread between layers of cake. (The remaining Lime Frosting is ample to cover top and sides of cake.) Yield: filling for a 2-layer cake.

ORANGE FILLING

⅓ cup sugar
2 tablespoons cornstarch
¼ teaspoon salt
¾ cup milk
2 egg yolks
¼ cup orange juice
1 teaspoon grated orange rind
1 tablespoon lemon juice
1 tablespoon butter

Mix the sugar, cornstarch, and salt in a saucepan. Add the milk gradually and cook, stirring constantly, for 5 minutes, until thickened. Pour a little of this into the well-beaten egg yolks and then pour the egg mixture back into the hot filling. Cook another 5 minutes, stirring constantly; do not allow to boil. Remove from heat. Add the orange juice, orange rind, lemon juice, and butter. Stir well. Cool. Yield: filling for a 2-layer cake.

STRAWBERRY FROSTING

½ package frozen strawberries
½ cup butter
1 pound confectioners' sugar
½ teaspoon vanilla

Thaw the strawberries. Beat the butter until smooth. Add the sugar alternately with the strawberries (including syrup) and beat until smooth. Add vanilla. If frosting is too thick, thin with a little milk or cream. Yield: frosting for a 2-layer cake.

STRAWBERRY CHEESE FROSTING

1 (8 oz.) package cream cheese
Cream or sour cream
2 teaspoons brown sugar
½ cup strawberry jam

Moisten the cheese with a little cream or sour cream. Blend in the sugar. Spread cake with jam and cover with the cheese mixture. Serve at once. Yield: frosting for a 13×9×2-inch cake.

PINK CHEESE FROSTING

1 (3 oz.) package cream cheese
¼ cup cranberry jelly
1 pound confectioners' sugar

Soften the cheese with the cranberry jelly and gradually add the sugar. Blend until very smooth. Yield: frosting for a 2-layer cake.

YELLOW FROSTING

2 cups sugar
¼ cup light corn syrup
4 egg yolks
¼ teaspoon salt
2 tablespoons cream
1 teaspoon lemon juice
1 teaspoon orange juice
½ teaspoon grated orange rind

Cook the sugar, corn syrup, and ½ cup water until it reaches the hard-ball stage (250°–255°). Beat the egg yolks until lemon-colored. Add the salt. Pour the syrup over the beaten yolks in a continuous stream, beating constantly. Beat until cool and fudge-like. Add the cream, lemon juice, and orange juice and rind. If the mixture should get too stiff before you finish, add a little more cream. Yield: frosting for a 2-layer cake.

SOUR-CREAM FILLING

1 cup sour cream
¼ cup sugar
1½ tablespoons flour
1 egg yolk
Pinch salt
Pinch cinnamon
½ teaspoon vanilla
¼ cup chopped nuts

Heat the sour cream a little. Mix the sugar and flour together and add to the slightly beaten egg yolk. Add the sour cream slowly. Cook over low heat, stirring constantly, until thickened. Remove from heat. Add the salt, cinnamon, and vanilla. Stir in the nuts. Yield: filling for a 2-layer cake.

PINEAPPLE ORANGE FROSTING

¼ cup frozen orange-juice concentrate
½ cup butter
1 pound confectioners' sugar
Pinch salt
½ cup well-drained crushed pineapple
¾ cup grated coconut (optional)

Heat the orange-juice concentrate. Add butter, remove from heat, and let stand until butter is just softened and mixture cooled. Stir in half the confectioners' sugar and the salt. When smooth, add the pineapple and remaining sugar. Mix well. Sprinkle frosted cake with coconut if you wish. Yield: frosting for a 3-layer cake.

PETITS-FOURS FROSTING

¼ cup melted butter
1 cup light cream
2 pounds confectioners' sugar
1 teaspoon almond flavoring

Add the melted butter and light cream to the sugar. Stir in the almond flavoring. Warm gently in a double boiler, stirring constantly, until shiny. Yield: frosting for about 25 petits fours.

PLAIN COOKY FROSTING

1 egg white
1¼ cups confectioners' sugar
1 teaspoon lemon juice
Few drops cooking oil

Beat the egg white until foamy. Add the sugar a little at a time, beating until thick and glossy. Stir in the lemon juice and oil. Drop by teaspoonfuls onto cookies. Yield: about 1 cup, enough frosting for 5 dozen small cookies.

BASIC GLAZE

1 egg white
2 cups confectioners' sugar
Pinch salt
1½ teaspoons light cream
¼ teaspoon cooking oil

Beat the egg white until foamy; then beat in the sugar and salt. Gradually stir in the cream until frosting reaches a spreading consistency. Stir in the oil. Yield: about ¾ cup, glaze for a 9-inch cake.

CHOCOLATE GLAZE

4 ounces semisweet or sweet chocolate
1 tablespoon butter
1 cup confectioners' sugar
Pinch salt
½ teaspoon vanilla

Melt the chocolate and butter with 3 tablespoons water over boiling water and remove from heat. Combine the sugar and salt and add to the chocolate mixture gradually, blending thoroughly. Add the vanilla. Pour evenly over the top of cake. Yield: ¾ cup, glaze for a 9-inch layer.

VANILLA GLAZE

1 teaspoon vanilla
2½–3 cups confectioners' sugar

Add the vanilla with ¼ cup water very gradually to the sugar while beating. Continue to beat until thick enough to spread. You may have to adjust the amount of confectioners' sugar to get a good spreading consistency according to the day's humidity. Yield: about 1⅓ cups.

LEMON GLAZE

¾ cup confectioners' sugar
½ teaspoon grated lemon rind
1 tablespoon heavy cream
¼ cup lemon juice

Beat all the ingredients together to make a thin frosting. Good as a cooky glaze. Yield: about ⅓ cup, enough for 2 dozen cookies.

PINEAPPLE GLAZE

1 (9 oz.) can crushed pineapple
2 teaspoons lemon juice
¼ cup sugar
1 tablespoon cornstarch

Heat the pineapple with the lemon juice and sugar until it comes to a boil. Blend the cornstarch with 1 tablespoon water and stir into the pineapple mixture. Cook over medium heat, stirring frequently, until clear and thickened. Cool and spread over the top of cooled cake; particularly good for cheesecake. Yield: about 1¼ cups.

ORANGE GLAZE (Plate 5)

1 cup confectioners' sugar
½ teaspoon grated orange rind
4 teaspoons orange juice
Yellow food coloring (optional)

Mix the sugar, orange rind, and orange juice until smooth and thick. Tint with a very little yellow food coloring if you wish. This is a good glaze for coffeecake, cookies, or plain cake. Yield: about ⅔ cup, enough for about 3 dozen cookies.

BERRY GLAZE

2½ cups confectioners' sugar
Pinch salt
¼ cup puréed strawberries or raspberries
1–2 teaspoons lemon juice

Add the sugar and salt to the berry purée, mixing very well. Add lemon juice until the frosting is the consistency to spread or to pour thinly on angel-food, chiffon, or other plain cake. Yield: 1 cup.

BASIC FROSTING FOR DECORATING

¼ cup butter
1 pound confectioners' sugar
1 egg white
Pinch salt
Light cream
Food coloring

Cream the butter until very soft. Gradually beat in some of the sugar. Add the egg white and salt. Mix well and then slowly add remaining sugar while stirring. Thin if necessary with a little cream. Divide into small portions and color each portion as desired. This frosting is put through a pastry tube. Yield: 1¼ cups.

ROYAL FROSTING (FOR DECORATING)

1 egg white
About 1 cup confectioners' sugar
1 teaspoon softened butter
Food coloring

Beat the egg white until frothy in an electric mixer. Add the sugar gradually, beating constantly until frosting will hold its shape. Stir in butter until well blended. Then divide into separate containers and color as desired. Cover these bowls with a damp cloth until needed. Using a pastry bag and the appropriate decorating tips, make any patterns you like. Yield: about 1 cup.

ROYAL ORNAMENTAL FROSTING

1 pound confectioners' sugar
3 egg whites
½ teaspoon cream of tartar

Put the sugar, egg whites, and cream of tartar into a bowl. Beat together for about 10 minutes. Keep covered, as this frosting hardens quickly. This is used mainly for decorating, especially appropriate for a wedding cake. This can also be used as a frosting for a wedding cake; double or triple the quantity. Yield: enough for ornamenting two 2-layer cakes or a wedding cake.

BRAZIL-NUT CURLS

Heat about ¼ pound of shelled Brazil nuts in boiling water for a few minutes to soften. Slice them lengthwise with a vegetable peeler. Use quick short strokes so that the pieces will curl as you slice. These curls make an attractive garnish on top of frosting of a contrasting color, such as chocolate. Yield: garnish for a large cake.

CHOCOLATE CURLS

Use a vegetable peeler on a cake of warm (a little warmer than room temperature but not too soft) chocolate. Use quick strokes so the chocolate will curl as you slice.

CHOCOLATE MEDALLIONS

Cut circles out of waxed paper and cover with melted sweet or semisweet chocolate. Apply the chocolate with a spatula and then chill. When the chocolate is firm, pull off the paper and you have medallions with which to decorate a cake.

CHAPTER FOUR

Perfect Pies and Pastry

Pie is a truly American dessert, most popular of all sweets. Many more pies are consumed in the United States than in all the rest of the world put together. Pie à la mode is an American innovation of combining pie with the second-most-popular dessert—ice cream.

You will find here not only the usual type of pastry for a one- and two-crust pie but various cheese crusts, several kinds of crumb crusts, nut crusts, hot-water crust, rich French galette crust, coconut and cornflake crusts, chocolate crust, puff paste, numerous tart shells, and meringue shells.

Pies take their names from the filling. There are many kinds: fruit pies, chiffon pies, meringue pies, deep-dish pies, cream pies, custard pies, angel pies, and ice cream pies. Not only must the filling be outstanding but it must be coupled with its most complementary crust. Here there are many new combinations.

But I, when I undress me
Each night upon my knees
Will ask the Lord to bless me
With apple pie and cheese.
EUGENE FIELDS

PASTRY FOR 2-CRUST PIE

8-Inch	1½–1¾ cups flour
	½ teaspoon salt
	½ cup shortening
9-Inch	2 cups flour
	¾ teaspoon salt
	⅔ cup shortening
10-Inch	2½ cups flour
	1 teaspoon salt
	1 cup shortening

To make the pastry for pie crust, the materials used should be very cold. Very cold water is the secret of good crust. Use about 4 tablespoons of ice water to 2 cups of flour. Too much water makes the crust tough; too little and it's crumbly. The pie dough should be handled as little as possible. Use a light touch with your hands and with the rolling pin.

Sift the flour and salt together. Cut in the shortening with a pastry blender or with 2 knives, used scissor fashion, until the pieces are a little larger than corn meal. Sprinkle water a tablespoon at a time over different parts of the mixture, tossing lightly with a fork until the dough is moistened and will form a ball. Wrap in waxed paper and chill the ball. Divide the dough in half and roll out on a lightly floured pastry cloth or board or between 2 pieces of waxed paper. Roll from the center to outside edges to form circles. Lift the rolling pin near the edge to keep dough from splitting. If edges split, pinch the cracks together. Roll the dough ⅛–¼ inch thick into a circle a little larger than the pie plate. Ease the lower crust into the plate; don't stretch it. Allow the pastry to hang over and trim evenly ½ inch beyond the plate edge. The upper crust should be gashed before or after placing it over the filling. This is done to let the steam out as the pie bakes. Seal the upper and lower crusts around the edge with a little cold water. Try rolling the edges together, or pinch or scallop the edge if you prefer. When the pie is ready to go into the oven, dot the crust with a bit of butter for extra flakiness; or try glazing it by brushing the top with a little water, milk, cream, or a mixture of 1 tablespoon water and an egg yolk.

You may wish to sprinkle the crust of fruit pies with sugar also.

For a lattice top, roll half the pastry into a rectangle and cut strips of pastry ½ inch wide. Use a pastry wheel if you have one. Weave the strips across the top of the pie in crisscross fashion, or braid them.

For a berry pie, to keep the juice from dripping out, make the edge of the crust high. Try putting a small funnel into the center of the pie so the juice will bubble into that.

Bake in a 450°–475° oven for 10 minutes to set the crust before reducing heat to about 350° for the main baking time.

CHEDDAR-CHEESE CRUST

Add 1 cup grated Cheddar cheese with the shortening to the recipe for Pastry for 9-Inch 2-Crust Pie.*

CINNAMON CRUST

Add 1 teaspoon cinnamon with the flour to Pastry for 9-Inch 2-Crust Pie.*

SPICY CRUST

Add 1 teaspoon cinnamon and 1 teaspoon nutmeg with the flour to Pastry for 9-Inch 2-Crust Pie.*

RUM CRUST

Add 2 tablespoons chilled rum in place of 2 tablespoons of the water in Pastry for 9-Inch 2-Crust Pie.*

BLACK-WALNUT CRUST

Add ½ cup ground black walnuts to the dough in Pastry for 9-Inch 2-Crust Pie.*

BAKED OR UNBAKED 9-INCH PIE SHELL

*½ recipe Pastry for 9-Inch 2-Crust Pie**

Proceed as above, rolling only one circle. Ease into the pie plate and pat out air bubbles. Allow the pastry to hang over the rim. Trim evenly ½ inch beyond the edge of the pie plate. Fold the overhang under. With your fingers crimp the edges to make a neat rim.

If you want a prebaked shell, prick the shell *thoroughly* with a fork. Bake in 450° oven for 12–15 minutes. Another way to prevent the pie shell from buckling is to fit a piece of waxed paper into the pie shell and spread about 1½ cups of raw rice or beans over the paper. Remove the rice or beans and the paper after about 5 minutes of baking. The rice or beans may be saved for future pie-shell baking.

SESAME CRUST

Add ½ cup toasted sesame seeds along with the flour to pastry for a 9-Inch Pie Shell.*

OATMEAL CRUST

Sprinkle ¼ cup quick-cooking rolled oats on the board before rolling out pastry for a 9-Inch Pie Shell.*

BAKED OR UNBAKED 8-INCH PIE SHELL

Proceed as for 9-Inch Pie Shell,* using ½ recipe Pastry for 8-Inch 2-Crust Pie.*

BAKED OR UNBAKED 10-INCH PIE SHELL

Proceed as for 9-Inch Pie Shell,* using ½ recipe Pastry for 10-Inch 2-Crust Pie.*

TART SHELLS

*½ recipe Pastry for 9-Inch 2-Crust Pie**

Proceed as for a 2-crust pie. Roll the pastry about ⅛ inch thick on a lightly floured board or pastry cloth and cut into 6–8 circles about 4 inches in diameter, or divide the pastry into equal parts and roll each into a circle. Fit the pastry into small tart pans and press firmly into place. Crimp the edges. If you want baked tart shells, prick the bottom of each shell with a fork. You may also use the waxed paper and raw rice technique, removing paper and rice after 5 minutes of baking. Bake in a 450° oven for 10–12 minutes. Yield: 6–8 tart shells.

CREAM-CHEESE CRUST

2 cups flour
Pinch baking powder
¾ teaspoon salt
3 (3 oz.) packages cream cheese
½ cup butter
½ cup shortening

Sift the flour, baking powder, and salt together. Add the cream cheese, butter, and shortening. Cut with two knives or a pastry blender until thoroughly blended; wrap in foil or waxed paper and refrigerate overnight. Roll to a little more than ⅛-inch thickness on a lightly floured board. Yield: two 9-inch pie shells.

CREAM-CHEESE TART SHELLS

*½ recipe for Cream-Cheese Crust**

Roll the pastry as for pie crust and cut into rounds about 4 inches in diameter. Proceed as for Tart Shells.* Yield: 8 tart shells.

CHEDDAR-CHEESE TART SHELLS

*½ recipe Pastry for 9-Inch 2-Crust Pie**
½ cup grated Cheddar cheese

Add the cheese to the dough with the shortening. Proceed as for Tart Shells.*

BAKED OR UNBAKED CRUMB CRUST

1½ cups graham-cracker or zwieback crumbs
¼ cup sugar
⅓–½ cup melted butter

Mix the crumbs and sugar thoroughly with ⅓ cup of melted butter. Press the crumb mixture evenly on the bottom and sides of a buttered 8- or 9-inch pie plate. Bake in a 350° oven for 5 minutes and chill. For an unbaked crust use ½ cup butter; chill about 1 hour until firm. Yield: one 8- or 9-inch pie shell.

CRUMB CRUST WITH ALMONDS

Add ¼ cup unblanched almonds, chopped fine, to the crumbs; add ¼ teaspoon cinnamon if you wish. Proceed as for Crumb Crust.*

CHOCOLATE CRUMB CRUST

Substitute rolled chocolate wafers for other crumbs and omit sugar in Crumb Crust.*

GINGERSNAP CRUST

Use gingersnap crumbs in place of other crumbs in Crumb Crust.*

CORNFLAKE CRUST

Proceed as for Unbaked Crumb Crust,* substituting 1½ cups crushed cornflakes for the crumbs.

MERINGUE SHELL

2 egg whites
⅛ teaspoon salt
⅛ teaspoon cream of tartar
½ cup superfine sugar
½ teaspoon vanilla

Beat the egg whites with the salt and cream of tartar until a peak forms. Gradually add the sugar, beating constantly until a very stiff meringue is formed and sugar is dissolved. Fold in the vanilla. Lightly butter and flour a 9-inch glass pie plate, including the rim. Spread the meringue across the bottom and up the sides of the pie plate—be sure that none goes on the rim. Bake in a 275° oven for 1 hour and 5 minutes. Cool at room temperature. Yield: one 9-inch meringue shell.

COCONUT MERINGUE SHELL

Proceed as for Meringue Shell,* adding 1 cup chopped flaked coconut with the vanilla.

FORGOTTEN MERINGUE

5 egg whites
¼ teaspoon salt
½ teaspoon cream of tartar
1½ cups sugar
1 teaspoon vanilla

Beat the egg whites until a peak forms. Add the salt and cream of tartar. Beat until the egg whites stand in soft peaks. Add the sugar very gradually and keep beating until the egg whites are stiff. Flavor with vanilla. Grease well and flour a 9-inch pie plate. Spread the meringue on the bottom, having it high around the edges and scooping it out in the center to form a shell. Place the meringue in a 400° oven and turn off the heat immediately. Leave it in the oven 4 or 5 hours or overnight. Yield: one 9-inch meringue shell.

MERINGUE PUFFS

2 egg whites
Pinch salt
Pinch cream of tartar
½ cup superfine sugar
Few drops lemon flavoring or ⅛ teaspoon grated lemon rind

Beat the egg whites with the salt and cream of tartar until a soft peak forms. Gradually add the sugar and lemon flavoring or lemon rind, beating all the while until stiff. Put through a pastry tube to form puffs; or drop by tablespoonfuls, swirling the mixture into peaks, onto lightly buttered heavy brown paper. Bake on the paper on a baking sheet in a 250° oven for about 45 minutes, until the puffs are firm and just lightly golden. Use for a garnish to top pies or tarts or serve as cookies. Yield: 8 puffs.

CHOCOLATE-CHIP MERINGUE TOPPING

3 egg whites
Pinch salt
6 tablespoons sugar
⅔ cup grated sweet or semisweet chocolate

Beat the egg whites until a stiff peak forms. Add the salt and the sugar a tablespoon at a time, beating thoroughly after each addition. Gently fold in the grated chocolate. Pile on a pie or pudding and bake in a 325° oven for about 15 minutes, until tinged with brown. Yield: topping for a 9-inch pie or pudding.

MAPLE MERINGUE TOPPING

3 egg whites
1 tablespoon sugar
5 tablespoons maple syrup
Pinch salt
Dash cinnamon
Dash nutmeg

Beat the egg whites until a soft peak forms. Add the sugar and the maple syrup a spoonful at a time, beating well after each addition. Add the salt, cinnamon, and nutmeg. Good for pumpkin pie. This meringue is not baked.

COCONUT CRUST

2–3 tablespoons soft butter
2 cups flaked coconut

Spread the butter evenly over the bottom and sides of a 9-inch pie plate. Press the coconut evenly into the butter. Bake in a 300° oven for 15–20 minutes, until coconut is golden. Cool before filling. Good with chiffon, cream, or ice cream. Yield: one 9-inch pie shell.

CHOCOLATE COCONUT CRUST

2 ounces unsweetened chocolate
2 tablespoons butter
2 tablespoons hot milk or water
⅔ cup confectioners' sugar
1½ cups flaked coconut

Melt the chocolate and butter in a double boiler. Mix the milk or hot water with the sugar. Stir into the chocolate mixture, add coconut, and mix well. Grease an 8- or 9-inch pie plate and press in the mixture along sides and bottom. Chill until firm. Yield: one 8- or 9-inch pie shell.

GALETTE CRUST

1 cup flour
½ teaspoon salt
1 tablespoon sugar
6 tablespoons butter
1 egg yolk
1½ tablespoons lemon juice or rum

Sift the flour, salt, and sugar together. Cut in the butter with a pastry blender or 2 knives, used scissor fashion. Beat the egg yolk with 1 tablespoon water and the lemon juice or rum and work it into the dough with your fingers. Form into a ball and chill. Roll to ⅛–¼-inch thickness. Put into a 9- or 10-inch pie plate and chill again. For a baked pie shell, bake in a 350° oven for 15 minutes. This crust is usually used for fruit pies. Handle galette dough as little as possible. Yield: one 9- or 10-inch pie shell.

MACAROON CRUST

2 dozen macaroons
½ cup soft butter

Buy the macaroons a few days ahead and let them dry out thoroughly. Roll to fine crumbs. Mix with the butter and press evenly into a 9-inch pie plate. Chill. Yield: one 9-inch pie shell.

RUM CAKE-SHELL

Slice poundcake quite thin and line a 9-inch pie plate completely. Sprinkle with 3 tablespoons rum. Cover with Saran and chill for several hours.

NUT CRUST

¾ cup ground Brazil nuts
¾ cup ground walnuts or black walnuts
3 tablespoons sugar
1 tablespoon butter

Mix the nuts and sugar. Spread the softened butter over the bottom and sides of a 9-inch pie plate. Press in the nut-sugar mixture with the back of a spoon. Bake in a 400° oven for 10 minutes, until crust is golden. You may double the quantity of walnuts and omit the Brazil nuts if you wish. Chill well before using. Yield: one 9-inch pie shell.

HOT-WATER PIE CRUST

⅔ cup shortening
2 cups cake flour
½ teaspoon salt
½ teaspoon baking powder

Put the shortening in a bowl and pour ⅓ cup boiling water over it. Beat until creamy. Chill by setting the bowl in a pan of ice water. Sift the dry ingredients together and combine with the shortening to make a smooth ball. Proceed as for Pastry for 9-Inch 2-Crust Pie.*

EASY BISCUIT PIE SHELL

1 cup biscuit mix
¼ cup butter

Put the biscuit mix and softened butter in a 9-inch pie plate. Pour in 3 tablespoons boiling water and stir mixture with a fork until dough forms a soft ball and leaves the sides of the plate. With your fingers pat the dough evenly over the bottom and sides of the plate, bringing it up over the rim and pressing it into a neat edge. Prick all over with a fork. Bake in a 450° oven for 10–12 minutes, until golden. Remove from oven and cool. Yield: one 9-inch pie shell.

COOKY CRUST

2 tablespoons flour
½ cup commercial cooky dough

Work the flour into the cooky dough. Chill. Roll out and carefully transfer to a 9-inch pie plate. Trim off even with the rim; the dough is too rich to make a fluted edge. Prick and bake in a 400° oven for about 8 minutes. This shell is especially good for chiffon pies. Yield: one 9-inch pie shell.

PUFF PASTE

1 cup flour
¼ teaspoon salt
½ cup butter

Put the flour on a slab or board and make a hole in the center. Add salt and ⅓–½ cup ice water gradually, working it into a paste with your fingers. Roll out about ½ inch thick and put the butter in the center. The butter should be soft, almost the same consistency as the paste, but not melted. Fold up from the sides and ends like a package.

Flatten it in 2 or 3 places with a rolling pin; then roll out into a long strip. Fold into thirds; then give the pastry a ¼ turn so the folds are at the sides. Roll again and fold again. Refrigerate 20 minutes. Repeat this process 3 times.

For an alternate, easier method: prepare the paste as given above; have the butter pliable. Roll out the paste and dab the butter on the paste to cover it evenly. Do not take the butter to the very edges of the pastry. Now fold into thirds and proceed as directed above. This method makes it easier to incorporate the butter into the paste without its breaking through.

Wrapped in waxed paper or foil, puff paste may be kept in the refrigerator for several days.

APPLE PIE

Pastry for 9-Inch 2-Crust Pie*
8 apples
1 cup brown sugar or ¾ cup granulated
¼ teaspoon nutmeg
Dash cinnamon
¼ teaspoon salt
1 tablespoon lemon juice
Grated rind ½ lemon
2 tablespoons butter
Cheddar cheese
Heavy cream (optional)

Line a 9-inch pie plate with half of the pastry. Peel, core, and slice the apples. Toss with a mixture of sugar, spices, salt, lemon juice, and rind. Fill the pie plate with apples, piling them high in the center. Dot with butter and cover with plain or lattice crust. Bake in a 450° oven for 15–20 minutes; reduce heat to 350° and bake for 20–30 minutes more, until the crust is brown and apples are tender. Serve hot or cold with good-sized pieces of cheese. Serve a pitcher of cream on the side if you wish. Serves 8.

DEEP-DISH APPLE PIE

½ recipe Pastry for 9-Inch 2-Crust Pie*

Proceed as for Apple Pie,* putting the apples directly into a 10×6×1¾-inch baking dish. Use top crust only.

OPEN APPLE PIE

Unbaked 9-Inch Pie Shell*
2 tablespoons flour
⅛ teaspoon nutmeg
¾ cup dark brown sugar
7 tart apples
1 tablespoon lemon juice
¼ cup heavy cream
¼ cup sugar
3 tablespoons butter

Mix the flour, nutmeg, and brown sugar. Pare, core, and slice the apples and arrange them in the pie shell in layers, sprinkling each layer with the brown-sugar mixture. Add lemon juice and heavy cream. Top with the sugar and dot with butter. Cover with a circle of foil, cut just to fit over the apples. Bake in a 450° oven for 10 minutes. Then reduce heat to 400° and continue baking for ¾–1 hour, until the apples are tender and the filling has bubbled up around them. Remove foil and serve warm or cold. Serves 6–8.

DUTCH APPLE PIE

Unbaked 9-Inch Pie Shell*
3 pounds tart apples
⅓ cup flour
¾ cup sugar
Pinch salt
1 cup heavy cream
¼ teaspoon nutmeg
½ teaspoon cinnamon
Cheese (optional)

Pare and core the apples and slice them into the pie shell. Sift the flour, sugar, and salt together. Add the cream and beat until smooth and thick. Mix in the nutmeg and cinnamon; add more to taste. Pour the mixture over the apples. Bake in a 450° oven for 20–25 minutes, until the edge of the custard begins to brown. Put a square of foil between 2 pie plates, press them together, trim edges of the foil, and lift off the top pie plate. You now have a perfect lightweight lid in the shape of a pie plate which won't stick. Cover the apples with the foil pie plate, reduce heat to 350°, and continue baking about 45 minutes, until filling thickens and becomes glossy. Better bake this pie with a pan underneath to catch the juices. Serve warm, with cheese, if you wish. Serves 6–8.

RAISIN APPLE PIE

Unbaked 9-Inch Pie Shell*
6–7 apples
1 cup cider
¾ cup sugar
¼ teaspoon salt
2 tablespoons cornstarch
2 tablespoons lemon juice
¼ teaspoon nutmeg
¼ teaspoon cinnamon
2 tablespoons butter
¾ cup raisins or white raisins
Crumb Topping*

Peel, core, and cut the apples into eighths; there should be about 6 cups. Heat the apples, cider, sugar, and salt to boiling. Cover and simmer until apples are barely tender. Drain and measure the liquid; if needed, add more cider to make 1½ cups. Blend the liquid with the cornstarch, lemon juice, spices, and butter. Simmer until thickened. Add the apples and raisins and turn into the pie shell. Sprinkle with the Crumb Topping. Bake in a 425° oven for 20–25 minutes. Serve warm or cold, topped if you wish with whipped cream or ice cream, or serve with cheese. Serves 6–8.

APPLE CHEESE-PASTRY SQUARES

2 cups flour
½ cup plus 2 tablespoons sugar
¾ teaspoon salt
⅔ cup shortening
1 (8 oz.) package cream cheese
3 pounds apples
¼ cup packaged dry bread crumbs
1 teaspoon cinnamon
1 tablespoon milk or cream
½ cup chopped walnuts
Heavy cream (optional)

Sift the flour with 2 tablespoons sugar and the salt. Cut in the shortening and cream cheese with a pastry blender. No liquid is needed, but be sure the cheese is worked in well. Put the dough in the refrigerator. Peel, core, and slice the apples. When the apples are ready, divide the dough in half. Roll out half the dough thin on a lightly floured board or pastry cloth. Fit into an 11×7×1½-inch pan and sprinkle with the bread crumbs. Lay the apple slices in the pastry, overlapping them in rows. Sprinkle with a mixture of cinnamon and ½ cup sugar. Roll out the remaining dough and fit over the apples. Cut gashes in the top and seal the edges. Brush top with milk or cream and sprinkle with the walnuts. Bake in a 425° oven for 15 minutes; reduce heat to 325° and bake 30–40 minutes longer, until the apples are tender and crust is golden brown. Cut into pieces and serve warm or cold, with or without heavy or whipped cream. Serves 8–10.

APPLE APRICOT PIE

Unbaked 10-Inch Pie Shell*
3 pounds tart green apples
1½ tablespoons lemon juice
½ cup sugar
½ cup dark brown sugar
3 tablespoons flour
1 teaspoon cinnamon
½ teaspoon nutmeg
¼ teaspoon salt
12 fresh or canned apricot halves
Superfine sugar
1 teaspoon vanilla
½ teaspoon almond flavoring
2 tablespoons butter
Heavy cream (optional)

Peel, core, and slice the apples thin. You should have about 2 quarts. Add the lemon juice. Mix the sugars, flour, cinnamon, nutmeg, and salt and toss with the apples. Arrange the fruit in the pie shell. Arrange the apricot halves cut side down in the top layer of apples. If using fresh apricots, sprinkle with a little superfine sugar. Sprinkle a mixture of the vanilla and almond flavoring over the pie and dot with butter. Bake in a 400° oven for 20 minutes. Cover with a 9-inch pie pan or foil and bake 40 minutes more, until the apples are tender. Baste once or twice with the pie juices. Serve with cream on the side if you wish. Serves 8–10.

APPLE STREUSEL PIE

*Unbaked 9-Inch Pie Shell**
7 tart apples
Lemon juice
¼ cup raisins
1 cup sugar
⅓ cup flour
2 tablespoons butter
⅔ cup light cream
1 teaspoon cinnamon

Pare, core, and slice the apples. Sprinkle with a little lemon juice to prevent their darkening. Soften the raisins for a few minutes in hot water. Mix all but 2 tablespoons sugar with the sifted flour. Cut in the butter until you have a fine crumb mixture. Sprinkle half in the bottom of the pie shell. Arrange apples and drained raisins on top. Over them sprinkle remaining crumbs. Pour the cream slowly over the mixture. Mix the remaining sugar with the cinnamon and sprinkle over the pie. Bake in a 425° oven for 25 minutes; lower heat to 375° and continue baking about 20 minutes, until apples are tender. Serves 6–8.

APPLESAUCE PIE

*Unbaked 9-Inch Pie Shell**
6 tart apples
1 teaspoon butter
2 eggs
3 tablespoons lemon juice
1 tablespoon grated lemon rind
1 cup sugar

Core and quarter the apples. Cook in ¼ cup water about 20 minutes, until tender; the time depends on the size and kind of apple. Rub through a sieve, add the butter, and cool. Add the slightly beaten eggs, lemon juice, lemon rind, and sugar to the cooled apple mixture. Pour into the pie shell and bake for 1 hour in a 375° oven. If there is any remaining pastry, roll it out and cut out a few small shapes. Bake. Decorate pie with the baked pieces of pastry. Serve cold. Serves 6–8.

APPLE PEACH BREAD-TART

6 slices white bread
4 tablespoons butter
1 (1 lb. 4 oz.) can sliced apples
¾ teaspoon cinnamon
¼ teaspoon nutmeg

1 package frozen sliced peaches
2 tablespoons dark brown sugar
Whipped cream (garnish)

Cut the crusts off the bread and brush 1 side of each slice thoroughly, using 3 tablespoons melted butter. Arrange buttered side down in a 1-quart casserole to form a crust that covers bottom and sides entirely; use little pieces if necessary to fill in. Mix the apples with cinnamon and nutmeg. Fill the casserole with apples and the drained, thawed peaches. Dot with remaining butter and sprinkle with the brown sugar. Bake in a 350° oven for ½ hour. Good served with whipped cream. Serves 6.

CRUSTLESS DEEP-DISH APPLE PIE

5–6 apples
½ teaspoon cinnamon
1 tablespoon grated lemon rind
Juice 1 large lemon
½ cup flour
½ cup brown sugar
½ cup sugar
½ cup butter
1 teaspoon salt
Cream or Custard Sauce (optional)*

Fill a 1½-quart baking dish with sliced, cored, peeled apples. Do not fill right up to the brim; leave room for the topping. Sprinkle apples with cinnamon, lemon rind, and juice. Mix the flour with sugars, butter, and salt until you have a smooth paste. Spread evenly over the apples. Bake in a 425° oven for about 40 minutes, until the apples are tender. Serve hot or warm. If you serve with a pitcher of cream, add a little additional cinnamon to the cream. Serves 4–6.

APRICOT PIE

*Pastry for 8-Inch 2-Crust Pie**
2 cups dried apricots
1½ cups sugar
2 tablespoons melted butter
3 tablespoons quick-cooking tapioca

Cook the apricots according to package directions. Drain and reserve 1 cup liquid. Mix the apricots with the liquid, the sugar, butter, and tapicoa. Boil 5 minutes. Line the pie plate with pastry, pour in the hot filling, cover with crust, and bake in a 425° oven for 30–40 minutes. Serves 6.

APRICOT LEMON PIE

Meringue Shell*
¼ cup flour
¼ teaspoon salt
2 tablespoons sugar
1 cup milk
2 egg yolks
1 teaspoon grated lemon rind
5 tablespoons lemon juice
¼ cup heavy cream
1 (1 lb. 14 oz.) can peeled apricots
¼ cup cherry jelly

Mix the flour, salt, and sugar together in a saucepan. Stir the milk and slightly beaten egg yolks together. Add gradually to dry ingredients. Add lemon rind and heat, stirring constantly, until slightly thickened. Add lemon juice and cook until quite thick. Cool to room temperature. Add the cream which has been whipped and turn into the meringue shell. Chill. Drain the apricots thoroughly and divide them into halves. Arrange on top of the filling. Force the jelly through a fine sieve and spoon over the apricots just before serving. Serves 8.

BLACKBERRY OR RASPBERRY PIE

Pastry for 9-Inch 2-Crust Pie*
2 pints blackberries or raspberries
1 cup sugar
2 tablespoons flour
1 tablespoon butter

Pick over the berries and toss with a mixture of the sugar and flour. Line a pie plate with half the pastry and heap the berries high into it. Dot with butter and cover with the upper crust or a lattice top. Bake in a 450° oven about 10 minutes; then reduce heat to 350° and bake 20–30 minutes longer. Serves 8.

GOOSEBERRY PIE

Pastry for 9-Inch 2-Crust Pie*
1 cup sugar
⅓ cup flour
1 tablespoon lemon juice
4 cups gooseberries
1½ tablespoons butter

Line a pie plate with half the pastry. Mix the sugar, flour, and lemon juice with the gooseberries and turn into the pie plate. Dot with butter and cover with a plain or lattice-top crust. Bake in a 425° oven for 35–45 minutes. Serves 8.

BLUEBERRY PIE

Substitute 3 cups blueberries for the blackberries, adding a pinch of salt and 1 tablespoon lemon juice or ¼ teaspoon grated lemon rind. Proceed as for Blackberry Pie.*

CHERRY PIE

Pastry for 8-Inch 2-Crust Pie*
1 (1 lb.) can pitted tart red cherries
2 tablespoons cornstarch
¾ cup sugar
Pinch salt
1 teaspoon lemon juice
1 tablespoon butter
¼ teaspoon almond flavoring

Drain the cherries. Mix the cornstarch, sugar, and salt with ¼ cup of the cherry liquid. Cook, stirring constantly, until mixture is thickened and clear. Add the cherries, lemon juice, butter, and almond flavoring. Cool slightly. Line a plate with pastry and fill with the cherry mixture. Cover with the top crust or, for a festive touch, make a lattice pastry top with pastry stars between. Bake in a 425° oven for 35–40 minutes. Serves 6.

LATTICE CHERRY PIE

Pastry for 9-Inch 2-Crust Pie*
2 (1 lb.) cans pitted tart red cherries
½ cup brown sugar
½ cup sugar
3 tablespoons quick-cooking tapioca
¼ teaspoon almond flavoring
1 tablespoon butter

Drain the cherries and reserve ½ cup of the liquid. Mix the liquid with the sugars, tapioca, and almond flavoring. Add the cherries and let stand 15 minutes. Line the pie plate with pastry. Pour in the cherry mixture and dot with butter. Form a lattice-top crust. Bake in a 425° oven for 35–40 minutes, until the crust is golden and the pie bubbly. This has its best flavor when served warm. Serves 6–8.

FRESH CHERRY PIE

Baked 9-Inch Pie Shell*
1 quart tart red cherries
1 cup sugar
¼ cup flour
Pinch salt
¼ teaspoon almond flavoring
Whipped cream (optional)

Pit the cherries. Stew the cherries with the sugar, flour, and salt until soft and the juice thickened. Add the almond flavoring and taste for sweetness. Some cherries require much more sugar than others. Fill the pie shell. Chill. Serve with whipped cream if you wish. Serves 6–8.

EASY CHERRY STREUSEL PIE

2 (10 oz.) sticks pie-crust mix
1 (1 lb. 6 oz.) can cherry pie filling
1 teaspoon lemon juice
½ cup brown sugar
½ teaspoon grated lemon rind
½ teaspoon cinnamon
⅓ teaspoon nutmeg

Using 1 stick of pastry mix, make crust for an 8-inch pie according to package directions. Mix the pie filling with lemon juice and pour into the unbaked pie shell. Blend the brown sugar, lemon rind, and spices with the remaining stick of pastry. Crumble over the filling. Bake for 10 minutes in a 425° oven; reduce heat to 350° and bake for 25–30 minutes, until topping is golden. Cool a little before serving. Serves 4–6.

CHERRY APPLE PIE

Pastry for 10-Inch 2-Crust Pie*
1 (1 lb.) can pitted tart red cherries
1 cooking apple
1 cup sugar
¼ cup quick-cooking tapioca
1 teaspoon almond flavoring
¼ teaspoon salt
¼ teaspoon nutmeg
Red food coloring

Drain and measure the liquid from the cherries. Add water to make ¾ cup. Peel, core, and slice the apple thin. Put cherries and liquid in a bowl and add sugar, tapioca, almond flavoring, salt, nutmeg, a few drops of food coloring, and the sliced apple. Stir gently. Line a 10-inch pie plate with pastry. Fill with the cherry-apple mixture. Cover with top crust. Bake in a 425° oven for about 45 minutes, until golden. Serve warm. Serves 8–10.

FRESH PEACH PIE

Pastry for 9-Inch 2-Crust Pie*
1 quart sliced, peeled peaches
1 tablespoon cornstarch
½ teaspoon salt
¾–1 cup sugar
1 teaspoon almond flavoring

Line a pie plate with half of the pastry. Toss the peaches with a mixture of cornstarch, salt, and sugar and add almond flavoring. Arrange in the pie shell and top with a lattice crust. Bake in a 450° oven for 10 minutes; reduce to 350° and bake 50 minutes longer. Serves 6–8.

OPEN PEACH PIE

Unbaked 8-Inch Pie Shell*
1 (1 lb. 13 oz.) can peaches
¾ cup sugar
¼ cup flour
2 tablespoons butter
Pinch salt
2 tablespoons lemon juice
⅛ teaspoon almond flavoring

Drain the peaches, reserving 2 tablespoons of the syrup. Mix the sugar, flour, butter, and salt until blended. Sprinkle ¼ of this mixture on the pastry. Then combine the drained peaches with the remainder. Mix together the lemon juice, almond flavoring, and reserved peach syrup. Add to the peaches and pour into the prepared pie shell. Bake in a 375° oven for 25–30 minutes, until filling is clear and bubbling. Cool before serving. Serves 4–6.

PEACH TARTS

8 baked Tart Shells*
4 large freestone peaches or 8 canned free-stone peach halves
½ cup sugar
1 tablespoon lemon juice
1 tablespoon cornstarch
2 tablespoons butter
Pinch salt

⅛ teaspoon almond flavoring
½ cup heavy cream (optional)

Peel the fresh peaches; this can be done easily by first dropping them into boiling water for a minute. Cut the peaches in half, remove the pits, and poach until tender in 1 cup water with the sugar and lemon juice. Set the peach halves aside to cool and save the syrup. If using canned peaches, drain and save 1 cup syrup. Mix the cornstarch with 2 tablespoons cold water until smooth; add to the syrup with the butter and salt. Cook until clear and thickened. Cool and add almond flavoring. Place a peach half, cut side up in each tart shell and cover with enough syrup to fill the shell. Chill. Whip the cream and top each with a fluff of it if you like. Serves 8.

PEACH MERINGUE TARTS

8 baked Tart Shells*
1½ cups sugar
½ teaspoon cream of tartar
Pinch salt
2 egg whites
8–12 peaches

Mix the sugar, ¼ cup water, cream of tartar, salt, and egg whites in a double boiler. Beat slightly with a rotary beater. Set over briskly boiling water and beat steadily with rotary beater for 6–8 minutes, until the meringue holds a soft peak. Remove from heat and beat 3 minutes. Fill the pastry shells as full as possible with the sliced, peeled peaches. Cover the peaches with the meringue, swirling it high. Put the tarts on a baking sheet under the broiler for 2–3 minutes, until delicately browned. Chill before serving. Serves 8.

DEEP-DISH PEACH ALMOND PIE

Pastry for 9-Inch Pie Shell*
2 (1 lb. 14 oz.) cans cling peach slices
⅓ cup sugar
½ cup chopped toasted almonds
2 tablespoons melted butter
¾ teaspoon almond flavoring
2 tablespoons quick-cooking tapioca

Drain the peaches and combine with all other ingredients except crust in an 8×8×2-inch pan. Top with pastry, sealing the edges to the sides of the pan. Cut slits in the top of pastry. Bake in a 425° oven for about ½ hour, until golden. Serve warm. Serves 6–8.

PEACH GLAMOUR PIE

ALMOND COCONUT CRUST
1 cup blanched almonds
1 cup flaked coconut
¼ cup sugar
¼ cup soft butter

PEACH FILLING
1 (1 lb. 14 oz.) can peach slices
Pinch salt
¼ cup superfine sugar
1 teaspoon orange juice
1 teaspoon coarsely grated orange rind
1 teaspoon vanilla
1 cup sour cream

Almond Coconut Crust. Put the almonds through a food chopper, using a medium blade. Then chop the coconut and combine with the ground almonds. Work in the sugar and butter. Press mixture evenly on the bottom and up the sides of a 9-inch pie plate, saving 2–3 tablespoons for the top. Bake in a 375° oven for 12–15 minutes, until light golden brown. Put the topping crumbs in a shallow pan and toast in the oven at the same time for about 5 minutes. Cool thoroughly.

Peach Filling. About 1 hour before serving time, drain the peach slices on paper toweling. Blend the salt, superfine sugar, orange juice, orange rind, and vanilla into the sour cream. Spread this mixture on the bottom and sides of the pie shell. Top with drained peaches. Sprinkle with the topping crumbs. Chill. Serves 8.

PINEAPPLE PIE

Baked 9-Inch Pie Shell*
Pinch salt
¾ cup sugar
1 (1 lb. 4 oz.) can crushed pineapple
2 eggs
3 tablespoons cornstarch

Add the salt, ½ cup sugar, and ½ cup hot water to the pineapple. Beat the egg yolks until thick and lemon-colored and stir into the pineapple mixture. Add the cornstarch which has been mixed with 2 tablespoons cold water. Cook over moderate heat, stirring constantly, until mixture thickens and no taste of cornstarch remains. Cool. Fill the pie shell. Make a meringue out of the egg whites beaten stiff with the remaining sugar. Cover the pie with the meringue and bake in a 350° oven for 15 minutes, until slightly browned. Serves 6–8.

INDIANA RAISIN PIE

Pastry for 8-Inch 2-Crust Pie*
2 cups raisins
½ cup orange juice
½ cup dark brown sugar
2 tablespoons cornstarch
1 teaspoon cinnamon
1 teaspoon grated orange rind
Pinch salt
1 tablespoon vinegar
2 tablespoons butter
Cinnamon-sugar (optional)

Line the pie plate with pastry. Simmer the raisins in 1¼ cups water and the orange juice for 5 minutes, covered. Combine the brown sugar, cornstarch, cinnamon, grated orange rind, salt, and ¼ cup water. Add to the raisins and bring to a boil, stirring well. Remove from heat and add vinegar and butter. Pour into the pie shell and cover with the top crust. Sprinkle lightly with a mixture of cinnamon and sugar if you wish. Bake in a 425° oven for 25 minutes. Serve warm. Serves 6.

RAISIN TARTS

1 recipe Tart Shells*
⅔ cup light brown sugar
3 tablespoons melted butter
1 egg
3 tablespoons light corn syrup
⅔ cup raisins
½ cup chopped pecans or walnuts
¾ teaspoon vanilla

Cut out the tarts with a 3½-inch round cutter and fit them into tart pans 3½ inches in diameter at the top (the pastry won't completely fill the pans). Mix together all of the filling ingredients and fill each tart ⅓ full (the mixture bubbles up while baking). Place the pans on a baking sheet and bake in a 375° oven for 20–25 minutes, until filling is bubbly and pastry golden. Cool slightly, remove from pans, and serve warm. Yield: about 8 tarts.

RHUBARB PIE I

Pastry for 9-Inch 2-Crust Pie*
6–8 tablespoons flour
1½–2 cups sugar
1 teaspoon grated orange rind
4 cups cut-up rhubarb
1 tablespoon butter

Line a pie plate with half the pastry. Mix the flour, sugar, and orange rind. If using hothouse rhubarb, which gives off more liquid, use 8 tablespoons flour. Toss with the rhubarb and pour into the pie plate. Dot with butter. Cover with a plain slitted or lattice crust and bake in a 450° oven for 10 minutes. Reduce heat to 350° and bake for 40 minutes, until crust is golden brown. Serves 8.

RHUBARB PIE II

Baked 9-Inch Pie Shell*
4 cups cut-up rhubarb
¼ teaspoon salt
1⅓ cups sugar
¼ cup cornstarch
1 teaspoon grated lemon rind
3 egg yolks

MERINGUE (optional)
3 egg whites
Pinch salt
6 tablespoons sugar

Cook the rhubarb in very little water and no sugar. Two cups cooked rhubarb is needed. Add the salt, sugar, and cornstarch and cook, stirring, about 10 minutes over medium heat, until very thick and no taste of cornstarch remains. Remove from heat and add lemon rind. Beat the egg yolks, add a little of the hot mixture, and then combine with the hot rhubarb. Cook about 1 minute. Cool and pour into the pie shell. If you wish, cover with a meringue made with the egg whites, salt, and sugar. Bake 20 minutes in a 300° oven until meringue is lightly browned. Serves 6–8.

RHUBARB STRAWBERRY PIE

Baked 9-Inch Pie Shell*
4 cups cut-up rhubarb
⅔ cup sugar
¼ cup honey
3 tablespoons cornstarch
1 tablespoon flour
Pinch salt
1 pint strawberries
Cream cheese, cream, and sugar (garnish)

Cut the rhubarb into ½-inch pieces and mix with the sugar and honey in a double boiler. Steam until tender—do not stir. Pour carefully, so the pieces will stay whole, into a sieve over a bowl to drain. There should be about 1½ cups syrup; if not, add a little hot water. Mix the cornstarch, flour, and salt. Blend to a smooth paste with 2–3 tablespoons cold water. Stir in the syrup and then cook until thickened, stirring constantly. Cool to room temperature. Add the hulled berries and gently fold in the rhubarb. Fill the pie shell. Garnish if you wish with cream cheese whipped with cream and a little sugar. Serves 6–8.

RHUBARB STRAWBERRY TARTS

Proceed as for Rhubarb Strawberry Pie,* using 8 baked Tart Shells* instead of the pie shell. Serves 8.

FRESH STRAWBERRY PIE

*Baked 9-Inch Pie Shell**
3 pints strawberries
1 cup sugar
3 tablespoons cornstarch
1 tablespoon lemon juice
¼ teaspoon almond flavoring
*1 cup Sweetened Whipped Cream**

Wash and hull the berries. Reserve half (the best-looking ones) and mash the rest. Add the sugar and cornstarch. Mix well and cook 5 minutes, stirring constantly, until thickened and clear. Stir in the lemon juice and almond flavoring. Cool. Add the remaining berries. Pour into the pie shell and chill. Before serving, top with a ruff of the Sweetened Whipped Cream. Serves 6–8.

FRESH STRAWBERRY TARTS

Proceed as for Fresh Strawberry Pie,* using 8 baked Tart Shells* instead of the pie shell. Serves 8.

STRAWBERRY GLAZE PIE

*Baked 8-Inch Pie Shell**
2 (3 oz.) packages cream cheese
1 tablespoon milk
⅓ cup plus 1 tablespoon sugar
2 teaspoons grated lemon rind
1 quart strawberries
2 tablespoons cornstarch
1 tablespoon lemon juice

Soften the cheese at room temperature and whip until smooth. Add milk, 1 tablespoon sugar, and 1 teaspoon grated lemon rind. Mix well. Spread evenly over the bottom of the baked crust. Hull the berries and stand the best ones on end in the cheese, covering it entirely. Crush the remaining berries or buzz in a blender. You should have 1 cup purée; if not, add water to make a cup. Mix the remaining ⅓ cup sugar and the cornstarch in a saucepan. Add strawberry purée, lemon juice, and remaining grated lemon rind. Heat and stir until glaze is thickened. Cool slightly, spoon over the berries, and chill. Serves 4–6.

STRAWBERRY WHIPPED-CREAM PIE

*Baked Easy Biscuit Pie Shell**
3 pints strawberries
1 cup sugar
2½ tablespoons cornstarch
1 tablespoon butter
Red food coloring
*Sweetened Whipped Cream** *(garnish)*

Hull the berries. Mix the sugar, cornstarch, and ½ cup water in a saucepan. Crush 2 cups of berries and add. Bring this mixture to a boil and cook 3–5 minutes, until clear. Add the butter and a few drops of coloring. Rub through a sieve. Arrange the remaining berries in the pie shell, mounding them up in the center. Spoon the warm glaze over, making sure all berries are covered. Cool. Before serving, arrange fluffs of cream on the pie. Serves 8.

STRAWBERRY LEMON TARTS

*6 baked Tart Shells**
3 eggs
¾ cup sugar
Pinch salt
Juice 1 lemon
Grated rind ½ lemon
15 large strawberries

Beat the egg yolks until thick. Add the sugar gradually and then the salt, lemon juice, and lemon rind. Cook in a double boiler for 10 minutes, stirring constantly, until thick. Cool. Fold in the egg whites, beaten until a soft peak forms. Fill the tart shells ¾ full. Chill. Just before serving, slice the unsweetened strawberries in an overlapping circle over the top. Serves 6.

STRAWBERRY CREAM-CHEESE PIE I
(Plate 16)

Unbaked 9-inch graham-cracker
 Crumb Crust*
1 (8 oz.) package cream cheese
½ cup sour cream
3 pints strawberries
¼ cup plus 1 tablespoon sugar
3 tablespoons cornstarch
⅛ teaspoon vanilla

Blend the cream cheese with ¼ cup sour cream. Measure ½ cup and spread it on the bottom of the chilled pie shell. Crush 1 pint of strawberries, sprinkle with ¼ cup sugar, and let stand until juicy. Rub through a sieve. Measure the juice and add water to make 1½ cups. Mix in the cornstarch and heat and stir until thick. Cool. Pour a thin layer of the sauce into the shell and add the remaining berries which have been hulled. Top with remaining sauce and chill. Add remaining sugar, sour cream, and vanilla to the rest of the cream cheese; chill and garnish the pie. Serves 6–8.

STRAWBERRY CREAM-CHEESE PIE II

Baked 9-Inch Pie Shell*
⅓ cup plus ½ cup sugar
1 tablespoon cornstarch
1 cup thawed frozen sliced strawberries
3 (3 oz.) packages cream cheese
2 eggs
1 teaspoon vanilla
¼ teaspoon salt

Blend ⅓ cup sugar with the cornstarch and add the strawberries, juice and all. Cook until mixture is thick and clear. Cool. Beat together with a rotary beater the softened cream cheese, ½ cup sugar, eggs, vanilla, and salt. Spread the cooled strawberry mixture over the bottom of the pie shell. Pour in the cheese mixture. Bake in a 350° oven for 40 minutes. Cool. Serves 6–8.

CRANBERRY CHEESE PIE

9-Inch Pie Shell* slightly underbaked
2½ (8 oz.) packages cream cheese
1 cup sugar
1½ tablespoons flour
¼ teaspoon grated lemon rind
¼ teaspoon grated orange rind
⅛ teaspoon salt
3 eggs plus 1 egg white

2 tablespoons evaporated milk or heavy
 cream
½ teaspoon vanilla
CRANBERRY TOPPING
1 (1 lb.) can whole cranberry sauce
2 tablespoons sugar
1½ tablespoons cornstarch
1 teaspoon lemon juice
1 teaspoon grated lemon rind

Beat the cream cheese until fluffy. Combine the sugar, flour, lemon and orange rinds, and salt. Add to the cream cheese and beat until thoroughly mixed. Add the eggs and egg white one at a time, beating well after each addition. Last, add the milk or cream and the vanilla, beating again until well blended. Pour into the slightly underbaked pie shell. Bake in a 450° oven for 7 minutes. Reduce heat to 200° and bake 15 minutes more. Cool.

Cranberry Topping. Combine the cranberry sauce, sugar, and cornstarch. Cook over low heat until thick and clear. Blend in the lemon juice and rind. Cool slightly and spread over the cooled cheese filling. Chill. Serves 6–8.

HONEY CHEESE PIE

Baked 9-inch Crumb Crust*
1 envelope unflavored gelatin
⅓ cup honey
⅛ teaspoon salt
1 egg
½ cup milk
½ teaspoon grated lemon rind
1½ teaspoons lemon juice
½ teaspoon vanilla
1 pound cottage cheese
2 tablespoons sugar
½ cup heavy cream

Mix the gelatin, honey, and salt in a double boiler. Beat the egg yolk and milk together and add to the gelatin mixture. Cook over boiling water, stirring constantly, about 10 minutes, until gelatin dissolves. Remove from heat and add lemon rind. Cool. Stir in the lemon juice, vanilla, and cottage cheese, which has been rubbed through a sieve. Chill. Stir occasionally until it thickens. Beat the egg white stiff, gradually adding the sugar, and beating well after each addition. Fold into the gelatin mixture along with the cream, whipped. Turn into the crust. Chill. Serves 6–8.

Plate 12. APPLE STRUDEL.

Plate 13. CROQUEMBOUCHE—a pyramid of small filled cream puffs. BUTTERFLY CAKE—made from a cake mix.

Plate 14.
MINCE PIE
lattice top.
PUMPKIN PIE
with cream.

Plate 15.
SOUTHERN
PECAN PIE.

Plate 16. STRAWBERRY CREAM-CHEESE PIE in a graham-cracker shell. NESSELRODE PIE in a nut crust.

FRENCH FRUIT TARTS (*Plate 1*)

6 baked Tart Shells*
3 tablespoons flour
¼ cup sugar
⅛ teaspoon salt
1 cup milk
½ teaspoon vanilla
2 egg yolks
¼ cup heavy cream
3 peaches
1 pint strawberries and/or blueberries

GLAZE

2 tablespoons sugar
4 teaspoons cornstarch
1 teaspoon lemon juice
Red food coloring (*optional*)

Mix the flour, sugar, and salt. Add a little of the milk and stir until smooth. Add remaining milk and vanilla and cook, stirring, in a double boiler until smooth and thickened. Beat the egg yolks slightly; stir in a little of the hot mixture. Return to double boiler and cook, stirring constantly, until thick. Cool thoroughly and fold in the cream, whipped. Meanwhile, peel, pit, and halve the peaches. Put a few spoonfuls of cold custard-cream mixture into each tart shell. Place a peach half cut side down in the center; arrange strawberries and/or blueberries around.

Glaze. Heat 1 cup water and the sugar. Add the cornstarch mixed with 2 tablespoons water and the lemon juice. Cook and stir until thick and clear. Tint pale pink. Cool.

Spoon a little glaze over the fruit. Keep in a cool place until serving time; do not refrigerate. Serves 6.

ALMOND PIE

Baked 9-Inch Pie Shell*
2 cups milk
3 eggs
1 cup brown sugar
3 tablespoons cornstarch
¼ teaspoon salt
¼ cup melted butter
½ cup toasted slivered blanched almonds
6 tablespoons sugar

Scald the milk. Beat the egg yolks until thick and add the brown sugar, cornstarch, and salt; then add the hot milk gradually. Put the mixture into a double boiler, add the melted butter, and cook until thick, stirring almost constantly. Cool and pour into the pie shell. Sprinkle with most of the almonds. Top with a meringue made by beating the egg whites very stiff while adding the sugar gradually and beating after each addition. Sprinkle the remaining almonds on top of the meringue and bake 15 minutes in a 350° oven. Serve cold. Serves 6–8.

RAISIN PECAN PIE

Unbaked 8-Inch Pie Shell*
2 eggs
1 cup sugar
1 teaspoon cinnamon
1 teaspoon cloves
½ cup pecan halves
½ cup raisins
1 tablespoon melted butter
1 tablespoon vinegar
Whipped cream (*garnish*)

Beat the egg yolks until light and thick. Sift the sugar with the cinnamon and cloves and add gradually to the egg yolks. Stir in the nuts, raisins, and butter. Fold in the egg whites which have been beaten to a soft peak. Fold in the vinegar; do not beat. Pour into the pie shell. Bake in a 450° oven for 10 minutes; then reduce heat to 350° and bake 25 minutes more. The top should be crisp and nicely browned. Serve cold, with whipped cream if you wish. Serves 4–6.

SOUTHERN PECAN PIE (*Plate 15*)

Unbaked 9-Inch Pie Shell*
1 cup pecan halves
3 eggs
1 tablespoon melted butter
½ cup dark corn syrup
½ cup light corn syrup
½ teaspoon vanilla
1 cup sugar
1 tablespoon flour

Arrange the pecan halves in the bottom of the pie shell. Beat the eggs until light; add the butter, corn syrups, and vanilla. Stir until well blended. Combine the sugar and flour and blend this with the egg mixture. Pour over the nuts in the pie shell. Let stand until the nuts rise to the surface. Bake in a 350° oven for 45 minutes. The nuts will glaze during baking. Serves 6–8.

PECAN PIE

Unbaked 9-Inch Pie Shell*
1 cup dark corn syrup
½ cup plus 1 teaspoon sugar
3 tablespoons butter
3 eggs
1 cup pecan halves
1 teaspoon flour

Heat the syrup and ½ cup sugar, stirring until boiling. Remove from heat and add butter. Stir hot mixture into the well-beaten eggs a little at a time. Add pecans. Sprinkle bottom of the pie shell with a mixture of the flour and remaining sugar. Fill with pecan mixture. Bake in a 325° oven for 40–50 minutes. Serves 6–8.

PECAN MACAROON PIE

Unbaked 9-Inch Pie Shell*
½ cup dark brown sugar
1 cup dark corn syrup
3 eggs
¼ cup butter
1 tablespoon vanilla
½ cup crumbled day-old macaroons
½ cup broken pecans
Whipped cream (optional)

Cook the sugar and syrup over low heat until the sugar is dissolved. Beat the eggs with a fork and slowly add the hot syrup, beating constantly. Add the remaining ingredients except whipped cream, stir well, and pour into the pie shell. Bake in a 450° oven for 10 minutes, then reduce to 300° for 25 minutes. Cool. Serve with whipped cream if you wish. Serves 6–8.

DATE WALNUT PIE

Unbaked 10-Inch Pie Shell*
3 tablespoons butter
5 tablespoons light brown sugar
2 tablespoons flour
1¼ cups light corn syrup
1 teaspoon salt
3 eggs
1 cup slivered pitted dates
1 cup broken walnuts
1 cup heavy cream (optional)

Cream the butter, sugar, and flour together. Add the corn syrup, salt, ¼ cup water, and the well-beaten egg yolks. Beat with a rotary beater until blended. Stir in the dates and wal-

nuts. Fold in the stiffly beaten egg whites and spoon the mixture into the pie shell. Bake in a 325° oven for 55 minutes. Serve very cold. Top if you wish with the unsweetened cream, whipped. Serves 8–10.

ANGEL PECAN PIE

3 egg whites
1 cup plus 2 tablespoons sugar
2 teaspoons vanilla
1 cup crisp cracker crumbs
1½ cups chopped pecans
1 cup heavy cream
¼ teaspoon almond flavoring

Beat the egg whites until foamy. Add 1 cup sugar a little at a time, beating after each addition. Add 1 teaspoon vanilla. Continue beating until mixture holds soft peaks. Mix cracker crumbs and 1 cup pecans. Fold into meringue mixture a little at a time. Spoon into an 8-inch pie plate to form a shell. Pull up mixture with back of spoon into peaks around the edge of the plate. Spread evenly. Bake in a 350° oven for ½ hour. Cool thoroughly on a rack. Mix the cream, remaining sugar and vanilla, and the almond flavoring. Whip until thick and shiny. Spoon into the cold pie shell. Sprinkle remaining chopped pecans around the edge of the cream. Serves 6–8.

SHOO FLY PIE

Unbaked 9-Inch Pie Shell*
1½ cups flour
1 cup brown sugar
¼ cup butter
¾ teaspoon baking soda
⅛ teaspoon nutmeg
⅛ teaspoon ginger
⅛ teaspoon cinnamon
⅛ teaspoon cloves
¼ teaspoon salt
¾ cup molasses

Mix the flour and sugar and cut in the butter to make crumbs. Add the soda, nutmeg, ginger, cinnamon, cloves, and salt to the molasses. Mix well and add ¾ cup hot water. Pour the molasses mixture into the pie shell and sprinkle the crumbs on top. This is the traditional way, but if you prefer, alternate layers of crumbs and molasses mixture in the pie shell, beginning and ending with crumbs. Bake in a 450° oven for 15 minutes. Reduce heat to 350° and bake 20 minutes. Serves 6–8.

MINCE PIE

Pastry or Cheddar-Cheese Pastry for 9-Inch 2-Crust Pie*
1 quart mincemeat
2–3 tablespoons brandy (optional)

Line a pie plate with pastry. Fill with mincemeat, with brandy added if you wish. Cover with the other half of pastry and slash the crust thoroughly. Bake in a 450° oven for 10–12 minutes; lower heat to 350° and continue baking 20–25 minutes longer, until crust is lightly browned. Serves 8.

BRANDIED MINCE PIE (Plate 14)

Pastry for 9-Inch 2-Crust Pie*
⅓ cup finely chopped walnuts (optional)
2 cups mincemeat
½ cup orange marmalade
1 cup peeled diced apple
2 tablespoons brandy
2 tablespoons flour
1 egg (optional)
Hard Sauce* (optional)

When preparing the pastry, add the nuts after blending the flour and shortening if you wish. Mix the mincemeat, marmalade, apple, and brandy. Sprinkle the flour over all and stir well. Spoon into the pie shell. Roll remaining pastry and cut into strips. Arrange on the surface of the pie in lattice fashion. Brush pastry and edge of pie with egg beaten with a little water. Bake in a 425° oven for 35–40 minutes, until crust is golden. Serve warm. This pie is good with Hard Sauce. Serves 8.

MINCEMEAT APPLE CRUMB PIE

Unbaked 9-Inch Pie Shell*
1 (1 lb.) jar mincemeat or
1 (9 oz.) package dry
2¼ cups peeled, cored, and sliced tart apples
1 cup sugar
½ teaspoon cinnamon
2 tablespoons butter
⅓ cup flour

If you use dry mincemeat, prepare according to package directions. Pour the mincemeat into the pie shell. Mix the apples with ½ cup sugar and the cinnamon. Arrange the apples over the mincemeat. Cut the butter into the flour and remaining sugar. When the mixture is in small pieces, lightly sprinkle it over the apples. Bake in a 450° oven for 15 minutes. Reduce heat to 350° and bake another ½ hour, until bubbly. Serves 6–8.

PUMPKIN MINCE PIE

Unbaked 9-Inch Pie Shell*
2 cups mincemeat
⅓ cup brown sugar
½ teaspoon salt
1 teaspoon cinnamon
¼ teaspoon ginger
¼ teaspoon cloves
1 cup canned pumpkin
2 eggs
¾ cup heavy cream or evaporated milk

Spread the mincemeat over the bottom of the pie shell. Bake in a 425° oven for 15 minutes. While this bakes, mix the sugar, salt, and spices together. Mix with the pumpkin. Beat the eggs slightly and add the cream or evaporated milk. Blend into the pumpkin mixture. Pour over the mincemeat. Bake in a 350° oven about 35 minutes, until the pumpkin custard is set. Serves 6–8.

PUMPKIN PIE (Plate 14)

Unbaked 9-Inch Pie Shell*
4 eggs plus 1 egg white
1½ cups canned pumpkin
⅔ cup brown sugar
½ teaspoon ginger
1 teaspoon cinnamon
Generous pinch salt
¼ teaspoon nutmeg
2 cups light cream or half-and-half
Whipped cream (optional)

Brush the pie shell with the slightly beaten egg white. Chill 1 hour or more. Mix the pumpkin, brown sugar, ginger, cinnamon, salt, and nutmeg. Scald the cream or half-and-half and add to the mixture. Add the slightly beaten eggs; mix well. Pour into the pie shell and bake in a 450° oven for 15 minutes. Reduce heat to 350° and bake about 30 minutes, until set. Top with whipped cream if you wish. Serves 6–8.

RICH PUMPKIN PIE

*Unbaked 10-Inch Pie Shell**
1 cup milk
⅔ cup raisins
1 cup light brown sugar
2 cups canned pumpkin
½ teaspoon cinnamon
¼ teaspoon nutmeg
¼ teaspoon ginger
¼ teaspoon allspice
½ teaspoon salt
2 cups heavy cream
4 eggs
1½ cups broken pecans

Scald the milk, add raisins and sugar, and let stand. Mix the pumpkin, cinnamon, nutmeg, ginger, allspice, salt, and 1 cup cream in a large bowl. Add the raisin-milk mixture and mix well. Add the slightly beaten eggs and mix again. Fold in the pecans. Fill the pie shell. Bake in a 350° oven for about 1 hour, until the center is set. Cool. Whip the remaining cream and decorate the pie. Serves 8–10.

MAPLE PUMPKIN PIE

Unbaked 9-Inch Pie Shell or Sesame Shell**
2 cups canned pumpkin
¼ cup maple syrup
2 eggs
1 cup heavy cream or evaporated milk
2 tablespoons butter
½ cup dark brown sugar
¼ teaspoon salt
1½ teaspoons cinnamon
¼ teaspoon nutmeg
¼ teaspoon ginger
⅛ teaspoon cloves
Maple Meringue Topping or*
  whipped cream (garnish)

Mix the pumpkin and maple syrup with slightly beaten eggs and ½ cup cream or evaporated milk. Heat remaining cream or milk and stir in the butter. Add to pumpkin along with brown sugar, salt, and the spices, mixing well. Pour into the pie shell and bake in a 425° oven for 15 minutes. Reduce heat to 350° and continue to bake for 50 minutes, until filling is set. Serve cold, garnished with Maple Meringue Topping or with fluffs of cream, which you may sweeten with a little maple syrup. Serves 8.

TOASTED-COCONUT PUMPKIN PIE

Proceed as for Pumpkin Pie,* adding 1 cup toasted shredded coconut just before pouring into the pie shell.

CHESS PIE

*Unbaked 8-Inch Pie Shell**
2 eggs
½ cup butter
1 teaspoon vanilla
1 cup light brown sugar
¼ cup broken walnuts
¼ cup broken pecans

Beat the eggs well and melt the butter. Then mix all of the ingredients together. Pour into the pie shell. Bake in a 375° oven for about 35 minutes. Serves 6.

LEMON CHESS PIE

*Unbaked 9-Inch Pie Shell**
1½ cups sugar
⅓ cup melted butter
Juice 3 lemons
Finely grated rind 3 lemons
5 eggs
Meringue Puffs or whipped cream*
  (garnish)
Chopped blanched pistachio nuts (garnish)

Mix together thoroughly all the ingredients. Pour into the pie shell and bake in a 425° oven for 5 minutes. Reduce temperature to 325° and bake 35–40 minutes longer, until filling is golden brown and set. Remove pie from oven and cool well. Decorate the pie with Meringue Puffs or fluffs of whipped cream and chopped pistachio nuts. Serves 8.

SWEET-POTATO PIE

*Unbaked 9-Inch Pie Shell**
4 sweet potatoes
1 cup brown sugar
½ cup butter
1½ teaspoons nutmeg
½ teaspoon cinnamon
½ teaspoon ginger
¼ teaspoon salt
3 eggs
1 cup heavy cream

Bake the sweet potatoes. Scoop the warm potatoes from the skins into a mixing bowl.

Mix with the brown sugar and butter. Add the spices and salt and beat until smooth. Add the slightly beaten egg yolks and cream. Blend well. Fold in the egg whites beaten until a stiff peak forms. Pour into the pie shell. Bake in a 350° oven for about 1 hour, until center is set when tested with a knife. Serves 6–8.

RAINBOW FRUIT TART

2 cups flour
½ cup superfine sugar
¼ teaspoon cinnamon
Grated rind 1 lemon
¾ cup butter
3 egg yolks

GLAZE
2 tablespoons sugar
4 teaspoons arrowroot or cornstarch
1 teaspoon lemon juice
Red food coloring

FILLING
1 cup heavy cream
¼ cup sugar
1½ teaspoons vanilla
1 pint strawberries
1 seedless orange
Small bunch black grapes
Small bunch white grapes

Sift the flour, sugar, and cinnamon together. Add lemon rind and mix well. Cut the butter into the flour mixture until it resembles fine crumbs. Add the slightly beaten egg yolks and mix until pastry forms a ball; use your hands and knead in the bowl 1–2 minutes. Wrap in waxed paper and chill for 1 hour. Roll out ⅛–¼ inch thick on a lightly floured board and line a 10-inch pie plate. Handle quickly, being careful not to stretch the pastry. Crimp the edge, but be sure the pastry does not hang over the rim. Chill for another hour. Prick well over bottom and sides. Put waxed paper in the pastry shell and fill ½ inch deep with dry rice or beans. Bake in a 450° oven for 5 minutes; remove from oven and lift out rice or beans and waxed paper. Reduce oven to 350° and bake 12 minutes more, until golden. Cool in pie plate on a rack.

Glaze. Heat 1 cup water and sugar until simmering. Mix the arrowroot or cornstarch with 2 tablespoons water and the lemon juice to form a smooth paste. Add to the syrup and cook and stir until smooth and clear. Tint pale pink. Cool.

Filling. Whip the cream, sugar, and vanilla until thick and glossy. Spread evenly over the bottom of the cold pie shell.

Hull the strawberries, section the orange, and cut the grapes in half and remove seeds, or use seedless grapes. Arrange the fruit on top of the cream. Spoon the glaze over the fruit. Keep in a cool place until time to serve; do not refrigerate. Serves 8.

COOKTIP

Roll pastry between two sheets of waxed paper. Remove the top paper, turn into pie plate, and peel off the other paper.

CUSTARD PIE

Unbaked 9-Inch Pie Shell*
3 cups milk
6 eggs
½ cup sugar
1 teaspoon vanilla
Pinch salt

Scald the milk. Mix the slightly beaten eggs, sugar, vanilla, and salt. Stir the milk gradually into the egg mixture. Strain into the pie shell. Bake in a 450° oven for 10 minutes. Reduce the heat to 325° and bake 30–40 minutes, until a knife comes out clean. Cool. Serves 6–8.

CUSTARD CREAM MERINGUE PIE

Forgotten Meringue*
⅓ cup flour
¾ cup sugar
Pinch salt
2 eggs
2 cups light cream
1½ teaspoons vanilla
Raspberries or strawberries (optional)

Mix the flour with the sugar and salt. Add the well-beaten eggs to the cream and beat together. Stir this mixture into the dry ingredients gradually, beating well. Cook in a double boiler, stirring constantly, until the mixture is thick and smooth. Cool and add the vanilla. Chill. Just before serving, pour the filling into the meringue and serve with fresh or frozen berries if you wish. Serves 6–8.

BLACK BOTTOM PIE

Crumb Crust*
2 cups milk
4 eggs
1 tablespoon cornstarch
1 cup sugar
Pinch salt
1 envelope unflavored gelatin
2 ounces unsweetened chocolate
1 teaspoon vanilla
¼ teaspoon cream of tartar
1–2 tablespoons rum
1 cup Sweetened Whipped Cream*
Shaved unsweetened chocolate

Heat the milk in a double boiler. Pour a little hot milk into the beaten egg yolks and return to double boiler. Add the cornstarch mixed with ¾ cup sugar and salt. Cook 15–20 minutes, until mixture coats a spoon. Mix the gelatin with ¼ cup water. Stir into hot custard mixture until gelatin dissolves. Chill but do not let it set. Pour off 1¼ cups mixture and stir in the melted chocolate and vanilla. Spoon into the pie shell. Beat the egg whites with the cream of tartar until frothy. Gradually add remaining ¼ cup sugar, beating constantly until a soft peak forms. Fold into the remaining custard and add the rum. Pour on top of the chocolate mixture and chill. Before serving, top with Sweetened Whipped Cream and chocolate curls. Serves 8.

PEAR CUSTARD TART

Baked 10-Inch Pie Shell*
2 egg yolks
1 tablespoon plus ¾ teaspoon cornstarch
1½ tablespoons sugar
⅛ teaspoon salt
⅛ teaspoon nutmeg
1 cup milk
½ teaspoon vanilla
1 cup softened red currant jelly
6 cooked pears or 1 (1 lb. 13 oz.) can
  pear halves
1 cup whipped cream
Toasted slivered blanched almonds

Mix the egg yolks, cornstarch, sugar, salt, and nutmeg in a double boiler. Scald the milk and add slowly to the egg-yolk mixture. Cook, stirring constantly, 8–10 minutes, until the custard coats a spoon. Remove from heat and add vanilla and cool. Spread the inside of the

pie shell with the jelly. Pour the custard into the pie shell. Quarter the pears and arrange in the filling. Spread the top with the whipped cream and sprinkle with the almond slivers. Chill 3–4 hours. Serves 8–10.

CHOCOLATE-GLAZED CUSTARD PIE

1 Custard Pie*
6 ounces semisweet chocolate
2½ tablespoons milk

Chill the pie well. Break up the chocolate and put into a double boiler. Add the milk, cover, and cook until the chocolate is melted. Stir until smooth and glossy. Spread a thin layer over the pie. Let stand in a cool place for about 1 hour, until the chocolate sets. Serves 6–8.

EGGNOG PIE

Baked 9-Inch Pie Shell*
4 eggs
½ cup plus ⅓ cup sugar
Pinch salt
1 cup milk
1 envelope unflavored gelatin
2 tablespoons rum or brandy or
  1 tablespoon rum flavoring
1 cup heavy cream
⅛ teaspoon nutmeg

Beat the egg yolks slightly with ½ cup sugar and the salt. Scald the milk and add slowly to the egg mixture. Cook in a double boiler until custard consistency, stirring constantly. Soften the gelatin in ¼ cup cold water. Add to the hot custard; stir until the gelatin is dissolved. Flavor with rum or brandy. Chill until the mixture begins to thicken. Beat the egg whites until a soft peak forms, gradually adding the remaining sugar. Fold into the cooled custard, fill the pie shell, and chill until set. To serve, top with the cream, whipped, and sprinkle with nutmeg. Serves 8.

MACAROON FRUITED-CUSTARD PIE

9-inch Macaroon Crust*
½ cup milk
2 eggs
⅓ cup sugar
Pinch salt
1½ teaspoons unflavored gelatin
4 marshmallows

1 slice pineapple
2 ounces mixed candied fruits
1 cup heavy cream
¼ cup finely chopped pecans
2 tablespoons macaroon crumbs

Combine the milk, slightly beaten eggs, sugar, and salt in a double boiler. Cook and stir until custard coats a spoon. Remove from heat. Soften the gelatin in ¼ cup cold water and stir into hot custard until dissolved. Cool. Cut up the marshmallows and pineapple, chop the candied fruits, and whip the cream. Fold the whipped cream into the cooled custard; then fold in the marshmallows, pineapple, candied fruits, pecans, and macaroon crumbs. If the fruit sinks to the bottom, put pudding in refrigerator to thicken; then stir until it begins to set. Pour into the macaroon pie shell and chill overnight. Garnish if you wish with additional whipped cream and chopped candied fruits. Serves 6–8.

LEMON MERINGUE PIE I

Baked 9-Inch Pie Shell*
1¼ cups plus 6 tablespoons sugar
6 tablespoons cornstarch
⅛ teaspoon salt
1 teaspoon grated lemon rind
¼ cup butter
3 eggs
⅓–½ cup lemon juice

Mix 1¼ cups sugar, the cornstarch, and a pinch salt together in a saucepan. Add 2 cups boiling water and the lemon rind. Cook over direct heat, stirring constantly, until thickened. Continue cooking and stirring for about 20 minutes. Remove from heat, add butter, and pour the hot mixture gradually over the slightly beaten egg yolks which have been mixed with the lemon juice. Beat until very smooth. Return to heat and allow to become steaming hot again, stirring to prevent scorching. Fill the pie shell and bake in a 400° oven for 5 minutes. Remove from oven and cover with a meringue made with the egg whites beaten stiff with a pinch of salt and the remaining sugar. Bake in a 350° oven for 10–12 minutes, until delicately browned. Serves 6–8.

LEMON MERINGUE TARTS

Proceed exactly as for Lemon Meringue Pie,* using 8 baked Tart Shells* instead of the pie shell.

LIME MERINGUE PIE

Proceed as for Lemon Meringue Pie,* substituting lime juice and lime rind for lemon.

CRUSTLESS LEMON MERINGUE PIE
(Low Calorie)

3 tablespoons cornstarch
3 eggs
¾ teaspoon granulated noncaloric sweetener
1 tablespoon butter
1 teaspoon grated lemon rind
¼ cup lemon juice
½ teaspoon cream of tartar
Pinch salt
2 tablespoons plus 1 teaspoon sugar
¼ teaspoon vanilla

Mix the cornstarch, 1½ cups water, egg yolks, and sweetener together in a small saucepan. Cook, stirring constantly, over low heat about 10 minutes, until mixture thickens. Remove from heat and stir in the butter, lemon rind, and juice. Pour into an 8-inch pie plate. Beat the egg whites with the cream of tartar and salt until a soft peak forms. Gradually add the sugar and continue beating until a glossy stiff meringue is formed. Fold in the vanilla. Cover the filling with meringue, making sure it touches the rim. Bake in a 350° oven about 10 minutes, until it is delicately browned. Cool. Serves 4 (about 135 calories per serving).

LEMON CURD TARTS   (Plate 35)

20 very small baked Tart Shells*

FILLING
2 cups sugar
Grated rind 2 lemons
Juice 3 lemons
½ cup butter
6 eggs

Use Tart Shells (double the recipe) or buy them.

Filling. Mix the sugar, lemon rind, and juice. Melt the butter in a double boiler. Add the sugar to the beaten eggs, beating continuously, and stir slowly into the melted butter. Cook and stir over just simmering water about 45 minutes, until very thick. Cool in refrigerator. Fill the tart shells. Yield: 20 tarts, (about 2½ cups filling).

CHOCOLATE MERINGUE PIE

Baked 9-Inch Pie Shell*
4 ounces unsweetened chocolate
2½ cups milk
2 cups sugar
2 tablespoons butter
½ teaspoon salt
5 tablespoons cornstarch
6 eggs
1½ teaspoons vanilla

Melt the chocolate and set aside. Scald 2 cups milk and add 1¼ cups sugar, butter, salt, and the cornstarch which has been mixed with ½ cup cold milk. Cook in a double boiler until thickened and smooth, stirring all the time. Continue to cook for 10–15 minutes, until mixture no longer tastes starchy. Add the melted chocolate and beat until smooth. Add the mixture to the slightly beaten egg yolks, stirring constantly. Return to double boiler. Beat thoroughly with a rotary beater and cook for 2 minutes over rapidly boiling water. The mixture should be very thick. Add vanilla and pour into the pie shell. Cool thoroughly. Pile high with a meringue made of the egg whites beaten stiff with a pinch of salt and ¾ cup sugar added a tablespoon at a time. Be sure the meringue touches the crust all the way around. Bake in a 350° oven for 12–15 minutes, not allowing the meringue to become too brown. Serve cold, but do not refrigerate. Serves 6–8.

CHOCOLATE PIE SUPREME

9-inch Chocolate Coconut Crust,* Crumb
  Crust,* or other crust
1 envelope unflavored gelatin
1 cup sugar
½ teaspoon salt
1⅓ cups milk
2 teaspoons instant coffee
3 squares unsweetened chocolate
3 eggs
1 teaspoon vanilla
3 tablespoons coffee liqueur or chocolate
  liqueur
Pinch cream of tartar
½ cup heavy cream

Mix the gelatin, ⅓ cup sugar, salt, milk, and coffee together in a double boiler. Add the chocolate and cook until chocolate is melted and gelatin dissolved. Remove from heat and stir. Beat the egg yolks slightly. Quickly stir in the chocolate mixture. Return to heat and cook about 5 minutes, until thickened. Pour into a bowl and add vanilla and liqueur. Chill until the mixture begins to jell. Beat the egg whites and cream of tartar until frothy; gradually beat in remaining sugar. Fold into the mixture, then fold in the cream, whipped. Chill about ½ hour, until quite thick but not set. Spoon into the pie shell, heaping it up in the center. Garnish with additional whipped cream if you wish. Serves 8.

SHORT-CUT MOCHA PIE

Baked 8-Inch Pie Shell*
1 package chocolate pudding mix
2 teaspoons instant coffee
Cinnamon
Whipped cream (optional)

Make the pudding mix according to package directions, adding the coffee to the mix. Pour into pie shell and chill. Sprinkle with cinnamon and garnish if you wish with whipped cream. Serves 4–6.

BUTTERSCOTCH PIE

Baked 9-Inch Pie Shell*
1 cup brown sugar
¼ cup butter
1 teaspoon light corn syrup
1⅓ cups milk
¼ cup sugar
3 tablespoons cornstarch
3 tablespoons flour
¼ teaspoon salt
3 egg yolks
Sweetened Whipped Cream* (garnish)

Combine the brown sugar, butter, corn syrup, and ¼ cup water and cook until very-hard-ball stage (265°). Scald the milk in a double boiler. Combine the sugar, cornstarch, flour, and salt. Add the milk gradually while stirring. Cook for 15 minutes, stirring constantly, until thick and smooth. Add the hot butterscotch mixture and stir until smooth again. Pour slowly over the slightly beaten egg yolks, beating constantly; return to double boiler and cook another minute. Cool and pour into the pie shell. Serve topped with whipped cream. Serves 6–8.

COCONUT CREAM PIE

Baked 9-Inch Pie Shell*
1 cup sugar
½ cup flour
¼ teaspoon salt
2 cups milk
3 egg yolks
2 tablespoons butter
½ teaspoon vanilla
½ cup flaked coconut
Whipped cream (optional)

Mix the sugar, flour, and salt together. Scald the milk and add gradually to the dry ingredients. Cook in a double boiler, stirring almost constantly, about 10 minutes, until thickened. Add the slightly beaten egg yolks and cook another 3 minutes. Add the butter and vanilla. Fold in the coconut. Cool, without stirring, for about 10 minutes. Pour into the pie shell. Chill until firm. Serve with whipped cream if you wish. Serves 6–8.

PEACH DEVONSHIRE-CREAM PIE

Baked 9-inch Crumb Crust*
1 (1 lb. 13 oz.) can sliced cling peaches
1 envelope unflavored gelatin
3 tablespoons sugar
½ cup milk
2 eggs
½ can frozen orange-juice concentrate
¼ teaspoon almond flavoring
¾–1 cup sour cream
1 teaspoon lemon juice
¼ teaspoon salt

Drain the peaches, saving the syrup. Add the gelatin and 2 tablespoons sugar to the milk and scald. Beat the egg yolks slightly; gradually add milk mixture. Pour into double boiler and cook, stirring constantly, about 10 minutes, until it coats a spoon. Remove from heat and stir in the orange concentrate, ¼ cup syrup from the peaches, and the almond flavoring. Set aside ½ cup peaches for garnish. Chop the rest coarsely and stir into the gelatin mixture. Cool until thickened. Stir in ½ cup sour cream and the lemon juice. Add salt to the egg whites and beat until very foamy. Gradually add remaining sugar and beat until a soft peak forms. Fold into peach mixture. Then spoon the filling into the pie shell. Chill. Garnish with spoonfuls of remaining sour cream and peach slices. Serves 6–8.

RHUBARB CREAM PIE

Unbaked 9-Inch Pie Shell*
1 cup sugar
⅓ cup flour
Pinch salt
½ cup heavy cream
1 quart cut-up rhubarb

Beat the sugar, flour, salt, and cream until smooth and thick. Put the rhubarb into the unbaked pie shell. Pour the sugar mixture over the rhubarb. Bake in a 450° oven for about 30 minutes, until the crust begins to brown. Reduce heat to 350° and continue baking 20–30 minutes, until the filling thickens slightly. Serves 6–8.

GINGER BAVARIAN TARTS

2 (4¾ oz.) packages vanilla wafers
½ cup soft butter
3 tablespoons sugar

FILLING
1 envelope unflavored gelatin
1½ cups milk
⅓ cup sugar
¾ teaspoon ginger
¼ teaspoon salt
3 eggs
1 tablespoon chopped crystallized ginger
1 cup heavy cream

Roll the vanilla wafers until very fine. Add the butter and sugar and mix thoroughly with a pastry blender. Pat into 6 smooth-sided (not fluted) tart pans, being sure to make a thick coating on the sides. Bake in a 375° oven for 8 minutes. Cool in the pans.

Filling. Soften the gelatin in the milk for 5 minutes. Place over boiling water. Add the sugar, which has been mixed with the ginger and salt, and stir until the sugar and gelatin are dissolved. Beat the egg yolks slightly. Slowly stir into them a small amount of the hot liquid. Return this to double boiler and add the crystallized ginger. Cook over hot— not boiling—water, stirring constantly, until mixture coats a spoon. Remove from heat. Chill until slightly thickened. Fold in the stiffly beaten egg whites and then fold in the cream, whipped. Spoon into the tart shells and chill until firm. To serve, loosen carefully around top edges with a thin-bladed knife and transfer tarts to dessert plates with a spatula. Serves 6.

BANANA CREAM PIE

Baked 9-Inch Pie Shell*
¼ cup sugar
¼ teaspoon salt
3 tablespoons flour
1½ cups milk
1 egg yolk
1 tablespoon butter
¼ teaspoon vanilla or ½ teaspoon lemon
flavoring
4 bananas
1 cup Sweetened Whipped Cream*
(optional)

Mix the sugar, salt, and flour. Add the milk gradually. Cook until thickened, stirring constantly. Continue to cook for 3 minutes. Add some of the hot mixture to the slightly beaten egg yolk while stirring. Return to hot mixture and cook for another minute. Add butter and flavoring. Cool. Slice the bananas into the pie shell and pour the mixture over them. Chill. Garnish with Sweetened Whipped Cream if you wish. Serves 6–8.

APRICOT CHIFFON PIE

Baked 10-Inch Pie Shell*
2 cups dried apricots
1 cup plus 2 tablespoons sugar
Juice 1 lemon
Juice 1 orange
1 blade mace
1 stick cinnamon
1 envelope unflavored gelatin
2 egg whites
½ cup heavy cream
½ teaspoon almond flavoring
Whipped cream (optional)
Toasted slivered blanched almonds
(optional)

Put the apricots (don't pack them into the measure) in a saucepan with 1 cup water, 1 cup sugar, fruit juices, mace, and cinnamon. Simmer for 20–30 minutes, until apricots are tender and liquid is syrupy. Stir occasionally. Meanwhile, stir the gelatin into 1¾ cups cold water and heat and stir until gelatin is dissolved. Remove the whole spices from the apricots and force the fruit and syrup through a food mill or buzz in a blender. Stir the gelatin mixture into the apricot purée. Chill until it is just beginning to set; then beat until frothy.

Beat the egg whites with remaining sugar until a soft peak forms. Whip the cream and fold into the apricot mixture with the egg whites. When well blended, add the almond flavoring, pour into the pie shell, and chill until firm. Garnish if you wish with fluffs of whipped cream and nuts. Serves 8–10.

PEACH ALMOND CREAM PIE

Baked 9-Inch Pie Shell*
1 package lemon-flavored gelatin
1 pint vanilla ice cream
1 cup chopped, peeled fresh or
frozen peaches
Sugar
6 day-old small macaroons
½ cup chopped salted almonds
Sliced peaches (garnish)

Add 1¼ cups boiling water to the gelatin and stir until dissolved. If using frozen peaches, thaw and drain off syrup; substitute this syrup for part of the water to make the 1¼ cups of liquid. Break up the ice cream and fold into the gelatin with a fork. Chill for 10 minutes. Sugar the fresh peaches to taste. Crumble the macaroons and fold into the ice cream mixture with the almonds and peaches. Pour into the pie shell and chill until set. Garnish with sliced peaches. Serves 6–8.

SOUR-CREAM RAISIN PIE

Unbaked 8-Inch Pie Shell*
1 tablespoon lemon juice or vinegar
1 cup heavy cream
¾ cup sugar
2 eggs
1 teaspoon cinnamon
½ teaspoon nutmeg
½ teaspoon cloves
Pinch salt
½ cup raisins
1 teaspoon grated lemon rind

Add lemon juice or vinegar to the cream and let stand a few minutes. Mix the soured cream with sugar and slightly beaten eggs. Add the spices and salt. Mix in the raisins and grated lemon rind. Pour into the pie shell and bake in a 350° oven for 40–45 minutes, until custard is set. Serves 6.

LEMON CHIFFON PIE

Baked 9-Inch Pie Shell*
2 teaspoons unflavored gelatin
⅓ cup plus ¼ cup sugar
⅓ cup lemon juice
Pinch salt
3 eggs
1 teaspoon grated lemon rind
Sweetened Whipped Cream* (garnish)

Mix the gelatin, ½ cup cold water, ⅓ cup sugar, and the lemon juice together. Add the salt to the egg yolks and beat until light and quite thick. Add the gelatin and lemon mixture to the yolks. Cook in a double boiler until the custard coats a spoon, stirring continuously. Pour into a bowl and add the lemon rind. Refrigerate just until it begins to thicken. Beat the egg whites until a peak forms, adding the remaining sugar a tablespoon at a time while beating. Fold into the custard. Pour into the pie shell and chill until set. Garnish with Sweetened Whipped Cream. Serves 6–8.

LEMON STRAWBERRY SOUFFLE PIE

23 vanilla wafers
1 (4 oz.) package lemon-flavored pie filling
1 envelope unflavored gelatin
1 teaspoon grated lemon rind or
  ½ teaspoon dried
⅓ cup sugar
2 eggs
1 package frozen sliced strawberries

Arrange the vanilla wafers in the bottom and round the sides of a 9-inch pie plate. Mix the pie filling, gelatin, and grated lemon rind. Add 2½ cups water gradually. Add the sugar and slightly beaten egg yolks. Mix well. Cook over medium heat, stirring until mixture thickens. Remove from heat immediately and cool. Chill until thick and syrupy. Beat the egg whites until a soft peak forms. Fold into the lemon mixture. Chill until thick. Spoon into the pie plate and chill until firm. Spoon some of the thawed sliced strawberries over the lemon filling and pass the rest. Serve immediately. Serves 6–8.

ORANGE CHIFFON PIE

Proceed as for Lemon Chiffon Pie.* Omit the water and substitute ¾ cup orange juice for the lemon juice and orange rind for the lemon rind.

LIME CHIFFON CREAM PIE

9-inch Crumb Crust* or Baked Pie Shell*
2 envelopes unflavored gelatin
½ cup hot milk
Pinch salt
2 strips lime peel (about 1 × ⅛-inch)
½ cup lime juice
½ cup sugar
2 eggs
2–3 drops green food coloring
1 (8 oz.) package cream cheese
1 cup light cream

Buzz the gelatin, hot milk, salt, lime peel, and juice in a blender for 1 minute at high speed. Turn off motor and add sugar, eggs, food coloring, and cheese and blend for 15 seconds. Add 1 cup finely chopped ice and then the cream. Continue blending 15 minutes more. Let stand 2–3 minutes, until slightly thickened; then pour into crust and chill until set. You may make this filling, using a rotary beater; however, substitute 1 teaspoon grated lime rind for the piece of peel. It will take a few minutes longer. Garnish if you wish with fresh strawberries or a few strips of lime peel. Serves 6–8.

LIME CHIFFON PIE

Proceed as for Lemon Chiffon Pie,* substituting ¼ cup lime juice for the lemon juice and lime rind for the lemon rind.

CHERRY CHIFFON PIE

Baked 9-Inch Pie Shell*
1 (1 lb.) can pitted tart red cherries
1 envelope unflavored gelatin
¼ cup sugar
Pinch salt
¼ teaspoon almond flavoring
1 tablespoon lemon juice
½ cup heavy cream

Drain the cherries, reserving the juice. Soften the gelatin in ¼ cup cold water and dissolve in ¾ cup hot cherry juice. Add the sugar, salt, almond flavoring, and lemon juice. Chill until syrupy. Fold in the cream, whipped, and the cherries. Pour into the pie shell. Chill. Serves 6–8.

PEACH CHIFFON PIE
(Low Calorie)

1¼ cups zwieback crumbs
2 tablespoons sugar
¼ cup melted butter

PEACH FILLING

1 envelope low-calorie lemon-flavored
   gelatin
1 (8 oz.) can water-pack sliced peaches
½ cup frozen orange-juice concentrate
½ teaspoon almond flavoring
2 egg whites
¼ cup sugar

Crush the zwieback crumbs with the sugar and butter. Pack into an 8-inch pie plate and bake for 10 minutes in a 325° oven. Cool.

Peach Filling. Dissolve the gelatin in ½ cup hot water and the juice drained from the can of peaches. Dice the peaches and set aside. When the gelatin is dissolved, add the orange-juice concentrate and almond flavoring. Chill until slightly thickened. Beat the egg whites, adding sugar a little at a time, until a stiff peak forms. Fold the egg whites and peaches into the gelatin mixture. Chill until thickened and then pour into the prepared crumb crust. Refrigerate until firm. Serves 6 (196 calories per serving).

RICH PUMPKIN CHIFFON PIE

Baked 10-Inch Pie Shell*
¾ cup milk
2¼ cups canned pumpkin
1½ cups brown sugar
⅛ teaspoon salt
¾ teaspoon ginger
¾ teaspoon cinnamon
⅓ teaspoon nutmeg
5 eggs
2 envelopes unflavored gelatin
1½ cups heavy cream
¾ teaspoon grated orange rind
⅓ cup sugar
Sweetened Whipped Cream* (garnish)
Grated orange rind (garnish)

Heat the milk in a double boiler with the pumpkin, brown sugar, salt, and spices. Beat the egg yolks slightly. Gradually add some of the hot mixture to the yolks, mixing rapidly. Return to the pumpkin mixture and cook until thickened, stirring constantly. Soften the gelatin in ⅓ cup cold water; add to the cus-tard, stirring until dissolved. Remove from heat and cool. Beat the egg whites until a soft peak forms, fold them into the filling, and then chill but don't let it set. Whip the cream until thickened, add the orange rind and sugar, and whip until stiff. Fold into pumpkin mixture. Chill until quite thick and then put into the pie shell. Before serving, garnish with Sweetened Whipped Cream and a little grated orange rind. Serves 8–10.

PEAR CHIFFON PIE

Baked 9-Inch Pie Shell*
1 (1 lb. 1 oz.) can pear halves
1 package lime-flavored gelatin
2 tablespoons lemon juice
1 tablespoon green crème de menthe
1 cup heavy cream
Green food coloring (optional)

Drain the pears, reserving syrup, and put them on paper toweling to dry. Measure 1 cup of the pear syrup, heat, and pour over the gelatin in a bowl. Add the lemon juice and crème de menthe. Chill until syrupy. Beat the gelatin mixture with a rotary beater until light. Fold in the cream, beaten until a soft peak forms. Chill. Tint the pears with a little more crème de menthe and/or a few drops green food coloring mixed with water if you wish. Heap the gelatin mixture into the baked pie shell. Chill until firm. Top with pear halves, arranging them spoke fashion. Serves 8.

MOCHA CHIFFON PIE

Baked 9-Inch Pie Shell* or Crumb Crust*
2 envelopes unflavored gelatin
1 cup hot strong coffee
½ ounce unsweetened chocolate
⅓ cup plus ¼ cup sugar
1½ cups heavy cream
2 eggs
1 teaspoon vanilla
⅛ teaspoon salt
Chocolate curls (garnish)

Soften the gelatin in ½ cup cold water. Add the hot coffee and chocolate. Heat and stir until the gelatin is dissolved and the chocolate is melted. Add ⅓ cup sugar and ½ cup cream. Pour mixture into the well-beaten egg yolks. Cook in a double boiler until thickened, stirring occasionally. Cool, add vanilla, and, when almost ready to set, beat with a rotary beater until light and fluffy. Meanwhile, whip the remaining cup of cream. Beat the egg whites with the salt until a soft peak forms, gradually adding the remaining sugar. Fold the whipped cream into the coffee mixture and last fold in the meringue. Pour into the pie shell or crumb crust. Chill before serving. Garnish with chocolate if you wish. Serves 6–8.

CHOCOLATE NUT ANGEL PIE

PECAN MERINGUE SHELL
 ½ cup sugar
 ⅛ teaspoon cream of tartar
 2 egg whites
 ½ cup chopped pecans

CHOCOLATE FILLING
 ¾ cup semisweet chocolate bits
 1 teaspoon vanilla
 1 cup heavy cream

Pecan Meringue Shell. Sift the sugar and cream of tartar together. Beat the egg whites until a peak forms. Add the sifted sugar gradually, beating after each addition. Continue beating until the meringue is stiff and glossy. Fold in the nuts. Butter a 9-inch pie plate and fill with the meringue. Do not bring out over the rim. Bake in a 275° oven about 1 hour, until delicately browned. Cool thoroughly.

Chocolate Filling. Melt the chocolate in a double boiler. Add 3 tablespoons hot water and cook until thickened. Cool slightly. The mixture will become quite thick. Add the vanilla. Whip the cream and fold into the chocolate. Pour the filling into the meringue shell and chill 2–3 hours. Serves 6–8.

PEACH ANGEL PIE

 Meringue Shell*
 2 packages frozen sliced peaches
 1½ cups heavy cream
 ½ teaspoon almond flavoring
 1 tablespoon sugar

Drain the thawed peaches. Just before serving, whip the cream with the almond flavoring and sugar. Spread a layer of the cream over the meringue shell, then a layer of the peaches, another layer of cream, and more peaches on top. Serve at once. Serves 8.

NESSELRODE PIE (Plate 16)

 9-inch Nut Crust*
 ⅓ cup finely diced candied fruit
 2 tablespoons slivered candied cherries
 ¼ cup light rum
 1 envelope unflavored gelatin
 2 cups light cream
 ½ cup sugar
 2 eggs

Put the fruit and cherries in a small bowl and pour the rum over. Soften the gelatin in ¼ cup cold water. Heat the cream in a double boiler. Add ¼ cup sugar and the gelatin. Stir until dissolved. Beat the egg yolks slightly; stir a little hot cream into them, then stir rapidly into the cream mixture. Cook over simmering water until mixture is thickened and coats a spoon. Pour into a bowl and chill, stirring often. Beat the egg whites until frothy. Gradually add the remaining sugar while beating. Continue to beat until a stiff peak forms. Fold into the cold custard along with the fruits and rum. Mix well. Chill, stirring several times. Spoon into the crust and garnish if you wish with additional fruits. Chill several hours before serving. Serves 8.

COCONUT CHIFFON PIE

 Baked 9-Inch Pie Shell*
 1 envelope unflavored gelatin
 4 eggs
 ½ cup sugar
 ¼ teaspoon salt
 1 cup milk
 1½ cups flaked coconut
 1 teaspoon vanilla
 2 cups heavy cream

Soften the gelatin in ¼ cup cold water. Beat the egg yolks slightly and add the sugar and salt. Scald the milk and stir gradually into the egg mixture. Return to saucepan. Cook and stir over low heat until thickened. Add the gelatin, stirring until dissolved. Cool. Beat the egg whites until a soft peak forms. Mix ½ cup coconut with the vanilla. Fold the coconut mixture, egg whites, and 1 cup cream, whipped, into the custard mixture. Sprinkle half of the remaining coconut on the bottom of the pie shell. Pour in the filling and chill well. Before serving, top with the remaining cream, whipped, and coconut. Serves 6–8.

LEMON ANGEL PIE

ANGEL CRUST

4 egg whites
Pinch salt
¼ teaspoon cream of tartar
1 cup sugar

LEMON FILLING

4 egg yolks
½ cup sugar
¼ cup lemon juice
Grated rind 1 lemon
1–2 cups heavy cream
Mint (garnish)

Angel Crust. Beat the egg whites with the salt and cream of tartar until stiff. Add 1 cup sugar a little at a time, continuing to beat until mixture is glossy and the sugar dissolved. Spread it into a well-buttered 9-inch pie plate, carrying it well out on the rim. Bake in a 275° oven for 25 minutes. Then raise the heat to 300° and bake 25 minutes more, until a faint brown tinge has appeared. Remove from the oven and let cool.

Lemon Filling. Beat the egg yolks until thick. Add the sugar, lemon juice, and rind. Stir and cook in a double boiler until the mixture thickens. Use a whisk or slotted spoon for this. Remove from heat and cool. Whip 1 cup cream. Fold it into the cooled filling and turn the mixture into the crust. Chill. When ready to serve, top the pie with the remaining cream, whipped, and garnish with mint, if you wish. Serves 8.

CHOCOLATE-FILLED MERINGUES

6 egg whites
⅛ teaspoon salt
½ teaspoon cream of tartar
1½ cups sugar
1 teaspoon vanilla

CHOCOLATE FILLING

1 pound sweet baking chocolate
2 cups heavy cream
2 teaspoons vanilla

Beat the egg whites with the salt and cream of tartar until frothy. Add the sugar a tablespoon at a time, beating well after each addition. Continue beating until all sugar is dissolved and the mixture stands in stiff peaks. Add the vanilla. Cut brown paper to fit 2 baking sheets. Brush with cooking oil. Draw twelve 3-inch circles on the paper. Then spread ¼ inch of meringue evenly in the circles. Fill a pastry bag fitted with a rosette tip with the remaining meringue. Outline each circle with 2 layers of the meringue. Bake in a 250° oven for about 1 hour; the meringues should not get brown. Cool. Remove from paper.

Chocolate Filling. Melt the chocolate with 6 tablespoons of water over hot water. Stir while melting. If any lumps persist, mix with a wire whisk after removing from the heat. Cool. Whip the cream until thick and glossy. Add the vanilla. Fold carefully into the cold chocolate mixture.

Fill the meringues. Swirl the top and then refrigerate for at least 2 hours. Serves 12.

MERINGUE RING MOLD

8 egg whites
Pinch salt
½ teaspoon cream of tartar
1 cup sugar

Beat the egg whites, salt, and cream of tartar until a peak forms. Add the sugar a tablespoon at a time, beating well after each addition. When the meringue will stand in stiff glossy peaks, spoon it into an ungreased 2½-quart ring mold. Fill carefully to eliminate air bubbles. Set the mold in another pan with 1 inch of hot water in it. Bake in a 250° oven for 45 minutes, until the meringue is set. Remove the ring mold from the water and let cool until the meringue settles. Just before serving, loosen the meringue from the pan with a knife that has been dipped in water to prevent its tearing the meringue. Invert on a serving dish. This meringue is not very sweet; it is therefore useful for a rich or creamy filling. Try it with berries and flavored whipped cream. Serves 8.

ANGEL PIE

Meringue Shell*
1 cup heavy cream
¼ cup sugar
2 tablespoons rum or brandy
Strawberries, raspberries, or shaved sweet chocolate

Whip the cream with the sugar and flavor with rum or brandy. Spread on meringue shell. Arrange sugared berries over the top or sprinkle generously with shaved chocolate. Serves 6.

FRUIT-FILLED APPLE DUMPLINGS

2½ cups flour
3½ teaspoons baking powder
¾ teaspoon salt
½ cup shortening
¾ cup milk

FILLING

1 pound mixed dried fruit
1½ cups sugar
2 teaspoons lemon juice
3 tablespoons butter
¼ teaspoon cinnamon
6 tart apples

Sift together the dry ingredients. Cut in the shortening. Stir in the milk with a fork. Turn the dough out onto a lightly floured board. Fold and turn lightly a few times. Chill.

Filling. Wash the dried fruit. Put in a saucepan and cover with about 3 cups water. Bring to a boil, lower heat, and simmer for ½ hour, until fruits are tender. During the last 5 minutes of cooking add ½ cup sugar. Cool and drain the fruit. Reserve 1 cup of the syrup. Pit the fruit if necessary and set aside. Put the syrup in a pan with the remaining sugar, 1 cup water, and rest of ingredients except the apples. Bring to a boil and cook for 3 minutes. Remove from heat. Peel and core the apples.

Roll the dough into an 18×12-inch rectangle. Cut into six 6-inch squares. Place an apple on each square and fill the center with the cooked dried fruit. Moisten edges of squares. Pull corners up over the apple and pinch the edges of dough together. Fold back the pastry points at the center to show the fruit filling. Place 2 inches apart in a large baking pan and pour the syrup around and over the dumplings. Bake in a 425° oven for 10 minutes, reduce oven to 350°, and bake for 30–35 minutes, until the apples are tender. Baste with syrup so the dumplings are nicely glazed. Serves 6.

TURNOVERS

½ recipe Pastry for 9-Inch 2-Crust Pie*
¾ cup jam, preserves, or applesauce

Roll the pastry about ⅛ inch thick and cut into 4-inch squares or circles. Put the filling on half of each piece of pastry and fold over to make a triangle or crescent. Wet the edges and press together. Prick on top. Bake on baking sheets in a 400° oven for about 20 minutes. Turnovers may be fried in deep hot fat, 360°, until browned. Yield: 6–8 turnovers.

APPLE DUMPLINGS

2½ cups flour
3½ teaspoons baking powder
¾ teaspoon salt
½ cup shortening
¾ cup milk

APPLE FILLING

2¾ cups sugar
Juice 1½ lemons
3 tablespoons butter
¼ teaspoon cinnamon
¼ teaspoon nutmeg
1½ quarts peeled, cored, sliced apples

Sift the flour, baking powder, and salt together. Cut in the shortening to the consistency of coarse meal. Stir in the milk with a fork. Turn out onto a floured board. Fold and turn lightly a few times. Chill. Roll into a thin rectangular sheet; cut into six 5-inch squares.

Apple Filling. Mix 2 cups sugar with 2 cups water, juice of 1 lemon, and the butter and cook to a thin syrup. Mix the remaining sugar with the juice of ½ lemon and add the cinnamon, nutmeg, and apples.

Put a mound of the apple mixture on each pastry square. Fold over the points and pinch the corners together on top. Arrange in a large shallow pan. Pour the syrup over the dumplings and bake in a 425° oven for 10 minutes. Reduce heat to 350° and bake 35 minutes more. Serves 6.

RAISIN TURNOVERS
(Banbury Tarts)

Pastry for 9-Inch 2-Crust Pie*
1 cup raisins
1 cup sugar
Juice 1 lemon
Grated rind 1 lemon
¼ cup cracker crumbs
1 egg
Light cream

Prepare the pastry as usual, rolling it to ⅛-inch thickness. Cut into 4-inch rounds or squares. Chop the raisins and mix with the sugar, lemon juice, and lemon rind. Add the cracker crumbs and well-beaten egg. Place a generous spoonful of raisin mixture to one side of each piece of pastry, wet the edges, fold in half, and press edges together with a fork. Cut a slit in the top to permit the steam to escape. Brush the tarts with cream and bake in a 375° oven for 15–20 minutes, until pastry is browned. Yield: 12–15 tarts.

PASTRY CREAM
(Crème Pâtissière)

1½ cups milk
Piece vanilla bean or ¼ teaspoon vanilla
4 egg yolks
½ cup sugar
¼ cup flour
Pinch salt

Scald the milk with the vanilla bean. Beat the egg yolks and sugar until fluffy. Add the flour and salt slowly, stirring until smooth. Add the milk. Cook and stir over boiling water until smooth and thick. Remove from heat. If using the vanilla bean, discard; if not, add vanilla. Beat for a minute or two. Chill, stirring occasionally to prevent a film from forming. Yield: 1½ cups.

CHOCOLATE PASTRY CREAM

Add 2 ounces unsweetened chocolate and 1 tablespoon sugar to the milk and proceed as for Pastry Cream.*

MOCHA PASTRY CREAM

Add 1 ounce unsweetened chocolate and 1 teaspoon instant coffee or 1 tablespoon hot triple-strength coffee to the milk. Proceed as for Pastry Cream.*

COFFEE PASTRY CREAM

Proceed as for Pastry Cream.* Add 1 teaspoon instant coffee to the Pastry Cream when it is removed from the heat.

CUSTARD WHIPPED-CREAM FILLING

1¼ cups milk
5 tablespoons flour
6 tablespoons sugar
¼ teaspoon salt
¾ cup heavy cream
2 eggs
1 teaspoon vanilla or other flavoring

Heat the milk in a double boiler. Sift the flour, sugar, and salt together and stir in half the cream. Add to the hot milk. Cook, stirring constantly, until thick and smooth. Beat the eggs and add the hot mixture gradually. Return to double boiler and cook 2–3 minutes more while stirring. Cool. Fold in the remaining cream, whipped, and flavor with vanilla or any flavoring you like. Yield: about 2½ cups.

CREAM PUFFS

½ cup butter
1 cup flour
Pinch salt
4 eggs
About 2 cups Pastry Cream, Custard
  Whipped-Cream Filling,* or Sweetened
  Whipped Cream**
Confectioners' sugar

Put the butter in a saucepan, add 1 cup water, and bring to a boil. Add the flour all at once and the salt. Beat until the mixture forms a ball that leaves the sides of the pan clean. Remove from heat and add the eggs one at a time, beating until smooth after each addition. Drop by spoonfuls onto a greased baking sheet. Bake in a 400° oven for 20 minutes, until the puffs have really puffed; then reduce heat to 350° and bake another 25 minutes. This prevents them from falling. Cool on wire racks. Then slit one side and fill with 3–4 tablespoons Pastry Cream, Custard Whipped-Cream Filling, or Sweetened Whipped Cream. Dust with confectioners' sugar or frost if you wish. Yield: 8–12 puffs.

PROFITEROLES

Use the recipe for Cream Puffs,* dropping from a small spoon to make midget puffs. Bake in a 375° oven for 30–35 minutes. The finished puffs should be about the size of a walnut. When cold, fill from the bottom with slightly softened vanilla or chocolate ice cream (it is easier if you use a pastry tube). Serve immediately with Chocolate Sauce.* Yield: about 60 puffs; serves 12–15.

NAPOLEONS

*Puff Paste**
2 eggs plus 1 egg white
¼ cup flour
3 tablespoons sugar
1 envelope unflavored gelatin
1 teaspoon vanilla
1 cup milk
2 tablespoons rum
1 cup whipped cream
Vanilla Glaze and melted chocolate or
  confectioners' sugar*

Roll out the puff paste ¼ inch thick and cut into 3 long strips about 4 inches wide. Lay strips on a baking sheet, prick with a fork, and refrigerate 15 minutes. Bake in a 450° oven for 15 minutes, until golden. Let cool. Put 1 egg and 1 yolk in a bowl with the flour and sugar and beat well. Add the gelatin and vanilla. Pour in the heated milk and bring to boiling point. Remove from heat and stir over ice until it begins to thicken. Add the rum. Fold in the remaining 2 egg whites, beaten until a stiff peak forms, and then the whipped cream. Split the puff-pastry strips lengthwise into halves. Spread the above cream filling or Pastry Cream* or Sweetened Whipped Cream* on 3 of the strips and pile up sandwich fashion. Traditionally, Napoleons are frosted with Vanilla Glaze and cross-striped with chocolate; the chocolate is melted and put through a small paper cornucopia to make the lines. Or spread the top with a thin layer of filling and dust with confectioners' sugar. Cut into about 3-inch serving pieces or leave whole and cut at table. Serves 9.

CROQUEMBOUCHE   (Plate 13)

1½ recipes Cream Puffs*

HONEY WHIPPED-CREAM FILLING

2½ cups heavy cream
⅓ cup confectioners' sugar
3 tablespoons honey
2 tablespoons grated orange rind

GLAZE

2 cups sugar
½ teaspoon cream of tartar
½ teaspoon butter

Sifted confectioners' sugar

Prepare the cream-puff batter as usual. Drop by rounded teaspoonfuls 2 inches apart on greased baking sheets. Bake in a 375° oven for 30–35 minutes, until puffs are browned and there are no beads of moisture on them. They should be crisp. If they seem soft, bake a few minutes longer. Cool on racks. With the tip of a knife, make a little hole in the bottom of each puff. Store in a container, covered loosely. You may prepare these several days in advance. You should have about 90 puffs.

Honey Whipped-Cream Filling. Whip the cream, which should be very cold, until just thick. Add the remaining ingredients and beat until the cream stands in a soft peak. Spoon some of the mixture into a pastry bag fitted with a large plain tube (No. 4–6). Fill each puff by inserting the tube point deep into the bottom of the puff. Refill the pastry bag as needed, keeping the cream chilled. Refrigerate the filled puffs on trays.

Cut a 9-inch circle from a piece of cardboard. Cover with foil. Set the circle on a larger piece of foil near the range so you can work quickly. Have some of the cream puffs close at hand.

Glaze. Put the sugar, cream of tartar, and 1½ cups of water in a heavy skillet. Bring to a boil, stirring until the sugar dissolves. Lower heat and cook until the syrup is just light amber. Lower heat until it is barely simmering.

To build the pyramid, lightly dip one side of a puff in syrup and place on the outer edge of the foil circle, glazed side down and the top facing out. Repeat with 9 or 10 more. The syrup will harden and act as an adhesive. For the second row, arrange a slightly smaller row of puffs over the spaces in between the puffs of the first row, inclining them inward. Fill in the center area behind the first two rows with more puffs; they will act as support. Continue building the pyramid in decreasing circles, filling in support area as needed, until you have 6 rows completed. Top with 1 puff. You will need to work quickly, always dipping puffs lightly in the syrup. If the syrup should thicken before the croquembouche is completed, add a little water and melt over low heat. Do not let the syrup burn. The croquembouche may be assembled on the morning of the party and refrigerated until serving time. Add 1 cup water to the remaining syrup in the skillet and the butter or margarine. Cook, stirring occasionally, to the thread stage (232°). Pour the syrup into a small bowl and let stand at room temperature.

At serving time, remove the croquembouche from the refrigerator. Lightly drizzle the reserved syrup on the pyramid, not covering it completely. Sift confectioners' sugar over the surface. To serve, use 2 forks or serving tongs and loosen the puffs one by one. Serve 4–5 puffs to each person and pass Butterscotch Rum Sauce.* Serves 15–20.

APPLE STRUDEL (Plate 12)
(Apfelstrudel)

2 cups flour
½ teaspoon salt
1 egg
2 tablespoons cooking oil
7 cups pared, cored, thinly sliced tart cooking apples
¼ cup melted butter
1½ cups white bread crumbs browned in ½ cup butter
¼ cup seedless raisins
¼ cup currants
¼ cup sugar mixed with ½ teaspoon cinnamon
Confectioners' sugar

Sift the flour with salt into a large bowl; make a well in the center and put in the slightly beaten egg and cooking oil. Stir while gradually adding ½ cup lukewarm water to make a soft, rather sticky dough. Work the dough in the bowl until it comes away from the sides; turn out and knead for about 15 minutes with little or no additional flour. Frequently slap the dough down hard on the board and work it until it is elastic and silky-smooth. It must not stick to the hands or board. Form into a ball, set on a towel, and let rest for 1 hour in a warm place, covered with a bowl which has been warmed in hot water. Warm your rolling pin. (This step is one key to success.) While the dough is resting, cover the kitchen table—or a card table—with a cloth (a pressed piece of sheeting will do) and rub in about 1–2 tablespoons flour, brushing off any excess. Then place the ball of dough in the center of the cloth and roll with the warm rolling pin into a sheet ⅛ inch thick. Lift and turn to prevent sticking to the cloth. Take off your rings! Now stretch the dough, using your floured hands palm side down under the dough. Work carefully, stretching from the center toward the outside. Don't raise your knuckles too high—make a fist and lift from the wrists only. Work gently or you'll puncture the dough (the holes aren't difficult to patch, though). Stretch as thin as possible, moving around the table. Austrian cooks say the dough should be "as thin as paper." It should cover the table and hang slightly over the sides—about 30×40 inches. Trim off the edges, which will be a little thick. If you've made a hole, moisten the area around it with a little water and patch with a thin piece of dough from the trimmings. Let the dough rest and dry for 15 minutes while you prepare the apples.

Now brush the entire surface with melted butter, then sprinkle with bread crumbs. Mix sliced apples, raisins, currants, and sugar mixed with cinnamon. About 3 inches from one edge of the pastry and running the long way, shape the fruit mixture into a bar, leaving 2-inch margins on each side. Fold the 3-inch end piece of dough over the apples, then fold the 2-inch margins in too. Now lift the corners of the cloth and let the pastry roll up. Stop after each turn, patting the filled pastry to keep the bar shape even. Brush with melted butter and slide the strudel onto a lightly buttered baking sheet, curving it into a U shape. Bake in a 375° oven for about 40 minutes, until golden brown. Sprinkle with confectioners' sugar and serve warm. Serves 10–12.

CHEESE STRUDEL

1½ pounds dry cottage cheese
1 egg plus 1 egg yolk
½ cup sugar
½ teaspoon vanilla
½ cup raisins (optional)

Smooth the cheese and add the other ingredients. Mix well and spread on the stretched strudel dough. Proceed as for Apple Strudel.*

CHERRY STRUDEL I

Pit and cut into quarters 2 pounds Bing cherries and use in place of apples in Apple Strudel.*

CHERRY STRUDEL II

2 pounds Bing cherries
2 tablespoons grated lemon rind
½ cup sugar
½ cup chopped nuts
¾ cup bread crumbs

Pit the cherries and cut into quarters. Mix with the lemon rind, sugar, and nuts. Spread the crumbs on the stretched dough. Cover with the cherry mixture and proceed as for Apple Strudel.*

POPPY-SEED STRUDEL

2 cups poppy seeds
½ cup raisins
1 cup sugar
2 tablespoons grated lemon rind
½ cup sour cream or heavy cream

Combine the ingredients and mix them thoroughly. Spread on the stretched strudel dough. Proceed as for Apple Strudel.*

HORNS OF PLENTY

5 tablespoons superfine sugar
2½ tablespoons flour
2 eggs plus 1 egg yolk

RUM FILLING
2 cups heavy cream
5½ tablespoons sugar
1–2 tablespoons rum

Beat the superfine sugar, flour, and eggs and egg yolk with a rotary beater until thick and lemon-colored. Grease a warm baking sheet and drop the mixture by teaspoonfuls onto it. Spread each to a diameter of about 2 inches. Bake only a few at a time in a 400° oven for 4–5 minutes, until golden around the edges. Remove from sheet while still hot and roll immediately into horns. Cool.

Rum Filling. Whip the cream, mix with the sugar and add flavoring.

Fill the horns with Rum Filling, Syllabub* or Sweetened Whipped Cream.* Yield: about 50 horns.

CHERRY PITA

1 package active dry yeast
1 cup butter
4 cups flour
3 tablespoons sugar
Pinch salt
Grated rind ½ lemon
2 eggs plus 2 egg yolks
½ cup sour cream

CHERRY FILLING
1 cup soft bread crumbs
3 (1 lb.) cans pitted tart red cherries
½ cup light brown sugar
1 cup sugar
1 teaspoon cinnamon

Put a pinch of sugar into a small bowl. Add 2 tablespoons warm water (110°–115°), stir in the yeast, and let stand for 10 minutes. Rub or work the butter into the flour along with the sugar, salt, and lemon rind until it resembles coarse crumbs. Mix 1 egg and 2 egg yolks, and the sour cream with the yeast. Add to the dry ingredients. Knead about 5 minutes, until the dough is smooth and elastic. Divide the dough in half and refrigerate one half. Roll out the other half into a 17×12-inch rectangle on a lightly floured board. Put into the bottom of a greased 15½×10½×1-inch jelly-roll pan. Shape to fit, bringing the dough up the sides and onto the rim. Prick well all over with a fork and bake for 10 minutes in a 450° oven.

Cherry Filling. Sprinkle the bread crumbs over the baked layer. Mix the drained cherries with the sugars and cinnamon and spoon evenly over the crumbs.

Roll the remaining dough to fit the top and place over the cherries. Turn the edges under and secure to the rim. Press edges with a fork. Prick well all over and brush with the remaining egg, slightly beaten. Bake in a 350° oven about ½ hour, until golden brown. Cool about 10 minutes, cut into squares, and serve warm. Good with Lemon Hard Sauce.* Serves 12.

ICE-CREAM-FILLED CREAM PUFFS

8 Cream Puffs or Eclairs**
4 ounces semisweet chocolate
¾ cup chocolate syrup
1½ pints coffee, vanilla, or chocolate
  ice cream
⅛–¼ cup confectioners' sugar

Open the puff shells carefully and remove any soft dough from the centers. Melt the chocolate over simmering water, mix with the chocolate syrup, and cool. Place spoonfuls of ice cream inside each shell and gently press the shell back into the original shape. Arrange cream puffs on a cake rack or chilled platter. Work quickly so the ice cream doesn't melt. Sprinkle each with a little sieved confectioners' sugar. Drizzle each one with about 1 tablespoon chocolate sauce. Serve immediately. Pass the remaining chocolate sauce, warm or cold. Serves 8.

ECLAIRS

Eclairs are made in the same fashion as Cream Puffs*; however, the dough is shaped in long ovals instead of rounds.

CHOCOLATE ECLAIRS are slit and filled as you would Cream Puffs.* Cover with Chocolate Frosting.* In France chocolate eclairs are filled with Chocolate Pastry Cream.*

COFFEE ECLAIRS are made exactly like chocolate ones; however, the frosting is coffee and the filling Coffee or Mocha Pastry Cream.*

VANILLA ECLAIRS are filled with Pastry Cream,* Boiled Custard,* or Sweetened Whipped Cream* and frosted with Vanilla Frosting.*

FROZEN ECLAIRS are filled with ice cream and served usually with Chocolate Sauce.*

COOKTIPS

Put a square piece of foil between two pie plates, press them together, trim edges of foil, and lift off the top plate. This makes a light-weight lid in the shape of a pie plate to use when baking a covered pie. A lid is often used for an open apple pie, and this one won't stick to the apples or crush them.

If you have a bakery apple pie or one that's a few days old, try serving with toasted cheese topping. Place serving-size pieces on a baking sheet; top each with a slice of processed cheese. Just before you're ready to serve, put the pie and cheese under the broiler until the pie is hot and the cheese melted.

When making Puff Paste,* save all the edges and extra bits, roll into a ball, and chill. Baked in crescents or squares, they garnish almost any dessert. They make wonderful additions on top of stewed or fresh fruit.

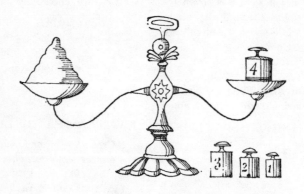

Plate 17. ENGLISH PLUM PUDDING and ORANGE HARD SAUCE.

Plate 19. ORANGE APRICOT GELATIN MOLD garnished with assorted fruits.

Plate 18. STRAWBERRY PINEAPPLE RICE PUDDING made in a mold.

Plate 20. CHESTNUT MOCHA LOG—the center of this log is chocolate-flavored chestnut purée and the frosting flavored with chocolate and coffee.

CHAPTER FIVE

Divers Desserts

Something for everyone! A refreshing whip or soufflé to follow a hearty meal; a rich custard or mousse after a light repast. Welcome the spring with a strawberry Bavarian; serve a dainty gelatin or chiffon on a hot summer night; an apple turnover or cobbler tastes especially good in the brisk fall; make a sumptuous Christmas pudding flambé to highlight the holidays. Here are adventures in desserts for the discriminating cook or hostess to choose from.

Beaten Egg Whites

To beat egg whites, have the eggs and bowl at room temperature. Use a dry, grease-free round-bottomed bowl of glass, china, copper, plastic, or stainless steel (aluminum is likely to make egg whites look slightly gray). A French-type wire whip works very well; if using a rotary hand or electric beater, turn the bowl as you whip. The whites should increase to about 6 times their volume. To make a meringue, add sugar a tablespoon at a time after a peak forms. Beat after each addition of sugar.

Whipped Cream

Have the heavy cream, bowl, and beater chilled (if you are in a hurry, set the bowl in an ice-water bath to whip the cream). Use a hand whip or rotary beater, being careful not to whip the cream too long as it will separate and make butter. If using an electric beater, turn the bowl as you whip. Test by dropping a little cream from the beater back onto the surface of the cream; it should keep its shape and make a soft peak. Cream should at least double in volume when whipped.

SWEETENED WHIPPED CREAM
(Crème Chantilly)

1 cup heavy cream
2–3 tablespoons superfine sugar
½ teaspoon vanilla or almond flavoring

Whip the cream until it begins to thicken, add the sugar and flavoring, and whip 2 or 3 minutes more. (For a garnish, half the recipe is usually sufficient.) Yield: 2 cups.

CHOCOLATE WHIPPED CREAM

Proceed as for Sweetened Whipped Cream.* Substitute 1 tablespoon cocoa for the flavoring.

COFFEE WHIPPED CREAM

Proceed as for Sweetened Whipped Cream.* Substitute 2 teaspoons instant coffee for the flavoring.

LEMON WHIPPED CREAM

1 cup heavy cream
4 teaspoons lemon juice
Grated rind 1 lemon
¼ cup sugar

Whip the cream until stiff. Fold in the lemon juice and then the rind mixed with the sugar. Yield: 2 cups.

WHIPPED LIGHT CREAM

To whip 1 cup light cream, soften 2 teaspoons gelatin in 2 tablespoons cream, add 3 tablespoons hot cream, and stir until dissolved. Add remaining cream and 2 tablespoons confectioners' or superfine sugar. Chill and whip. Yield: about 2 cups.

WHIPPED SKIM MILK

In a chilled bowl sprinkle ½ cup nonfat dry milk over ½ cup ice water mixed with 1 teaspoon lemon juice. Whip until thick. Fold in ¼ cup confectioners' or superfine sugar. Use at once. Yield: about 2½ cups.

WHIPPED EVAPORATED MILK I

Freeze 1 cup evaporated milk until ice crystals form around the edge. Then whip until a soft peak forms. Yield: 2 cups.

WHIPPED EVAPORATED MILK II

Soften 1 teaspoon gelatin in 2 tablespoons cold water, add ¼ cup hot evaporated milk, and stir until gelatin is dissolved. Chill. Add 1 cup cold evaporated milk and 2 tablespoons confectioners' or superfine sugar and whip until a soft peak forms. Yield: about 2½ cups.

CUP CUSTARD

1 quart milk
6 eggs
½ cup sugar
Pinch salt
1 teaspoon vanilla

Scald the milk. Beat the eggs slightly with a fork, just enough to break up the whites and yolks. Add the sugar and salt. Gradually add the scalded milk, stirring as you add it. Flavor with vanilla and strain into 8 buttered custard cups. Set in a pan of hot water, having the water come up to about ½ the height of the cups. Bake in a 350° oven for 30–35 minutes, until a knife inserted in the center of the custard comes out clean. Chill. Serves 8.

BAKED CARAMEL CUSTARD

1 quart milk
½ cup plus 2 tablespoons sugar
6 eggs
½ teaspoon salt
2 teaspoons vanilla

Scald the milk. Caramelize ½ cup sugar by heating in a skillet over low heat, stirring constantly, until the sugar melts and is quite brown. Be careful not to let it burn. Pour the hot milk into the sugar. The sugar will become brittle. Heat and stir the mixture about 2–3 minutes, until the caramel dissolves. Beat the eggs with salt and the remaining sugar and gradually add to the hot milk mixture, stirring constantly. Flavor with vanilla. Strain into a buttered 2-quart baking dish or individual custard cups. Put dish or cups in a pan of hot water; have the water ½ the height of the cups or dish. Bake in a 325° oven until a knife inserted in the center of the custard comes out clean. Individual custards take 30–35 minutes; a large one, about 40 minutes. Chill. Serves 8.

HONEY CUSTARD

2 cups milk
½ cup honey
4 eggs
2 tablespoons sugar
¼ teaspoon nutmeg or mace
1 teaspoon vanilla
Pinch salt

Scald the milk. Butter 6 custard cups and divide the honey among them. Beat the eggs slightly. Add the sugar, nutmeg or mace, vanilla, salt, and the milk. Mix thoroughly and pour slowly into the cups. Pour against a spoon so it will stay on top of the honey. Bake in a hot-water bath in a 350° oven for ½ hour. Test with a knife in the center of the custard; if it comes out clean, the custard is done. Cool, then chill. Serves 6.

MOLASSES CUSTARD

3 eggs
¼ cup molasses
¼ teaspoon salt
1 teaspoon vanilla
2 cups milk

Beat the eggs slightly; add molasses, salt, and vanilla. Scald the milk and gradually stir into the molasses and egg mixture. Pour into a greased 1-quart baking dish. Bake in a pan of hot water in a 325° oven for 30–40 minutes, until knife comes out clean. Serves 6.

WHITE CUSTARD

3 cups milk
1 cup egg whites (about 8)
6 tablespoons sugar
¼ teaspoon salt
1½ teaspoons vanilla
1–2 teaspoons almond flavoring
Berries or fruit sauce (optional)

Scald the milk. Mix together the egg whites, sugar, salt, vanilla, and almond flavoring. Gradually add the hot milk and beat with rotary beater until well mixed. Pour into ungreased custard cups. Set cups in a pan of hot water. Bake in a 325° oven for 45–50 minutes, until a knife inserted in the center of the custard comes out clean. Chill the custards and then loosen around the edges and turn upside down on a serving platter. Serve with sugared berries or fruit sauce. Serves 6–8.

BOILED CUSTARD
(Custard Sauce)

1 quart milk
6–8 egg yolks
½ cup sugar
Pinch salt
1 teaspoon vanilla

Scald the milk in a double boiler. Beat the egg yolks slightly with a fork and add the sugar and salt. Gradually stir in the milk. If you have added the milk too fast, bits of egg will float in the mixture; strain if this happens. Return to double boiler and cook, stirring constantly, for 6–8 minutes, until mixture coats a spoon. Cool slightly; add the vanilla. Chill at once, unless you are using this as a warm sauce. Yield: about 5 cups.

ZABAGLIONE

6 egg yolks
⅔ cup superfine sugar
⅔ cup Marsala or sweet sherry

Beat the egg yolks with a rotary beater until lemon-colored. Continue to beat while gradually adding the sugar and then the Marsala or sherry. Transfer to a double boiler and cook and beat about 7 minutes, until the mixture foams up and becomes quite thick. Be sure that the water in the bottom of the double boiler doesn't touch the upper pan. Serve at once. However, if you want it cold, let stand at room temperature to cool before refrigerating. Serves 6.

FLOATING ISLAND I

*½ recipe Boiled Custard**
3 egg whites
Pinch salt
6 tablespoons sugar
⅛ teaspoon cinnamon (optional)

Beat the egg whites until very stiff. Add the salt and then the sugar gradually while beating. Take it up by tablespoonfuls and drop one at a time into boiling water or milk. When set—a couple of minutes—take out carefully, using a skimmer or perforated spoon, and place on top of the chilled custard in a serving bowl. The islands may be made by just dropping the meringue in fluffs on top of the custard instead of poaching it first. The islands are less good this way but much easier to make. For a change, flavor with cinnamon. Serves 6.

FLOATING ISLAND II

1 quart plus 2 tablespoons milk
3 eggs
2 tablespoons cornstarch
½ cup sugar
Pinch salt
1 teaspoon vanilla
2 tablespoons honey
Few spoonfuls grape or currant jelly
  (optional)

Scald 1 quart milk in a double boiler. Stir in the beaten egg yolks. Add the cornstarch mixed with the remaining milk. Add the sugar, salt, and vanilla. Cook, stirring constantly, until smooth and thickened. Cook 5–10 minutes more, until the mixture coats a spoon. Cool a little. Pour into a serving bowl and chill. Beat the egg whites until a stiff peak forms, adding the honey at the end. Make islands of this on the custard. Top with jelly. Serves 4.

Stolen sweets are always sweeter.
Leigh Hunt,
Song of Fairies Robbing an Orchard

BREAD PUDDING

6 slices white bread
Butter
3 cups milk
3 eggs
½ cup sugar
1 teaspoon vanilla
Pinch salt
½ cup raisins or currants
1 teaspoon nutmeg
Whipped cream (optional)
Strawberry jam (optional)

Trim the crusts from the bread. Butter each slice and cut into 1-inch squares. You will need about 3 cups bread cubes. Place in the bottom of a 6×10×2-inch baking dish. Heat the milk. Beat the eggs slightly and add the sugar, vanilla, and salt. Slowly add the hot milk and pour the mixture over the bread. Stir in the raisins or currants and ½ teaspoon nutmeg. Let stand about ½ hour. Sprinkle top with remaining nutmeg and bake in a 350° oven for 45 minutes. Cool slightly and serve with fluffs of whipped cream and spoonfuls of strawberry jam if you wish. Serves 6.

BREAD PUDDING WITH MERINGUE

3½ cups milk
1 cup raisins
¼ teaspoon salt
12 tablespoons sugar
4 teaspoons grated orange rind
2 teaspoons grated lemon rind
1½ tablespoons butter
3 eggs
3 cups (½ inch) bread cubes
Orange sections (garnish)

Scald the milk and pour over the raisins. Let stand 10 minutes and add salt, 6 tablespoons sugar, orange rind, lemon rind, 1 tablespoon melted butter, and the slightly beaten egg yolks. Add bread cubes and mix well. Pour into a 2-quart baking dish and dot with remaining butter. Cover and bake in a 325° oven for 1 hour. Remove from oven and pile on top of the pudding a meringue made with the egg whites beaten stiff with the remaining sugar. Return the pudding to oven and bake 15 minutes more, until the meringue is golden. A garnish of orange sections is attractive and adds flavor. Serve warm. Serves 6–8.

BUTTERSCOTCH BREAD PUDDING

3 tablespoons butter
½ cup dark brown sugar
¼ teaspoon baking soda
2 cups milk
2 eggs
Pinch salt
2 cups (½ inch) stale bread cubes

Melt the butter in a skillet. Add the sugar and heat until they are blended together. Dissolve the soda in the milk and slowly add to the sugar mixture. Stir until blended and then cool. Beat the eggs slightly. Add the salt to the eggs and then the milk mixture. Put the bread cubes in a greased 1½-quart casserole. Pour the custard mixture over and bake in a 350° oven for about 45 minutes. Serves 6.

CUSTARD JELLY BREAD PUDDING

2 cups small bread cubes (no crusts)
1 quart milk
¼ cup butter
½ cup sugar
2 eggs
1 teaspoon vanilla

½ cup flaked coconut
6 tablespoons currant jelly

Place the bread cubes in a 1½-quart shallow baking dish, 10×6×2-inches. Put the milk, butter, and sugar in a saucepan, bring to simmering point, and add slowly to the slightly beaten eggs, stirring constantly. Pour this over the bread cubes. Cover the baking dish and let stand 10 minutes. Remove cover; stir in the vanilla. Bake in a hot-water bath in a 350° oven for about ½ hour. Sprinkle with coconut. Return to oven and bake ½ hour longer, until the custard is firm. Cool. Decorate with jelly just before serving. Serves 6.

RICE IMPERIAL
(Riz à l'Imperatrice)

1½ cups rice
4½ cups milk
1½ tablespoons grated orange rind
4¾ teaspoons vanilla
¼ teaspoon salt
6 egg yolks
1 cup sugar
1½ envelopes unflavored gelatin
1½ cups slivered glacéed fruits
6 tablespoons kirsch or orange juice
2 cups heavy cream
1 cup currant jelly (garnish)
Glacéed cherries (optional)
Angelica (optional)

Add the rice to 6 cups boiling water, bring to a boil again, and drain. Return rice to saucepan and add 2 cups milk, the orange rind, 2 teaspoons vanilla, and salt. Cover and simmer for ½ hour, until the rice is very tender and the liquid has all been absorbed. Set aside. Meanwhile, make a soft custard with the egg yolks, ¾ cup sugar, and 2½ cups milk. Cook in double boiler until mixture coats a spoon. Add 2 teaspoons vanilla and remove from heat. Soften the gelatin in ⅓ cup cold water and stir into the hot custard mixture until dissolved. Add to the rice and cool to room temperature. Marinate the glacéed fruit in 3 tablespoons kirsch or orange juice. Add to the pudding and taste for sweetness. Add remaining sugar to taste to the cream, flavor with ¾ teaspoon vanilla, and whip until stiff and shiny. Fold ¾ of the cream into pudding and turn into a 2-quart mold. Chill well for at least 4 hours. Unmold onto serving plate and top with more whipped cream. Spoon the currant jelly, which has been thinned with remaining kirsch or orange juice, over the top. Garnish with more cream and decorate with cherries and bits of angelica if you wish. Serves 12.

BROWNED-HONEY RICE PUDDING

1 cup rice
¾ cup honey
¼ cup raisins
1¾ cups heavy cream or evaporated milk
2 tablespoons butter
½ teaspoon cinnamon
¼ cup chopped nuts
Juice 1 lemon

Cook the rice by your favorite method. Heat the honey in a skillet until light brown, being careful not to let it burn. Mix the drained rice with the honey, raisins, cream or milk, butter, cinnamon, and nuts. Put in a 1½-quart casserole. Bake in a 375° oven about 20 minutes, until the pudding is golden. Add the lemon juice, stir, and bake another 15 minutes. Serves 4–6.

SNOW-CAPPED RICE PUDDING

2 cups freshly cooked rice
2 eggs plus 1 egg yolk
¼ cup raisins
¼ cup chopped pitted dates
¼ cup chopped pecans
2½ cups milk
1 teaspoon vanilla
1 tablespoon melted butter
⅛ teaspoon nutmeg
3 tablespoons sugar

MERINGUE TOPPING
1 egg white
Pinch salt
2 tablespoons sugar

Mix the warm rice with the remaining ingredients, stirring gently but thoroughly. Spoon into 8 custard cups. Bake in a hot-water bath in a 350° oven for about 25 minutes, until the center is almost firm.

Meringue Topping. Beat the egg white with salt until frothy. Gradually add the sugar and continue beating until a stiff, glossy peak forms.

Drop the meringue in fluffs on top of puddings and bake again just until light brown. Serve warm. Serves 8.

RICE PUDDING I

⅓ cup rice
1 quart milk
Pinch salt
⅓ cup sugar
¾ cup raisins
1 teaspoon vanilla
½ cup heavy cream

Put the rice in a 1½-quart baking dish with the milk, salt, sugar, raisins, and vanilla. Bake in a 275° oven for 2 hours, stirring occasionally. Add the cream, raise the heat to 350°, and bake ½ hour longer, until the top is golden. Serves 4–6.

RICE PUDDING II

2¼ cups milk
½ cup sugar
Pinch salt
1 egg
1⅔ cups cooked rice
⅓ cup raisins
1 teaspoon vanilla
½ teaspoon grated lemon rind

Mix the milk with the sugar and salt. Stir in the slightly beaten egg, rice, raisins, vanilla, and lemon rind. Pour into a greased 1½-quart baking dish. Set dish in a hot-water bath and bake in a 350° oven for 1–1¼ hours, stirring twice during the last ½ hour of baking. Serves 6.

ORANGE RICE RING

1 cup rice
¾ cup sugar
1 cup orange juice
1½ tablespoons grated orange rind
3 eggs
½ cup heavy cream
1 teaspoon vanilla
Toasted almonds (garnish)
Sections 2 oranges (garnish)

Cook the rice in your favorite way until tender. When the rice is cooked and drained, mix with the sugar, orange juice, and orange rind. Heat gently until the rice has absorbed most of the liquid, stirring now and then. This takes about 15 minutes. Beat the eggs slightly and spoon a little hot rice into them. Then stir this into the remaining rice and heat for 2 minutes, stirring constantly. Do not boil. Cool for 1 hour. Whip the cream until a soft peak forms, add the vanilla, and fold into the cooled rice mixture. Pour into a 1-quart mold and chill until set. When ready to serve, unmold onto a serving platter. Top with toasted almonds and garnish with oranges. Serves 4.

GLAZED RASPBERRY CREAM RING

(Plate 22)

1 cup rice
1 envelope plus 2 teaspoons unflavored
  gelatin
½ cup sugar
3 cups milk
Pinch salt
1½ teaspoons vanilla
2 tablespoons kirsch
3 cups raspberries
1½ cups heavy cream
¾ cup red currant jelly

Cover the rice with water and bring to a boil. Cook gently for 5 minutes. Drain. Stir the gelatin into the sugar and then into the cold milk. Heat in a double boiler. Add the partially cooked rice, salt, and vanilla. Cover and cook over simmering water about ½ hour, until the rice is very tender. Stir once or twice. Not all the liquid will be absorbed. Remove from heat and mix in the kirsch. Cool. Press 1 cup raspberries through a strainer to remove the seeds. You should have about ⅔ cup purée. Whip the cream until it stands in a glossy peak. When the rice mixture is at room temperature, stir in the cream, whipped, and the purée. Turn into a 1½-quart mold, cover, and chill about 8 hours, until set. When about ready to serve, melt the currant jelly over low heat, cool slightly, and pour over the remaining berries. Loosen edges of the mold with a knife and carefully turn out on a large serving plate. Garnish with the glazed berries. Serves 8–10.

STRAWBERRY PINEAPPLE RICE
PUDDING
(Plate 18)

3 cups strawberries
⅓ cup sugar
15 large marshmallows
¼ cup glacéed cherries
1 cup crushed pineapple
½ teaspoon almond flavoring

1½ cups cooked rice, cooled
1 package lemon-flavored gelatin
½ cup finely chopped blanched almonds
1 cup heavy cream
Red food coloring (optional)
1 tablespoon cornstarch

Reserve a few whole berries and purée the rest. Add sugar to the purée and stir until dissolved. Cut the marshmallows and cherries into small pieces. Add ¾ cup purée, marshmallows, cherries, pineapple, and ¼ teaspoon almond flavoring to the rice. Dissolve the gelatin in 1 cup boiling water, add 1 cup cold water, and chill until almost set. Then whip to a foam. Add to rice mixture with chopped almonds. Whip the cream until thick and shiny, tinting with red food coloring if you like. Fold into rice mixture. Chill until thick, stirring occasionally. Spoon into a 2-quart mold and chill until firm. Mix the cornstarch with ¼ cup cold water. Heat the remaining strawberry purée, ½ cup water, and remaining almond flavoring. Add cornstarch and cook, stirring constantly, until clear and thickened. Add a little sugar if you wish. Add whole strawberries and chill. Unmold the chilled rice onto a serving plate and pour a little of the sauce over it. Pass the remaining sauce. Serves 8.

TAPIOCA PEACH PUDDING   (Plate 21)

2 tablespoons quick-cooking tapioca
¼ cup sugar
¼ cup brown sugar
⅛ teaspoon nutmeg
2 teaspoons lemon juice
4 cups sliced peaches (fresh, frozen, or drained canned)
1 tablespoon butter (optional)
6 small rounds white bread (optional)

Mix the tapioca, sugar, brown sugar, nutmeg, lemon juice, peaches, and butter. Turn into a 1½-quart shallow baking dish. Cover and bake in a 400° oven 25–30 minutes, until the peaches are soft. Stir once while baking. Take from the oven, remove cover, and cool. Butter the bread very lightly on each side and brown on both sides in a skillet. Cut each in half and press the curved edges into each serving of pudding, butterfly fashion. This is especially appropriate for a children's party. Serve each with a fluff of whipped cream if you wish. Serves 6.

TAPIOCA PUDDING

3 tablespoons quick-cooking tapioca
1 egg
⅓ cup sugar
⅛ teaspoon salt
2¾ cups milk
½–1 teaspoon vanilla
Cream (optional)

Mix the tapioca with the slightly beaten egg, sugar, salt, and milk in a saucepan. Stir and let stand a few minutes. Bring to a full boil while stirring. Remove from heat when slightly thickened, 6–7 minutes. Stir in the vanilla. Serve slightly warm or chill. Pass the cream if you wish. Serves 4.

APPLES WITH TAPIOCA

½ cup quick-cooking tapioca
Pinch salt
6–8 tart apples
¼ cup sugar
½ teaspoon cinnamon
¼ teaspoon nutmeg

Put the tapioca, 2½ cups boiling water, and salt in a double boiler and cook until transparent. Meanwhile, place the peeled, cored apples in a greased shallow 2-quart baking dish. Fill the centers with sugar mixed with cinnamon and nutmeg. Pour the tapioca over the apples and bake in a 350° oven until apples are tender. Serves 6–8.

CHERRY TAPIOCA PUDDING

¼ cup quick-cooking tapioca
½ cup sugar
¼ teaspoon salt
1 (1 lb.) can pitted tart red cherries
¾ teaspoon almond flavoring
2 teaspoons lemon juice
Heavy cream (optional)

Mix the tapioca, sugar, and salt in a saucepan. Mix the liquid from the cherries with enough water to make 2½ cups; add to the tapioca mixture and let stand 5 minutes. Cook, stirring frequently, until it comes to a full boil. Cool and stir in the cherries, almond flavoring, and lemon juice. Pour into sherbet glasses and chill. Serve with cream if you wish. Serves 6.

STRAWBERRY TAPIOCA PUDDING

*1 quart strawberries or 3 packages frozen
   sliced strawberries*
1 cup sugar
¼ cup quick-cooking tapioca
½ teaspoon salt
½ cup heavy cream

Hull and slice the fresh strawberries, sprinkle with the sugar, and let stand for ½ hour. (If using frozen strawberries, thaw and do not add sugar.) Drain and measure the juice; add enough water to make 3 cups. Cook the juice, tapioca, and salt over medium heat until the mixture comes to a boil. Cool, stirring occasionally. Fold in the strawberries and chill. Spoon half of the mixture into parfait glasses. Whip the cream, fold into remaining strawberry mixture, and spoon lightly into parfait glasses. Serves 6–8.

APPLE BROWN BETTY

4 slices dry bread
¼ cup melted butter
4–6 apples (1½ pounds)
⅔ cup dark brown sugar
¼ teaspoon nutmeg
¼ teaspoon cinnamon
1 tablespoon lemon juice
Heavy cream or Hard Sauce* (optional)

Cut the dry bread into very small cubes. Toss together with the melted butter. Put ⅓ of these cubes in the bottom of a shallow 1½-quart baking dish. Cover with half the apples which have been peeled, cored, and sliced and half of the other ingredients. Repeat and top with the last of the bread cubes and ¼ cup water. Bake in a 375° oven for 40 minutes, until apples are tender. Serve with cream or Hard Sauce if you wish. Serves 4–6.

APPLE PUDDING

5–6 tart apples
¼ cup sugar
½ teaspoon cinnamon
¼ teaspoon nutmeg
2 tablespoons butter

BATTER
1 egg
½ cup sugar
2 tablespoons melted butter

⅓ cup flour
1 teaspoon baking powder
Pinch salt

Peel, core, and slice the apples and arrange in a 1½-quart casserole. Sprinkle with a mixture of the sugar, cinnamon, and nutmeg. Dot with butter and pour ¼ cup hot water over all.

Batter. Beat the egg; add the sugar gradually, beating until thick. Stir in the melted butter. Sift the flour, baking powder, and salt together and fold into the egg mixture.

Spread the batter over the apples. Bake ½ hour in a 375° oven, reduce heat to 350°, and bake 10 minutes more. Serve hot. Very good with Lemon Sauce* or heavy cream. Serves 4–6.

APPLE LEMON PUDDING

2½ cups peeled, cored, sliced apples
2 tablespoons butter
½ plus ⅓ cup sugar
¼ cup sour cream
4 eggs
1 tablespoon flour
1 tablespoon grated lemon rind
1½ tablespoons lemon juice
¼ teaspoon salt
1 teaspoon cinnamon
½ cup crushed cornflakes
½ cup grated blanched almonds
Cream, Sweetened Whipped Cream, or ice
   cream (optional)*

Cook the apples with butter in a covered skillet over low heat until tender. Beat ½ cup sugar, sour cream, egg yolks, flour, and lemon rind and juice together. Add to apples and cook over low heat until mixture thickens, stirring constantly. Remove from heat and cool. Beat the egg whites with salt until a soft peak forms. Fold into apple mixture. Combine the remaining sugar with cinnamon, cornflakes, and almonds. Spread about ⅔ of this mixture on the bottom of a greased 8×8×2-inch pan. Pour in the apple mixture and sprinkle remaining crumbs over the top. Bake in a 325° oven for about 45 minutes. Serve warm with cream, Sweetened Whipped Cream, or ice cream if you wish. Serves 6.

APPLE PECAN PUDDING

2 eggs
1½ cups sugar
6 tablespoons flour
2½ teaspoons baking powder
1 teaspoon vanilla
Pinch salt
1 cup peeled, cored, finely chopped tart
apples
1 cup broken pecan meats
Whipped cream (optional)

Beat the eggs until very thick. Fold in the sugar, flour, baking powder, vanilla, and salt. Stir in the apples and nuts. Mix thoroughly and pour into a well-buttered 8×8×2-inch pan. Bake in a 325° oven for 45 minutes, until top is brown and crusty. Serve warm with whipped cream if you wish. Serves 6.

APPLE FRITTERS

4 large apples
⅓ cup lemon juice
¼ cup sugar
1 cup flour
¼ teaspoon salt
¾ cup milk
1 tablespoon melted butter
2 eggs

Peel, core, and cut the apples into ¼-inch rounds. Marinate for 15 minutes in a mixture of the lemon juice and sugar. Meanwhile, make a thin batter by mixing the flour with the salt, milk, melted butter, and egg yolks. Stir in the lightly beaten egg whites. Dip the apples into batter and fry in melted shortening or cooking oil until golden brown and apples are tender. Good served with Hard Sauce.* Serves 6.

YANKEE APPLE JOHN

6–7 tart apples
¾ cup sugar
¾ teaspoon cinnamon
1 teaspoon nutmeg
2 tablespoons butter
2 cups flour
½ teaspoon salt
1 tablespoon baking powder
½ cup shortening
⅔ cup milk

Peel, core, and slice the apples thin. Arrange them in the bottom of a 13×9½×2-inch baking dish. Mix the sugar with the cinnamon and nutmeg. Sprinkle over the apples. Dot with butter. Sift the flour with salt and baking powder. Cut the shortening into the dry ingredients. Add the milk all at once. Mix with a fork just enough to blend the ingredients. Knead lightly for 1 minute on a slightly floured board. Roll out to fit the baking dish and cut gashes in the dough to allow steam to escape. Fit the dough over the apples and brush the top with milk. Bake in a 425° oven for 25 minutes. Reduce the heat to 350° and bake 20 minutes more. Serve warm with or without cream, Nutmeg Sauce,* or Hard Sauce.* Serves 6.

APPLE CRISP

6–8 apples
2 tablespoons lemon juice
¾ cup flour
1 cup brown sugar
1 teaspoon cinnamon
½ cup butter

Peel, core, and slice the apples. Put them in a shallow 2-quart baking dish and add ⅛–½ cup water; the amount will depend upon how juicy the apples are. Add the lemon juice. Mix the flour, sugar, and cinnamon. Cut the butter into the dry ingredients with a pastry blender or 2 knives until crumbly. Sprinkle over the apples. Bake in a 375° oven 30–40 minutes, until apples are tender and top is golden. Serves 4–6.

APPLE CRISP PUDDING I

6 tart apples
1 cup graham-cracker crumbs
1½ cups dark brown sugar
1 teaspoon cinnamon
½ teaspoon nutmeg
¼ cup butter
1 cup heavy cream (optional)

Peel and core the apples and slice ½ inch thick. Mix the crumbs, sugar, and spices. Add 1 cup of crumb mixture to the apples. Place in a buttered 2-quart casserole. Top with remaining crumbs and dot with butter. Bake in a 350° oven for about 1 hour, until apples are tender. Serve with whipped cream if you wish. Serves 6.

APPLE CRISP PUDDING II

1 cup graham-cracker crumbs
1 tablespoon flour
1 cup chopped nuts
1 cup light brown sugar
¼ cup sugar
1 tablespoon grated orange rind
Pinch salt
½ teaspoon cinnamon
½ teaspoon nutmeg
½ cup melted butter
4 large tart apples
Juice 1 lemon
Heavy cream

Mix the crumbs, flour, nuts, and the sugars together. Season with orange rind, salt, cinnamon, and nutmeg. Moisten with melted butter. Cover the bottom of a lightly buttered 9×9×2-inch baking dish with a layer of peeled, cored, sliced apples. Scatter some of the crumb mixture over the top and sprinkle with lemon juice. Repeat, ending with crumbs. Bake in a 350° oven for 45 minutes. Serve warm and pass the cream. Serves 6.

APPLES BAKED IN CUSTARD SAUCE

4 firm apples (Rome Beauty or Golden
    Delicious)
2 cups sugar
½ teaspoon vanilla
CUSTARD CREAM SAUCE
⅓ cup flour
¾ cup sugar
Pinch salt
2 eggs
2 cups light cream
1½ teaspoons vanilla

½ cup chopped toasted blanched almonds

Peel and core the apples and cut in half lengthwise. Put 3 cups water, the sugar, and vanilla in a skillet. Bring to a boil. Lay the apples in the syrup and cook uncovered for 10 minutes, until just tender but still firm. Lift out apples carefully and place side by side in a greased 13×9½×2-inch baking dish.

Custard Cream Sauce. Mix the flour with sugar and salt. Add the well-beaten eggs to the cream and beat together. Then beat this cream mixture into the dry ingredients gradually. Cook in a double boiler, stirring constantly,

until the mixture is thick and smooth. Add the vanilla.

Pour the sauce over the apples. Sprinkle with almonds and bake in a 350° oven for 20 minutes. Serve hot. Serves 8.

APPLE BLUEBERRY CRISP

3 cups peeled, cored, sliced apples
2 cups thawed and drained frozen blueberries
5 tablespoons brown sugar
1 cup plus 2 tablespoons flour
¾ cup sugar
1 teaspoon baking powder
½ teaspoon salt
½ teaspoon cinnamon
1 egg
½ cup melted butter
Cream

Put the apples in a greased 1½-quart baking dish or casserole. Add the blueberries. Mix the brown sugar with 2 tablespoons flour and sprinkle over the fruit. Sift the sugar, baking powder, salt, cinnamon, and remaining cup of flour together. Add the egg and mix with a fork until crumbly. Sprinkle the mixture over the fruit; do not pat it down. Pour the melted butter evenly over the top. Bake in a 350° oven for about 1 hour, until the top is golden brown and the apples are tender. Serve warm with cream. Serves 6–8.

APPLE COBBLER PUDDING

4 apples
3 tablespoons butter
½ cup raisins
½ cup coarsely chopped nuts
½ cup dark brown sugar
¾ cup flour
1 teaspoon baking powder
Pinch salt
2 eggs
½ cup sugar

Peel and core the apples and cut into eighths. Melt the butter in a skillet and add the apples, raisins, nuts, and brown sugar. Stir until the sugar is dissolved. Pour into a greased 9×5× 2¾-inch loaf pan. Sift the flour, baking powder, and salt together. Beat the egg yolks until light and stir in the sugar and 3 tablespoons water. Stir into the flour. Beat the egg whites until a soft peak forms and fold into the batter. Pour the batter over the apples and bake in a 325° oven for about 40 minutes. Good served with Custard Sauce* or heavy cream. Serves 6–8.

APPLE COBBLER

1 egg
1 cup sugar
½ teaspoon grated lemon rind
1 teaspoon vanilla
1 cup flour
1 teaspoon baking powder
½ teaspoon salt
¼ cup milk
¼ cup melted butter
3 cups peeled, cored, thinly sliced apples
1 tablespoon lemon juice
1 teaspoon cinnamon (optional)
Dash nutmeg (optional)
1 cup sour cream or heavy cream, plain or whipped (optional)

Beat the egg well and add ½ cup sugar gradually, beating well after each addition. Add lemon rind and vanilla. Sift the flour with baking powder and salt. Add to egg mixture alternately with the milk. Next add the melted butter and pour into a greased and floured 9-inch cake pan, spreading evenly. Sprinkle the sliced apples with lemon juice and arrange on top of batter. Sprinkle the top with remaining sugar, and the cinnamon and nutmeg if you wish. Bake in a 350° oven for 1 hour and 10 minutes, until cake is golden brown and pulls away from the sides of the pan. Cool in the pan for 20 minutes. Serve warm with cream if you wish. Serves 6.

CHERRY COBBLER I

2 (1 lb.) cans pitted tart red cherries
1⅔ cups sugar
6 tablespoons quick-cooking tapioca
¼ cup butter
⅜ teaspoon salt
2 eggs
¼ teaspoon cream of tartar
½ cup cake flour

Put the cherries with their juice in a saucepan and add 1⅓ cups sugar, the tapioca, butter, and ⅛ teaspoon salt. Stir until well blended, bring to a boil, and cook 5 minutes, stirring constantly. Pour into an 8×8×2-inch

pan. Beat the egg yolks until thick. Gradually add the remaining sugar, beating well after each addition. Add remaining salt to egg whites and beat until foamy. Put in the cream of tartar and beat until a soft peak forms. Fold the whites into the sugar-yolk mixture. Then fold in the flour lightly. Pour evenly over the hot cherry mixture and bake in a 350° oven 35–40 minutes, until done. Serve warm. Serves 6–8.

CHERRY COBBLER II

3 (1 lb.) cans pitted tart red cherries
1 cup sugar
¼ cup cornstarch
½ teaspoon salt
Red food coloring (optional)
1 tablespoon butter
1 teaspoon vanilla
½ teaspoon almond flavoring

TOPPING
1 cup cake flour
2 tablespoons confectioners' sugar
1 tablespoon sugar
1 tablespoon grated lemon rind
1 teaspoon baking powder
¼ teaspoon salt
6 tablespoons butter
¼ cup evaporated milk

Drain the cherries, reserving 1 cup liquid. (You will need about 1 quart cherries.) Mix the sugar, cornstarch, and salt together. Combine with the cherry liquid and a few drops red coloring. Cook, stirring constantly, until thick and clear. Add the butter, vanilla, almond flavoring, and the cherries. Cook slowly, stirring occasionally, for 15 minutes. Pour into a 1½-quart casserole.

Topping. Mix together the flour, sugars, lemon rind, baking powder, and salt. Cut in the butter until the mixture is like coarse meal. Blend in the evaporated milk with a fork. Turn onto a floured board and roll ¼ inch thick. Cut circles with a biscuit cutter.

Arrange the circles on the cherries. Bake in a 450° oven for 15 minutes, until golden brown. Serves 6.

BLUEBERRY COBBLER

Use 2 cups fresh or frozen blueberries and proceed as for Apple Cobbler.*

PEACH OR NECTARINE COBBLER

Use 3 cups sliced, peeled fresh nectarines or peaches or 3 packages frozen peaches in place of the apples and proceed as for Apple Cobbler.* If frozen peaches are used, drain thoroughly.

PEAR AND APRICOT CRISP

*3 large pears or 1 (1 lb. 12 oz.) can pear
  halves
1 (1 lb. 14 oz.) can apricot halves
¼ cup orange juice
1 cup crushed cornflakes
1 cup sugar
½ cup melted butter
½ teaspoon grated orange rind*

If using fresh pears, peel and core them and cut into eighths. Drain and slice the canned pears and apricots. Arrange the fruit in the bottom of a 9×9×2-inch baking dish. Pour the orange juice over the fruit. Toss the cornflakes, sugar, melted butter, and orange rind together until well blended. Sprinkle over the fruit and bake in a 350° oven for 30–40 minutes, until the topping is golden. Serves 6.

BAKED PEACH DESSERT

*3 tablespoons butter
1 cup sugar
2 eggs
1 cup flour
⅛ teaspoon salt
1 tablespoon baking powder
½ teaspoon vanilla
6 peaches sliced or 4 packages frozen
1 pint vanilla ice cream or Sweetened
  Whipped Cream**

Cream the butter; then add sugar gradually and the eggs. This should not be beaten, just mixed until blended. Stir in the flour which has been sifted with salt and baking powder; then add the vanilla. Place the peach slices in the bottom of a buttered 1½-quart casserole. (If using frozen peaches, thaw and drain them thoroughly.) Pour the batter over them and bake in a 350° oven for 1 hour. Serve with vanilla ice cream or with almond-flavored Sweetened Whipped Cream. Serves 6.

PEACH CRISP

*½ cup dark brown sugar
1 cup graham-cracker crumbs
2 tablespoons melted butter
1 tablespoon lemon juice
2 cups drained sliced peaches (fresh, frozen,
  or canned)
Light cream*

Combine the sugar, cracker crumbs, melted butter, and lemon juice. Blend this gently with the peaches. Place in a greased shallow baking dish, about 6½×10×2 inches. Bake in a 350° oven for 25 minutes. Serve with light cream. Serves 6.

RAISIN PUDDING

*3 tablespoons butter
½ cup sugar
½ cup milk
1 cup flour
½ teaspoon baking soda
½ teaspoon nutmeg
¼ teaspoon salt
½ cup raisins
¼ cup chopped walnuts
1 teaspoon vanilla
1 cup dark brown sugar
Cream*

Cream 1 tablespoon butter with the sugar. Add the milk. Sift the dry ingredients together and blend into the creamed mixture. Then add the raisins, walnuts, and vanilla. Spread in the bottom of a 1½-quart casserole. Mix the brown sugar with the remaining butter and 2 cups boiling water in a saucepan. Stir over medium heat until dissolved. Pour carefully over the top of the batter and bake for ½ hour in a 375° oven. Spoon into serving dishes and serve warm with cream. Serves 4.

GRAHAM-CRACKER WALNUT PUDDING

*3 eggs
2 cups graham-cracker crumbs
1½ cups sugar
1 teaspoon baking powder
2 teaspoons vanilla
1 cup finely chopped walnuts
Heavy cream or Custard Sauce* (optional)*

Beat the egg yolks with ¼ cup cold water until frothy. In a separate bowl mix the crumbs, sugar, and baking powder. Add to the egg yolks and flavor with vanilla. Beat the egg whites until stiff and fold into the mixture along with the nuts. Spoon pudding into a buttered 1½-quart casserole and bake in a 325° oven for 45 minutes. Serve warm with cream or Custard Sauce if you wish. Serves 6.

INDIAN PUDDING I

⅓ cup yellow corn meal
1 quart milk
½ cup dark molasses
½ teaspoon salt
½ teaspoon cinnamon
2½ teaspoon nutmeg
1 egg
Ice cream, cream, or maple syrup

Mix the corn meal with ⅓ cup cold water. Scald the milk. Add the corn meal and cook in a double boiler for 25 minutes, until thickened, stirring occasionally. Add the molasses, salt, cinnamon, nutmeg, and the beaten egg. Turn into a 1½-quart baking dish. Bake in a 325° oven for 45 minutes. Serve with ice cream, cream, or maple syrup. Serves 6–8.

INDIAN PUDDING II

1 quart plus 1 cup milk
⅓ cup corn meal
1 cup dark molasses
¼ cup butter
1 teaspoon salt
1 teaspoon ginger
1 egg
Cream or vanilla ice cream

Scald 1 quart milk in a double boiler; then stir in the corn meal and cook 15 minutes. Stir in the molasses and cook 5 minutes longer. Remove from heat and add the butter, salt, ginger, and the beaten egg. Pour the batter into a greased 2-quart baking dish and pour the remaining milk over it. Bake in a 300° oven for 1½–2 hours. Serve with cream or vanilla ice cream. Serves 8.

MERINGUE FOR FRUIT

6 egg whites
¼ teaspoon salt
2 cups sugar
2 teaspoons vanilla
2 teaspoons lemon juice

Beat the egg whites with the salt until a peak forms. Add 1 cup sugar a tablespoon at a time, beating well after each addition. Add the vanilla and another cup of sugar gradually, alternating with the lemon juice. Beat until the sugar is dissolved and the meringue stiff and glossy. Put the meringue into a well-greased and floured 9- or 10-inch pie plate. Spread it higher in the middle than around the edges; it should look like a dome. Bake 1½ hours in a 275° oven and then for ½ hour at 300°. Don't worry if it puffs and cracks. Cool at room temperature. As it cools, the center will sink somewhat. Good filled with berries, sliced peaches, or other fruit and, if you wish, with Sweetened Whipped Cream.* Serves 8.

MERINGUE MACAROON RING WITH FRUIT

5 egg whites
½ teaspoon cream of tartar
⅛ teaspoon salt
1¼ cups sugar
1 cup crumbled day-old macaroons
2 cups heavy cream
Frozen strawberries or cut-up fresh fruit

Cut brown paper to fit a 15½×12-inch baking sheet. Draw one circle 8¾-inches in diameter and a 5½-inch circle inside. (If you have kitchen bowls the right size, use them for marking.) Brush the paper with cooking oil. Beat the egg whites with the cream of tartar and salt until a soft peak forms. Add the sugar 2 tablespoons at a time, beating well after each addition. Continue beating 15–20 minutes, until the sugar dissolves and the mixture becomes very stiff and glossy. Using a spoon and spatula, arrange the meringue between the circles on the brown paper. Pile the mixture high, keeping the sides as straight as possible (about 1½ inches high). Bake in a 250° oven for about 2 hours, until crisp to the touch. Cut away the meringue from the brown paper with a sharp knife or broad spatula. Cool on a rack. Add the crumbled macaroons to the cream and let stand for about 1 hour. Then beat the mixture until very thick. Just before serving, place the meringue on a large serving plate and coat the outside generously with the macaroon-cream mixture. Fill the center with strawberries or cut-up fresh fruit. Decorate the base of the ring with fruit. Serves 8.

APRICOT CHARLOTTE

1 (1 lb. 14 oz.) can apricots
2 envelopes unflavored gelatin
2 cups heavy cream
½ cup superfine sugar
Grated rind ½ lemon
About 2 dozen ladyfingers or Spongecake*

Drain the apricots, remove pits, and reserve ½ cup syrup. Purée apricots; you should have 1 cup. Stir the gelatin into the syrup and 1 cup water. Heat until dissolved. Remove from heat and cool until mixture is slightly thickened. Add the puréed apricots and beat until light and frothy. Whip the cream with sugar and lemon rind until a soft peak forms and fold into the apricot mixture. Chill until a spoonful mounds. Line a 10-inch spring-form mold with halves of ladyfingers, rounded side out, or with strips of Spongecake. Fill the mold with the apricot mixture and refrigerate until firm. Unmold to serve. Serves 8–10.

BANANA SUPREME

2 bananas
¼ cup butter
1 teaspoon vanilla
1 tablespoon lemon juice
2 teaspoons grated lemon rind
⅔ cup confectioners' sugar
4 (½ inch) slices poundcake
Whipped cream

Mash the bananas with softened butter. Add vanilla, lemon juice, and lemon rind. Mix in the sugar. Put the 4 slices of cake in a baking pan and spread with the banana mixture. Place under preheated broiler until mixture becomes golden brown. Serve hot or cool, topped with whipped cream. Serves 4.

CUSTARD COTTAGE PUDDING
WITH BANANA (*Plate 21*)

2 cups milk
2 teaspoons cornstarch
¼ cup sugar
Pinch salt
1 egg
2-inch strip lemon peel
16 (1 inch) squares day-old white cake
2 small bananas

Scald the milk. Combine the cornstarch, sugar, and salt and stir into the egg. Gradually add the hot milk, stirring until smooth. Add the lemon peel and cook in a heavy saucepan over low heat, stirring constantly, about 10 minutes, until mixture coats a spoon; do not boil. Cool and remove peel. Divide the cake among 4 dishes. Slice half a banana into each dish and cover with sauce. Garnish with gumdrops if you wish. Serves 4.

BLUEBERRY COTTAGE PUDDING
(*Plate 21*)

¼ cup butter
1 cup sugar
1 egg plus 1 egg white
2 cups flour
2½ teaspoons baking powder
½ teaspoon salt
⅔ cup milk
1 teaspoon vanilla
3½ cups blueberries or 2 packages
  unsweetened frozen
Lemon Sauce* or heavy cream

Cream the butter with the sugar. Add the egg and egg white and beat well. Sift the flour, baking powder, and salt together. Add alternately to the creamed mixture with the milk and vanilla. Fold in the berries very gently and turn into a greased 2-quart baking dish. Bake in a 350° oven for 50–60 minutes; the time will depend upon the depth of the dish. Cut into squares and serve while still warm. Serve with Lemon Sauce or cream. Serves 6–8.

COCOA MERINGUE

5 egg whites
1 cup sugar
2 tablespoons cocoa
1 teaspoon vanilla
Pinch salt
Sweetened Whipped Cream* (optional)

Beat the egg whites until a peak forms. Sift the sugar and cocoa together and add to egg whites a tablespoon at a time, beating constantly. Add vanilla and salt and continue beating until mixture holds a stiff peak. Spoon into a buttered 1½-quart ring mold or soufflé dish. Fill carefully to eliminate large air bubbles. Place in a baking pan half full of warm water and bake in a 350° oven for ½ hour. Turn out of the mold or serve in the soufflé dish immediately. Serve with the Sweetened Whipped Cream if you wish. Serves 6.

ENGLISH TRIFLE

CAKE

½ cup butter
1 cup sugar
1 egg plus 5 egg yolks
1¾ cups cake flour
2½ teaspoons baking powder
¼ teaspoon salt
½ cup milk
½ teaspoon vanilla

CUSTARD SAUCE

1 quart milk
2 tablespoons cornstarch
1 cup sugar
½ teaspoon salt
8 egg yolks
2 teaspoons vanilla

Sherry
Whipped cream (garnish)
Currant jelly (garnish)

Cake. Cream the butter and sugar, adding the sugar a little at a time. When smooth and creamy, add the egg and yolks which have been beaten until thick and lemon-colored. Sift the cake flour, baking powder, and salt together. Add alternately with the milk to the first mixture. Flavor with vanilla and turn into a greased and floured 9×9×2-inch pan. Bake in a 350° oven for ½ hour. Cool.

Custard Sauce. Scald the milk. Mix the cornstarch, sugar, and salt and add to the hot milk, stirring until smoothly blended. Cook for ½ hour in a double boiler. Add the beaten egg yolks. Cook a few minutes, stirring constantly, until thickened. Add the vanilla. Chill. Both the cake and custard may be made a day in advance.

To serve, cut the cake into 2-inch squares. Split the squares in half and pour some sherry on each piece. Arrange the cake and custard in a serving dish and chill several hours. Top with whipped cream and dabs of currant jelly. Serves 12.

TRADITIONAL TRIFLE

CAKE

3 eggs
¾ cup sugar
½ teaspoon vanilla
⅛ teaspoon salt
¾ cup flour

FILLING

1 (1 lb. 14 oz.) can peeled whole apricots
1 (11 oz.) can mandarin oranges
½ cup Marsala or sweet sherry
1 (1 lb.) can pineapple chunks

CUSTARD

1½ cups milk
¼ cup cornstarch
2 tablespoons sugar
3 eggs
1 cup crumbled day-old macaroons

GARNISH (optional)

2½ cups heavy cream
½ cup sugar
½ teaspoon vanilla

Cake. Make the cake the day before. Beat the eggs, sugar, vanilla, and salt together until thick and lemon-colored and the consistency of mayonnaise. Fold in the flour. Pour into an 8×8×2-inch pan lined on the bottom with waxed paper. Bake in a 350° oven for about 45 minutes, until surface is lightly browned. Turn out on a rack, remove waxed paper, and cool. The resulting cake will be a spongy porous one.

Filling. Drain the syrup from the apricots. Remove pits and buzz the apricots in a blender or purée in a food mill. Cut the cake into 2 layers, spread half the apricot purée between the layers and assemble the cake again. Cut into pieces 2 inches long and 1 inch wide. Place in the bottom of a 2½-quart serving dish. Drain the oranges. Pour the Marsala or sherry, mixed with a little syrup from the oranges, over the cake. Spread the remaining purée on top. Drain the pineapple. Arrange orange sections and pineapple to form the next layer.

Custard. Mix 2 tablespoons of the milk with the cornstarch to make a paste; combine with the remaining milk and sugar in a double boiler. Cook, stirring constantly, until thickened. Remove from heat, add the slightly beaten eggs, and beat well. Cook and stir over just simmering water for 10 minutes. Add the macaroons and let soak until soft. Beat until macaroons dissolve. Cool.

Pour the custard over the fruit and refrigerate for about an hour. Whip the cream with sugar and vanilla until thick and glossy. Cover the custard with the whipped cream. You may omit the cream or whip half the quantity as a garnish. Serves 8–10.

CHARLOTTE RUSSE

24 ladyfingers or strips of Genoise*
2–3 tablespoons sherry (optional)
5–6 cups Sweetened Whipped Cream*
* or Bavarian**

Line a 7-inch spring-form mold with the ladyfingers or strips of Genoise. Lightly sprinkle with the sherry if you wish. Fill the mold with the Sweetened Whipped Cream or Bavarian, piling it up in the center. Chill well. Carefuly remove the mold just before serving. Serves 6.

COEUR A LA CREME I

3 (8 oz.) packages cream cheese
2 pounds creamed cottage cheese
Strawberries or other berries
Confectioners' sugar

Allow the cream cheese and cottage cheese to stand at room temperature until softened. Press both cheeses through a sieve together. Cut a piece of cheesecloth to fit a 9-inch spring-form cake pan or 2-quart mold, a heart-shaped mold or basket if available. Dip the cheesecloth in cold water, wring out the excess moisture, and fit the cheesecloth into the mold. Fill with the cheese mixture, press gently, and fold the edges of cheesecloth over the top of the mold. Refrigerate overnight. Unmold on a serving platter and remove cheesecloth. Serve with berries and a bowl of confectioners' sugar. Serves 12–15.

COEUR A LA CREME II

2 (8 oz.) packages cream cheese
¼ cup heavy cream
2 tablespoons superfine sugar
½ teaspoon vanilla
Strawberries, raspberries, or strawberry or
* currant preserves*

Soften the cheese and mix it with the cream and sugar until smooth. Flavor with vanilla. Proceed as for Coeur à la Crème I,* using a 1-quart mold. Serve with berries or preserves. Serves 6.

COEUR A LA CREME III

2 (8 oz.) packages cream cheese
1 cup sour cream
Fresh fruit or Spicy Bing-Cherry Sauce*

Blend together the cream cheese and sour cream until very smooth and creamy. Proceed as for Coeur à la Crème I,* using a 1-quart mold. Serve with sugared fruit or topped with Spicy Bing-Cherry Sauce. Serves 6.

PEACH COEUR A LA CREME

2 envelopes unflavored gelatin
1 cup light cream
6 (3 oz.) packages cream cheese
2 cups heavy cream
1 cup sugar
1 package frozen sliced peaches
Red and yellow food coloring (optional)
Fresh or frozen sliced peaches (garnish)

Mix gelatin with ¼ cup cold water. Scald light cream; add softened gelatin and stir until dissolved. Cool. Soften the cream cheese. Beat until it is light. Slowly add the heavy cream, beating until mixture is very smooth. Add the sugar and the peaches, which have been thawed and buzzed in a blender or puréed through a food mill. Mix well. Combine both mixtures and stir in a little red and yellow food coloring for a peach color if you wish. Pour into a lightly oiled 1½-quart mold. Refrigerate several hours or overnight until set. Unmold and spoon sliced peaches over and around the mold. Serves 8–10.

CREAM PUDDING

1 envelope unflavored gelatin
1½ cups milk
½ cup sugar
⅛ teaspoon salt
2 eggs
1 teaspoon vanilla
1 cup heavy cream
Fruit sauce

Mix the gelatin with the milk. Add ¼ cup sugar and the salt and heat in a double boiler. Beat the egg yolks lightly. Stir the hot milk into the egg yolks; return to double boiler and cook until slightly thickened. Remove from heat and add the vanilla. Cool until mixture is slightly thick. Stir occasionally. Beat the egg whites until they stand in soft peaks; gradually beat in the remaining sugar. Fold the egg whites and the cream, whipped, into the cooled custard. Turn into a 1½-quart serving dish or individual dishes and chill thoroughly. Serve with any fruit sauce. Serves 6.

SYLLABUB

1 egg white
¼ cup confectioners' sugar
2 tablespoons crème de menthe or
½ teaspoon mint flavoring
1 cup heavy cream
Green food coloring

Beat the egg white until a stiff peak forms and fold in the sugar. Add the crème de menthe or mint flavoring. Fold in the cream, whipped. Add a few drops of food coloring if you wish. This rich dessert may also be used as a filling for horn pastry. Serves 4–6.

HONEY CREAM WITH ORANGES

3 eggs plus 3 yolks
1½ cups honey
2 cups heavy cream
8 oranges sectioned or 2 (11 oz.) cans
mandarin oranges

Beat the egg yolks until thick and lemon-colored. Add the honey gradually while beating. Pour mixture into a double boiler and cook over low heat for about 1¼ hours, until very thick. Stir with a wire whisk occasionally. Remove from heat and cool. Beat 3 egg whites stiff and fold in. Add the cream, whipped. Spoon into a serving bowl and chill for at least 5 hours. Serve with orange sections or mandarin orange sections. Serves 8–10.

Crème Brûlée

Crème Brûlée is one of the great party desserts; it is rich, caloric, and delicious—also pretty to look at. There are many versions, but all require fresh egg yolks and good cream. The brittle crust on top is the distinctive and the tricky part; the custard should be velvety smooth.

CREME BRULEE I

4 egg yolks
2 cups heavy cream
Pinch salt
1 teaspoon vanilla
½ cup brown sugar

Beat the egg yolks until lemon-colored. Heat the cream to boiling point and simmer 1 minute. Pour slowly over the egg yolks, stirring constantly. Return to heat and cook over water, stirring constantly, until just thickened. Add salt and vanilla. Pour into an 8-inch shallow ovenproof casserole, cover, and chill for 5–6 hours, or preferably overnight. Half an hour to an hour before serving, sift the brown sugar and sprinkle evenly ¼ inch deep over the custard. Work quickly so that the sugar remains on top. Place immediately under broiler, 6 inches away from high heat. Broil until the sugar melts. When sugar has melted evenly, remove at once. Leave the door open and watch carefully; the sugar should melt quickly and bubble a little but not burn. You may put the casserole in a pan of ice water or on cracked ice; however, if you work quickly and the sugar melts fast, you should have no difficulty keeping the crème cool and firm so that the sugar crust stays on top. Refrigerate until the crust hardens. Serves 6.

CREME BRULEE II

2 cups milk
2 cups heavy cream
6 eggs
½ cup sugar
Pinch salt
2 teaspoons vanilla
Brown sugar

Scald the milk and cream. Mix the slightly beaten eggs with the sugar and salt. Add the scalded milk and cream gradually to the eggs. Cook in a double boiler, stirring constantly, until the mixture thickens and coats a spoon. Remove from heat at once and add the vanilla. Chill and pour into a shallow 1½-quart casserole. Chill, uncovered, overnight. Proceed as for Crème Brûlée I.* Serves 8.

CREME BRULEE III

1 quart light cream
8 egg yolks
2 tablespoons sugar
½ teaspoon vanilla
Brown sugar

Scald the cream. Beat the egg yolks lightly with a whisk. While beating gently, stir in the warm cream. Add sugar and vanilla. Pour into a 1½-quart shallow ovenproof glass dish. Set in a large pan of hot water and bake in a 300° oven for 45 minutes, until the surface feels set when lightly touched. Remove from oven and bath and cool. Cover and chill overnight. Proceed as for Crème Brûlée I.* Serves 8.

PEACH OR GREENGAGE CREME BRULEE

2 (1 lb. 1 oz.) cans cling-peach halves or
  greengage plums
1½ quarts heavy cream
12 egg yolks
¾ cup sugar
½ cup strawberry or currant jelly
  (optional)
1½ cups light brown sugar

Drain the fruit and dry on paper toweling.
Heat the cream in a double boiler over just
simmering water. Beat the egg yolks and sugar
until light and thick. Add to the cream and
cook, stirring constantly, until mixture thickens
and coats a spoon. Remove from heat and continue to stir for a minute or two. Pour into a
bowl and chill. Stir from time to time. Arrange
peach halves cup side up or the plums in the
bottom of a shallow 3-quart casserole. If using peaches, put about 1 teaspoon jelly in
each if you wish. Pour the chilled cream mixture over the fruit and refrigerate overnight.
About 1 hour before serving, sprinkle the surface with the brown sugar; be sure the entire
surface is covered with a layer ¼ inch thick.
Place in a bed of crushed ice in a baking pan.
Broil 6–9 inches away from the heat with
the door open until the sugar melts and is bubbly; watch carefully. Remove at once and chill
again for about 15 minutes, until the crust
hardens. Serves 10–12.

RICH ALMOND CREAM

4 envelopes unflavored gelatin
2 quarts light cream
1⅓ cups sugar
2 cups light corn syrup
1 teaspoon salt
2 teaspoons almond flavoring
4 cups blanched almonds
Whipped cream (garnish)
Candied cherries (garnish)

Mix the gelatin with the cream. Add sugar
and scald. Add the corn syrup, salt, and almond flavoring. Refrigerate until mixture begins to thicken. Then add the almonds, chopped
fine. Pour into a steeple mold if you have one,
or any 4-quart mold or two 2-quart molds, and
chill until firm. Unmold by dipping in warm
water and turn out on a serving plate. Garnish
with whipped cream and bits of candied cherries if you wish. Serves 12–15.

FARINA CREAM PUDDING

1 quart milk
2 tablespoons plus 1 teaspoon farina
1 cup sugar
4 teaspoons unflavored gelatin
1 teaspoon vanilla
1 teaspoon grated lemon rind
1 cup heavy cream
Fruit sauce (optional)

Heat the milk in a large saucepan. Mix the
farina, sugar, and gelatin. Add to the milk,
stirring constantly, and cook for 10 minutes.
Cool until it begins to thicken; then flavor with
vanilla and lemon rind. Fold in the cream,
whipped, and pour into a 1½-quart mold.
Chill several hours until set. Unmold to serve.
This is good with any favorite fruit sauce; try
it with Orange Strawberry Sauce.* Serves 6–8.

SPICED COFFEE JELLY

3 cloves
1½ sticks cinnamon
6 cups hot very strong coffee
1 cup sugar
3 envelopes unflavored gelatin
¾ cup toasted shaved Brazil nuts
1 tablespoon minced preserved ginger

Add the cloves and cinnamon to the coffee.
Simmer 10 minutes and then strain. Add the
sugar and the gelatin that has been softened in
½ cup cold water. Stir until gelatin is dissolved. Chill until the jelly begins to set. (To
shave Brazil nuts, boil them for a few minutes;
then, while still warm, shave with a vegetable
peeler; toast after cutting.) Stir in the Brazil
nuts and ginger. Chill until very firm, break up
with a fork, and serve in a bowl. Good with
Custard Sauce* or whipped cream. Serves 8.

RED-WINE JELLY

2 envelopes unflavored gelatin
1 cup claret, sherry, or Madeira
1 tablespoon lemon juice
⅓ cup orange juice
About 1 cup sugar
Sour cream or whipped cream (optional)

Add the gelatin to 2 cups cold water; heat
and stir until the gelatin is dissolved. Add the
wine, lemon and orange juices, and sugar. If
using sweet sherry or Madeira, cut the amount

of sugar in half. Pour into a 1-quart ring mold. Chill until firm. Turn out and serve with sour or whipped cream if you wish. Serves 4.

CHERRY RED-WINE JELLY

Proceed as for Red-Wine Jelly,* omitting the orange juice and adding 2 cups pitted tart red cherries with their juice. Use a 1½-quart mold. Serves 6.

WHIPPED LIME JELLY
(Low Calorie)

2 envelopes low-calorie lime-flavored gelatin
1¼ cups noncaloric lemon-flavored gelatin
1 tablespoon lime juice
½ teaspoon grated lime rind
1 teaspoon sugar
1 egg white
Pinch salt

Dissolve the gelatin in 1 cup hot water. Stir in the soda, lime juice, rind, and sugar. Chill until mixture is syrupy. Beat until very fluffy, using a rotary or electric mixer. Fold in the egg white, beaten until stiff with the salt. Spoon into 4 dessert glasses and chill about 1 hour, until set. Serves 4 (18 calories per serving).

COFFEE JELLY
(Low Calorie)

1 envelope unflavored gelatin
1¾ cups cold strong coffee
6 cloves
½ stick cinnamon
1 teaspoon sugar
2 tablespoons brandy or 2 teaspoons brandy
    flavoring
½ teaspoon liquid noncaloric sweetener

WHIPPED MILK TOPPING
1 teaspoon lemon juice
½ cup nonfat powdered milk
2 tablespoons sugar
¼ teaspoon vanilla

Mix gelatin and cold coffee in a saucepan. Add cloves and cinnamon and heat, stirring until gelatin is dissolved. Add sugar and stir until dissolved. Cool. Remove cinnamon and cloves. Add brandy or flavoring and liquid sweetener. Pour into a 9×9×2-inch pan and chill until firm, about 2 hours.

Whipped Milk Topping. Mix together ⅓ cup ice water, the lemon juice, and powdered milk. Beat until a soft peak forms. Add sugar and vanilla; beat until stiff and glossy.

Cut gelatin into ½-inch cubes. Alternate gelatin and topping in 4 parfait glasses or serving dishes. Serves 4 (65 calories per serving).

PINEAPPLE MANDARIN MOLD
(Low Calorie) (*Plate 31*)

4 envelopes low-calorie lime gelatin
1 (1 lb.) can dietetic pineapple
2 tablespoons lime juice
2 cups yoghurt
Mandarin oranges, pineapple chunks, and
    mint (garnish)

Dissolve the gelatin in 2 cups hot water. Drain the pineapple and measure the liquid. Add water to make 1 cup. Add the lime juice and gelatin. Chill until syrupy. Fold in the yoghurt and beat smooth. Chop the pineapple fine and add. Stir, pour into a 1½-quart mold, and chill until set. Unmold on a platter and garnish if you wish with mandarin oranges, pineapple, and mint. Serves 8 (100 calories per serving without garnish).

PLUM MOLD

2 (1 lb. 14 oz.) cans greengage (or purple)
    plums
3 packages lemon-flavored gelatin
2 tablespoons lemon juice
½ cup flaked coconut

GARNISH (optional)
Berries
Pineapple slices
Sour cream
Grated orange rind
*Custard Sauce**

Drain the plums and reserve 2½ cups syrup. Dissolve the gelatin in 1 cup hot water and add the plum syrup. Chill until thick and syrupy. In the meantime, pit the plums and put through a food mill or strainer; you should have 2½ cups. Mix the plum purée with the thickened gelatin and add lemon juice and coconut. Mix thoroughly. Pour into a 1½-quart mold and chill overnight. Dip the mold in hot water to loosen before turning upside down on a serving dish. Surround the mold with berries and pineapple slices and serve with a bowl of sour cream sprinkled with grated orange rind, or with Custard Sauce if you wish. Serves 6.

ORANGE APRICOT GELATIN MOLD
(Plate 19)

4½ cups orange juice
⅓ cup sugar
3 envelopes unflavored gelatin
1¼ cups apricot nectar
Almond flavoring
2 egg whites
Drained pears, peaches, and/or apricots
  (pitted); seeded grapes; thawed or fresh
  berries

Heat 1 cup orange juice with the sugar and the gelatin in a saucepan. Stir until gelatin is dissolved. Add remaining orange juice and the apricot nectar. Add a few drops of almond flavoring. Chill until syrupy. Whip the egg whites until frothy and stir into the juices. Pour into a 1½-quart mold. Chill until firm, 5–6 hours or overnight. When ready to serve, unmold onto a serving dish and surround with the fruits of your choice. Serves 6.

COCONUT BAVARIAN WITH FRUIT

1½ envelopes unflavored gelatin
1¾ cups milk
½ cup sugar
Pinch salt
½ teaspoon almond flavoring
1 cup flaked coconut
1 cup heavy cream
Berries or peaches

Mix the gelatin with the milk; stir and heat to dissolve. Add the sugar, salt, almond flavoring, and flaked coconut. Cool until it begins to thicken. Whip the cream until a soft peak forms. Fold the cream into the coconut mixture. Spoon into a 1-quart mold and chill overnight. Turn out and serve with sugared fruit. Serves 6.

BAVARIAN-CREAM MOLD WITH FRUIT

2 envelopes unflavored gelatin
2½ cups milk
¾ cup sugar
¼ teaspoon salt
1½ teaspoons vanilla
8 day-old macaroons
1 cup heavy cream
Fresh or frozen strawberries, other berries,
  or sliced peaches

Mix the gelatin with ¼ cup cold water. Scald the milk and add the sugar and salt. Stir the gelatin into this mixture until dissolved. Chill. When it begins to thicken, flavor with the vanilla. Beat with a rotary beater until fluffy. Fold in the macaroons, crumbled, and the cream, whipped until stiff. Put into a 1½-quart ring mold and chill. Serve with fruit in the center and around the sides. Serves 6.

LEMON LIME BAVARIAN

2 packages lemon-lime-flavored gelatin
1 tablespoon lime juice
2 cups heavy cream
1 package frozen mixed fruit or berries

Empty the contents of the gelatin packages into a bowl. Add the lime juice and 1 cup very hot water and stir until the gelatin is dissolved. Add 1 cup cold water and chill until syrupy. Whip with a rotary beater until very fluffy. Carefully fold in the cream, whipped. Spoon the mixture into a 1½-quart mold and chill several hours, until set. Unmold and serve with mixed fruit or berries, thawed a little but still icy. Serves 6.

MAPLE ALMOND BAVARIAN

6 tablespoons sugar
1 cup maple syrup
3 egg whites
1½ cups heavy cream
1 teaspoon grated orange rind
1½ envelopes unflavored gelatin
¾ cup toasted blanched almonds, chopped
  fine
Toasted slivered almonds (garnish)
Orange sections (garnish)

Mix the sugar, maple syrup, and ½ cup water together. Cook to soft-ball stage (235°). Beat the egg whites until a soft peak forms. Pour the hot syrup gradually over the egg whites, beating constantly as syrup is added. Cool. Whip the cream and flavor with orange rind. Fold into the egg-white mixture. Mix the gelatin with 6 tablespoons water and heat until gelatin is dissolved. Cool to lukewarm and pour gradually into the maple cream. Fold together until mixed evenly. Stir in the chopped almonds and turn into a 1½-quart mold. Chill until firm. To serve, turn out on a platter and garnish with slivered almonds and orange sections. Serves 8.

Plate 21. Puddings especially appropriate for children—top to bottom: VANILLA PUDDING with ladyfingers, CUSTARD COTTAGE PUDDING WITH BANANA, CHOCOLATE PUDDING, BLUEBERRY COTTAGE PUDDING, TAPIOCA PEACH PUDDING.

Plate 22. GLAZED RASPBERRY CREAM RING decorated with fresh berries glazed with melted currant jelly.

ALMOND BAVARIAN

4 teaspoons unflavored gelatin
2½ cups milk
⅔ cup sugar
Pinch salt
½ cup finely ground toasted blanched
almonds
1 teaspoon almond flavoring
1 cup heavy cream
Chocolate Sauce* (optional)
Additional ground almonds (optional)

Sprinkle the gelatin on the milk and heat with the sugar and salt. When hot, add the almonds, cover, and remove from heat. Allow to stand for 15 minutes. Add the almond flavoring. Cool until it begins to thicken, then beat with rotary beater until fluffy. Fold in the cream, whipped, and spoon into a 5-cup ring mold. Chill. When firm, turn onto a deep platter. You may coat with Chocolate Sauce (or a sauce of your choice) and serve the rest of the sauce on the side. Sprinkle almonds over the top of the ring if you wish. Serves 8.

BUTTERSCOTCH BAVARIAN

1¾ cups light brown sugar
6 tablespoons butter
2 envelopes plus 1 teaspoon unflavored
gelatin
1 quart milk
1 cup heavy cream (optional)
½ cup coarsely chopped toasted walnuts
(optional)

Put the sugar and butter in a heavy saucepan and cook over low heat, stirring constantly. When butter has melted, turn heat up a little and watch carefully; it should not darken. Cook about 8 minutes. Put the gelatin in the milk; then heat and stir until the gelatin is dissolved. Add milk to the butterscotch and stir until the sugar is completely melted. Cool until it begins to thicken and beat with a rotary beater for about 5 minutes, until fluffy. If you wish, fold in the cream, whipped; this makes a smooth rich mixture but is not necessary. Transfer to the bowl in which it will be served and chill. Sprinkle with walnuts if you wish. Serves 6.

This dessert can be used as a filling in a baked pie shell or tarts. If you use it as a filling, be sure to spread it before it sets.

STRAWBERRY BAVARIAN

1 quart strawberries
2 envelopes unflavored gelatin
1 tablespoon lemon juice
3 tablespoons Cherry Heering
2 cups heavy cream

Force the hulled berries through a food mill or buzz in a blender and then strain. Soften the gelatin in ¼ cup cold water and add to the purée. Heat and stir until the gelatin is dissolved. Cool and add lemon juice and Cherry Heering. Chill, stirring occasionally, until thickened. Fold in the cream, whipped. You may put into a mold or serving bowl. Chill until set. Serves 6.

COFFEE CHIFFON

2 envelopes unflavored gelatin
2 cups milk
1 cup light cream
2 generous tablespoons instant coffee
5 eggs
1 cup sugar
½ teaspoon salt
Chopped pistachio nuts or grated chocolate
(garnish)
Whipped cream (optional)

Heat the gelatin, milk, cream, and coffee in a double boiler. Beat the egg yolks until thick and add ½ cup sugar slowly, beating after each addition. Add gradually to the hot coffee mixture and cook until custard coats a spoon. Remove from heat and chill until syrupy. Beat the egg whites with the salt until a soft peak forms. Gradually beat in the remaining sugar. Fold this into the custard and pour into a 2-quart mold. Chill until set. Unmold and sprinkle with the nuts or chocolate curls. Surround with fluffs of whipped cream if you wish. Serves 6–8.

COFFEE RUM DESSERT

1 cup heavy cream
1 tablespoon instant coffee
1 tablespoon rum
6 tablespoons confectioners' sugar
2 cups gingersnap and chocolate-wafer
crumbs

Whip the cream and fold in the instant coffee, rum, and sifted sugar. Layer into parfait or dessert dishes with a mixture of gingersnap and chocolate crumbs. Chill. Serves 4–6.

CHERRY WHIP

1 (1 lb.) can pitted tart red cherries
2 teaspoons unflavored gelatin
½ cup sugar
2 egg whites
Pinch salt

Heat the cherries to boiling point in a saucepan. Meanwhile, soften the gelatin in ¼ cup cold water. Add the sugar to cherries and stir until dissolved. Remove from heat. Drain, reserving the juice. Dissolve the gelatin in the hot juice. Chill until thickened. Beat the egg whites and salt until a soft peak forms and fold with the cherries into the thickened juice mixture. Pour into dishes. Chill. Serves 4.

LEMON CHIFFON WHIP

8 eggs
1¼ cups sugar
1 envelope unflavored gelatin
1 teaspoon grated lemon rind
6 tablespoons lemon juice
Pinch salt
Fresh fruit (optional)

Beat the egg yolks until thick and lemon-colored. Add the sugar slowly and continue to beat. Soften the gelatin in ¼ cup cold water and then dissolve it over hot water. Add the gelatin, lemon rind, and juice to the egg mixture. Chill, stirring occasionally, until it gets thick and syrupy. Beat the egg whites with the salt until a soft peak forms. Fold into the yolk mixture. Cover and chill overnight. This will not turn out but may be served in sherbets or a serving dish. Top with sugared fresh fruit if you wish. Serves 10–12.

ORANGE FLUFF

3 cups milk
6 tablespoons sugar
3 tablespoons cornstarch
1 tablespoon grated orange rind
3 eggs
1 teaspoon butter
½ teaspoon salt
½ teaspoon vanilla
2 seedless oranges (garnish)

Scald the milk in a double boiler. Mix ¼ cup sugar and the cornstarch together, add the grated orange rind, and mix in the egg yolks. Stir in ⅓ cup of the scalded milk and add

sugar mixture to the remaining hot milk. Cook about 10 minutes, stirring constantly, until smooth and thickened. Add the butter, salt, and vanilla. Cool in a pan of cold water. Peel and section the oranges and chill. When the custard has cooled, add 2 tablespoons sugar to the egg whites and beat until a soft peak forms. Gently fold into the custard and spoon into a serving bowl. Chill 1 hour. Garnish with orange sections. Serves 8.

LEMON CHIFFON RING

4 teaspoons unflavored gelatin
1 cup sugar
⅔ cup lemon juice
Pinch salt
6 eggs
2 tablespoons grated lemon rind
Seedless grapes
Fresh strawberries or other fruit
Whipped cream (optional)
Chopped mint (optional)

Mix the gelatin with ½ cup cold water. Meanwhile, mix ⅔ cup sugar with the lemon juice. Add the salt to the egg yolks and beat until thick and light. Add the lemon-juice mixture to the egg yolks, stirring constantly. Cook in a double boiler until mixture coats a spoon. Remove from heat, add the gelatin, and stir until dissolved. Add the grated lemon rind. Chill until it begins to thicken. Beat the egg whites until a soft peak forms and add remaining sugar a tablespoon at a time, beating well after each addition. Fold into the gelatin mixture. Pour into a 2-quart ring mold and chill until set. Unmold and fill the center with grapes and fresh strawberries or your favorite fruits. The ring may be frosted with whipped cream and garnished with mint if you wish. Serves 6–8.

PRUNE WHIP I

1 envelope unflavored gelatin
½ cup sugar
2 tablespoons lemon juice
½ teaspoon grated lemon rind
¾–1 cup prune purée
4 egg whites

Soften the gelatin a few minutes in ¼ cup cold water; add ¾ cup boiling water and stir until dissolved. Stir in the sugar, lemon juice, lemon rind, and prune purée. Chill until syrupy. Beat until frothy and fold in the stiffly beaten egg whites. Chill until set. Spoon into individual serving glasses or a dessert dish to serve. Serves 6–8.

PRUNE WHIP II

4 egg whites
½ teaspoon grated lemon rind
4 teaspoons lemon juice
⅔ cup sugar
1 cup sweetened puréed prunes

Combine the egg whites, lemon rind, and lemon juice with the sugar in a double boiler. Heat, beating steadily with a rotary beater, until the mixture fluffs up and holds its shape when you lift the beater out of the mixture. Fold in the prunes and cool. This is good served with cream or with Custard Sauce.* Serves 4.

STRAWBERRY WHIP MOLD

2 packages frozen strawberries
2 cups milk
2½ envelopes unflavored gelatin
¼ cup sugar
Juice 1 lemon
1 teaspoon orange flavoring
1½ cups heavy cream

While the berries are thawing, heat together the milk, gelatin, and sugar, stirring until the gelatin and sugar are dissolved. Remove from heat and cool. Save a few berries for garnish if you wish. Purée the remaining partially thawed berries or buzz in blender. Strain to remove seeds. When the milk mixture is cool, stir in the purée. Flavor with lemon juice and orange flavoring. Chill until mixture begins to thicken. Beat until fluffy. Fold in the cream, whipped, and chill until mixture thickens, stirring occasionally. Pour into a 2-quart mold and chill until firm. To serve, unmold on a platter and garnish with berries if you wish. Serves 8–10.

TANGERINE CREAM MOLD

2 cans frozen tangerine-juice concentrate
4 envelopes unflavored gelatin
¾ cup sugar
2 cups heavy cream
2 tablespoons orange liqueur—Curaçao, Cointreau, or Grand Marnier (optional)
Tangerine sections (garnish)

Mix the tangerine-juice concentrate with 4 cups cold water. Heat ½ cup water with the gelatin and the sugar until the sugar dissolves. Mix with the diluted tangerine juice. Chill until thick and syrupy. Whip the cream until a soft peak forms. Fold the cream into the tangerine mixture. Add the orange liqueur if you wish. Pour into a 2-quart mold and chill until firm. Unmold and garnish with tangerine sections. Serves 8.

RICH BLANCMANGE
(Cornstarch Pudding)

2 cups heavy cream
2 cups milk
6 tablespoons cornstarch
¼ teaspoon salt
⅔ cup sugar
2 teaspoons almond flavoring
Fruit (optional)

Scald the cream and 1 cup milk in a double boiler. Mix the cornstarch, salt, and sugar with the remaining milk until smooth. Combine with the cream and milk mixture and cook in double boiler over low heat for 10 minutes, stirring constantly, until thick and smooth. Cover and cook another 15 minutes, stirring occasionally. Remove from heat, add almond flavoring, and beat until creamy. Pour into a 1-quart mold or individual molds. Chill until firm, overnight if you wish. Unmold and serve garnished with berries or stewed fruit if you wish. Serves 6–8.

Peeling Chestnuts

To peel chestnuts, make a slit through the shell around each nut or cut an X through the shell in the convex side. Put in a saucepan with water to cover. Boil 1 minute, remove from heat, and peel while still hot, leaving the nuts in the water until peeled. Be sure to remove the inside skin as well as the shell. Another method is to slit the shells and put the nuts in a pan with a little water in a 500° oven for 8–10 minutes. Cool a little before removing shells and inner skin. It is always a tedious job to remove the chestnut skins; there is no short cut.

MONT BLANC

2 pounds chestnuts or 2 (1 lb.) cans
About ¾ cup sugar
2-inch piece vanilla bean
About 3 cups milk
Sweetened Whipped Cream*

Peel the chestnuts (see above). Simmer them, uncovered, with sugar and vanilla bean in milk to cover until very soft, about ½ hour. (If using canned chestnuts, drain and simmer, covered, in about 1½ cups milk for 15–20 minutes, stirring frequently. Canned are much less satisfactory.) Most of the milk will evaporate or be absorbed; drain if there is any moisture left. Remove vanilla bean and mash the chestnuts until smooth. Add more sugar and/or a little vanilla to taste. Rub through a coarse strainer, pushing with a wooden spoon, or put through a potato ricer or pastry tube with a very small hole. Pile onto the platter in a circle with the center empty, or let the purée fall into a greased ring mold and turn out onto the platter, which is more difficult to do. Chill. Fill the center with Sweetened Whipped Cream; pile the cream up to resemble a mountaintop. Serves 6.

CHESTNUT MOCHA LOG   *(Plate 20)*

1 (2 lb.) can water-pack whole chestnuts
½ cup butter
4 ounces unsweetened chocolate
½ cup sugar
2 teaspoons vanilla
¼ teaspoon cinnamon
Mocha Butter Frosting*
Leaves cut from angelica or lime rind
  (garnish)
Glacéed cherries (garnish)

Drain and purée the chestnuts by rubbing through a sieve. Melt the butter and chocolate in a double boiler. Remove from heat and add the sugar, ¼ cup water, vanilla, and cinnamon. Mix well. Add this mixture to the chestnut purée a little at a time, beating well after each addition. Make sure the mixture is thoroughly blended. Turn out onto waxed paper and chill slightly. Then roll into a log shape, approximately 12×3 inches. Wrap in waxed paper and chill about 4 hours, until quite solid. Unwrap the chestnut roll and place on a serving platter. Spread the surface with Mocha Butter Frosting, running the back of a spoon

lengthwise in a wavy pattern over the entire surface to give the appearance of bark. Trim the ends; garnish with leaves and glacéed cherries if you wish. Chill for ½ hour before serving. Serves 8–12.

MAPLE SPONGE PUDDING

2 envelopes plus 1 teaspoon unflavored
  gelatin
2 cups maple syrup
6 egg whites
1 cup crumbled macaroons
Whipped cream (garnish)
Grated maple sugar (garnish)

Mix the gelatin with ½ cup cold water. Boil the maple syrup 3 minutes. Add the gelatin and stir until dissolved. Chill until it begins to thicken. Meanwhile, beat the egg whites until a soft peak forms. Beat the gelatin mixture with a rotary beater about 3 minutes, until frothy. Fold in the egg whites, add the macaroon crumbs, and blend well. Spoon into a 2-quart ring mold, making sure that no air bubbles form. If any pudding is left over, put into custard cups. Chill. To serve, unmold on a platter. Fill the center with whipped cream and garnish with grated maple sugar. Have the maple sugar cold and use a coarse grater. Decorate edges of platter with mounds of cream and maple sugar if you wish. Serves 8.

STRAWBERRY ALMOND MOLD

3 pints strawberries
1 cup sugar
3 envelopes unflavored gelatin
1 tablespoon lemon juice
1 teaspoon almond flavoring
½ cup toasted chopped blanched almonds
2 cups heavy cream

Rub 1 quart hulled berries through a sieve or food mill, or buzz in blender. You need about 2½ cups of purée. Add the sugar and let stand ½ hour. Soften the gelatin in ½ cup cold water and heat to dissolve. Stir into the purée. Add lemon juice, almond flavoring, and almonds. Chill until mixture begins to thicken. Then fold in the cream, whipped. Pour into a 6½-cup ring mold and chill until firm. To unmold, dip the ring into warm water and loosen edges with a spatula. Invert on serving dish; garnish with hulled berries. Serves 8–10.

CHOCOLATE ORANGE SPONGE

2 eggs
¼ cup sugar
1 tablespoon grated orange rind
¼ teaspoon salt
1 cup chocolate milk
¼ cup orange juice
1½ tablespoons melted butter
Whipped cream (garnish)

Combine the egg yolks with sugar, orange rind, and salt. Mix well. Add the chocolate milk, orange juice, and melted butter gradually. Beat until well blended. Fold in the egg whites beaten until a soft peak forms. Spoon into a greased 1-quart baking dish. Bake in a hot-water bath in a 350° oven for 40–45 minutes. Serve with whipped cream if you wish. Serves 4.

LEMON SPONGE

2 tablespoons cornstarch
1 cup sugar
2 tablespoons butter
¼ teaspoon salt
¼ teaspoon grated lemon rind
4 eggs
½ cup lemon juice

Mix the cornstarch and sugar in a double boiler. Add 1½ cups boiling water and cook over direct heat, stirring constantly, until clear. Add the butter, salt, and grated lemon rind. Add the slightly beaten egg yolks and cook over hot water until mixture thickens, stirring constantly. Remove from heat and add lemon juice. Fold in the egg whites which have been beaten until a soft peak forms. Cool and serve in chilled sherbet glasses or a serving dish. Serves 4–6.

LEMON SPONGE PUDDING

Grated rind 1½ lemons
Juice 1½ lemons
3 eggs
2 tablespoons flour
1 cup sugar
1 cup milk

Add the lemon rind and juice to the egg yolks which have been beaten until thick. Mix the flour with sugar and stir smoothly into the egg mixture. Add the milk gradually. Beat the egg whites until a soft peak forms and fold into pudding mixture. Pour into a shallow 1-quart baking dish. Set in a pan of cold water and bake 45 minutes in a 325° oven. This will have a cake-like top with custard on the bottom. Serves 4–6.

STRAWBERRY MACAROON MOLD

2 quarts strawberries
1½ cups sugar
1½ cups crumbled macaroons
2 cups heavy cream
3 (8 oz.) packages cream cheese
¼ cup milk
2 tablespoons grated orange rind
½ cup orange juice
3 envelopes unflavored gelatin

Hull and cut 1 quart berries in half. Mix with the sugar and let stand at room temperature for 2 hours, stirring occasionally. Soak the macaroons in cream until soft. Allow the cheese to soften at room temperature. Stir the milk into the cheese; add orange rind and juice and beat smooth. Heat the gelatin in ½ cup water until dissolved. Drain the berries, add syrup from berries to gelatin, stir, and beat into cheese mixture. Fold in the berries. Whip the cream-macaroon mixture until thick and shiny. Fold into the strawberry mixture. Pour into a 2½-quart mold. Chill until firm. Unmold and serve surrounded with remaining strawberries, hulled. Serves 12.

SPANISH CREAM

2½ cups milk
1 envelope unflavored gelatin
¼ teaspoon salt
½ cup sugar
3 eggs
2 teaspoons vanilla

Mix the milk, gelatin, salt, and sugar in a double boiler. Heat and stir until the gelatin and sugar are dissolved. Pour slowly into the slightly beaten egg yolks. Return to double boiler and cook until slightly thickened, stirring constantly. Remove from heat. Pour into a bowl and add vanilla. Fold in the egg whites beaten until a soft peak forms. Turn into a 1-quart mold. Chill until firm. Unmold. Spanish Cream may be served with whipped or plain heavy cream or with berries. Serves 4–6.

SPANISH VELVET CREAM

2 envelopes unflavored gelatin
1 cup milk
2 cups light cream
3 eggs
¾ cup sugar
2-inch piece of vanilla bean
    or 1 teaspoon vanilla
Pinch salt
Cherry Strawberry Sauce*

Mix the gelatin with ½ cup cold water. Mix the milk, cream, slightly beaten egg yolks, sugar, and vanilla bean together in a double boiler. (Slice the vanilla bean down the center to add flavor.) Cook over simmering water until mixture coats a spoon. Remove vanilla bean; if using vanilla extract, add it. Remove from heat and stir in the gelatin. Cool. Beat the egg whites with the salt until a stiff peak forms. Fold into the custard. Spoon the mixture into a 1½-quart ring mold; chill until firm. To serve, unmold on a platter, spoon Cherry Strawberry Sauce around the base, and pass the rest. Serves 6–8.

Hot Soufflés

Soufflés should be baked in a moderate oven for about 40 minutes. One does not usually grease a soufflé dish. When a knife inserted in the center comes out clean, the soufflé is ready and anxious to be served; don't keep it waiting.

APRICOT SOUFFLE

¼ pound dried apricots
2 tablespoons butter
2 tablespoons flour
½ cup milk
Pinch salt
6 tablespoons light brown sugar
2 eggs plus 2–3 egg whites
1 teaspoon grated lemon rind

Simmer the apricots in enough water to cover for about 15 minutes, until soft. Drain thoroughly and buzz in blender or rub through a sieve. You need ½ cup thick purée. Melt the butter in a heavy saucepan and add the flour, then milk and salt. Cook, stirring constantly, until smooth and thick; mix in the sugar and cool slightly before adding the beaten egg yolks, then the apricot purée and

lemon rind. Make sure you have at least ½ cup egg whites before you beat them until a stiff peak forms. Fold into the mixture and spoon into a 1½-quart soufflé dish. Bake in a pan of hot water in a 350° oven for 40 minutes. Serves 6.

CHOCOLATE SOUFFLE

2 cups milk
2 ounces unsweetened chocolate
⅓ cup flour
½ teaspoon salt
½ cup sugar
1 tablespoon butter
1 teaspoon vanilla
6 eggs
Chocolate Sauce,* Custard Sauce,* or
    whipped cream (optional)

Scald the milk in a double boiler. Add the chocolate, grated or in pieces. Heat and stir until blended. Mix the flour, salt, and ¼ cup sugar and add the chocolate mixture gradually, blending until smooth. Return to double boiler and cook about 5 minutes, until thickened, stirring constantly. Add butter and vanilla. Cool mixture but do not chill. You may do this part of the soufflé hours ahead of time if you wish. Beat the egg yolks until very thick and lemon-colored and fold into the chocolate mixture. Beat the egg whites until a very soft peak forms. Add remaining sugar gradually, beating after each addition. Fold into the chocolate mixture lightly and quickly. Pour into a 1½-quart soufflé dish. Set in a pan of hot water and bake in a 325° oven for about 50 minutes, until the center of soufflé springs back to the touch. Serve with a sauce or cream if you wish. Serves 6.

EASY CHOCOLATE SOUFFLE

1⅓ cups milk
½ cup sugar
2 ounces unsweetened chocolate
Pinch salt
1 teaspoon vanilla
4 eggs
Whipped cream (optional)

Heat the milk, sugar, and chocolate in a double boiler. When the chocolate is melted, add the salt and vanilla and beat smooth. Add the eggs and beat hard for 2 full minutes with a rotary beater. Cook, covered, for 40 minutes. Be sure that there is plenty of water in the bottom of the double boiler and do not lift the lid. Serve plain or with whipped cream. This chocolate soufflé is good hot or cold. Serves 4.

ORANGE SOUFFLE

½ cup butter
¾ cup flour
1½ cups milk
1½ teaspoons grated orange rind
1 teaspoon orange flavoring
6 eggs plus 2 egg whites
¾ cup sugar
3 seedless oranges
Orange Custard Sauce* and/or whipped
  cream

Melt the butter in a saucepan, add the flour, and mix well. Gradually add milk, orange rind, and flavoring. Cook and stir until mixture becomes very thick. Remove from heat. Beat together the egg yolks and sugar until lemon-colored. Add to the sauce a little at a time, beating constantly. Cook and stir over low heat 4–5 minutes. Cool thoroughly. Section the oranges and arrange over the bottom of a buttered and floured 2-quart soufflé dish. Beat the egg whites until a stiff peak forms. Carefully fold into cold sauce mixture a little at a time, making sure no specks of egg white are visible. Spoon into soufflé dish. Bake in a 350° oven for 10 minutes. Raise the heat to 450° for 15 minutes, then lower the heat to 350°, and bake 30–35 minutes more, until set. The soufflé is done when the mixture is firm to the touch, lightly browned, and a knife inserted in the center comes out clean. Serve immediately with Orange Custard Sauce and/or whipped cream. Serves 8.

VANILLA SOUFFLE

½ cup flour
¼ cup sugar
2½ cups milk
¼ cup butter
5 eggs
½ cup chopped nuts (optional)
1 teaspoon vanilla
¼ teaspoon salt

Sift the flour with the sugar and stir in ½ cup cold milk. Scald the remaining milk. Stir in the flour mixture with a wire whisk. Cook over low heat until thickened, stirring constantly. Remove from heat. Stir in the butter, add the well-beaten egg yolks, and mix thoroughly. Cool. Add the nuts if you wish and the vanilla. Beat the egg whites with the salt until a soft peak forms and fold lightly into the milk mixture. Bake in an ungreased 2-quart baking dish in a 325° oven for 1 hour. Serves 8.

GINGER SOUFFLE

Proceed as for Vanilla Soufflé,* substituting ¼ cup ginger syrup for the sugar and ¼ cup chopped preserved or crystallized ginger for the vanilla.

LEMON SOUFFLE

Proceed as for Vanilla Soufflé,* substituting the finely grated rind of 1 lemon and the juice of ½ lemon for the vanilla. Add to the mixture just before folding in the beaten egg whites.

ORANGE SOUFFLE

Proceed as for Vanilla Soufflé.* Omit the vanilla, and before folding in the egg whites, add the finely grated rind of a small orange and 1 tablespoon Cointreau or 2 tablespoons orange juice.

GRAND MARNIER SOUFFLE

3 tablespoons butter
3 tablespoons flour
¾ cup milk
3 tablespoons orange marmalade
4 eggs plus 2 egg whites
¼–⅓ cup Grand Marnier

Butter a 1½-quart soufflé dish; then sprinkle the bottom and sides with sugar. Melt the butter in a saucepan and stir in the flour. Add the milk gradually, stirring constantly, and cook over low heat until thick and smooth. Remove from heat. Stir in the marmalade, lightly beaten egg yolks, and Grand Marnier. Blend thoroughly. Beat the egg whites until a stiff peak forms and fold them into the marmalade mixture. Spoon into the soufflé dish. Bake in a 375° oven for about 45 minutes, until well risen and golden brown. Serves 6.

COLD APRICOT SOUFFLE
(Low Calorie)

1 (1 lb.) can dietetic apricot halves
1 envelope unflavored gelatin
4 eggs
1 teaspoon plus 1 tablespoon lemon juice
⅛ teaspoon salt
¼ teaspoon almond flavoring
1½ teaspoons noncaloric liquid sweetener
¼ cup sugar
½ cup nonfat dry milk powder

Drain the juice from apricots and put into double boiler; sprinkle gelatin on the juice and let it soften. Beat the egg yolks with ¼ cup water and add to gelatin. Cook over simmering water, stirring constantly, about 5 minutes, until gelatin is dissolved. Remove from heat and stir in 1 teaspoon lemon juice, salt, almond flavoring, and the sweetener. Purée the apricots in blender or through a sieve and add to the mixture. Beat the egg whites until a soft peak forms. Gradually add the sugar a tablespoon at a time and continue beating until a soft meringue is formed. Fold into the apricot mixture. Sprinkle the dry milk over ½ cup ice water and beat until thickened. Add remaining lemon juice and continue to beat until consistency of whipped cream. Fold this into the apricot mixture. Cut a strip of brown paper 5 inches deep and long enough to go around a 1-quart soufflé dish. Fasten the paper around the outside, letting it extend 3 inches above the top. Brush the inside of the strip with oil. Turn the mixture into the dish and chill at least 4 hours, until firm. To serve, loosen paper collar and pull it gently away. Serves 8 (108 calories per serving).

COLD COFFEE SOUFFLE

1½ envelopes unflavored gelatin
1 cup milk
¾ cup sugar
¼ teaspoon salt
2 tablespoons instant coffee (espresso or half and half)
3 eggs
1 teaspoon vanilla
Chocolate curls (optional)

Mix the gelatin with 1½ cups water, the milk, sugar, salt, and coffee in a double boiler. Heat until mixture is scalded and gelatin dissolved. Add the slightly beaten egg yolks and cook until mixture coats a spoon. Remove from heat, add vanilla, and chill until syrupy. Fold in the stiffly beaten egg whites. Pour into 6 sherbet glasses or a serving bowl and chill until firm. Garnish with chocolate curls if you wish. These are made by scraping unsweetened chocolate, which has been kept at room temperature, with a vegetable peeler. Serves 6.

DATE NUT LEMON SOUFFLE

2¼ cups sugar
5 tablespoons flour
¼ teaspoon salt
5 tablespoons softened butter
6 eggs
2 cups milk
¾ cup lemon juice
Grated rind 3 lemons
1 cup chopped dates
¾ cup broken walnuts

Sift the sugar, flour, and salt together. Add the butter, and cream until blended. Beat the egg yolks until light. Add with the milk to the sugar and flour mixture and stir. Blend in the lemon juice and rind. Beat the egg whites until a stiff peak forms. Fold them into the mixture and add the dates and nuts. Pour into a lightly buttered 2-quart baking dish, set in a pan of hot water, and bake in a 325° oven for 50 minutes. This soufflé will not rise as much as some. When done, the top will have a fluffy cake-like consistency and the bottom a thick lemon sauce. Let cool and then refrigerate for about 1 hour before serving. Try serving it hot sometimes. Serves 6–8.

WEIGHTLESS SOUFFLE
(Low Calorie)

4 egg whites
2 tablespoons superfine sugar
2 tablespoons currant jelly
2 tablespoons chopped toasted blanched almonds

Beat the egg whites until they stand in soft peaks. Sprinkle sugar on top and gently fold in. Break up jelly lightly with a fork and fold in; the jelly does not have to be evenly mixed. Spoon into a 1-quart soufflé dish that has been greased and floured. Sprinkle almonds on top. Bake in a 400° oven for 10–12 minutes, until soufflé is high and golden. Serve at once. Serves 6 (65 calories per serving).

EASY LEMON SOUFFLE

5 eggs
½ cup sugar
5 tablespoons frozen lemonade concentrate
1 teaspoon grated lemon rind

Beat the egg yolks slightly. Add the sugar gradually while beating. Add thawed lemonade concentrate and lemon rind. Beat again for 2–3 minutes. Beat the egg whites until very stiff. Fold into the yolk mixture. Mix until no egg white is visible. Pour into an ungreased 1½-quart casserole. Place in a warm-water bath and bake in a 325° oven for 50–60 minutes. Serve at once, or allow to cool and then chill for about 2 hours before serving. Good with Rum Custard Sauce.* Serves 8.

The proof of the pudding is in the eating.
Miguel de Cervantes,
Don Quixote

DESSERT OMELET

1 cup blueberries or raspberries
Superfine sugar
¼ teaspoon salt
2 eggs plus 2 egg whites
¼ cup of confectioners' sugar
½ teaspoon grated lemon rind
2 teaspoons butter

Sprinkle the fruit with superfine sugar and set aside in a bowl. Sprinkle about ⅛ teaspoon salt in a skillet with a removable or ovenproof handle, warm it, and rub vigorously with paper toweling. Discard the salt. Beat the egg yolks until light and lemon-colored. Add the confectioners' sugar gradually while beating. Flavor with the lemon rind. Beat the egg whites and ⅛ teaspoon salt and fold into the yolk mixture. Melt the butter in the skillet and let it coat the bottom and sides. When the butter is warm and foamy, pour the egg mixture into the skillet and cook over low heat until nicely browned around the edges. Place in 350° oven for 5 minutes, until the center is just set. Drain the sugared fruit. Remove

omelet from oven and cover half of it with the fruit. Slash the edges of the omelet at the center to facilitate the turning and flip the other half over the fruit. Serve at once sprinkled with a little superfine sugar. Serves 2–3.

PUFFY BANANA OMELET

4 eggs
½ teaspoon salt
¼ cup milk
2 tablespoons butter
2 bananas
2 tablespoons marmalade
2 teaspoons sugar

Beat the egg yolks until thick and light. Add the salt and stir in the milk. Beat the egg whites until a soft peak forms. Fold in the yolk mixture carefully. Heat the butter until foamy in a 9-inch or 10-inch skillet with a removable or ovenproof handle. Pour in the omelet mixture. Cook over low heat until it puffs. Set in a 350° oven for about 5 minutes, until top is set. Crease through center; put the bananas, sliced thin, and a little marmalade on half the omelet. Fold over and turn out on a warm platter. Sprinkle the top with sugar and, if you wish, put under a broiler for about 2 minutes to glaze. Serves 2–3.

CHOCOLATE-CHIP PUDDING

5 cups ½-inch cubes day-old cake (any
   flavor)
1 quart milk
4 eggs
½ cup sugar
¼ teaspoon salt
½ cup broken pecans or walnuts
1 teaspoon vanilla
½ teaspoon nutmeg
1 cup chocolate bits
Cream

Put the cake cubes into a lightly greased 2½-quart casserole. Scald the milk. Beat the eggs slightly with the sugar and salt. Stir in the hot milk and nuts. Flavor with vanilla and nutmeg. Pour over the cake and mix well. Set the casserole in a pan of hot water and bake in a 350° oven for 50 minutes, until just set. Sprinkle the chocolate bits over the top and bake 15 minutes more, until firm. Serve warm with cream. Serves 8.

CHOCOLATE MOUSSE I

½ pound sweet baking chocolate
1 cup sugar
8 eggs
2 tablespoons rum or brandy

Melt the chocolate in a double boiler. Heat the sugar with ½ cup water until syrupy. Pour the syrup into the chocolate in a slow steady stream, beating constantly. Add egg yolks one at a time, beating after each addition. Remove from heat and add rum or brandy. Fold in the beaten egg whites and pour into a serving dish or individual cups or pot de crèmes. Chill overnight. Serves 8–10.

CHOCOLATE MOUSSE II

4 ounces unsweetened chocolate
6 eggs
1 cup sugar
2 cups heavy cream
About 3 tablespoons rum (optional)

Melt the chocolate in a double boiler and cool slightly. Beat the egg yolks until thick and lemon-colored. Add sugar gradually while beating. Stir in the melted chocolate. Beat the egg whites until a stiff peak forms. Whip the cream. Fold both into the chocolate mixture and blend well. Add the rum if you wish. Spoon into a 2-quart bowl or individual cups or dishes. Chill at least 4 hours. Garnish if you wish with additional whipped cream. Serves 8–10.

POT DE CREME I

½ pound semisweet or sweet baking
*   chocolate*
1 cup heavy cream
5 eggs
2 tablespoons butter
1 teaspoon vanilla
Pinch salt

Melt the chocolate in a double boiler with ¼ cup hot water. Remove from heat and add the cream gradually. Mix well. Beat the egg yolks until thick and stir into chocolate mixture; cook until thickened. Remove from heat and fold in the egg whites which have been beaten just to hold a soft peak. Return to heat and stir until mixture thickens again. Remove

from heat and add butter, vanilla, and salt. Pour into pot-de-crème cups or a serving bowl. Demitasses may be used instead of pot de crèmes. Chill in refrigerator 2–3 hours or overnight. Serves 6–8.

POT DE CREME II
(Low Calorie)

1 ounce semisweet chocolate
1 envelope low-calorie chocolate-flavored
*   pudding mix*
¾ cup skim milk
¼ cup strong coffee
2 egg yolks
1 teaspoon vanilla

Grate the chocolate into a saucepan. Add the pudding mix, skim milk, coffee, and egg yolks and mix well. Cook over low heat until smooth and thickened, stirring often. Add the vanilla. Cool a little, stirring occasionally, and pour into 4 pot-de-crème cups, after-dinner coffee cups, or other individual serving dishes. Cover and chill several hours. Serves 4 (109 calories per serving).

FUDGE PUDDING CAKE

1 cup flour
2 teaspoons baking powder
1 teaspoon salt
⅔ cup sugar
¼ cup plus 2 tablespoons cocoa
½ cup milk
1 teaspoon vanilla
2 tablespoons melted butter
½ cup chopped walnuts
1 cup dark brown sugar
Ice cream or whipped cream (optional)

Sift the flour, baking powder, salt, sugar, and 2 tablespoons cocoa together 3 times. Combine the milk, vanilla, and melted butter. Add to the dry ingredients and beat until smooth. Stir in the chopped walnuts. Spread in a buttered 1½-quart casserole. Mix the brown sugar with remaining cocoa and sprinkle over the batter. Pour 1½ cups boiling water over the entire cake. Bake in a 350° oven for 50 minutes. Do not attempt to turn this cake out; the bottom is full of fudge sauce. Serve warm with ice cream or whipped cream if you wish. Serves 6.

CHOCOLATE VELVET WITH COFFEE CREAM

½ pound sweet baking chocolate
2 cups milk
1½ envelopes unflavored gelatin
½ cup sugar
⅛ teaspoon salt
½ cup light cream
½ teaspoon vanilla
¼ teaspoon almond flavoring
1 cup heavy cream

COFFEE CREAM
2 teaspoons instant coffee
¾ cup heavy cream
¼ teaspoon vanilla
3 tablespoons sugar
Chocolate curls (garnish)

Cut the chocolate into pieces and scald with 1½ cups milk in a double boiler until the chocolate is melted. Mix the gelatin with ½ cup milk. Beat the chocolate-milk mixture with a rotary beater. Add the gelatin mixture, sugar, and salt. Stir until dissolved. Cool until it begins to thicken. Add the light cream, vanilla and almond flavoring, and the heavy cream, whipped. Mix until smooth. Chill until it begins to thicken again. Beat with a rotary beater and pour into a 5-cup ring mold. Chill until firm.

Coffee Cream. Sprinkle the instant coffee over the cream. When most of the coffee has dissolved, add the vanilla and whip the cream until a stiff peak forms, adding the sugar as you beat.

Unmold the dessert, frost with coffee cream, and garnish with chocolate curls. Serves 6.

Steamed Puddings

Steamed puddings are festive desserts, particularly suitable for winter holidays. They repay the time, about 3 hours, it takes to steam them. They don't require attention once you've put the pudding in a closed mold and the mold in a tightly covered pot or steamer with water. The water must be kept about halfway up the mold and will need replenishing. To unmold, loosen edge with a knife or spatula; place serving plate over the pudding and invert.

BASIC STEAMED PUDDING

¼ pound ground suet
1 cup dark brown sugar
½ cup milk
2 eggs
¾ cup flour
1 teaspoon baking soda
1 teaspoon cinnamon
2 cups raisins
¼ cup chopped candied orange peel
¼ cup chopped candied lemon peel
½ cup finely cut citron
½ cup chopped Brazil nuts
¼ cup soft bread crumbs
Hard Sauce* or Foamy Eggnog Sauce*

Combine the suet with sugar, milk, and well-beaten eggs. Sift the flour, soda, and cinnamon together. Mix the raisins, orange and lemon peels, citron, and nuts with flour and bread crumbs. Add dry ingredients and fruit mixture to the suet mixture; blend well. Pour into a well-greased and floured 1½-quart mold; cover with a tight-fitting cover or with foil tied in place securely. If you do not have a steamer, place mold on a rack in a deep kettle. Pour boiling water to half the depth of the mold. Cover and steam 3 hours, adding more boiling water if necessary. Cool slightly, loosen edge with a spatula, and unmold. Serve with sauce. Serves 6–8.

STEAMED MARMALADE PUDDING I

2 tablespoons grated orange rind
⅓ cup orange juice
1 cup orange marmalade
2½ cups soft bread crumbs
¼ pound ground suet
2 tablespoons flour
2 eggs
½ teaspoon baking soda
Foamy Eggnog Sauce* (optional)

Heat the orange rind, juice, and marmalade and simmer gently for 15 minutes. Toss the bread crumbs, suet, and flour together. Add eggs beaten with the soda; then add the orange mixture. Pour into a well-greased 1-quart mold and cover tight. Set mold on a rack in a deep kettle, fill to half the height of the mold with hot water, cover kettle, and bring to a boil. Boil gently for 3½ hours. Remove from steamer, uncover, and allow to stand 5 minutes. Loosen edge with a knife and unmold. Good with Foamy Eggnog Sauce. Serves 6.

STEAMED MARMALADE PUDDING II

1 loaf stale unsliced firm white bread
½ pound ground suet
2 tablespoons grated orange rind
⅔ cup orange juice
½ cup sugar
2 cups orange marmalade
1 teaspoon baking soda
3 eggs
Eggnog Sauce*

Trim the crusts from the bread. Grate the bread on coarse side of grater or pull apart with a fork. Measure 5 cups crumbs. Mix with the suet and set aside. Cook together the orange rind and juice, sugar, and marmalade. Simmer for 15 minutes, then pour over the bread crumbs and suet, and mix well. Add soda to the beaten eggs and mix into the pudding. Pour into a well-greased 2-quart melon-shaped pudding mold. Cover tight and place the mold on a rack in a steamer. Steam 3½ hours; replenish boiling water if necessary. Loosen around the edges and unmold on a platter. Serve with Eggnog Sauce. Serves 8.

STEAMED APPLE PUDDING

3 apples
¾ cup molasses
⅓ cup butter
2½ cups flour
¼ teaspoon salt
1 teaspoon cinnamon
¼ teaspoon cloves
¼ teaspoon nutmeg
¼ teaspoon allspice
1½ teaspoons baking soda
1 egg
Lemon Sauce* or Custard Sauce* (optional)

Peel, core, and slice the apples and cook with the molasses over low heat until tender. Add the butter and cool. Sift the dry ingredients together. Add the cooled apple mixture, ½ cup water, and the slightly beaten egg. Stir well. Turn into a well-greased 1½-quart mold and cover tight. Place mold on a rack in a deep kettle and bring to a boil. Boil gently for 1½ hours. Remove from steamer, uncover, and let stand at least 5 minutes. Loosen edge of pudding with a knife, plunge mold quickly into and out of cold water, and unmold. Serve with Lemon Sauce or Custard Sauce if you wish. Serves 8–10.

STEAMED GINGER PUDDING

2¼ cups flour
½ teaspoon salt
1 teaspoon baking soda
⅓ cup shortening
½ cup sugar
3 eggs
¾ cup milk
¾ cup dark molasses
⅓ cup chopped crystallized ginger
Peach Sauce,* Foamy Eggnog Sauce,* or heavy cream (optional)

Sift the flour, salt, and soda together. Cream the shortening with sugar until light and fluffy. Stir in the well-beaten eggs. Add dry ingredients alternately with milk. Stir well after each addition. Add the molasses and ginger. Pour into a well-greased 1½-quart mold and cover tight. Place mold on a rack in a deep kettle, fill to half the height of the mold with hot water, cover kettle, and bring to a boil. Boil gently for about 2 hours, adding boiling water if necessary. Remove from steamer, uncover, and allow to stand for at least 5 minutes. Loosen edge of pudding with a knife and unmold. Good served hot with Peach Sauce, Foamy Eggnog Sauce, or cream. Serves 8.

STEAMED GINGER FRUIT PUDDING

1 cup flour
¾ cup dark brown sugar
1 quart dry bread crumbs
¼ pound ground suet
1½ teaspoons baking powder
¾ teaspoon ginger
¼ teaspoon salt
1 egg
½ cup milk
1 teaspoon grated orange rind
½ cup drained crushed pineapple
Sauce or ice cream (optional)

Mix the flour, sugar, crumbs, suet, baking powder, ginger, and salt. Add the well-beaten egg and the milk, orange rind, and pineapple —be sure the pineapple is well drained. Stir well but do not beat. Turn into a well-greased 1½-quart mold, cover tight, and place on a rack in a deep kettle. Partially fill the kettle with boiling water to half the height of the mold. Cover and steam for 3 hours. Be sure water is always halfway up the mold; add more when needed. Unmold on a hot platter. Good with Hard Sauce,* ice cream, or Orange, Lemon, or Custard Sauce.* Serves 6–8.

STEAMED CRANBERRY PUDDING

3 cups fresh or frozen cranberries
¾ cup raisins
2½ cups flour
1 tablespoon baking soda
¾ cup dark molasses

Put the berries and raisins in a bowl. Sift the flour and soda over them. Add the molasses mixed with ½ cup hot water. Stir until well blended. Pour into a well-greased 2-quart mold, cover tight, and steam for 2½ hours. Loosen edges with a spatula and unmold on a serving plate. This is a quite tart pudding and is good served with a sweet sauce. Serves 8.

Flambé Puddings

It is traditional to serve plum puddings and other holiday puddings ablaze. This is easily done if the brandy, rum, or even whiskey is warmed. Pour the liquid over a warm pudding and ignite immediately. Turn out the dining-room lights for an effective entrance of the dessert glowing with blue flames.

ENGLISH PLUM PUDDING   (*Plate 17*)

2 cups seedless raisins
3 cups currants
⅓ cup chopped candied citron
⅓ cup chopped candied orange peel
⅓ cup chopped candied lemon peel
1 quart soft bread crumbs
¼ cup chopped blanched almonds
1½ cups sugar
1 teaspoon nutmeg
¼ teaspoon ginger
1 teaspoon cinnamon
¼ pound ground suet
¾ cup milk
2 eggs
½ cup brandy
Hard Sauce* or Brandy Hard Sauce*

Toss the fruits, bread crumbs, nuts, sugar, and spices together. Add suet to fruit mixture. Stir in the milk and beaten eggs. Add the brandy and blend well. Pack into a well-greased 2-quart pudding mold and cover tight. Place mold on a rack in a deep kettle, fill to half the height of the mold with hot water, cover kettle, and bring to a boil. Boil for 8 hours. Replenish boiling water if necessary. Remove from the steamer, uncover, and let stand 10–15 minutes. Loosen edge of pudding with a knife and unmold. Serve with Hard Sauce or Brandy Hard Sauce. Serves 8–10.

PLUM PUDDING

2 cups raisins
½ cup finely chopped citron
Grated rind 1 orange
Grated rind 1 lemon
½ cup sliced candied cherries
¼ cup chopped pitted dates
1 apple
1 cup orange marmalade
½ cup orange juice
3 eggs
½ cup sugar
1 cup molasses
1½ cups fine dry bread crumbs
¼ pound ground suet
1 cup coarsely chopped filberts
1 cup flour
1 teaspoon salt
¼ teaspoon baking soda
1 teaspoon baking powder
1 teaspoon cinnamon
½ teaspoon allspice
½ teaspoon cloves
Hard Sauce* or Brandy Hard Sauce*

Mix the raisins, citron, orange and lemon rinds, candied cherries, dates, and the peeled, cored, chopped apple. Add the marmalade and orange juice. Let stand overnight. Beat the eggs until very light. Add sugar and molasses gradually. Now add the bread crumbs, suet, filberts, and the soaked fruits. Sift the flour, salt, soda, baking powder, and spices together. Stir into pudding mixture. Pour into 2 greased 1-quart pudding molds. Cover tight and steam 3½–4 hours on a rack over boiling water. Let stand for 5 minutes before unmolding. Serve with Hard Sauce or Brandy Hard Sauce. Serves 12–14.

This pudding may be frozen. In that case, after 3 hours of steaming, cool, wrap with foil, seal, and freeze in the molds. Thaw and steam 1½ hours before serving.

BAKED PLUM PUDDING

1 cup finely chopped suet
1 cup peeled, cored, chopped apple
1 cup molasses
½ cup brown sugar
⅔ cup milk
¼ cup candied cherries
1 cup raisins
1 cup currants
½ cup chopped blanched almonds
¼ cup shredded citron
2 tablespoons finely shredded orange peel
3½ cups flour
1 teaspoon salt
1 teaspoon baking soda
½ teaspoon nutmeg
¼ teaspoon cloves
2 tablespoons lemon juice
Hard Sauce*

Put the suet and apple through a food chopper. Put into a bowl and add the molasses, brown sugar, and milk. Cut the cherries in halves and mix with the raisins, currants, almonds, citron, and orange peel. Dredge with ½ cup flour. Sift the remaining flour with the salt, soda, nutmeg, and cloves. Add to liquid mixture and blend smooth. Add the prepared fruits and lemon juice. Mix thoroughly. Fill a greased 1½-quart casserole ⅔ full, cover tight, and bake in a 300° oven for 2 hours. Serve warm with Hard Sauce. Serves 8.

TUTTI-FRUTTI DATE PUDDING

2 cups flour
1 tablespoon baking powder
1 teaspoon salt
1 cup butter
2 cups stale bread crumbs
½ cup sugar
2 teaspoons grated orange rind
⅓ cup quartered candied cherries
2 cups slivered candied fruits (mixture of candied orange rind, pineapple, and citron)
½ cup pitted dates quartered
1⅓ cups milk
2 eggs
½ teaspoon almond flavoring
⅛ teaspoon nutmeg
Honey Lemon Sauce* (optional)

Sift the flour, baking powder, and salt together into a large bowl. Cut in the butter with a pastry blender. Add the bread crumbs, sugar, orange rind, and fruits. Mix the milk and well-beaten eggs together. Add the almond flavoring and nutmeg. Stir into the fruit mixture. Blend well. Pour into a well-greased 2-quart ring mold and cover tight. Set mold on a rack in a deep kettle, fill to halfway up the mold with hot water, cover kettle, and bring to a slow boil. Boil for about 3 hours, replenishing water if necessary. Remove from steamer and let stand 5 minutes. Turn onto a hot platter and serve with Honey Lemon Sauce if you wish. Serves 8.

WINTER FRUIT PUDDING

½ pound dried figs
2½ cups soft bread crumbs
¾ cup milk
4 eggs
⅓ cup ground suet
½ cup finely chopped walnuts
½ cup chopped raisins
1 cup dark brown sugar
¾ teaspoon cinnamon
½ teaspoon nutmeg
1 teaspoon salt
2 tablespoons flour
2 teaspoons baking powder

Slit the figs, scrape out part of the seeds, and remove stems. Chop the figs coarse. Add bread crumbs to milk and slightly beaten eggs; then add figs and other ingredients. Blend well and pour into a greased 1½-quart mold. Cover tight. Set the mold on a rack in a deep kettle, fill to half the height of the mold with hot water, cover kettle, and bring to a boil. Boil for 3–3½ hours. Replenish boiling water if necessary. Remove from steamer, uncover, and let stand for at least 5 minutes. Loosen the edge of pudding with a knife and unmold. Good with Ambrosia Sauce.* Serves 8.

COOKTIP

To remove a dessert from a mold: press the dessert gently away from the edge of the mold, or run a thin-bladed paring knife around the top, ⅛ inch deep. Dip the mold in lukewarm water to the depth of the dessert, or place a hot moist towel around the mold. Place serving plate on top of the mold and invert. Tilt the mold slightly and insert the edge of a knife until the dessert drops to the plate.

CHAPTER SIX

Ice Creams, Ices, and Iced Sweets

An ice-cream freezer was at one time as important a kitchen utensil as a second skillet. Ice creams and sherbets are still worth the trouble required by ice, salt, and a dasher-type machine. With modern freezers and freezing compartments, many desserts such as mousses, ice creams, and ices are as easy as they are delicious. The technique of partly freezing, beating, and refreezing is almost foolproof.

Commercial ice creams are a boon. Naturally, some brands appeal more than others; choose the kind you like best and personalize it. Combine different flavors and textures, such as pistachio ice cream and lemon sherbet; serve strawberry ice cream with chilled crème de menthe, or coffee ice cream with crushed berries. You can add something to the ice cream itself: stir some instant coffee into commercial chocolate ice cream for a mocha taste, add a little liqueur to vanilla ice cream, or rum to lemon or pineapple, and refreeze. Almost all of them gain something from your personal touch. Make molds, baked Alaska, or ice-cream pies. Put the ice cream into parfait glasses with sauces to complement the flavor; read the paragraph on parfaits and discover these easiest-of-all glamorous party desserts.

Flavored water ices date back to the earliest times. The Chinese claim to have taught the Arabs; Marco Polo brought "milk ice" from Japan; the Romans served snow from their mountains mixed with syrup and fruits; a Sicilian, Procopio, introduced ice cream and water ice to France in about 1660. By the eighteenth century good quality frozen desserts were being made and sold everywhere. In spite of all its history, ice cream is considered an American dessert, almost an American invention! The amount consumed in the United States is beyond belief.

Dasher Ice Cream

Ice cream and sherbet are still best made in a crank-type freezer. Smooth ice cream results from the dasher machine, whether hand-turned or electric. The mixture should be cold and the container should be no more than ¾ full. Pack the freezer with a mixture of 1 part rock salt to about 5 parts cracked ice. Turn the crank until very stiff. Remove the dasher and give it to your child while you push the ice cream down, cover the container with a piece of foil or waxed paper, and replace the lid securely. Repack with ice and salt and let stand for several hours to rest and mellow.

Refrigerator Ice Cream

You can make very satisfactory ice cream in freezing trays. After the mixture is partially frozen, scrape into a cold bowl, beat until smooth, and refreeze until firm.

VANILLA ICE CREAM
(Basic)

1 quart light cream
¾ cup sugar
¼ teaspoon salt
1 tablespoon vanilla

Scald the cream and add the sugar and salt. Stir until the sugar is dissolved. Cool. Flavor with vanilla and freeze in a crank-type ice-cream freezer. This may be frozen in a freezing compartment, following the directions for Refrigerator Ice Cream.* Serves 8.

FRENCH VANILLA ICE CREAM

4 egg yolks
¾ cup sugar
⅛ teaspoon salt
2 cups milk
2 cups heavy cream
1 teaspoon vanilla

Mix the slightly beaten egg yolks with sugar and salt. Scald the milk and cream in a double boiler. Add a little milk slowly to the egg mixture, return to double boiler, and cook, stirring constantly, about 5 minutes, until mixture coats a spoon. Remove from heat and add vanilla. Cool and freeze in a crank-type ice-cream freezer, or follow directions for Refrigerator Ice Cream.* Serves 10.

CHOCOLATE ICE CREAM

Proceed as for French Vanilla Ice Cream,* adding 2 ounces melted chocolate before removing from heat. Stir until well blended.

VARIATIONS ON VANILLA ICE CREAM

Soften 1 quart vanilla ice cream, stir in the flavoring, and refreeze until firm. Serves 6.

ALMOND ICE CREAM
Add 2 teaspoons almond flavoring and proceed as above.

COFFEE ICE CREAM
Add 2 tablespoons instant coffee, dissolved in a little milk or cream, and proceed as above.

GINGER ICE CREAM
Add 1 tablespoon ginger syrup (from preserved ginger) and proceed as above.

LEMON ICE CREAM
Add the juice of 1 lemon and 1 teaspoon grated rind and proceed as above.

CHOCOLATE-CHIP ICE CREAM
Stir in ½ cup chopped semisweet chocolate and proceed as above.

BLUE RIPPLE ICE CREAM
Rub 1 quart blueberries or 1 package frozen blueberries through a coarse sieve or buzz in a blender. Ripple the purée through the softened ice cream. Refreeze until firm.

RASPBERRY RIPPLE ICE CREAM
Rub 1 package thawed frozen raspberries or 3 cups fresh raspberries through a sieve. Ripple spoonfuls of the purée through the softened ice cream and refreeze.

CHOCOLATE-CRACKLE ICE CREAM
Melt 1 cup semisweet chocolate bits with ¼ cup hot water, or use 4 ounces semisweet chocolate and melt in a double boiler with no water. Stir smooth and let cool a little. Pour and spread over the softened ice cream in freezing trays and return to freezer compartment. The chocolate hardens on the ice cream.

DATE NUT ICE CREAM

Cut ½ cup dates into small pieces and mix with ½ cup broken nut meats and ½ teaspoon grated orange rind. Add 1–2 tablespoons brandy if you wish. Stir this into the slightly softened ice cream and refreeze until firm. Serves 6–8.

MACAROON ICE-CREAM CAKE

Put a layer of day-old crumbs from sponge-cake or plain cake into 2 freezing trays. Sprinkle with macaroon crumbs and pat down lightly. Spread the softened ice cream evenly over the crumbs, 1 pint in each tray. Add more cake and macaroon crumbs and freeze until firm. Serves 6–8.

BUTTER-CRISP ICE CREAM

Mix 2 cups ready-to-eat cereal, such as grapenuts or wheat flakes, with ¼ cup brown sugar and ¼ cup coarsely chopped nuts. Cook for 2–3 minutes in 2 tablespoons melted butter until the sugar caramelizes a little. Stir as it cooks. Cool and crumble into bits. Stir into the softened ice cream and refreeze until firm. Serves 6–8.

CANTALOUPE ICE CREAM

1¼ cups milk
1 cup sugar
1 very ripe cantaloupe
⅓ cup lemon juice
Red and yellow food coloring (optional)
3 egg whites
1 cup heavy cream

Heat the milk and sugar until the sugar dissolves. Cool. Freeze until mushy. Scoop the pulp from the cantaloupe and buzz in a blender or chop very fine or purée, using the juice. You should have about 2 cups purée. Spoon the partially frozen mixture into a cold bowl and beat until light and fluffy but still thick. Add the cantaloupe purée and lemon juice while beating. This ice cream is pale in color; add a few drops of red and yellow food coloring if you like. Blend well. Pour into trays and partially freeze again. Beat the egg whites until a peak forms. Whip the cream and fold into the egg whites. Beat the partially frozen mixture just to soften. Carefully fold in the egg-white mixture. Freeze until firm. Serves 8–10.

BURNT-ALMOND ICE CREAM

½ cup milk
½ cup sugar
2 eggs
⅛ teaspoon salt
2 teaspoons vanilla
1 cup heavy cream
¾ cup chopped blanched almonds
3 tablespoons butter

Heat the milk and sugar in a double boiler, stirring until the sugar is dissolved. Pour slowly over the beaten egg yolks. Return to double boiler and cook, stirring, until the mixture coats a spoon. Cool. Beat the egg whites and salt until a soft peak forms. Fold into the cold custard and add vanilla. Fold in the cream, whipped. Meanwhile, brown the almonds in the butter. Add to the ice cream mixture. Pour into a freezing tray and freeze until firm. Serves 4.

APRICOT RIPPLE ICE CREAM

1 (11 oz.) package dried apricots
¼ cup sugar
½ teaspoon almond flavoring
1 quart vanilla ice cream

Wash the apricots, cover with water, and bring to a boil. Cook for 10 minutes, uncovered. Cover and simmer 15 minutes more, adding the sugar during the last 5 minutes of cooking. Rub the apricots and juice through a sieve or buzz in a blender and add almond flavoring. Cool. Make ribbons of apricot purée between spoonfuls of ice cream. This may be spooned directly into parfait glasses if you wish. Freeze until firm. Serves 6–8.

AVOCADO ICE CREAM

1 large or 2 small avocados
¼ cup sugar
4–6 tablespoons lime juice
1 pint vanilla ice cream

Peel the avocado and purée the flesh with a fork. Add the sugar and lime juice and mix at once with the purée to prevent discoloration. Combine with the slightly softened ice cream. Stir until very smooth. Put into a freezing tray and leave until almost frozen. Do not let freeze too firm. Serves 6.

ORANGE ICE CREAM

2 eggs
¼ cup sugar
½ cup light corn syrup
2 cups light cream
2 tablespoons lemon juice
⅓ cup frozen orange-juice concentrate
Red and yellow food coloring (optional)

Beat the eggs until light, adding the sugar gradually while beating. Then add the corn syrup, cream, lemon juice, and orange-juice concentrate. Add a few drops each of red and yellow food coloring if you wish. Pour into a freezing tray and freeze until almost firm but still soft in the center. Scrape into a cold bowl, beat smooth, refreeze until firm. Serves 4–6.

ORANGE APRICOT ICE CREAM

16 large marshmallows
1 (1 lb. 14 oz.) can apricots
¼ cup sugar
⅛ teaspoon salt
½ teaspoon grated lemon rind
1 cup orange juice
¼ cup light corn syrup
¼ teaspoon almond flavoring
2 cups light cream

Combine the marshmallows with 1 cup of syrup drained from the apricots. Add the sugar, salt, and lemon rind. Cook and stir over low heat until marshmallows are melted. Cool. Purée the apricots. Add ¾ cup of the purée to the marshmallow mixture with the orange juice, corn syrup, and almond flavoring. Chill. Stir in the cream, pour into freezing trays, and freeze until mushy. Scrape into a cold bowl and beat smooth. Pour back into the trays and freeze until firm. Serves 8.

COCONUT ICE CREAM

1 (15 oz.) can sweetened condensed milk
1½ teaspoons vanilla
1 cup heavy cream
1 (3½ oz.) can flaked coconut
1 tablespoon grated orange rind

Combine the milk, ⅔ cup water, and vanilla. Chill in a freezing tray. Whip the cream until a stiff peak forms, fold in the chilled milk mixture, and freeze until mushy. Scrape into a cold bowl and beat until smooth. Fold in coconut and orange rind. Freeze until firm. Serves 8.

LEMON ICE CREAM I

2 eggs
½ cup sugar
½ cup light corn syrup
1 teaspoon grated lemon rind
¼ cup lemon juice
2 cups milk or half-and-half
3 tablespoons green crème de menthe (optional)

Beat the eggs until thick; add the sugar gradually while beating. Then add the corn syrup, lemon rind and juice, and the milk or half-and-half. Mix well and pour into freezing trays. When the mixture is frozen around the edges, scrape into a cold bowl, add the crème de menthe if you wish, and beat until smooth. Freeze until firm. Serves 4–6.

LEMON ICE CREAM II

A smooth, easy refrigerator ice cream which has the virtue of not having to be whipped in the half-frozen stage.

½ cup lemon juice
4 teaspoons grated lemon rind
2 cups sugar
1 quart light cream
Yellow food coloring (optional)

Add the lemon juice and rind to the sugar and blend well. Slowly stir in the cream. Add a few drops coloring if you wish. Pour into 2 freezing trays and freeze quickly for 3 hours. *Do not stir.* Serves 6–8.

LEMON PINEAPPLE ICE CREAM

2 cups milk
½ cup sugar
1 cup heavy cream
1 (9 oz.) can crushed pineapple
½ teaspoon lemon flavoring

In a large saucepan heat the milk and sugar until the sugar is dissolved. Cool. Pour into a freezing tray and freeze until mixture is soft and mushy. Whip the cream and fold in the partially frozen mixture. Return to trays and freeze until mushy. Scrape into a cold bowl and beat smooth. Fold in the crushed pineapple and the lemon flavoring. Freeze until firm. Serves 6.

LIME MINT BUTTERMILK ICE CREAM

2–3 tablespoons finely chopped mint leaves
2 eggs
½ cup sugar
½ cup light corn syrup
1½ cups buttermilk
3 tablespoons lime juice
Green food coloring (optional)
Mint flavoring (optional)

Chop the mint and pour ⅔ cup boiling water over it. Cover and simmer 2–3 minutes, until the mint is wilted. Strain, and cool the liquid. Beat the eggs until very light and thick, adding the sugar gradually while beating. Then stir in the corn syrup, buttermilk, lime juice, and ½ cup mint juice. Add a few drops of the coloring if you wish. You may add a drop or two of mint flavoring to taste. Pour into a freezing tray and freeze until mushy. Scrape into a cold bowl, beat smooth, and refreeze until firm. Serves 6.

BUTTERMINT ICE CREAM

1 (7 oz.) package buttermints
1 (14½ oz.) can evaporated milk
Green food coloring (optional)
2 cups heavy cream

Crush the mints with a rolling pin or mallet; there should be about 1 cup. Put into the hot milk and let stand about 10 minutes, until fairly well dissolved. Stir in a few drops of food coloring to make a delicate shade of green if you wish. Add the cream, stir well, and pour into 2 freezing trays. Freeze until almost firm. Scrape into a cold bowl and beat with a rotary beater until fluffy but still thick. Return to freezer and refreeze until almost firm. Beat again until smooth and freeze until firm. Serves 8–10.

PEPPERMINT ICE CREAM

1 pound thin red-and-white peppermint-stick candy
2 cups milk
2 cups heavy cream

Place the peppermint sticks between sheets of waxed paper and crush with a rolling pin until very fine. Soak in the milk for about 1 hour, stirring from time to time. Mix with the whipped cream, pour into freezing trays, and freeze 3–4 hours. Serves 10.

MAPLE BUTTERMILK ICE CREAM

1 cup maple-blended syrup
1 cup buttermilk
1 tablespoon lemon juice
⅛ teaspoon salt
1 cup heavy cream

Mix the syrup, buttermilk, lemon juice, and salt. Pour into freezing tray and freeze for about 2 hours, until firm. Break into pieces and scrape into a cold bowl. Beat until smooth. Fold in the cream, whipped. Return to the tray and freeze about 2 hours, until firm. Serves 6.

MOLASSES-PRALINE ICE CREAM

4 egg yolks
½ cup molasses
1 cup milk
1 cup heavy cream
2–3 tablespoons toasted chopped nuts

Beat the egg yolks with the molasses. Scald the milk and add slowly. Cook in a double boiler, stirring constantly, until thickened. Remove from heat and continue stirring as it cools. When cold, fold in the cream, whipped, and the nuts. Freeze in an ice-cream freezer or freezing tray. If the latter, stir vigorously several times while it freezes. Serves 6.

FRESH PEACH ICE CREAM

2 cups heavy cream
2 cups light cream
¾ cup sugar
Pinch salt
2 cups crushed fresh peaches (or 1 package frozen sliced)
½ teaspoon almond flavoring
½ teaspoon vanilla

Scald the creams with the sugar and salt. Cool. Sweeten the crushed peaches to taste. Add to the cream and flavor with almond flavoring and vanilla. Freeze in a crank-type ice-cream freezer. Serves 10–12.

FRESH BERRY ICE CREAM

Proceed as for Fresh Peach Ice Cream,* substituting 2 cups crushed berries and adjusting sugar to taste.

PISTACHIO ICE CREAM

2 cups light cream
4 egg yolks
¾ cup sugar
Pinch salt
1 envelope unflavored gelatin
2 cups heavy cream
½ teaspoon pistachio flavoring
¼ teaspoon almond flavoring
½ cup pistachio nuts

Scald the cream. Mix the slightly beaten egg yolks with the sugar and salt. Add the cream gradually and cook in a double boiler, stirring constantly, until the mixture coats a spoon. Soften the gelatin in ¼ cup cold water; stir into custard until dissolved. Cool in a pan of ice water until it begins to thicken. Fold in the cream, whipped, and flavor with pistachio and almond flavorings. Add the nuts, blanched and ground fine. Pour into freezing trays and freeze until mushy. Scrape into a cold bowl, beat smooth, and refreeze until firm. If you wish, pack into a 1½-quart mold and freeze until firm. Serves 8–10.

STRAWBERRY ICE CREAM

1½ cups milk
1 cup sugar
1 package frozen strawberries
¼ cup lemon juice
3 egg whites
1 cup heavy cream

Heat the milk and sugar until the sugar is dissolved. Cool. Pour into a freezing tray and freeze until mushy. Meanwhile, thaw the berries and rub through a sieve to remove seeds. Scrape the partially frozen mixture into a cold bowl and beat until smooth. Fold in the berry purée and lemon juice. Pour into 2 freezing trays and freeze until mushy again. Again scrape into a cold bowl and beat only to soften. Beat the egg whites until a stiff peak forms, whip the cream, and combine. Fold into the berry mixture and return to same trays and freeze until firm. Good with Cherry and Strawberry Sauce.* Serves 6–8.

GREENGAGE ICE CREAM

Proceed as for Strawberry Ice Cream.* Drain, pit, and purée 2 (1 lb. 1 oz.) cans greengage plums and substitute for the strawberries. Add a few drops green food coloring if you wish.

PINEAPPLE ICE CREAM

1(1 lb. 13 oz.) can pineapple chunks
1 cup sugar
6 eggs
1 cup heavy cream
2 cups milk
2 tablespoons lemon juice
1 tablespoon grated lemon rind

Drain the pineapple. Heat the syrup with the sugar until dissolved. Cool. Pour into a freezing tray and freeze until mushy. Beat the egg yolks slightly and add the cream and milk. Cook in a double boiler, stirring constantly, until thickened. Cool. Pour into a freezing tray and freeze until mushy. Buzz the pineapple chunks in a blender or force through a food mill. Scrape the contents of both trays into a cold bowl and beat smooth. Add the puréed pineapple, lemon juice, and lemon rind. Return to the trays and freeze again until mushy. Beat the egg whites until a soft peak forms. Beat the ice cream until smooth and fold in the egg whites. Pour quickly into 3 freezing trays and freeze until firm. Serves 12.

EASY STRAWBERRY ICE CREAM

1 package sliced frozen strawberries
1 cup sugar
1 pint sour cream

Thaw the berries until mushy; add sugar and cream. Stir well and put into freezing tray. Stir 3 or 4 times while it freezes. Serves 4.

STRAWBERRY RHUBARB ICE CREAM

2 packages frozen cut rhubarb
1⅓ cups sugar
2 packages frozen sliced strawberries
2 cups heavy cream

Put the thawed rhubarb in a baking dish with the sugar. Cover and bake in a 300° oven for 35–45 minutes, until rhubarb is soft and juicy. Stir occasionally. Cool. Force rhubarb and thawed strawberries through a food mill or buzz in a blender. Add the cream to the purée and freeze to a mush. Scrape into a cold bowl and beat until fluffy. Refreeze. Serves 8.

RASPBERRY ICE CREAM

Proceed as for Strawberry Ice Cream,* substituting 1 package frozen raspberries for the strawberries.

Plate 23.
FROZEN
STRAWBERRY
GRAND-
MARNIER
SOUFFLE.

Plate 24.
ICE CREAM CAKE.

Plate 25.
ICE CREAM
CAKE BOMBE.

Plate 26. PARFAITS—a variety of ice creams and sherbets used singly or in combination, with or without the addition of sauces, fruit, or liqueur. Layered into glasses ahead of time, parfaits make an easy, effective, and colorful dessert.

Plate 27. Flowers
in a casserole, on a
table set for dessert.

Plate 28. Dessert
and coffee served
on a gay cloth
in the patio.

Refrigerator Sherbet

Refrigerator freezing is quite satisfactory, since new refrigerators are colder and, therefore, freeze more quickly. The mixture should be cold when poured into freezing trays. Set the refrigerator at the coldest point. When partially frozen, about 1 inch around the edges, scrape into a cold bowl and beat quickly with a rotary beater until smooth and creamy. Return to freezing compartment, in freezing trays or in a serving bowl, and refreeze until firm. Sherbet melts easily, so the serving dishes should be chilled. Frozen desserts may also be made in freezers.

APRICOT SHERBET

1 cup apricot purée
1 cup milk
1 cup sugar
¾ cup light corn syrup
1 cup orange juice
¼ cup lemon juice
1 teaspoon grated orange rind
1 teaspoon grated lemon rind
2 egg whites

To make the apricot purée, buzz peeled, pitted fresh or canned apricots in a blender or force through a food mill. Put the milk, sugar, and syrup into a saucepan and bring to a boil. Cool. Blend the cold mixture with the purée; add orange and lemon juices and the grated rinds. Mix well and pour into freezing trays. Freeze until almost firm. Scrape into a cold bowl and beat until smooth. Fold in the egg whites, beaten until a soft peak forms. Refreeze until firm. Serves 6–8.

AVOCADO SHERBET

1 cup canned unsweetened pineapple juice
1 cup sugar
5 tablespoons lemon juice
⅓ teaspoon salt
1 cup sieved avocado
2 egg whites

Mix the pineapple juice with ¾ cup water, ¾ cup sugar, lemon juice, and salt. Boil for 5 minutes. Cool. Add the avocado, pour into a freezing tray, and freeze until almost firm.

Beat the egg whites until a stiff peak forms, gradually adding ¼ cup sugar while beating. Scrape the frozen mixture into a cold bowl, beat until smooth, and fold in the egg whites. Refreeze until firm. Serves 6.

CREAMY BANANA SHERBET

6 bananas
3 tablespoons lemon juice
1 (15 oz.) can sweetened condensed milk
2 cups milk
2 egg whites

Rub the bananas through a sieve. Add the lemon juice, condensed milk, and whole milk. Beat with a rotary beater until smooth. If using an electric blender, slice the bananas into it, add some of the milk, buzz until smooth, and mix with other ingredients. Pour into freezing trays and freeze until mushy. Beat smooth. Fold in the egg whites, beaten until a soft peak forms, and continue freezing—about 3 hours in all. During the freezing, beat several times, scraping the sides and bottom of the pan so that a smooth, even consistency is reached. Serves 8.

MARASCHINO SHERBET

⅔ cup sugar
6 tablespoons lemon juice
1 tablespoon grated lemon rind
2 cups milk or half-and-half
⅓ cup maraschino cherries
1 tablespoon maraschino syrup

Mix the sugar, lemon juice, and lemon rind and stir until sugar is dissolved. Add the milk slowly while beating. Add the cherries, chopped fine, and syrup. Mix well and pour into a freezing tray. Freeze until firm, stirring once or twice during the freezing process. Serves 4–6.

BLUEBERRY SHERBET

1 package frozen blueberries
  or 1 (15 oz.) can
1 quart lemon sherbet
1 cup toasted grated coconut (optional)

Rub the berries through a sieve. Stir into the softened lemon sherbet. Freeze in freezing trays. After about 1½ hours stir and refreeze. When ready to serve, sprinkle coconut over the sherbet if you wish. Serves 6–8.

CHERRY SHERBET   (Plate 1)

1 quart fresh cherries or 2 (1 lb.) cans
  pitted tart red cherries
⅔–1 cup sugar
1 envelope unflavored gelatin
⅓ cup orange juice
2 egg whites
Cherries or raspberries (garnish)

Pit and chop the fresh cherries (or chop the drained canned cherries). Mix with the sugar; the amount will depend on the sourness of the cherries. Let stand 1 hour. Strain the liquid and heat with the gelatin and orange juice. Combine with chopped cherries. Freeze until mushy. Scrape into a chilled bowl and beat until light and fluffy but still thick. Freeze partially again. Beat the egg whites until a soft peak forms. Beat cherry mixture until fluffy and soft. Fold in the egg whites. Spoon into a 1½-quart mold or individual molds. Freeze until firm. Dip mold into warm water and turn out. Garnish with fresh cherries or raspberries. Serves 6.

CHAMPAGNE SHERBET

2 cups sugar
2 tablespoons grated lemon rind
¼ cup lemon juice
¼ cup light corn syrup
3 cups champagne (brut)
4 egg whites
¼ cup confectioners' sugar

Boil 2 cups water and the sugar together until the sugar is dissolved. Add the lemon rind, juice, and corn syrup. Cool and then stir in the champagne. Pour into freezing trays and freeze firm. Beat the egg whites until a soft peak forms; then add the confectioners' sugar gradually while beating to form a soft meringue. Scrape the frozen mixture into a cold bowl. Beat smooth. Stir in the meringue and return to freezer. Freeze until almost firm. Beat once again and refreeze. Serves 8.

CRANBERRY SHERBET I

2 cups cranberries
1 cup sugar
1 teaspoon unflavored gelatin
2 tablespoons lemon juice

Cook the cranberries in 1¼ cups water until the skins pop. Rub through a sieve. Add the sugar to the pulp and cook until sugar is dissolved. Remove from heat. Add the gelatin, which has been mixed with ¼ cup water, and the lemon juice. Mix well. Pour into a freezing tray and freeze until firm, stirring twice while freezing. Serves 4.

CRANBERRY SHERBET II

1 (1 lb.) can jellied cranberry sauce
Juice 1 orange
Juice 1 lemon
Grated rind 1 lemon
2 egg whites
¼ cup sugar

Beat the cranberry sauce with a rotary beater until smooth. Add fruit juices and lemon rind. Mix well and freeze until almost firm. Scrape into a cold bowl and beat until smooth. Beat the egg whites with sugar to form a soft meringue. Fold into the cranberry mixture and refreeze until firm. Serves 4.

GINGER-ALE SHERBET
(Low Calorie)

1 envelope unflavored gelatin
⅔ cup plus 2 tablespoons sugar
¼ cup orange juice
6 tablespoons lemon juice
¼ cup pineapple juice
2 pints noncaloric ginger ale
2 egg whites

Soften the gelatin in 1 cup cold water and heat with ⅔ cup sugar until gelatin and sugar are dissolved. Cool and add the fruit juices and ginger ale. Freeze until almost firm. Remove to a cold bowl and beat until mushy. Return to freezer. When quite firm, break into chunks; add the egg whites which have been beaten with the remaining sugar until a peak forms. Quickly beat again until smooth and refreeze. Serves 12 (61 calories per serving).

GRAPE SHERBET
(Low Calorie)

2 teaspoons unflavored gelatin
1 cup grape juice
1 tablespoon corn syrup
1 teaspoon lemon juice
½ teaspoon grated lemon rind
Granulated noncaloric sweetener
1 egg white

Mix the gelatin with 2 tablespoons cold water. Add ½ cup boiling water and stir until dissolved. Add the grape juice, corn syrup, and lemon juice and rind. Mix well. Add a few shakes of sweetener to taste. Pour into freezing tray and freeze until almost firm. Scrape into a cold bowl and beat until smooth. Quickly fold in the egg white, beaten until a soft peak forms. Return to tray and freeze until firm. About 10–15 minutes before serving, break up sherbet with a fork and spoon into a cold bowl. Beat at high speed with electric mixer until sherbet is pale grape-colored and very fluffy. Mound into chilled serving dishes and serve at once. Serves 4 (about 59 calories per serving).

LIME SHERBET
(Low Calorie)

2 envelopes low-calorie lime-flavored
  gelatin
½ cup sugar
3 cups skim milk
½ teaspoon grated lime rind
¼ cup lime juice

Dissolve the gelatin in 1 cup hot water. Add the sugar, milk, and lime rind and juice. Mix well and pour into freezing trays. Freeze until firm. Scrape into a cold bowl, break up the pieces, and beat until smooth. Refreeze until firm. Serves 6 (113 calories per serving).

For a change, serve with 4 peaches, peeled and sliced (146 calories per serving).

FRESH LIME SHERBET

¾ cup lime juice (juice 6 large limes)
½ teaspoon grated lime rind
1¾ cups sugar
1½ teaspoons unflavored gelatin
Green food coloring (optional)
2 egg whites
Pinch salt

Strain the lime juice. Add the rind, 1½ cups sugar, the gelatin, and 1¾ cups water. Boil for 3 minutes. Add a few drops green coloring if you wish. Pour into freezing trays. Freeze to a mush. Meanwhile, beat the egg whites until a peak forms. Add a pinch of salt and the remaining sugar a tablespoon at a time, beating until all sugar is dissolved. Scrape the sherbet into a cold bowl, beat until smooth, and fold in the meringue. Freeze until firm. Serves 4–6.

JAMAICAN LIME SHERBET

1 cup sugar
1 envelope unflavored gelatin
2 cups milk
¼–⅓ cup lime juice
2 teaspoons grated lime rind
Green food coloring
2 tablespoons light rum
2 egg whites

Mix the sugar, gelatin, and milk together. Bring just to boiling point. Cool. Stir in the lime juice and rind, a few drops of coloring, and the rum. Pour into freezing trays and freeze until almost firm. Scrape into a cold bowl, add the egg whites, and beat until smooth but still thick. Return to trays and freeze until firm. Serves 4.

MELON SHERBET
(Low Calorie)

4 packages frozen melon balls
Juice 1 lemon
1 teaspoon grated lemon rind
½–¾ cup sugar or liquid noncaloric
  sweetener to taste
Red food coloring (optional)

Thaw the melon balls and buzz in a blender or rub through a sieve. Add the lemon juice and rind, and sugar or sweetener to taste. Stir in a drop or two of food coloring if you like. Pour into freezing trays and freeze until mushy. Scrape into a cold bowl, beat smooth, and refreeze to the mushy stage. Beat smooth again and freeze until firm. Serves 4 (53 calories per serving).

CANTALOUPE SHERBET

2 large cantaloupes
1 cup sugar
1 envelope unflavored gelatin
Juice 3 lemons or 1 lemon and 2 limes
2 tablespoons light corn syrup
¼ teaspoon salt

Buzz the meat from the melons in a blender or rub through a sieve. You need about 3 cups of purée. Heat and stir the sugar with 1 cup water and the gelatin until dissolved. Remove from heat. Add the fruit juices, melon purée, corn syrup, and salt. Mix well and pour into freezing trays. Freeze until mushy. Scrape into a cold bowl and beat until smooth. Refreeze until firm. Serves 6.

HONEYDEW SHERBET
(Low Calorie)

1 large or 2 small honeydew melons
¼ cup lemon juice
Pinch salt
½ cup sugar
2 teaspoons liquid noncaloric sweetener
Yellow food coloring (optional)

Purée the pulp of the honeydew melon, using a sieve or blender. Add lemon juice and salt. Make a syrup of the sugar and 2 cups water. Cool; add the sweetener and melon purée. Stir in a few drops of food coloring if you wish. Freeze until mushy. Scrape into a cold bowl and beat until smooth. Refreeze until firm. Serves 6 (95 calories per serving).

MELON BALLS WITH MELON SHERBET
(Low Calorie)

3 cantaloupes
1 honeydew melon
Juice 1 lemon
1 teaspoon lemon rind
¼ teaspoon liquid noncaloric sweetener
Red and yellow food coloring (optional)

Cut the cantaloupes in half, saw-tooth fashion. Pull halves apart and remove seeds. Cut as many melon balls as possible. Cut the honeydew in half and make melon balls. Scrape out remaining fruit with a spoon. Refrigerate the balls and cantaloupe shells while you make the sherbet. Rub the melon scrapings through a sieve or buzz in a blender. Add lemon juice, lemon rind, sweetener to taste, and a few drops red and yellow coloring if you wish. Pour into a freezing tray and freeze for ½ hour. Scrape into a cold bowl and beat smooth. Return to freezer for ½ hour more, until mushy. Serve the cantaloupe shells heaped with melon balls and topped with sherbet. You may serve this dessert in chilled dishes if you prefer. Serves 6 (73 calories per serving).

ORANGE SHERBET

1 package orange-flavored gelatin
1 cup orange juice
2 tablespoons lemon juice
¾ cup sugar
1 tablespoon grated lemon rind
2 cups milk

Dissolve the gelatin in 1 cup hot water and add the fruit juices, sugar, and grated lemon rind. Chill until syrupy. Add the milk and freeze until mushy. Scrape into a cold bowl, beat until smooth, and refreeze. Serves 6.

TANGERINE BUTTERMILK SHERBET

1 envelope unflavored gelatin
¾ cup sugar
1 can frozen tangerine-juice concentrate
2¼ cups buttermilk

Mix the gelatin with ½ cup cold water. Place over boiling water, add sugar, and stir until dissolved. Pour into a large bowl. Add the juice concentrate and buttermilk. Mix well and pour into freezing trays. When almost firm, scrape into a cold bowl and beat until smooth. Return to trays and freeze until firm. Serves 6.

PINEAPPLE SHERBET

4 eggs
⅛ teaspoon salt
⅔ cup sugar
1 cup light corn syrup
1 quart milk
1 (1 lb. 13 oz.) can crushed pineapple
⅔ cup lemon juice
2½ teaspoons grated lemon rind

Beat the eggs and salt until light, gradually adding the sugar and corn syrup. Add the milk, pineapple, lemon juice and rind; mix well and pour into 3 freezing trays. Freeze until frozen about ½ inch around the edges. Scrape into a cold bowl and beat until smooth. Return to freezing trays and refreeze. Serves 12–15.

MINTED PINEAPPLE SHERBET

½ cup sugar
¼ teaspoon mint flavoring
Green food coloring (optional)
⅓ cup lemon juice
½ cup canned crushed pineapple
1 cup ginger ale

Put the sugar, ½ cup water, mint flavoring, and a few drops green food coloring if you wish in a saucepan and simmer for 10 minutes. Cool. Add the lemon juice, crushed pineapple, and ginger ale. Mix thoroughly. Pour into a freezing tray. Freeze until mushy, stir, and freeze until firm. Serves 2–4.

PEACH SHERBET   (*Plate 31*)
(Low Calorie)

1 package frozen peaches
¼ cup sugar
¼ cup frozen orange-juice concentrate
¼ teaspoon granulated noncaloric
 sweetener
¾ cup liquefied nonfat dry milk
1 egg white
½ teaspoon almond flavoring
1 peach (*garnish*)

Thaw, drain, and chop the peaches. Mix 2 tablespoons sugar with the peaches. Heat until sugar is dissolved. Cool and add the orange-juice concentrate and sweetener. Freeze the milk until mushy. Pour into a cold bowl and beat until the consistency of whipped cream. Beat the egg white until frothy. Add remaining sugar while beating. Fold in the whipped milk. Add peach mixture. Pour into freezing trays and freeze until almost firm. Beat smooth and freeze overnight. Beat until smooth, add almond flavoring, and refreeze until firm. Garnish with slices of peach if you wish. Serves 6 (125 calories per serving).

RASPBERRY SHERBET

3 packages frozen raspberries
¾ cup sugar
2 tablespoons light corn syrup
3 cups milk
3–5 tablespoons lemon juice

Buzz the thawed berries in a blender and strain or force through a sieve. Heat the sugar, syrup, and milk, stirring until sugar is dissolved. Cool. Add to the purée with the lemon juice. Pour into freezing trays and freeze until almost firm. Scrape into a cold bowl and beat until smooth. Freeze again until almost firm. Repeat the beating and refreeze until firm. Serves 8–10.

RASPBERRY SHERBET WITH BLUE-BERRIES

1 quart raspberry sherbet
1 pint fresh, 1 package frozen, or 1 (1 lb.)
 can blueberries

Spoon the sherbet into a serving dish and sprinkle with fresh berries, thawed frozen, or partially drained canned blueberries. The color combination is attractive. Serves 6.

STRAWBERRY SHERBET

3 quarts strawberries
3 cups sugar
1 tablespoon lemon juice
Dash cayenne

Hull the berries; cut in half or slice them and mix with the sugar. Let stand about 3 hours, stirring occasionally. Buzz in a blender or crush and rub through a sieve. Add 2½ cups water, the lemon juice, and cayenne. Mix well and freeze in freezing trays until thick but not frozen solid; stir occasionally. Scrape into a cold bowl and beat until smooth. Cover with Saran or foil and freeze. This sherbet is better frozen in a crank-type freezer. Serves 8–12.

STRAWBERRY HONEY SHERBET
(Low Calorie)

2 packages frozen sliced strawberries
½ cup honey
Pinch salt
1½ teaspoons unflavored gelatin
Juice 1 lemon
¼ teaspoon rose flavoring (*optional*)
2 egg whites

Thaw the berries and rub through a sieve. There should be 3 cups purée. Heat and add the honey and salt. Simmer 5 minutes. Add the gelatin and stir until dissolved. Cool. Add the lemon juice, and the rose flavoring if you wish. Pour into a freezing tray. Freeze until solid around the edges. Scrape into a chilled bowl and beat until smooth. Quickly fold in the egg whites, beaten until a soft peak forms, and return at once to freezer. Freeze until firm. Serves 6 (198 calories per serving).

THREE-FRUIT SHERBET

3 ripe bananas
1½ cups orange juice
½ cup lemon juice
2 cups sugar

Peel and mash the bananas. Add the fruit juices, sugar, and 2 cups water. Stir until the sugar is dissolved or buzz in a blender. Pour into freezing trays. During the freezing time, stir every 20 minutes until mixture becomes mushy, about 2 hours. Continue freezing until firm. Serves 8.

PURPLE PLUM SHERBET

2 cups purple plums
Juice 1½ lemons
Grated rind 1 lemon
1 cup sugar
1½ cups buttermilk
⅛ teaspoon salt

Put the plums in a pan with ½ cup water, cover, and simmer gently for 10 minutes. Cool; pit and purée the plums. You need about 1 cup of purée. If you use canned plums, drain and purée; reduce the amount of sugar to ¾ cup. Add lemon juice and rind and the sugar; simmer all together until sugar is dissolved. Cool and add the buttermilk and salt. Mix well, pour into freezing trays, and freeze until almost firm. Scrape into a cold bowl and beat smooth. Return to trays and freeze until firm. Serves 4.

RHUBARB SHERBET

2 pounds rhubarb
2¼ cups sugar
1 tablespoon light corn syrup
2 egg whites
1 cup heavy cream

Trim the rhubarb, cut into 1-inch pieces, and put into a saucepan with the sugar and ½ cup water. Bring to a boil and cook gently until very tender. Force through a food mill or sieve; you will have about 4 cups of purée. Stir in the corn syrup, cool, and freeze until hard around the edges but still soft in the center. Scrape into a cold bowl and beat until smooth. Whip the egg whites until they hold a soft peak and fold into the sherbet along with the cream, whipped. Freeze until firm. Spoon into a chilled serving dish. Serves 8–10.

WATERMELON SHERBET   . *(Plate 34)*

¼ of a 25-pound watermelon or 1
    (6–7 lb.) midget watermelon
1 can frozen lemonade concentrate
¼ teaspoon salt
Sugar
Lemon juice
2 envelopes unflavored gelatin
Red food coloring (optional)

Remove seeds and rind from the melon. Buzz the pulp in a blender or chop and rub through a fine sieve. You need 6 cups purée. Stir in the lemonade concentrate and salt. Add sugar and lemon juice to taste; the amount will depend upon the sweetness of the melon. Mix the gelatin with ½ cup water and heat to dissolve. Add to the melon mixture. Mix well and pour into 2 freezing trays. Freeze until frozen ½ inch around the edges. Scrape into a cold bowl and beat until smooth. Add a few drops of the red coloring if you wish. Return to freezer until firm. For a party dessert, serve garnished with melon balls and a sprinkling of blueberries. Serves 8–10.

Mousse

Frozen mousse contains whipped cream and is made in the freezing compartment of the refrigerator. Because the mixture is thick, it does not usually need to be beaten during the freezing process. This rich, creamy dessert is a suitable ending for a party dinner or when the meal is light. Serve rather small helpings.

ANGEL MOUSSE

¾ cup sugar
Pinch salt
3 egg whites
1 cup heavy cream
2 teaspoons vanilla
Fresh or frozen raspberries (garnish)

Bring the sugar, salt, and ⅓ cup water to a boil in a covered saucepan. Uncover and boil the syrup to the soft-ball stage (238°). Beat the egg whites until a stiff peak forms. Add the syrup gradually while beating. Cool. Fold in the cream, whipped, and the vanilla. Pour the mixture into a freezing tray and freeze until firm. Serve with sugared fresh berries, crushed or whole, or use frozen berries without sugar. Serves 6.

CHOCOLATE MOUSSE I

1 (6 oz.) package semisweet chocolate bits
6 eggs
½ cup sugar
1 teaspoon vanilla
½ teaspoon cinnamon
Pinch salt
1 cup heavy cream

Melt the chocolate in a double boiler. Add ½ cup hot water and stir until smooth. Cool slightly. Beat the egg yolks until very thick. Stir in the melted chocolate. Beat the egg whites until a soft peak forms and gradually add the sugar, beating continuously. Add the vanilla, cinnamon, and salt. Fold in the chocolate mixture and the cream, whipped. Pour into 2 freezing trays and freeze until mixture is mushy. Stir gently but thoroughly and refreeze until firm. Serves 6.

CHOCOLATE MOUSSE II

1 teaspoon unflavored gelatin
1 cup milk
2 ounces unsweetened chocolate
¾ cup sugar
1 teaspoon vanilla
2 cups heavy cream

Stir the gelatin into the milk and then add the chocolate and ¼ cup sugar. Heat until the milk is scalded, chocolate is melted, and gelatin is dissolved. Beat until well blended. Add the vanilla and pour into freezing trays or a bowl. Chill until the mixture thickens; whip until light. Beat the remaining sugar into the cream and whip until stiff. Fold the cream into frozen mixture. Return to freezing trays. Freeze until firm. Serves 8.

EASY CHOCOLATE MOUSSE WITH HOT SAUCE

1 (14 oz.) package chocolate-fudge-flavor frosting mix
2 cups heavy cream
2 tablespoons chocolate- or coffee-flavored liqueur or brandy
2 tablespoons butter

Put half the contents of the frosting in a large mixing bowl with the cream. Mix, then whip with rotary beater until fluffy and thick. Be careful not to overbeat. Stir in the liqueur. Spoon the mousse into 6 after-dinner coffee cups or small dishes. Freeze several hours until firm. In a small saucepan mix the remaining frosting mix with butter and ½ cup water. Bring to a boil and simmer for 10 minutes. Serve this sauce quite hot with the mousse. Serves 6.

COCOA MOUSSE

1½ cups sugar
1 cup Dutch or breakfast cocoa
Pinch salt
1 teaspoon vanilla
2 cups heavy cream

Mix the sugar with ½ cup water and heat slowly, without stirring, to the soft-ball stage (234°). Cool slightly without stirring. Then beat in the cocoa and salt until smooth. Cool thoroughly. Flavor with vanilla and fold in the cream, whipped. Pour into freezing trays and freeze until mushy. Scrape into a cold bowl, beat smooth, and freeze until firm. Serves 6–8.

COFFEE MOUSSE

2 envelopes unflavored gelatin
1 quart milk
4 teaspoons instant coffee
½ cup sugar
½ cup light corn syrup
Pinch salt
2 cups heavy cream
4 egg whites

Mix the gelatin and the milk. Cook and stir over low heat until the gelatin dissolves. Add the instant coffee and stir well. Add the sugar, corn syrup, and salt. Stir until the sugar dissolves. Chill until thick. Fold in the cream, whipped. Beat the egg whites until a soft peak forms and fold into the cream mixture. Pour into freezing trays and freeze until mixture is mushy. Scrape into a cold bowl and beat quickly until smooth. Return to trays and freeze until firm. Serves 12.

APRICOT MOUSSE WITH SAUCE

2 (1 lb. 13 oz.) cans apricots
2 cups heavy cream
½–1 cup sugar
Rum or rum flavoring (optional)

Drain the apricots, reserving the syrup. Rub the fruit through a sieve; you need about 3 cups purée. Fold in the cream, whipped. Pour into freezing trays and freeze until firm.

For sauce, add sugar to the apricot syrup and boil until quite thick. Cool. Just before serving, stir in rum or rum flavoring to taste. Serves 8.

APRICOT HONEY MOUSSE

3 cups apricot purée
6 egg yolks
⅔ cup honey
Juice 2 lemons
2 cups heavy cream

Use canned or stewed fresh or dried apricots. Drain before puréeing. Beat the egg yolks until thick and lemon-colored. Add the honey gradually, beating the mixture until very thick. Fold in the apricot purée, lemon juice, and cream, whipped. Pour into 3 freezing trays. Freeze until firm. Serves 10–12.

HONEY MOUSSE

2 egg whites
Pinch salt
⅓ cup honey
1 cup heavy cream
¼ teaspoon almond flavoring

Beat the egg whites with the salt until a stiff peak forms. Add the honey and beat thoroughly. Fold in the cream, whipped, and also the almond flavoring. Pour into a freezing tray and freeze until firm. Serves 4–6.

LEMON MOUSSE

1 envelope unflavored gelatin
2¼ cups sugar
3 cups milk
Juice 3 lemons
2 teaspoons grated lemon rind
3 cups heavy cream
1 egg white
4 cups sliced fresh, frozen, or canned
* peaches (optional)*

Mix the gelatin, sugar, and milk. Heat until sugar dissolves. Cool. Add the lemon juice and rind. Freeze until almost firm. Whip the cream until thick and glossy and fold in the egg white, beaten until a stiff peak forms. Meanwhile, beat the lemon mixture in a cold bowl until smooth. Quickly fold in the cream mixture. Freeze overnight or until firm in a 3-quart ring or decorative mold. To unmold, loosen edges with a knife, dip bottom of mold quickly into hot water, and invert on a baking sheet. Unless serving at once, return mousse to freezer. To serve, transfer mold to a plate, using a broad spatula. Fill center and decorate with sliced peaches if you wish. Serves 12–14.

CURRANT JELLY MOUSSE

3 egg whites
Pinch salt
½ cup currant jelly
1½ tablespoons lemon juice
1 cup heavy cream

Beat the egg whites with the salt until a soft peak forms. Add the currant jelly by spoonfuls, beating after each addition. Add the lemon juice. Whip the cream to a custardlike consistency—not too stiff—and fold into the jelly whip. Pour the mixture into a freezing tray and freeze, without stirring, 2–3 hours, until firm. Serves 4–6.

MAPLE MOUSSE I

1 cup maple syrup
4 eggs
1 cup heavy cream
1 teaspoon vanilla
Pinch salt

Heat the maple syrup. Beat the egg yolks until thick and lemon-colored. Stir in the hot syrup gradually and cook in a double boiler until thickened, stirring constantly. Cool. Beat the egg whites until a soft peak forms and fold into the custard. Whip the cream with the vanilla and salt and add. Pour into a freezing tray. When partly frozen, stir well and continue freezing until firm. Serves 6.

MAPLE MOUSSE II

1–1½ cups maple syrup
Pinch salt
2 cups heavy cream

Bring the syrup to a boil, add salt, and simmer for 5 minutes. Cool. Whip the cream and fold in the cold syrup. Freeze in freezing tray until firm. Serves 8.

ORANGE MOUSSE

⅔ cup orange juice
⅔ cup sugar
Pinch salt
3 egg yolks
1 cup heavy cream

Heat the orange juice with sugar and salt in a double boiler. Beat the egg yolks until thick and lemon-colored. Add to the orange-juice mixture gradually and cook until thick, stirring constantly. Cool thoroughly. Whip the cream and fold into the orange mixture. Pour into freezing trays or muffin-size fluted paper cups and freeze until firm. Serves 8.

ORANGE LEMON MOUSSE

⅔ cup orange juice
¼ cup lemon juice
¼ cup pineapple juice
1 teaspoon grated orange rind
1 cup sugar
1 cup heavy cream

Mix together the fruit juices, orange rind, and sugar. Stir until the sugar is dissolved. Fold into the cream, whipped, and pour into a freezing tray. Stir once when partially frozen. Serves 6.

PINEAPPLE MOUSSE

1⅓ cups sugar
2 (9 oz.) cans crushed pineapple
½ cup lemon juice
2 cups heavy cream
4 egg whites

Mix the sugar, 1 cup water, and ½ cup syrup drained from the pineapple. Heat about 5 minutes, until sugar is thoroughly dissolved. Add 1½ cups drained pineapple and the lemon juice. Cool, then pour into freezing trays and freeze until mushy. Scrape into a cold bowl and beat until smooth. Add the cream, whipped, and fold in the stiffly beaten egg whites. Return to freezing trays and refreeze. Serves 10–12.

GINGER PINEAPPLE MARSHMALLOW MOUSSE

16 large marshmallows
1 (1 lb. 14 oz.) can crushed pineapple
1 tablespoon grated preserved ginger
1 cup heavy cream

Place the marshmallows and 2 tablespoons water in a double boiler and heat and stir until melted. Cool slightly. Combine with the drained pineapple, ginger, and 3 tablespoons of syrup from the pineapple. Fold in the cream, whipped, and pour into a 1-quart mold, bowl, or freezing tray. Freeze for 3–4 hours, until firm. Serves 6.

STRAWBERRY MOUSSE

1 quart strawberries
1 cup sugar
2 envelopes unflavored gelatin
2 cups heavy cream

Crush the strawberries, cover with the sugar, and let stand 1 hour. Rub through a sieve. Mix the gelatin with ½ cup cold water. Heat until gelatin is dissolved. Add to the strawberries and chill until syrupy. Whip the cream and fold into strawberry mixture. Pour into freezing trays and freeze until set. Serves 6–8.

RASPBERRY MOUSSE

Substitute raspberries for the strawberries and proceed as for Strawberry Mousse.*

BANANA FROST

4–5 ripe bananas
¼ cup lemon juice
½ cup orange juice
½ cup pineapple juice
1 cup milk
1½ cups heavy cream
Yellow food coloring (optional)
2 seedless oranges (garnish)

Purée 3 bananas in a food mill or buzz in a blender. You need 1 cup purée. Add lemon juice at once to prevent darkening. Add orange and pineapple juices and the milk; mix well. Fold in the cream, whipped. Add a few drops of coloring if you wish. Pour into freezing trays and freeze until firm. When ready to serve, slice 1–2 bananas and sprinkle with lemon juice. Cut sections from the oranges. Spoon the frost into a serving dish and decorate with bananas and oranges. Serves 8.

PINEAPPLE FROST

2 (1 lb.) cans crushed pineapple
1 envelope unflavored gelatin
¾ cup mint-flavored apple jelly
2 cups heavy cream
2 teaspoons confectioners' sugar

Drain the pineapple, reserving 1 cup of the liquid. In this soften the gelatin. Melt the jelly over low heat, add the gelatin, and heat until it is dissolved. Stir in the pineapple and chill. Whip the cream with the sugar and fold into the pineapple mixture. Pour into freezing trays and freeze until just mushy. Serves 10.

BING-CHERRY FROST

1½ pints vanilla ice cream
3 cups heavy cream
2 tablespoons rum or
  2–3 teaspoons rum flavoring
1 (1 lb. 4 oz.) can Bing cherries
1½ tablespoons cornstarch
1½ tablespoons sugar

Let the ice cream soften a little. Whip the cream, mix with the ice cream, and continue whipping until mixture stands in soft peaks. Flavor to taste with rum or rum flavoring. Pour into 2 freezing trays and freeze until firm. Meanwhile, drain the cherries and chill the fruit. Add the cornstarch mixed with the sugar to the cherry syrup. Heat and stir until thickened, about 10 minutes. Chill. Heap spoonfuls of frozen cream into a chilled serving bowl. Spoon the fruit and sauce over it. Serves 12–14.

PEAR GINGER FROST

1 (1 lb. 13 oz.) can pear halves
1 tablespoon lemon juice
⅓ cup syrup drained from preserved
  ginger
2 egg whites

Drain the pear halves and buzz in a blender or force through a food mill. Add the lemon juice and ginger syrup. Fold in the egg whites which have been beaten until a soft peak forms. Pour into a freezing tray and freeze until mushy. Scrape into a cold bowl and beat until smooth. Return to tray and freeze until firm. Serves 3.

FRUIT FROST

12 fresh or canned apricots or nectarines
Lemon juice
½ pint vanilla ice cream
2 cups heavy cream
½ teaspoon vanilla
Toasted coconut chips

Peel, halve, and pit the fresh fruit; drain if using canned. Arrange the fruit in a bowl and sprinkle the fresh fruit with lemon juice. Chill. Let the ice cream get a little soft; then whip together with the cream which has been whipped and flavored with vanilla. Keep in freezer until ready to use, but don't let it freeze too hard. Heap the cream on the fruit and top with coconut chips. Serves 8.

Parfaits (*Plate 26*)

Parfaits are a boon to the hostess since they are made ahead and take only a moment to bring to the table from the freezer. In chilled glasses, combine two kinds of ice cream, ice cream and sherbet or mousse, using commercial or homemade. Use a fruit or other sauce in layers in the parfait glass or add a liqueur for a festive touch.

In chilled parfait glasses, alternate equal parts of:

Chocolate Ice Cream and Lemon Sherbet

Chocolate Ice Cream and Mint Ice Cream

Chocolate Ice Cream and Coffee Ice Cream

Chocolate Mousse and Raspberry Sherbet

Coffee Ice Cream and Lemon Sherbet

Coffee Ice Cream and Strawberry Ice Cream

Coffee Mousse and Orange Sherbet

Vanilla Ice Cream and Strawberry Ice Cream

Vanilla Ice Cream and Chocolate-Chip Ice Cream

Vanilla Ice Cream and Mint Ice Cream

Vanilla Ice Cream and Melon Sherbet

Vanilla Ice Cream and Lemon Sherbet

Strawberry Ice Cream and Pineapple Sherbet

Strawberry Ice Cream and Peach Ice Cream

Lemon Ice Cream and Rum Bisque

Lemon Mousse and Lemon Sherbet

Layer ice cream, mousse, or sherbet with sugared crushed fruit or a sauce:

Chocolate Ice Cream and Lemon Sauce

Chocolate Ice Cream and Marshmallow Mint Sauce

Chocolate Ice Cream and Chocolate Fudge Sauce

Chocolate Ice Cream and Fluffy Mint Sauce

Coffee Ice Cream and Strawberry Purée

Coffee Ice Cream and Ginger Sauce

Coffee Ice Cream and Three-Fruit Sauce

Lemon Ice Cream and Raspberry Sauce

Lemon Sherbet and Apple Lemon Sauce

Lemon Ice Cream and Crushed Pineapple

Orange Sherbet and Raspberry Orange Sauce

Orange Ice Cream and Chocolate Sauce

Peach Ice Cream and Crushed Peaches

Peach Ice Cream and Three-Fruit Sauce

Peach Ice Cream and Special Melba Sauce

Pineapple Sherbet and Crushed Peaches

Pineapple Ice Cream and Butterscotch Sauce

Pineapple Mousse and Crushed Strawberries

Pistachio Ice Cream and Peach Sauce

Raspberry Sherbet and Raspberry Sauce

Raspberry Sherbet and Strawberry Purée

Strawberry Ice Cream and Strawberry Purée

Strawberry Ice Cream and Macaroon Sauce

Strawberry Ice Cream and Bing-Cherry Sauce

Vanilla Ice Cream and Satiny Mocha Sauce

Vanilla Ice Cream and Tutti-Frutti Sauce

Vanilla Ice Cream and Maple Sauce

Vanilla Ice Cream and Jubilée Sauce

Fill parfait glasses with mousse, ice cream, or sherbet and make a hole down the center, the size of a pencil, almost to the bottom of the glass. Fill the space with chilled sauce or liqueur:

Chocolate Ice Cream and Chocolate Sauce

Chocolate Mousse and Crème de Cacao

Chocolate Ice Cream and Coffee Sauce

Chocolate Ice Cream and Curaçao or Cointreau

Coffee Ice Cream and Chocolate Sauce

Coffee Ice Cream and Irish Whiskey

Coffee Mousse and Brandy

Vanilla Ice Cream and B&B

Vanilla Ice Cream and Dark Rum

Vanilla Ice Cream and Green Crème de Menthe

Vanilla Ice Cream and Apricot-Nectar Sauce

Strawberry Ice Cream and Red Wine

Strawberry Ice Cream and Light Rum

Strawberry Ice Cream and White Crème de Menthe

Lemon Ice Cream and Chocolate Sauce

Lemon Ice Cream and Mocha Fudge Sauce

Lemon Ice Cream and Orange Sauce

Peach Ice Cream and Apricot Brandy

Pineapple Mousse and Light Rum

Orange Mousse and Curaçao

If you want your parfaits to look fancier still, top with a little Sweetened Whipped Cream,* nuts, chocolate curls, crushed mint candies, berries, grated orange or lemon rind, or crushed fruit.

LIME PEACH STRAWBERRY PARFAITS

1 pint lime sherbet
1 pint peach ice cream
1 cup sugared sliced strawberries
1 cup Sweetened Whipped Cream*
(optional)

Soften the sherbet and ice cream slightly so that they can be spooned easily. Then alternate the sherbet with the ice cream and strawberries in chilled parfait glasses and repeat. Top with whipped cream if you wish. Freeze. Serves 6.

CHOCOLATE ICE-CREAM CUPS

1 (6 oz.) package chocolate bits
1 quart ice cream

Melt the chocolate. Coat the inside of 6 paper cupcake liners as evenly as possible. Cool. When ready to serve, pull off the paper and fill with the ice cream. Choose the flavor you wish; coffee is recommended. Try filling the cups with tiny scoops of assorted ice creams. Serves 6.

BISCUIT TORTONI

2 egg whites
½ cup superfine sugar
2 cups heavy cream
1 cup crumbled day-old macaroons
2 tablespoons brandy

Beat the egg whites until a peak forms and gradually add the sugar, beating until stiff and glossy. Fold in the cream, whipped. Reserve ¼ cup of the macaroon crumbs and fold the rest into the cream mixture. Add the brandy. Spoon into 12–14 paper baking cups and sprinkle with the reserved macaroon crumbs. Freeze until firm. Serves 12–14.

QUICK TORTONI

2 quarts vanilla ice cream
1½ cups macaroon crumbs
½ cup diced candied cherries
1 cup chopped toasted blanched almonds

Put the ice cream in a bowl and break it up with a spoon. Let it soften a bit. Add the macaroons, cherries, and almonds. Stir quickly together. Pack into pint or quart molds or into individual fluted paper cups and refreeze. Serves 12–15.

MACAROON FRUIT PARFAIT

½ cup macaroon crumbs
½ cup chopped mixed candied fruit
2 tablespoons sherry or 1 tablespoon
* maraschino cherry syrup*
1 tablespoon orange flavoring
8 egg yolks
1 cup sugar
1½ cups heavy cream

Mix the macaroon crumbs and fruit and soak for ½ hour in the sherry or maraschino cherry syrup and orange flavoring. Beat the egg yolks with sugar until thick and lemon-colored. Fold in the fruit and macaroon crumbs. Whip 1 cup cream until thick and shiny. Fold into the fruit mixture and pour into a bowl or trays. Freeze until firm. The mixture will not become too hard but just velvety, since it is very rich. Serve in parfait glasses with alternate spoonfuls of the remaining cream, whipped. Serves 8.

ICE-CREAM CAKE   (Plate 24)

20 standard-size ladyfingers
2 quarts vanilla ice cream
1 can frozen orange-juice concentrate
2 packages frozen raspberries
2 (9 oz.) cans crushed pineapple
1 tablespoon frozen lemonade concentrate
1 teaspoon almond flavoring
2 tablespoons rum
3 tablespoons chopped blanched pistachio
* nuts*
6 maraschino cherries
Sweetened Whipped Cream* (garnish)
Sugared strawberries (garnish)
Mint leaves (optional)

Line the bottom and sides of a 10-inch spring-form pan with ladyfingers split in half. Mix 1 quart vanilla ice cream with the frozen undiluted orange juice. Pour into mold over the bottom layer of ladyfingers. Work quickly to prevent ice cream from becoming too soft. Freeze firm. Meanwhile, buzz the raspberries and pineapple in a blender with the lemonade concentrate, or purée through food mill. Strain to remove seeds and freeze until mushy. Scrape into a cold bowl and beat slightly. Spoon over the orange layer and freeze. To the other quart of ice cream add the almond flavoring, rum, nuts, and cherries, chopped. Pour this over the raspberry layer and freeze overnight. Transfer to refrigerator 1 hour before serving. Final frills: garnish with Sweetened Whipped Cream, sugared fresh strawberries, and mint if you wish. Serves 12.

ANGEL ICE-CREAM CAKE

1 recipe Angel-Food Cake*
2 quarts strawberry ice cream
1 package frozen strawberries
4 teaspoons cornstarch
Sugared sliced peaches or strawberries
(optional)

Bake the cake in two 9×5×2¾-inch loaf pans in a 300° oven for 40–50 minutes. Cool. Wrap one loaf and save for later use. With a sharp knife slice the other cake the long way in 4 layers. Let the ice cream stand at room temperature until soft enough to cut. Cut off slices of ice cream and fit them together on the cake. Put the next slice of cake on the ice cream and press it down. Repeat until the loaf is complete with 4 layers of cake and 3 of ice cream. Work as fast as possible. Wrap the loaf in foil and freeze while you make the glaze. Rub the thawed strawberries through a sieve. Mix cornstarch and ½ cup water, add to puréed berries, bring to a boil, and boil 2 minutes. Chill. Spread the top of the cake with the glaze and return to freezer for a few minutes until the glaze freezes. Again wrap in foil, return to freezer, and it is ready to serve when you wish. About 20 minutes before serving time, remove from freezer to let it thaw slightly. The ice-cream cake is easier to slice if you dip the knife in hot water. Surround the cake with the peaches or berries if you wish. Serves 8.

ORANGE CHOCOLATE CREAM CAKE

¼ cup instant cocoa
¾ cup chocolate-wafer crumbs
1¼ cups confectioners' sugar
1 quart heavy cream
¼ cup orange juice
2 teaspoons vanilla
Grated rind 1 orange
Mandarin orange sections (garnish)

Stir the cocoa into the crumbs. Add sugar to the cream, whipped. Then add the orange juice, vanilla, and orange rind. To make the cake, place alternate thin layers of cream and crumbs in freezing trays. Build up until trays are full.

Be sure the top layer of each is cream. Freeze until firm. When ready to serve, either spoon into serving dishes or cut into squares and serve. Garnish with mandarin orange sections. Serves 8.

ICE-CREAM CAKE WITH FRUIT

2 quarts vanilla ice cream
2 packages frozen raspberries
1 (9 oz.) can crushed pineapple
1½ teaspoons frozen lemonade concentrate
1 pint fresh raspberries or 1 package frozen
(garnish)
1 pound fresh peaches or 1 package frozen
(garnish)
Special Melba Sauce* (optional)

Soften 1 quart ice cream and beat until smooth. Pour into an 8-inch spring-form pan and freeze until firm. Crush the raspberries or buzz in a blender. Strain to remove seeds. Add the crushed pineapple and lemonade concentrate. Mix well, pour into a freezing tray, and freeze until mushy. Scrape into a cold bowl and beat slightly. Pour over ice cream in the mold to form a second layer and return to freezer. When layer is frozen, add a layer of softened ice cream which has been beaten until smooth. Cover and freeze. To serve, set the cake in the refrigerator 1 hour before serving so it is easier to slice. Garnish the cake with raspberries and sliced peaches. Top if you wish with some Special Melba Sauce and pass the rest. Serves 8–10.

CHOCOLATE MINT-CREAM LOAF

12–16 chocolate wafers
3 tablespoons butter
2 tablespoons confectioners' sugar
1 cup small white after-dinner mints
1 cup heavy cream

Crush enough chocolate wafers to make 1¼ cups. Cream the butter with some of the chocolate crumbs and the confectioners' sugar. Work in the rest of the crumbs. Spread half of this mixture on the bottom of a freezing tray. Crush the mints fine and fold them into the stiffly whipped cream. Spread cream mixture over the layer of chocolate-crumb mixture. Cover with remaining chocolate-crumb mixture. Freeze until firm. Cut in slices for serving. Serves 4–6.

CHAMPAGNE COUPE

2 peaches
Lemon juice
Small bunch seedless grapes
1 pint strawberry ice cream
1 split pink champagne

Peel, pit, and slice the peaches. Sprinkle with a little lemon juice to prevent darkening. Divide the peaches among 4 champagne or sherbet glasses. Add a few stemmed grapes and a large scoop of ice cream to each glass. Fill to the brim with chilled champagne. Serve at once. Serves 4.

TRIPLE RASPBERRY DESSERT

1 quart raspberry sherbet
2 pints raspberries or 2 packages frozen
¼ cup Framboise, Himbeergeist, or kirsch

Spoon the sherbet into a serving bowl or into sherbet glasses. Top with the raspberries, fresh or partially thawed frozen. Pass the liqueur. Serves 6–8.

CHESTNUT ICE-CREAM TORTE

CHESTNUT TORTE
4 eggs
1 cup canned puréed chestnuts
¾ cup sugar
1 teaspoon vanilla
*1 tablespoon rum or 1 teaspoon rum
flavoring*

FILLING
1 cup heavy cream
1 teaspoon grated orange rind
*1 tablespoon rum or 1 teaspoon rum
flavoring*
¼ teaspoon nutmeg
1 pint vanilla ice cream

Chestnut Torte. Add the beaten egg yolks to the puréed chestnuts; beat in the sugar until smooth. Flavor with vanilla and rum or rum flavoring. Fold in the egg whites beaten until a soft peak forms. Line three 8-inch cake pans on the bottom with waxed paper and spread ⅓ of the batter in each. Bake for 20-25 minutes in a 375° oven, until the cake is light brown and has pulled away from the sides of the pans. Invert immediately on cake racks, remove pans, and peel off the waxed paper. Cool. The cake will be soft and spongy since it was made without flour.

Filling. Whip the cream and flavor with orange rind, rum or rum flavoring, and nutmeg. Quickly beat in the vanilla ice cream which is slightly softened. You will have to work fast.

Put the cake together, using the ice-cream mixture as the filling and frosting. Freeze until firm. If the ice cream gets too soft while working, put it with the partially prepared cake into the freezer to harden a bit. To make it easier to cut, transfer the cake from freezer to refrigerator 15 minutes before serving. Serves 10.

ICE-CREAM CHOCOLATE ROLL

3 eggs
1 cup sugar
¾ cup cake flour
¼ cup cocoa
2 teaspoons baking powder
¼ teaspoon salt
1 teaspoon vanilla
Confectioners' sugar
1 quart coffee or vanilla ice cream

Beat the eggs very light and add the sugar gradually, beating after each addition. Add ¼ cup cold water. Sift the flour, cocoa, baking powder, and salt together. Add to the egg mixture, beating slowly. Flavor with vanilla. Line a greased 15½ × 10½ × 1-inch jelly-roll pan with waxed paper and grease again. Pour in the batter, spread smooth, and bake in a 425° oven for 12–15 minutes. Turn out on a towel which has been sprinkled with confectioners' sugar. Remove the waxed paper and trim crisp edges. Roll up in the towel. Cool. Unroll and spread with coffee or vanilla ice cream softened enough to spread. Roll up quickly, wrap in foil, and keep in freezing compartment until ready to serve. Slice and serve with or without Chocolate Sauce.* Serves 6–8.

FROZEN STRAWBERRY CREAM CAKE

1 pint strawberries
¼ cup sugar
1 teaspoon orange flavoring
8 ladyfingers
1 cup heavy cream
¼ cup confectioners' sugar

Set aside 7 or 8 of the best berries. Hull the rest and buzz in a blender or force through a food mill. Strain through a fine sieve to remove all seeds from the purée. Stir in the sugar and orange flavoring and chill. Line the bottom of a round dish or pan about 8 inches in diameter and 2 inches deep with waxed paper. Split the ladyfingers lengthwise and make a star design in the bottom of the dish; save half for a second layer. Hull the whole berries, cut them in half lengthwise, and place them cut side down with points out between the ladyfingers and in the center of the star. Mix the cream and sugar and whip until stiff. Fold in the berry purée. Spoon half of the mixture over the ladyfingers, being sure to spread to the edges of the pan. Now make a second star design, using the rest of the ladyfinger halves. Top with remaining strawberry cream and freeze until firm. Unmold on a serving plate and remove paper. Serves 6.

ORIENTAL SHERBET MOLD

1 quart lemon sherbet
1 tablespoon minced preserved ginger
2 tablespoons finely chopped, pitted
    preserved kumquats
1 quart orange sherbet
Poached or canned pear halves (garnish)
Melon balls (garnish)
Mint sprigs (garnish)

Soften the lemon sherbet and mix with the ginger. Spread over the bottom and up the sides of a very-well-chilled 2-quart melon mold to form a hollow shell. Freeze. Add the kumquats to the orange sherbet, mix well, and fill the hollow shell of the molded lemon sherbet. Freeze until firm. When ready to serve, dip the mold quickly into and out of hot water. Turn out on a platter and garnish with pears, melon balls, and mint. Serves 12.

CARIBBEAN ICE-CREAM MOLD

3 pints coffee ice cream
2 pints chocolate ice cream
Sweet baking chocolate
Crème de cacao

Chill a 2-quart mold or metal bowl. Soften half the coffee ice cream slightly. Spread it over the bottom and up the sides of the mold in a layer about ¾ inch thick. Freeze until firm. Soften the chocolate ice cream and spread it the same way, mounding it a little in the center. Freeze until firm. Soften the remaining coffee ice cream and pack it in the mold, filling it to the brim. Cover with waxed paper and freeze until firm. To serve, unmold onto a serving plate. Garnish with chocolate curls and pass the cool or chilled crème de cacao separately. Serves 10–12.

TUTTI-FRUTTI ICE-CREAM MOLD

¼ cup sugar
1½ cups heavy cream
¼ cup dark rum
1 (1 lb. 14 oz.) can crushed pineapple
¼ cup finely chopped citron
2 tablespoons chopped red glacéed cherries
2 tablespoons chopped green glacéed
    cherries
9 pitted dates
2½ pints vanilla ice cream

Add the sugar to the cream and whip. Fold in the rum. Spread evenly over the bottom and up the sides of a thoroughly chilled 2-quart mold. Freeze 2–3 hours, until firm. Meanwhile, drain the pineapple and mix with the citron and cherries. Add the dates, cut fine. Let stand for ½ hour. Let the ice cream soften until it can be easily stirred with a spoon. Add the fruit to the ice cream. Mix well, pour into freezing trays, and freeze until almost solid. Pack it into the mold and freeze until firm. Unmold 10 minutes before serving and keep chilled. Serves 8–10.

MINT SHERBET RING WITH STRAWBERRIES

3 pints lemon sherbet
⅓ cup crème de menthe or ¾ teaspoon
    mint flavoring
Green food coloring (optional)
1 quart strawberries
Coconut (garnish)
Leaves (garnish)

Put the slightly softened lemon sherbet in a bowl. Beat quickly with a rotary beater. Mix in the crème de menthe or mint flavoring. Add a few drops green coloring if you wish. Pack the sherbet into a 5-cup ring mold. Freeze until firm. To serve, unmold and transfer the ring to a serving plate or shallow bowl. Fill the center of the ring with sweetened hulled strawberries. Sprinkle with coconut and garnish with leaves if you wish. Serves 6–8.

NEAPOLITAN RING

1 pint orange sherbet
2 tablespoons minced candied ginger
1 pint vanilla ice cream
2 tablespoons finely chopped Brazil nuts
2 teaspoons butter
1 pint lemon sherbet
Green food coloring
⅓ cup crushed pineapple
Sugared grapes (garnish)
Leaves (garnish)

Soften the orange sherbet and add the candied ginger. Pour into a 1½-quart mold. Freeze solid. Soften the vanilla ice cream; fold in the Brazil nuts which have been sautéed in the butter and pour into the mold. Refreeze. For the third layer, use the lemon sherbet which has been tinted pale green and mixed with the pineapple. Freeze firm. Turn out and garnish with grapes and leaves if you wish. Serves 6–8.

MERINGUE RING

4 egg whites
Pinch salt
Pinch cream of tartar
1¼ cups superfine sugar
1 teaspoon vanilla
¼ teaspoon almond flavoring
⅓ cup slivered blanched almonds (optional)
Fruit and ice cream

Beat the egg whites with salt and cream of tartar until a peak forms. Add the sugar a tablespoon at a time, beating well after each addition. When the sugar is completely dissolved, add the vanilla and almond flavoring. Grease a baking sheet. With a pastry bag and rosette tube end, make a circle of meringue on the sheet 8–9 inches in diameter or to fit the size of your serving plate or platter. Go around again with tube to make a base about 2 inches wide. Go round and round, building up to form a ring 2 inches high. Sprinkle with almonds if you wish. Bake in a 250° oven for about 1½ hours, until light beige in color. Turn the oven off and allow to cool in the oven for another hour. Loosen from sheet with a spatula. This meringue ring makes a delicious dessert filled with sugared fruit and ice cream. Serves 8.

Ice-Cream Pies

It is easy to make an ice-cream pie, using a crumb or nut crust or a meringue shell. Soften commercial or homemade ice cream and spread it on the crust. Then freeze until firm. You may serve this plain or topped with chocolate curls, candy sprinkles, a meringue, or sugared, slivered, or chopped nuts. Use two kinds of ice cream in layers if you wish. A 9-inch shell will hold 2 to 3 pints of ice cream. Serves 6–8.

BRAZIL-NUT ICE-CREAM PIE

½ pound shelled Brazil nuts
3 tablespoons sugar
1 quart coffee, chocolate, or other ice cream

Grind the nuts fine. There should be 1½ cups ground. Mix with the sugar. (Reserve ¼ cup.) Press the mixture into the bottom and up the sides of a 9-inch pie plate. Fill the shell with the slightly softened ice cream. Sprinkle the remaining sugared nuts over the top. Freeze until firm. Cut as you would any pie. Serves 6.

FROZEN STRAWBERRY MERINGUE PIE
(Low Fat)

9-inch Meringue Shell*
1 package frozen strawberries
6 tablespoons sugar
⅓ cup frozen lemonade concentrate
1½ cups skim milk
Red food coloring (optional)
1 egg white
Fresh strawberries (garnish)
Mint sprigs (garnish)

Combine the frozen strawberries with ¼ cup sugar and heat until the sugar is dissolved. Cool. Add the lemonade. Pour the skim milk into a freezing tray and freeze until edges are mushy. Scrape into a cold bowl and beat until consistency of whipped cream. Add a few drops of red coloring if you wish. Beat the egg white until a soft peak forms. Add the remaining sugar slowly, beating after each addition. Fold into the whipped milk. Add the strawberry mixture. Pour into freezing trays and freeze until mushy. Scrape into a cold bowl and beat smooth. Return to trays and freeze overnight.

The next day, beat again until consistency of ice cream. Freeze until firm. Scoop into the meringue shell and garnish with strawberries and mint. Serves 8.

NEAPOLITAN BOMBE

1 quart chocolate ice cream
2 tablespoons brandy (optional)
1½ pints vanilla ice cream
1 pint strawberry ice cream
1 (1 lb.) package fudge brownie mix or
*   butterscotch squares mix*
½ cup chopped walnuts

MERINGUE
5 egg whites
Pinch salt
⅔ cup sugar

Line a 2-quart metal mixing bowl with foil, having about 2 inches extending over the rim. Place the bowl in freezer. Soften the chocolate ice cream slightly and work in the brandy if you wish. Working quickly, spread an even layer over the bottom and up the sides of the foil-lined bowl. Return bowl to freezer. Soften the vanilla ice cream, spread it evenly to form a layer over the chocolate ice cream. Freeze until firm. Soften the strawberry ice cream slightly and pack into the center. Level off the top, cover, and freeze until firm. Prepare the brownie or butterscotch mix according to package directions, adding the nuts. Bake in a greased 8-inch cake pan for 35–40 minutes. Remove from pan and cool.

Meringue. Beat the egg whites with the salt until a stiff peak forms. Add the sugar a little at a time, beating after each addition.

To assemble the meringue bombe, let the ice cream stand at room temperature a few minutes. Place the brownie layer on a wooden board or baking sheet. Remove the cover from the bowl and invert onto the brownie base. Lift off the bowl and peel off the foil. Working quickly, cover the ice cream and brownie base with meringue, swirling it with the back of a spoon to form peaks. Place on the lowest rack of a 500° oven and bake for 3–4 minutes for the meringue to brown. Remove from the oven and let stand a few minutes for easier cutting. The entire bombe can be assembled and frozen the day before, removing it from the freezer and browning in the oven just before serving. Serves 10–12.

ICE-CREAM CAKE BOMBE   (*Plate 25*)

½ gallon vanilla ice cream
1 cup Nesselrode Sauce*
1 package white cake mix
2 tablespoons minced maraschino cherries
2 tablespoons maraschino cherry syrup

MERINGUE FROSTING
2 cups sugar
¼ teaspoon cream of tartar
4 egg whites
Green food coloring (optional)
Red cinnamon candies (optional)

Line both an 8-inch round cake pan and a mixing bowl measuring 7–8 inches across at the top with strips of waxed paper. Arrange strips so ends come over the edge of pan and bowl about 2 inches. Soften the ice cream and stir in the Nesselrode Sauce. Divide the ice cream equally between pan and bowl. Freeze 2–3 hours, until firm. Prepare the cake mix according to package directions, adding maraschino cherries and syrup to batter. Pour into two 8-inch round cake pans which have been greased and floured. Bake in a 350° oven for about ½ hour, until cake tests done. Turn out of pans onto racks and remove paper. Chill thoroughly while making the frosting.

Meringue Frosting. Put the sugar, cream of tartar, and ⅔ cup water into a 1-quart saucepan. Bring to a boil and continue boiling until the bubbles are large and syrup forms thick drops (about 200°). Beat the egg whites until creamy (very soft peaks). Gradually add the hot syrup in a fine thread, beating continually, until the meringue is thick and glossy and will hold swirls. Tint with green food coloring if you wish.

Working quickly, remove the frozen ice cream from molds. Place one layer of cake on a large serving plate and cover with the ice cream layer. Add the second layer of cake and top with the ice cream molded in the bowl, round side up. Quickly frost the entire surface, using less than half the meringue, to seal in the coldness. Shape into a beehive effect. Return to the freezer for about 3 hours. Cover and place remaining meringue in the refrigerator. Before frosting the second time, beat the meringue until thick and glossy again. Remove the ice-cream cake from the freezer and once more cover with meringue, working rapidly. Dot with cinnamon candies if you wish. Return to freezer and continue to freeze for several hours or overnight. Serves 10–12.

MARDI GRAS BOMBE

3 eggs
¾ cup sugar
¾ cup light corn syrup
3 cups buttermilk
6 tablespoons lemon juice
1½ tablespoons grated lemon rind
1 cup mixed candied fruits
¾ cup strawberry preserves
½ cup canned crushed pineapple
1 tablespoon rum or 1 teaspoon rum flavoring
Glacéed fruit (optional)

Beat the eggs slightly and add the sugar a little at a time, beating steadily. Then add the corn syrup, buttermilk, and lemon juice and rind. Pour into freezing trays. Freeze until almost firm, scrape into a cold bowl, and beat until smooth. Return to trays and refreeze. Meanwhile, mince the candied fruits and mix together with the strawberry preserves, pineapple, and rum or flavoring; let stand several hours at room temperature. Layer the sherbet and fruit alternately into a 2-quart mold, beginning and ending with sherbet. Freeze until solid, at least overnight. Turn onto a serving platter and decorate with glacéed fruit if you wish. Serves 10–12.

FROZEN SOUFFLE

1 pint vanilla ice cream
2 macaroons
4 teaspoons Grand Marnier or other orange liqueur
½ cup heavy cream
1–2 tablespoons chopped toasted blanched almonds
1–2 teaspoons confectioners' sugar
*½ recipe Strawberry Liqueur Sauce**

Soften the ice cream slightly. Stir in the macaroons, crumbled, and the Grand Marnier. Fold in the cream, whipped. Spoon into a 3-cup serving dish or mold. Sprinkle the surface with nuts and sugar. Cover with foil or Saran and freeze until firm, 4–5 hours or overnight. To unmold, wrap the dish for 4–5 seconds in a towel wrung out of very hot water and loosen the edges with a spatula. Turn out onto a chilled serving dish. Serve the sauce in a separate bowl. Serves 4–6.

BAKED ALASKA

4 egg whites
Pinch salt
½ cup sugar
1 (9-inch) spongecake layer
1 quart chocolate or fruit-flavored ice cream

Beat the egg whites with the salt until a peak forms and add the sugar a tablespoon at a time, beating well after each addition. Beat until the sugar is dissolved and the meringue is stiff and glossy. Place the cake on a board or baking sheet. Use firm ice cream and pile it onto the cake to within ½ inch of the edge. Spread the meringue over the top and sides of the ice cream and cake, covering them completely; leave no holes. Place in a 500° oven for 3–5 minutes, until the meringue is delicately browned. Serve immediately. This is very impressive although it is easy to make. Serves 6–8.

ORANGE RASPBERRY ALASKAS
(Low Calorie)

4 oranges
3 packages frozen raspberries
⅛ teaspoon mint flavoring
3 egg whites
2 tablespoons superfine sugar
1 teaspoon finely grated orange rind

Cut the oranges in half and squeeze. Scrape out as much pulp as possible. Set the orange shells aside. Thaw the berries and force through a food mill or buzz in the blender; then strain through a fine sieve to remove seeds. Stir in ¼ cup orange juice and the mint flavoring. Pour into a freezing tray and freeze until mushy. Remove and beat smooth. Spoon this purée into the orange shells, making the tops fairly level. Freeze until firm. (These can be made ahead and brought from the freezer when you want to serve them.) To serve, beat the egg whites with the sugar until a peak forms. Add 2 tablespoons orange juice and continue to beat until stiff. Fold in the orange rind and swirl the meringue on top of the shells, covering the filling. Put on a baking sheet and broil quickly until meringue is golden brown. Serve at once. Serves 8 (158 calories per serving).

CRANBERRY BAKED-ALASKA PIE

10 ladyfingers
2 pints vanilla ice cream
¼ cup brandy
½ cup whole cranberry sauce
3 egg whites
⅛ teaspoon cream of tartar
Pinch salt
¾ cup superfine sugar
Brandy Cranberry Sauce* (optional)

Separate the ladyfingers and trim them so they will stand up around the edge of a 9-inch pie plate. Cut the remaining ones into pieces and cover the bottom of the plate as completely as possible. Chill. Have the ice cream slightly softened and turn it into a cold bowl. Add brandy to the cranberry sauce and swirl into the mixture (refrigerate if too soft). Spoon into the pie shell and freeze firm. Just before serving, beat the egg whites with the cream of tartar and salt until a peak forms. Gradually add the sugar while beating to form a stiff meringue. Cover the pie with this, pulling up peaks with the back of a spoon. Put into a 500° oven for 4–5 minutes, until the meringue is tinged with brown. Serve at once with or without Brandy Cranberry Sauce. Serves 8.

LEMON ICE-CREAM PIE

9-inch Cornflake Crust* or Crumb Crust*
1 quart vanilla ice cream
½ cup frozen lemonade concentrate
1 tablespoon thinly slivered lemon rind
⅓ cup sugar

Let the ice cream stand at room temperature until mushy. Add the thawed lemonade concentrate and mix well. Fill the pie shell with ice cream and place in freezing compartment for about 4 hours, until frozen. Take from freezer 20 minutes before serving. Have ready a topping made by putting the yellow slivers of lemon rind in a saucepan with ¼ cup water. Boil, covered, for 10 minutes, until nearly all the water has evaporated. Add the sugar and cook another 5 minutes, until the rind is transparent. If the sugar does not dissolve easily, add a teaspoon of water. Stir occasionally. Chill. Dribble over the ice cream just before serving. This pie may be made with lemon ice cream instead of vanilla and lemonade. Serves 6.

ICE-CREAM GINGER PIE
WITH BERRIES

3 pints vanilla ice cream
3 tablespoons finely chopped crystallized
  ginger
1 package frozen raspberries or sliced
  strawberries

Spread 1 quart vanilla ice cream evenly in a 9-inch pie plate. Sprinkle with the ginger. Freeze until firm. Top with the remaining ice cream and freeze again until firm. When firm, place the thawed berries at random on the top. Serves 8.

FROZEN COCONUT VELVET

2 cups grated fresh or flaked coconut
2 cups fresh coconut milk or milk or
  combination
1 cup sugar
1 envelope unflavored gelatin
Pinch salt
6 egg whites
½ teaspoon vanilla
Berries (optional)

Add the coconut to the milk, sugar, gelatin, and salt. Stir well and simmer for 10 minutes. Strain and pour into a freezing tray and freeze about 1½ hours, until mushy around the edges. Scrape into a cold bowl and beat until softened. Fold in the egg whites, beaten until a peak forms, and add the vanilla. Pour into a 1½-quart ring mold or 2 freezing trays and freeze until firm. Serve with fresh berries if you wish. Serves 8.

Curly-locks, curly-locks,
Wilt thou be mine?
Thou shalt not wash dishes
Nor yet feed the swine,
But sit on a cushion
And sew a fine seam,
And feed upon strawberries,
Sugar and cream.

Anonymous, *Curly-Locks*

FROZEN STRAWBERRY GRAND-MARNIER SOUFFLE   (*Plate 23*)

2 packages frozen sliced strawberries
6 eggs
2 cups sugar
½ cup Grand Marnier
⅓ cup orange juice
3 cups heavy cream
Red food coloring
1 cup chopped walnuts (garnish)
Whipped cream (garnish)
Strawberries (garnish)

Prepare the mold first. Using a 2-quart soufflé dish, make a collar to extend about 3 inches above the top of the dish; use a double strip of foil about 4–5 inches wide and long enough to go around the dish. Secure with paper clips and a large rubber band to hold in place. Thaw and purée the strawberries. Beat the egg yolks until thick and lemon-colored with 1 cup sugar. Stir in half of the strawberry purée. Cook in a double boiler about 15–20 minutes, until the mixture thickens. Remove from heat and cool. Stir in the Grand Marnier. Combine the remaining sugar and the orange juice in a small saucepan. Heat, stirring, until the sugar dissolves. Then cook, without stirring, to the thread stage (232°–234°). Beat the egg whites until very stiff. Very slowly pour a thin stream of hot syrup over them, beating at high speed until all the syrup is used and the mixture stands in stiff peaks. Cool. Beat the cream until thick and glossy. Fold into the cooled strawberry mixture along with the remaining purée. Fold in the meringue, mixing well. Stir in a few drops of red food coloring. Turn into the prepared soufflé dish and freeze several hours or overnight. To serve, remove the collar and press walnuts into the sides of the soufflé. Decorate the top edge with fluffs of whipped cream and mound a few whole strawberries in the center. You may serve with Strawberry Liqueur Sauce.* Serves 12.

Plate 29. A tower of STRAWBERRIES GLACEES.

Plate 30. ORANGE FLOWERS garnished with clusters of grapes.

Plate 31. PINEAPPLE MANDARIN MOLD, PEACH SHERBET with peaches, and SNOWY MERINGUE WITH FRUIT MELANGE.

CHAPTER SEVEN

Fabulous Fruits

Don't apologize because "there's only fruit for dessert." Fruit is just about the most delicious, versatile, and satisfactory dessert there is. A famous French food authority suggests that it should be included in every well-planned meal. If you don't serve fruit in the early part of the meal—such as a fruit cup, melon, or half grapefruit as a starter—or have applesauce with the pork or prunes with the veal, by all means consider fruit for dessert.

A bowl of fresh fruit, which doubles as a centerpiece, contributes pleasure to the eye and, subsequently, to the palate. Serve it "as is" or with cheese. Suggestions for fruits with appropriate cheese accompaniments are in the following text.

Fruit makes a wonderful sauce or purée for puddings or frozen desserts. Fruit salads are a refreshing conclusion to a meal. Fruit offers great variety of treatment: a macédoine of cut-up fresh fruits with or without sugar and liqueur added; a compote of cooked or frozen fruits; single cooked fruits with or without a sauce, such as *poached* pears or apricots, *stewed* rhubarb or cherries, *baked* apples or peaches, or *broiled* grapefruit or bananas; and, of course, all the permutations and combinations of fruits, liqueurs, and gelatin.

Peeling and Sectioning Grapefruit and Oranges

To peel and section oranges or grapefruit, slice the peel off with a sharp knife, cutting round and round and being sure to remove all white membrane. To section, run the knife down the side of a section close to the tissue, turn the knife, and scoop the section loose from the other side, leaving the connecting tissue attached to the core. Hold the fruit loosely so as not to squeeze juice out as you work. After the sections are removed, you may squeeze the remainder to get the juice.

BAKED GLAZED APPLES

8 large baking apples
1¼ cups canned unsweetened pineapple juice
½ cup butter
1 cup sugar
Red food coloring
Cream (optional)

Core the apples. About a third of the way down, score the skin around the apples; try not to cut into the fruit. Steam just long enough (about 10 minutes) to permit you to lift off the skin like a cap. Arrange the apples in a shallow baking dish. Bring the pineapple juice, butter, and sugar to a boil. Add a few drops of red coloring and boil 5 minutes, until of syrupy consistency. Pour a little over each apple and place the dish in the broiler as far away from the heat as possible. Have the heat moderate. Baste every few minutes with the syrup. When the syrup is used up, baste with syrup in the pan. The apples are done when they are thoroughly tender and transparent. Cool. Fill centers with jellied syrup from the pan. Serve with cream if you wish. Serves 8.

APPLES IN BLOOM

6 large red apples
1 cup orange juice
Grated rind 1 orange
2 tablespoons lemon juice
1 cup sugar
Cream (optional)

Core the apples and cut through the apple skin from top to bottom with the tip of a paring knife so that the skin is divided in 6 sections. Try not to cut into the fruit. Place the apples in a skillet, add 1 cup water, cover, and steam 20–25 minutes, until tender. Remove apples and carefully work off the skins. Add the orange juice, orange rind, lemon juice, and sugar to the water in the pan. Boil the liquid until about 1½ cups remain. Place the apples in a dish and pour the sauce over them. Chill. Serve with cream if you wish. Serves 6.

APPLE COMPOTE

3 pounds tart apples
1½ cups sugar
Juice 4 lemons
1 lemon
1 stick cinnamon
¼ cup red cinnamon candies

Peel, core, and cut the apples into eighths. Add the sugar, lemon juice, sliced lemon, cinnamon, and 4 cups water. Simmer until apples are tender. Remove from heat. Take out cinnamon stick. Add the candies and stir very gently until dissolved. Serve warm or cold. Serves 6.

APPLESAUCE MOLDS

1 envelope unflavored gelatin
2 cups applesauce
2–3 tablespoons red cinnamon candies
2 tablespoons lemon juice
2 tablespoons sugar

Mix the gelatin with ¼ cup water. Add to the applesauce with the cinnamon candies. Heat and stir until the gelatin and candies are dissolved. Add the lemon juice and sugar. Pour into small individual molds and chill until firm. This is good served with cream. Serves 4.

APPLES IN MAPLE SYRUP

6 baking apples
¾ cup maple syrup
¾ teaspoon salt
2 tablespoons butter
Ice cream or cream (optional)

Peel, core, and quarter the apples and arrange in a shallow buttered 12×8½×2-inch pan. Pour the syrup over them, sprinkle with salt, and dot with butter. Bake in a 350° oven about 40 minutes, until barely tender. Baste occasionally with syrup as they bake. Serve warm or cold. Good served with generous spoonfuls of ice cream or with plain cream. Serves 6.

APPLESAUCE WITH PLUM JELLY

3 cups applesauce (fresh or canned)
½ teaspoon nutmeg
½ teaspoon cinnamon
1 (8 oz.) jar plum jelly
Juice 1 large lemon

Heat the applesauce with the spices. Add the jelly and stir until it is melted and blended with applesauce. Remove from heat and add the lemon juice. Chill well. Serves 4.

COUNTRY APPLE DESSERT

6 large tart apples
1½ tablespoons butter
1 cup sugar
⅓ teaspoon cinnamon
⅓ teaspoon nutmeg
½ cup heavy cream

Core and slice the apples. Arrange in a shallow baking dish and dot with butter. Mix the sugar, cinnamon, nutmeg, and cream together and pour over the apples. Bake in a 350° oven for ½ hour, until apples are tender. Serve warm. Serves 6.

JELLIED APPLES

3 cups sugar
14 drops red food coloring
8 cooking apples
2 tablespoons grated lemon rind
2 tablespoons grated orange rind
2 (3-inch) sticks cinnamon

Mix 3 cups water, sugar, and food coloring together in a skillet with a tight lid. Cover and heat. Pare the apples but do not core or stem. As each is ready, add it to the hot syrup. When all the apples are in the pan, simmer, covered, for 10 minutes. Then uncover and cook, just below the simmering point, for about ¾ hour. Never allow the syrup to come to a boil. Turn the apples from time to time. After about 20 minutes add the flavorings and continue cooking. Cool in the syrup and serve warm or cold. Serves 8.

CANDIED APPLESAUCE

12 large green apples
3 cups sugar
4 cloves
¼ teaspoon cinnamon
⅛ teaspoon nutmeg

Peel, core, and cut the apples into eighths. Mix the sugar with cloves, cinnamon, nutmeg, and 2 cups water in a heavy kettle. Add the apples, cover, and bring to a boil. Simmer gently, uncovered, until the apples are transparent. Stir only occasionally and carefully; you do not want the apples to cook into a sauce. Cool. Serves 8.

JELLIED APRICOT AND BANANA RING

1 (1 lb. 13 oz.) can apricot halves
3 envelopes unflavored gelatin
Juice 1 lemon
¾ cup sugar
2 eggs
Pinch salt
1½ cups milk
1 teaspoon vanilla
2 bananas
Apricot halves (garnish)
Banana slices (garnish)
Fresh mint (garnish)

Drain the apricots, reserving 1½ cups syrup. Mix 2 envelopes gelatin with the apricot syrup. Heat syrup and stir until gelatin is dissolved. Purée enough apricots to make 2 cups. Add to apricot gelatin with the lemon juice and ½ cup sugar. Chill until thick and syrupy. Put half the apricot mixture into a 1½-quart mold and chill until firm. Beat the eggs slightly; add remaining sugar and the salt. Scald the milk and add to egg mixture. Cook in double boiler, stirring constantly, until mixture coats a spoon. Remove from heat and add vanilla. Mix remaining gelatin with ¼ cup cold water, add to hot mixture, and stir until dissolved. Cool quickly in ice water and add the mashed bananas. Pour banana-gelatin mixture into mold and chill until firm. Add the rest of the apricot mixture and chill several hours or overnight. When ready to serve, turn out and garnish with apricot halves, banana slices, and mint if you wish. Good with Lemon Sauce I* or whipped cream. Serves 6.

DEVONSHIRE APRICOTS

1 (3 oz.) package cream cheese
¼ teaspoon grated lemon rind
1 tablespoon lemon juice
⅓ cup heavy cream
1½ teaspoons sugar
12 fresh stewed or canned apricots

Soften the cream cheese at room temperature. Blend in the lemon rind, lemon juice, cream, and sugar. If too thick, thin with a little apricot syrup. Serve 2 or 3 apricots with syrup in sherbet glasses. Spoon cream-cheese sauce over them, or place apricots and syrup in a serving bowl and spoon the sauce over them. Serves 4.

HONEY BANANAS

8 bananas
Lemon juice
1 cup honey

WHIPPED-CREAM DATE SAUCE
1 cup heavy cream
15 pitted dates
1 teaspoon vanilla
3 tablespoons brandy or rum (optional)

Peel the bananas, sprinkle with a few drops of lemon juice, and arrange them in a buttered shallow baking dish. Pour the honey mixed with 2 tablespoons hot water over them. Bake in a 350° oven for about ½ hour, until tender. Baste frequently with the honey. Serve hot or chilled.

Whipped-Cream Date Sauce. Whip the cream and fold in the cut-up dates; flavor with vanilla, or with brandy or rum if you wish. Serve the sauce on the side. Serves 8.

BAKED BANANAS

6–8 large not-too-ripe bananas (red
  bananas if available)
½ cup lemon juice
1 tablespoon butter
1 cup sugar
3 tablespoons rum (optional)

Peel, scrape, and cut the bananas in half lengthwise. Place not too close together in a buttered shallow glass baking dish. Mix the lemon juice, butter, and sugar and heat until mixture simmers. Add the rum if you wish and a little more sugar to taste. Pour the syrup

over the bananas and bake in a 350° oven about ½ hour, until tender. The syrup should be greatly reduced and quite heavy. Serves 6–8.

BAKED BANANAS AND PLUMS

4 bananas
1 teaspoon grated lemon rind
1–2 tablespoons lemon juice
1 (1 lb. 13 oz.) can purple plums

Cut the bananas in half lengthwise, place in a shallow baking dish, and sprinkle with the lemon rind and juice. Drain the plums, reserving 1 cup syrup. Pit the plums and arrange over the bananas. Pour plum syrup over all. Bake in a 350° oven for 20 minutes. Serve hot or cold. Serves 6–8.

BANANAS A LA MODE

1 cup heavy cream
2 egg yolks
1 tablespoon light brown sugar
¼ teaspoon nutmeg
4 bananas

Beat the cream with egg yolks, sugar, and nutmeg until very thick and shiny. Slice the bananas into ½-inch rounds. Add to the mixture and stir gently. Be sure that there are no uncovered pieces of banana—they will darken. Put the dessert into a serving dish and chill at least 1 hour. Sprinkle with a bit more nutmeg just before serving if you wish. Serves 4.

BANANAS WITH TANGERINE SAUCE

1 orange
1 lemon
½ cup sweet butter
½ cup sugar
¼ cup frozen tangerine concentrate
½ cup Curaçao (optional)
8 bananas

Grate very lightly the rind of the orange and lemon. Squeeze juices and strain. Melt the butter over low heat and gradually stir in the sugar. Then add the fruit juices, grated rinds, and the Curaçao if you wish. Bring to a simmer and set aside until serving time. At that point, cut the bananas in half lengthwise. Add them to sauce and simmer until softened a bit but not mushy. Baste frequently but turn only once. Serve with the sauce. Serves 8.

BLACKBERRY FLUMMERY

3 pints blackberries
2 cups sugar
2–3 tablespoons cornstarch
Whipped cream

Simmer the berries with sugar for 15 minutes. Stir in the cornstarch mixed with a little cold water and cook slowly about 10 minutes, until clear. Rub through a sieve, pour into a bowl, and chill. Traditionally, this is served with whipped cream. For a change, try it as a sauce for ice cream. Serves 6–8.

HOT CINNAMON CHERRIES

1 (1 lb. 14 oz.) can Bing cherries
¼ teaspoon cinnamon
1 tablespoon lemon juice
2 tablespoons red wine
Whipped cream (optional)

Drain the cherries. Boil the syrup with the cinnamon to reduce to half. Add the cherries, lemon juice, and wine. Serve piping hot. Top with whipped cream if you like. Serves 4.

WHITE GRAPES AND SOUR CREAM

6 cups (about 2½ pounds) stemmed
  seedless white grapes
1½ cups sour cream
¾ cup light brown sugar

Wash the grapes and dry them thoroughly. Chill for several hours. Sweeten the sour cream to taste—about ½ cup of the sugar. Toss the grapes and cream together. Serve with the remaining brown sugar sprinkled over the top. Serves 8.

BROILED GRAPEFRUIT

3 grapefruit
6 teaspoons honey
3 tablespoons sugar
Crystallized ginger (optional)
Rum (optional)

Cut the grapefruit in half and remove the core and membranes. Put 1 teaspoon of honey on each half and sprinkle with sugar. Brown under the broiler for several minutes. Garnish with slivers of ginger or 1 teaspoon rum before serving if you wish. Serves 6.

GRAPEFRUIT IN LEMON JELLY

3–4 grapefruit
2 envelopes unflavored gelatin
⅔ cup sugar
¼ teaspoon salt
⅔ cup lemon juice
Fresh berries (garnish)

Peel and section the grapefruit. Mix the gelatin with the sugar, salt, and 2¾ cups water. Heat and stir until dissolved. Stir in the lemon juice and chill until quite thick. Fold in the grapefruit sections and chill until firm. Serve with raspberries or other berries sprinkled over the top if you wish. Serves 8.

PEARS, CHERRIES, AND GRAPEFRUIT

1 (1 lb. 13 oz.) can pear halves
2 (1 lb.) cans pitted tart red cherries
1 cup red raspberry jelly
¼ cup slivered crystallized ginger
3 large grapefruit
Sherry (optional)

The day before, drain the juice from the pears and put cut side up in a flat-bottomed dish. Drain the cherries and pour the cherry juice over the pears. Place in refrigerator and occasionally turn the pears so they will be red all over. Some hours before you will serve the fruit, melt the raspberry jelly and add to the drained cherries with the crystallized ginger. Peel the grapefruit, removing all white membrane, and section, avoiding all connecting tissue. Make a mound of cherries in the center of a platter and surround it with sections of grapefruit. Make a border of pears cut side down with additional slivers of crystallized ginger in between. Sprinkle some sherry over the fruit if you wish. Serves 6–8.

SLICED ORANGES

6 seedless oranges
2–3 tablespoons sugar
Mint leaves

Peel the oranges with a sharp knife. Be sure to remove all outside white membrane. Save the juice. Slice the oranges thin and arrange in overlapping layers on a plate. Mix a little sugar (the amount will depend on the sweetness of the oranges) with the reserved juice and sprinkle over the oranges. Sprinkle liberally with finely cut fresh mint. Serves 6.

MELON WITH CHEESE

1 large or 2 small melons
½ pound yellow or Swiss cheese

Chill the melon; quarter and remove seeds and rind. Slice thin and arrange slices on dessert plates alternately with thin slices of cheese. Serves 6.

AMBROSIA

3 large seedless oranges
3 bananas
½ cup sugar
3 tablespoons orange juice
⅔ cup flaked coconut

Peel the oranges and cut into pieces; slice the bananas. Mix the sugar with the orange juice, add the coconut, and stir into the fruit. Refrigerate for several hours before serving; stir occasionally. Serves 4.

ORANGES PIQUANTES

8–10 large oranges or 4 (10 oz.) jars or cans
  mandarin orange sections
1 (8 oz.) jar orange marmalade
1 cup sour cream

If using fresh oranges, cut skin off with a sharp knife and divide into sections, avoiding all connecting membranes. Whichever you use, fresh or mandarin oranges, be sure that they are icy cold. Arrange the orange sections attractively in individual compote glasses. Melt the orange marmalade in a double boiler. Spoon over the oranges and top with sour cream. Serve at once. Serves 8.

ORANGES GRAND MARNIER

8 seedless oranges
3 cups sugar
½ cup Grand Marnier

Peel the oranges with a sharp knife, removing all white membrane, and cut into ¼-inch slices. Mix the sugar with 1½ cups water, bring to a boil, and cook for 5 minutes. Add the oranges and simmer for a few minutes. Baste the oranges as they simmer. Remove from heat and add the Grand Marnier. Chill. Serves 8.

SLICED ORANGES WITH CARAMEL SAUCE

1½ cups sugar
1 teaspoon butter
6 seedless oranges
½ cup toasted slivered almonds

Caramelize the sugar over low heat, stirring constantly, until all sugar is melted and dark. Remove from heat and add ¾ cup boiling water and the butter. Stir to a smooth syrup. Peel the oranges with a sharp knife, removing all white membrane, and slice. Arrange in overlapping layers on a platter. Pour the cool syrup over the oranges and sprinkle with almonds. Serves 6.

ORANGES AND PEACHES IN RASPBERRY SAUCE

7 large seedless oranges
2 packages sliced frozen peaches or 6 fresh
  peaches
1 cup grapefruit juice (optional)
2 packages frozen raspberries

Peel the oranges with a sharp knife, removing all the white membrane. Cut into sections, being careful to avoid all connecting tissue. Put the frozen peaches with the oranges; if you can get good fresh ones, peel and slice them and immerse in grapefruit juice to prevent discoloration. Buzz the thawed raspberries in a blender or just thaw and, either way, press through a fine sieve to remove seeds. Arrange the fruit in a shallow bowl or on dessert plates and spoon the sauce over them. Serves 8.

BAKED ORIENTAL ORANGES

8 oranges
16 pitted dates
8 figs
8 large marshmallows
2–3 tablespoons flaked coconut
½ teaspoon cloves
1 tablespoon honey, brown sugar, or
  coconut syrup
½ teaspoon cinnamon
½ teaspoon nutmeg
Pinch ginger
Juice ½ lemon
¾ cup toasted slivered blanched almonds

Cut off the tops of the oranges. Remove flesh and scrape out membrane. Drain the juice into a bowl. Cut the flesh into bite-size pieces, removing as much membrane as possible. Cut the dates, figs, and marshmallows into small pieces. Mix all ingredients together except almonds. Put 1 tablespoon orange juice in each orange cup, fill with the fruit mixture, and top with almonds. Arrange in a pan with a little water. Cover and bake in a 350° oven for ½ hour. Serves 8.

ORANGE FLOWERS (*Plate 30*)
(Low Calorie)

¼ cup sugar
1 tablespoon cornstarch
½ cup orange juice
½ teaspoon finely slivered orange peel
Pinch salt
1 teaspoon butter
6 seedless oranges
Grape clusters, mint (garnish)

Mix the sugar, cornstarch, ½ cup water, and orange juice together. Cook over low heat, stirring constantly, until clear and thickened. Remove from heat and stir in orange peel, salt, and butter. Chill. Cut through only the rind of the oranges from the stem end almost to the bud end, forming 5 petal-shaped pieces. Carefully peel back each piece of rind without breaking it; leave it attached to the orange and curl it inward so that you can tuck the top under the fruit at the base. Loosen the sections of the orange so that they can be pulled apart and also loosen the sections at the base enough so that they will come out easily when eaten with a knife and fork. Trim away any excess membrane. Just before serving, spoon some of the sauce over the orange sections and garnish with small grape clusters and mint. Serves 6 (117 calories per serving).

ORANGE COMPOTE I

6 seedless oranges
⅓ cup sugar
1½ cups orange juice
Grated rind 1 orange

Peel the oranges with a sharp knife, being careful to remove the white membrane. Cut horizontally into ⅓-inch slices. Cook the sugar, orange juice, and rind until sugar has dissolved and liquid comes to a boil. Cool and pour over the oranges. Serves 6.

ORANGE COMPOTE II

4 seedless oranges
½ cup sugar

Peel the oranges with a sharp knife, being sure to remove the white membrane. Save the rind of 2 oranges and shred it. Cut the oranges into thick slices. Make a syrup by bringing to a boil the sugar, 1¾ cups water, and the shredded orange rind. Pour boiling syrup over oranges. Let stand for at least 15 minutes. Drain syrup, bring to a boil again, and again pour it hot over the fruit. Cool the compote and place in a glass or china serving dish. Chill before serving. Serves 4.

ORANGE GELATIN
(Low Calorie)

2 envelopes low-calorie orange-flavored gelatin
½ cup orange juice
½ cup noncaloric ginger ale
1 seedless orange
2 tablespoons sour cream

Mix the gelatin with 1 cup hot water and stir until completely dissolved. Add the orange juice and ginger ale. Pour into a 8×8×2-inch pan and chill until firm. Peel and section the orange. Cut the gelatin into cubes and spoon into serving glasses. Top with orange sections and garnish with the sour cream. Serves 4 (66 calories per serving).

PEACHES WITH MELBA SAUCE

10–12 peaches
3 tablespoons lemon juice
1 pint strawberries or 1 package frozen
1 pint raspberries or 1 package frozen
1 (8 oz.) jar Melba sauce
⅓ cup Cointreau or Curaçao (optional)

Peel, pit, and slice the peaches and sprinkle immediately with 1 tablespoon lemon juice. Hull the strawberries and combine with the raspberries. Buzz the berries in a blender or force through a food mill. Strain to remove seeds. Add to the Melba sauce with the remaining lemon juice, and the orange liqueur if you wish. Arrange the peaches in a bowl or sherbet glasses and pour the sauce over them. Serves 8.

COUNTRY-STYLE PEACH MELBA

2 packages frozen raspberries
Juice ½ lemon
2 teaspoons cornstarch
8 peaches
16 macaroons
½ cup toasted slivered blanched almonds
Vanilla ice cream

Thaw the raspberries. Drain the juice; you should have about 1 cup. Add 1 teaspoon lemon juice, stir in the cornstarch, and cook until clear and slightly thickened. Chill. Dip the peaches briefly into boiling water, slip off skins, and sprinkle with remaining lemon juice. Put a layer of macaroons in a serving dish, then a layer of peach halves cut side down (cut them and remove the pits just before using), and top with raspberries, raspberry juice, and a sprinkling of almonds. Cut several macaroons into small pieces and sprinkle over the top of the nuts. Repeat this layering twice more, making three layers in all. If you wish, save a little of the fruit to garnish the top of the bowl. Refrigerate for 2 hours before serving. Just before it goes to the table, spoon softened vanilla ice cream on top and garnish with the reserved fruit. Serves 8.

FROZEN PEACHES IN ORANGE SAUCE

2 packages frozen peaches
3 tablespoons frozen orange-juice
    concentrate
1 tablespoon brandy, rum, or orange liqueur
1 teaspoon grated orange rind (optional)

Thaw the peaches, add the orange-juice concentrate, and gently stir in the brandy, rum, or liqueur. Sprinkle orange rind over the top if you wish. Serves 4.

PEACHES ROMANOFF

6 egg yolks
1 cup sugar
¾ cup sherry
¾ cup orange juice
1 cup heavy cream
2½ pounds peaches
Lemon juice
Strawberries or Bing cherries (garnish)
Confectioners' sugar (optional)

Beat the egg yolks until frothy. Add the sugar and continue beating until thick and lemon-colored. Stir in the sherry and orange juice. Cook in a double boiler over just simmering water, stirring constantly, until thick and smooth. Cool and chill. Whip the cream until thick and shiny. Fold into chilled custard mixture. As near serving time as possible, peel the peaches and dip at once into lemon juice mixed with a little water to prevent darkening. Slice the peaches fairly thick. Reserve a few slices for garnish. Fold the rest into the custard-cream mixture. Heap in the center of a cold serving dish and garnish with the reserved peach slices and hulled strawberries or pitted cherries dipped in confectioners' sugar if you wish. Serves 8.

PEACHES WITH RASPBERRY SAUCE ON MERINGUES

1 cup sugar
8 peaches
2 packages frozen raspberries
½ cup almond-flavored Sweetened Whipped
    Cream*

MERINGUE PEDESTALS
2 egg whites
Pinch salt
6 tablespoons sugar
¼ teaspoon almond flavoring

Put 2 cups water and the sugar in a saucepan. Bring to a boil and cook 5 minutes. Meanwhile, peel the peaches, cut in half, and remove the pits. Simmer peach halves in the syrup about 10 minutes, until tender. The time will vary, depending on how ripe the peaches are and their size. Drain and chill.

Meringue Pedestals. Beat the egg whites with the salt until a soft peak forms. Add the sugar a tablespoon at a time, beating well after each addition. Add the almond flavoring and continue beating until sugar is completely dissolved and meringue is glossy. Using a pastry bag, shape into 8 rings about 2½ inches in diameter on greased brown paper on a baking sheet. Bake in a 250° oven for 30–40 minutes, until crisp. Cool. Remove meringues from paper carefully.

Thaw raspberries, crush or buzz in a blender, and rub through a sieve to remove seeds. To serve, arrange meringue pedestals on serving dish. Put 2 peach halves together with about 1 tablespoon whipped cream and place on top of each meringue. Pour the raspberry purée over and around the peaches. Serves 8.

PEACH SNOW CAPS

2 (1 lb.) cans cling peach halves
1 tablespoon melted butter
1⅓ cups macaroon crumbs (12 macaroons)
1 tablespoon sugar
1 tablespoon cornstarch
Red and yellow food coloring
Vanilla ice cream

Drain the peaches, reserving the syrup. Arrange halves hollow side up in a shallow baking dish. Add 3 tablespoons peach syrup and the melted butter to the macaroon crumbs. When the syrup has all soaked into the macaroons, fill the peach hollows with the crumbs. Pour about ¼ cup peach syrup into the dish, cover, and bake in a 350° oven about ½ hour. Blend the sugar and cornstarch into the remaining syrup. Cook over medium heat, stirring constantly, until clear and slightly thickened. Tint a delicate amber color with a few drops of food coloring. Serve the peaches warm topped with a scoop of ice cream. Pass the hot peach sauce. Serves 8–10.

GINGER PEACH GELATIN

4 cups peach nectar
2 packages lemon-flavored gelatin
1 package peach-flavored gelatin
1½ cups ginger ale
¼ cup lemon juice
Cream or Custard Sauce*

Heat the peach nectar. Put the gelatins in a bowl, add the hot liquid, and stir until gelatins are dissolved. Mix in the ginger ale and lemon juice. Pour into a 1½-quart mold and chill several hours until set. Unmold and serve with cream or Custard Sauce. Serves 6–8.

SNOWY MERINGUE WITH
FRUIT MELANGE   (Plate 31)
(Low Calorie)

8 egg whites
½ teaspoon cream of tartar
1 cup sugar
6 cups fruit—strawberries, blueberries,
  grapes

Beat the egg whites and cream of tartar until a stiff peak forms. Add the sugar a tablespoon at a time, beating well after each addition. When the meringue stands in glossy peaks and all sugar is dissolved, spoon into a 2½-quart ring mold. Pack in carefully to eliminate any large air bubbles. Set the mold in a shallow pan with 1 inch of hot water in it. Bake in a 250° oven for about 45 minutes, until the meringue is set. Remove mold from water and allow to cool until meringue settles. Just before serving, loosen the edges of the meringue with a small spatula which has been dipped in cold water. Invert on serving dish and arrange the fresh fruit in and around meringue. Serves 12 (137 calories per serving).

BAKED PEARS

4 pears
1 cup light brown sugar
3 tablespoons butter
½ cup rum or orange juice
1 cup sour cream (optional)

Peel, halve, and core the pears. Place the pear halves cut side down in a shallow casserole. Sprinkle each half generously with brown sugar and dot with butter. Pour the rum or orange juice in at the side of the casserole so as not to wash off the sugar. Cover and bake in a 350° oven for 20 minutes. Remove cover, baste well, and continue to cook for 15 minutes more, basting frequently. If the pears are very ripe, remove the cover sooner. Serve hot, with sour cream if you wish. Serves 4.

BAKED PEARS WITH MARMALADE
SAUCE

1 (1 lb. 13 oz.) can pears
4 cloves
1-inch stick cinnamon
4 slices lemon
2 tablespoons sugar
⅓ cup orange marmalade

Drain the pears and place cut side down in a shallow 1½-quart baking dish. Simmer the syrup from the pears with the cloves, cinnamon, lemon slices, sugar, and marmalade for 10 minutes. Pour over the pears and bake in a 350° oven for 20 minutes. Serves 4.

PEARS HELENE

Serve Vanilla Stewed Pears* over vanilla ice cream and top with Chocolate Sauce.*

RASPBERRY POACHED PEARS

10 pears
1 cup sugar
6 slices lemon
2 tablespoons lemon juice
1 cup bottled raspberry syrup

Cut the pears in half lengthwise; leave the stem on one side. Peel and core. Place them cored side down in a large skillet. Add the sugar, lemon slices, lemon juice, and 1 quart water. Cover and simmer about 15 minutes until almost tender. Turn the pears and add the raspberry syrup. Continue cooking until tender but not too soft. Serves 10.

VANILLA STEWED PEARS

2 cups sugar
1 tablespoon vanilla
8 pears

In a large skillet boil 3 cups water, the sugar, and vanilla for 5 minutes. Peel, halve, and core the pears. Add to syrup. Cover and simmer until pears are just tender. Let cool in syrup. These pears are especially good drained and served with Cardinal Sauce.* Serves 8.

PEARS WITH CHERRIES

12 strips orange peel
10 large pears
1 cup orange juice
½ cup sugar
½ teaspoon salt
½ cup slivered preserved ginger
2 pounds fresh or canned pitted Bing cherries

Boil the orange peel in salted water for 10 minutes. Meanwhile, peel, halve, and core the pears. Drain the orange peel and put it in a large kettle with 1 cup water, the orange juice, sugar, and salt. Bring to a boil, add the pears, and cook gently 5 minutes; then add the slivered ginger and cook about 2 minutes, until the fruit is almost tender. Do not overcook, since pears can turn mushy with disconcerting abruptness. When cold, pour 1 cup of the orange and pear syrup over the cherries. Refrigerate overnight. To serve, heap pears in the center of a platter and make a border of the cherries. Serve cold. Serves 12.

PEARS WITH RASPBERRY SAUCE
(Pears Christine)

(Plate 1)

1 cup sugar
1 teaspoon vanilla
3-inch stick cinnamon
2-inch strip lemon rind
2 tablespoons lemon juice
8 pears
2 pints fresh raspberries or 2 packages frozen

Simmer 2 cups water with the sugar, vanilla, cinnamon, lemon rind, and 1 tablespoon lemon juice for 5 minutes in a deep pan. Peel the pears, leaving them whole and with stems on. After peeling, sprinkle pears with remaining lemon juice. Cook in the prepared syrup over low heat, turning them often, until tender. Remove with a slotted spoon to a bowl. Dice 2 of the pears. Cover 6 pears with Saran or foil. Boil the remaining syrup rapidly, uncovered, to reduce to 1 cup. Remove cinnamon and lemon rind. Add the hulled raspberries or thawed frozen raspberries and boil rapidly 7–8 minutes, until sauce turns red and thickens. Strain and pour over pears. Cover and chill, turning pears often. Place the whole pears in serving dishes and garnish with diced pear and a spoonful of sauce. Serve with cream if you wish. Serves 6.

PEARS WITH CHOCOLATE CUSTARD SAUCE

4 pears
1⅓ cups sugar
¼ teaspoon vanilla
3 egg yolks
1 cup milk
1-inch strip lemon peel
3 ounces semisweet chocolate
1 ounce unsweetened chocolate

Peel the pears, cut in half lengthwise, and core. Place 2 cups water in a saucepan with 1 cup sugar and the vanilla. Bring to a boil and cook for 5 minutes; add pears and cook 5–10 minutes, until tender. Drain pears and cool. Save the syrup. Beat egg yolks with remaining sugar until thick and lemon-colored. Scald the milk and blend into the egg yolks with the lemon peel. Pour into a saucepan. Cook over low heat or in double boiler, stirring constantly, until mixture coats a spoon. Do not boil. Melt chocolate and add to egg mixture. Discard lemon peel. Cool the chocolate mixture, stirring occasionally. Arrange pears cored side down on a serving dish. Pour chocolate mixture over them and chill. Serves 4–6.

PEARS WITH SPICED SOUR-CREAM SAUCE

1 (1 lb. 13 oz.) can pear halves
1 cup sour cream
½ cup softened vanilla ice cream
⅓ teaspoon cinnamon
⅛ teaspoon nutmeg
Maraschino cherries (garnish)

Drain the syrup from the pears and arrange them in a serving dish. Mix the sour cream, ice cream, cinnamon, and nutmeg. Spoon about 3 tablespoons of this mixture over each pear half. Chill until serving time. Decorate with small pieces of maraschino cherry if you wish. Serves 4.

PEARS WITH LIQUEUR SAUCE

6 pears
1½ cups sugar
¼ teaspoon cinnamon
⅛ teaspoon cloves
Dash nutmeg
3–4 tablespoons brandy
3–4 tablespoons Grand Marnier, Curaçao,
*   or Cointreau*

Peel, halve, and core the pears. Heat 3 cups water with the sugar and spices in a large saucepan. Place the pears in the liquid and simmer very gently until tender. Remove pears to a serving dish and reduce syrup to half. Pour hot syrup over the pears. Warm the brandy and liqueur, ignite, pour over the pears, and serve flaming or chilled. Serves 6.

PINEAPPLE AND STRAWBERRIES

3 pineapples
⅔ cup peach or apricot brandy or syrup
*   from can of peaches*
2 quarts strawberries
1 large or 2 small coconuts or 2 (3¾ oz.)
*   cans flaked coconut*
Superfine sugar

Peel, core, and slice the pineapples into bite-size pieces and pour some peach or apricot brandy or peach syrup over them. Hull the strawberries and sprinkle with a little sugar. If using fresh coconut, grate it. Make mounds of pineapple around a large platter. Pile the strawberries in between; make a fluffy mound of grated coconut in the middle. Pour some of the brandy or peach syrup over the strawberries. Sprinkle the fruit with a little superfine sugar if you wish. Serves 12.

MAPLE PINEAPPLE AND STRAWBERRIES

1 pineapple or 2 (1 lb. 4 oz.) cans pineapple
*   chunks*
2 packages frozen whole strawberries
Kirsch (optional)
About 1 cup maple syrup
½ cup sour cream

Peel the fresh pineapple, cut into chunks, and chill. If using canned pineapple, drain. Put the pineapple on cold dessert plates or a platter. Cover with the berries, leaving them slightly icy. Add a little kirsch if you wish. Pour 2 tablespoons maple syrup over each serving. Add a dollop of sour cream and a teaspoon of maple syrup in the center of the cream. Serves 6.

MELANGE OF PLUMS AND GINGER

1 (1 lb. 13 oz.) can purple plums
1 (1 lb. 13 oz.) can greengage plums
½ cup slivered crystallized ginger

Chill the fruit thoroughly and drain the purple plums. Put the greengages with their juice in a serving bowl. Add the purple plums and sprinkle with half the ginger; stir gently and sprinkle remaining ginger on top. Serves 6.

STEAMED RHUBARB

4 cups diced rhubarb
1 cup sugar

Mix the rhubarb with sugar in a double boiler. Cover and let steam about 45 minutes, until tender. Don't add any water; it makes its own juice. Stir once very gently after ½ hour. The rhubarb will stay attractive in color, in unbroken pieces, and will not get stringy. Serves 6.

STRAWBERRIES GLACEES   (Plate 29)

50 large perfect red strawberries with stems
2 cups sugar
¼ teaspoon cream of tartar
Red food coloring
⅛ teaspoon lemon juice

Wash the strawberries early enough to allow them to dry completely. Gently pull leaves back from each berry and lay them out ready to be dipped. Put the sugar, 1 cup water, cream of tartar, and a few drops of food coloring in a heavy saucepan over high heat. Rapidly boil until it reaches the hard-crack stage (300°), add lemon juice, and immediately set the pan in cold water for a few seconds until the syrup stops boiling. Then place pan on low heat. Dip each berry into hot syrup almost up to the stem. Allow excess syrup to drain back into the pan and then lay the berry on a baking sheet or on foil to cool. Work rapidly; if the syrup becomes too thick, turn heat up until it thins again. The berries should be served within 1½ hours after they are glazed (much sooner on a hot, humid day). Yield: 50 strawberries.

STRAWBERRIES WITH SOUR-CREAM DIP

1 cup sour cream
1 teaspoon grated orange or lemon rind
¼ cup superfine sugar
1 tablespoon rum, brandy, or kirsch
1 quart strawberries

Mix the cream, orange or lemon rind, and the sugar together; beat with a rotary beater until light. Add liqueur and beat ½ minute more. Make a mound in center of platter or individual plates and circle with berries, washed but not hulled. Serves 4.

RUBY STRAWBERRIES

1 package frozen raspberries
½ cup sugar
1 tablespoon lemon juice
1 quart strawberries
Grand Marnier or kirsch (optional)
⅓ cup toasted slivered blanched almonds
* (optional)*

Thaw the raspberries enough to put through a sieve or food mill, or buzz in blender. Strain

to remove seeds. Add ¼ cup sugar and lemon juice; chill. Wash, hull, and drain the strawberries. Sprinkle with remaining sugar. Add a little liqueur to the raspberry sauce if you wish, pour the sauce over the strawberries, and chill until ready to serve. Sprinkle with almonds before serving if you wish. Serves 4.

STRAWBERRIES IN LEMON JELLY

2 envelopes unflavored gelatin
1 cup sugar
Pinch salt
½ cup lemon juice
3 pints strawberries
Custard Sauce* or whipped cream

Mix the gelatin with the sugar, salt, and 2½ cups water. Heat and stir until dissolved. Add the strained lemon juice and chill until thick and syrupy. Hull the strawberries. Pour a thin layer of the gelatin into the bottom of a 1½-quart mold. Chill until firm by setting the mold in a pan of ice cubes and water. Cover the gelatin with a layer of whole berries and add enough gelatin to cover. Chill until firm and repeat the layering process until all the berries are used. Cover and refrigerate overnight. Serve with Custard Sauce flavored with sherry or vanilla, or with whipped cream if you prefer. Serves 6.

What beautiful fruit! I love fruit when it's expensive.

Sir Arthur Wing Pinero,
The Second Mrs. Tanqueray

BERRIES WITH BRANDY

1 quart strawberries, blackberries,
* raspberries, or blueberries*
¼ cup honey
¼ cup brandy
Sour cream or heavy cream

Prepare the berries and dry thoroughly. Blend the honey and brandy and pour the mixture over the berries. Roll the berries around gently so that all are coated. Chill for 2 hours or more, stirring them very gently once or twice. Serve with a bowl of sour or plain or whipped cream on the side. Serves 4.

Fruits with Raspberry Sauce

If the fresh or frozen fruit is not sweet, sprinkle with a little sugar before adding the sauce. You will not need sugar with canned fruit.

RASPBERRY SAUCE

2–3 packages frozen raspberries
¼–⅓ cup sugar
1–3 tablespoons liqueur (optional)
1 teaspoon grated lemon rind (optional)

Thaw the raspberries and rub through a fine sieve to remove the seeds. If you buzz the berries in a blender, it facilitates the straining. Chill unless you use at once. If you wish, you may add 1–3 tablespoons of liqueur such as kirsch, brandy, rum, Eau de Vie, Curaçao, or Cointreau; don't use too much or you will dull the raspberry flavor. Add the lemon rind if you wish. Yield: sauce for about 8 servings.

STRAWBERRIES

Hull 3 pints fresh berries. Chill and cover with the cold Raspberry Sauce.* You may make this with frozen whole berries, but the fresh are preferable. If using frozen fruit, thaw and drain. If you wish, you may add the juice to the Raspberry Sauce. If using liqueur, try brandy or kirsch.

RASPBERRIES

Pick over 3–4 boxes fresh raspberries. If you wash them, do so very carefully and dry by spreading on paper toweling. Pour the Raspberry Sauce* over the berries. This makes a most intense raspberry flavor. A little kirsch or Eau de Vie de Framboise may be added.

PEACHES

Peel and slice 12 peaches or thaw 3 packages frozen ones. Cover at once with the Raspberry Sauce.* If there is to be a delay, sprinkle the peaches with grapefruit, orange, or lemon juice to prevent discoloration. If using canned peaches, drain before adding the sauce.

ORANGES AND PEACHES

Peel 7 large seedless oranges with a sharp knife, removing all white membrane. Cut into sections, avoiding the connecting tissue. Peel and slice 5–6 large peaches and sprinkle with about ½ cup grapefruit juice. Arrange the fruit attractively on a serving plate and spoon Raspberry Sauce* over them. If you use a liqueur in the sauce, the orange ones such as Curaçao or Cointreau are appropriate. If fresh peaches are not available, use 2 packages frozen sliced peaches.

GRAPEFRUIT AND ORANGES

Peel 4 grapefruit and 7 seedless oranges with a sharp knife, removing all white membrane. Cut into sections, avoiding the connecting tissue. Arrange the fruit on a dessert plate or in a bowl and pour Raspberry Sauce* over. A little rum flavoring or rum in the sauce would be a good choice.

RUBY RHUBARB MOLD

2½ pounds rhubarb
2 cups sugar
3 packages strawberry-flavored gelatin
1–2 tablespoons lemon juice
1 cup ginger ale
1 tablespoon Cherry Heering (optional)
1 quart strawberries
Custard Sauce or heavy cream (optional)*

Trim the rhubarb and cut into 1-inch pieces. Put into a heavy saucepan with ½ cup water and the sugar. Bring to a boil, cover, and cook until very tender. Force through a food mill or sieve. You should have about 5 cups of purée. Add the strawberry gelatin and heat, stirring constantly, about 5 minutes, until gelatin is dissolved. Allow to cool slightly and add lemon juice to taste, ginger ale, and the Cherry Heering if you like. Chill. When mixture begins to thicken, stir and pour into a 1½-quart mold, cover, and chill 6–8 hours. Turn out onto serving dish and arrange berries around mold. Serve with Custard Sauce or with cream if you wish. Serves 8.

RHUBARB PINEAPPLE COMPOTE

2 pounds rhubarb
1½ cups sugar
Grated rind 1 orange
2 cups strawberries
2½ cups thinly sliced fresh pineapple
½ cup grenadine

Trim the rhubarb, cut into 1-inch pieces, mix with the sugar and grated orange rind, and place in a shallow baking dish. Hull and purée 1 cup strawberries and pour over the rhubarb. Cover with foil and bake in a 325° oven for about ½ hour, stirring twice during this time. The rhubarb should be crisp-tender when removed from the oven, for it will continue to cook slightly after it has been taken out. Set aside, still covered, to cool to room temperature; then chill thoroughly. Mix the pineapple and grenadine and chill at least 2 hours. Drain the rhubarb and pineapple, reserving the syrups, and arrange in a serving bowl. Pile the remaining hulled strawberries in the center. Mix the syrups and spoon over the fruit. Serves 6–8.

MACEDOINE OF FRESH FRUITS

(*Plate 1*)

Melon balls (cantaloupe, honeydew, Spanish, watermelon, casaba, etc.)
Strawberries or raspberries
Blackberries or blueberries
Grapefruit
Oranges
Peaches
Bing cherries
Bananas
Seedless white grapes
Pineapple
Pears
Apples
Lime juice (optional)
Maple syrup (optional)
Brown sugar (optional)
Yoghurt (optional)

Any fresh fruit can be used, and the greater the variety and contrast in color and flavor, the better. Allow 1 cup per person. If you serve your fruits on a platter, you can make attractive designs and vary the colors. The combination might be melon balls (both pale green and orange or pink), a pile of strawberries or raspberries in the middle, sections of grapefruit and oranges on each side. Perhaps a garnish of nuts. Try pitted Bing cherries in the center and leave off the melon balls and use sliced peaches and bananas. For pale colors use seedless grapes, small pieces of pineapple, or thin slices of peeled pears or apples. You can make all kinds of combinations. This platter should be made as soon before serving as possible, particularly if using bananas, which will darken. You might serve some lime juice, sweetened to taste with maple syrup, in a small pitcher with the fruit. Yoghurt and brown sugar are good served on the side. It is great fun to make various platters of fresh fruits in this manner, the effect is lovely, and the delightful refreshing taste of cold fruits is a perfect climax to a summer dinner.

THREE-FRUIT GARLAND   (*Plate 33*)

1 fresh pineapple or 3 cups frozen or canned
1 tablespoon shredded fresh mint
¼–½ cup sugar
1 quart strawberries
1½ cups seedless or seeded white grapes
3 tablespoons Cointreau or other orange liqueur (optional)
Mint sprigs (garnish)

Peel, quarter, and core the fresh pineapple and cut into thin fan-shaped pieces. Add the shredded mint and a little sugar to taste. Sweeten the strawberries with sugar. Arrange the grapes in the center of a shallow bowl. Circle the grapes with the strawberries and make an outer circle of pineapple. Pour Cointreau or other liqueur over fruit if you wish. Garnish with mint. Serves 6–8.

FRESH FRUIT WITH COCONUT

2 cantaloupes
1½ pounds seedless white grapes
1 pint raspberries
6 oranges
⅓ cup sugar or brown sugar
¾ cup flaked coconut

Make cantaloupe balls. Pull the grapes from their stems. With a sharp knife cut the peel from the oranges, being careful to remove all white membrane; section, avoiding connecting tissue. Put all of the fruit in a serving bowl, sprinkle with the sugar, and fold in the coconut. Serves 8.

THREE-FRUIT MEDLEY
(Low Calorie)

*½ cup sugar or 1 tablespoon liquid
    noncaloric sweetener*
Juice 1½ oranges
⅔ cup ginger ale (low calorie if you wish)
½ teaspoon orange flavoring
2 pints strawberries
3 cups blueberries
1 tablespoon grated preserved ginger
4 peaches
Mint sprigs (garnish)

Mix the sugar or sweetener and orange juice. Pour a third of the sweetened juice, ⅓ cup ginger ale, and the orange flavoring over the hulled and thinly sliced strawberries. Chill. In another bowl pour another third of sweetened orange juice over the blueberries and chill. Mix the remaining orange juice, ginger ale, and the grated ginger and pour over the thinly sliced, peeled peaches. Chill. To serve, mound the blueberries in the center of a large plate and surround with clusters of peaches and strawberries. Garnish with mint sprigs if you wish. Serves 6–8.

SPICED FRUIT COMPOTE

1 grapefruit
3 seedless oranges
1 pint strawberries
2 apples
1 (14 oz.) can frozen pineapple chunks

HONEY FRUIT SAUCE
½ cup honey
2 cardamom seeds
½ teaspoon salt
8 mint leaves
1–2 tablespoons lemon juice

Peel the grapefruit and oranges, removing all white membrane, and cut into sections, avoiding connecting tissue. Save the juice. Hull the strawberries. Peel, core, and slice the apples. Drain the thawed pineapple, reserving the juice. Mix with the apples, orange and grapefruit sections, and strawberries.

Honey Fruit Sauce. Mix the honey and ½ cup water with the cardamom seeds, peeled and crushed. Simmer 5 minutes. Add the salt and mint, cut fine. Cool and strain. Add the lemon juice and ½ cup mixed juice from the grapefruit, oranges, and pineapple.

Pour the sauce over the fruit and chill ½ hour or more. Serves 6.

COMPOTE WITH AVOCADO

1 apple
1 banana
1 grapefruit
2 oranges
1 avocado
2 tablespoons lemon juice
½ cup grapefruit juice
¼ cup honey

Chill the fruit. Mix the lemon and grapefruit juice with the honey. Peel, core, and slice the apple. Slice the banana. Peel grapefruit and oranges, cutting off all white membrane; section, avoiding the connecting tissue. Mix all the fruit together with the avocado which has been peeled and diced. Add the honey mixture and toss gently. Serve chilled. Serves 4.

FRUIT COMPOTE NESSELRODE

*2 large grapefruit or 3 cups frozen or canned
    sections*
1 (1 lb. 4 oz.) can sliced cling peaches
2 teaspoons lemon juice
½ teaspoon grated lemon rind
1 teaspoon orange bitters
½ jar Nesselrode sauce
1 pint strawberries

Peel the grapefruit with a sharp knife, removing all white membrane; section, avoiding connecting tissue, and save any juice squeezed out from the membrane; or drain frozen or canned grapefruit. Drain the peaches and save the syrup. Mix 1 cup peach syrup with the grapefruit juice, lemon juice, lemon rind, orange bitters, and Nesselrode sauce. Add grapefruit sections and peaches to the sauce. Chill well and add strawberries, sliced or cut in half. Serves 6.

FRUIT MOLD

1 package apple-flavored gelatin
1 package lemon-flavored gelatin
1½ cups ginger ale
½ cup dry white wine
1 cup seedless white grapes
1 package frozen melon balls

Dissolve the gelatins in 2 cups hot water. Stir in the ginger ale and wine. Chill until thick and syrupy. Stir in the grapes and the drained, thawed melon balls. Spoon into a 1½-quart mold; chill until firm. Unmold. Serves 6–8.

FRESH FRUIT PLATTER

1 large pineapple
½ pound seedless white grapes
2 pints strawberries
2 pints blueberries and/or raspberries
2 cups sour cream
5 tablespoons superfine sugar
1 tablespoon brandy or kirsch

Cut the top off the pineapple about ¾ inch below where the leaves sprout—lower if very large. With a sharp thin knife hollow out the center of the pineapple, leaving a firm shell. The shell will be a good sauceboat. Cut the pineapple into small pieces, discarding the hard core. Place the pieces of fruit on one side of the platter. Pull the stems off the grapes and place opposite the pineapple. Fill the platter with hulled strawberries and blueberries and/or raspberries. Do not sugar the fruit. Fill the center of the pineapple with a mixture of the sour cream, superfine sugar, and brandy or kirsch. You can make as many more servings as you like by adding more of any fruit or more varieties of fruits. Serves 8.

FRUIT WITH CREAM TOPPING

9 peaches
1 pint raspberries
½ pound seedless white grapes
½ cup sugar
¼ cup orange liqueur or orange juice
1 cup heavy cream
1 ounce unsweetened chocolate

Peel and thinly slice the peaches and put them in a pottery or china serving bowl. Sprinkle the raspberries over the peaches. Stem the grapes and place on top of the raspberries. Sprinkle with sugar and then with orange liqueur or orange juice. Chill. Just before serving, heat the broiler. Whip the cream. Spoon it on the fruit and sprinkle with the grated chocolate. Broil just until the chocolate melts—about ½ minute. Serve immediately. Serves 6.

FILLED WATERMELON

1 small long watermelon
Berries, grapes, pineapple, peaches, etc.
Mint sprigs (garnish)
½ cup apricot brandy (optional)

Make a cardboard scallop pattern 2 inches long and 1 inch high and draw scallops around the melon a third from the top. Cut around the scallops with a sharp knife and remove the top piece. Scoop out the fruit and the seeds and cut the rind back of the scallops fairly thin. Make melon balls of the red flesh. Use a combination of sugared fresh fruits of varying colors. Heap the shell high with the mixed fruit and garnish with mint. Pour apricot brandy over the fruit if you wish. Serves 12.

GINGER FRESH-FRUIT MELANGE

1 cup pitted Bing cherries
1 cup blueberries
1 cup fan-shaped pieces pineapple
1 cup orange sections
1 cup thinly sliced cored apples (unpeeled)
1 cup orange marmalade
1 tablespoon minced preserved ginger
2 tablespoons ginger syrup
1 cup raspberries

Mix the cherries and blueberries. Cover and chill. Mix the pineapple, orange sections, and apple slices. Cover and chill. Two hours before serving, mix the marmalade with the minced ginger and ginger syrup that has been drained from a jar of preserved ginger. Stir into the fruits mixed together and then add the raspberries. Chill until ready to serve. Serves 6–8.

FRUIT COMPOTE

6 peaches
2 cups sugar
2-inch strip lemon peel
6 pears
8 apricots
8 red plums
8 purple plums
Mousseline Sauce*

Peel the peaches by dropping them one at a time into boiling water for a second or two, then running cold water over them. The skins should slip off easily, leaving the peaches smooth. Drop them into cold water containing a little lemon juice to prevent darkening. Mix the sugar, 2 cups water, and lemon peel in a large pan. Boil for 5 minutes. Place the peaches in the syrup, lower heat, and simmer gently until they can be pierced easily with a fork. Remove with a slotted spoon to a large compote or serving dish. Peel, core, and halve the pears, placing them also in the lemon water to prevent darkening. Cook in the syrup until just tender. Remove with slotted spoon and arrange around the peaches. Next, cook the apricots (whole with the skins) and, finally, the red and purple plums. Turn the plums in the syrup often so the skins won't pop open too much. The apricots and plums take just a short while; don't overcook. Arrange the apricots and plums here and there between the peaches and pears. Boil the remaining syrup so it is reduced by half. Cool. Pour over the fruits and chill. Serve with Mousseline Sauce. Serves 8.

MULLED FRUIT

2 grapefruit
2 large seedless oranges
2 pears
2 bananas
½ cup dark brown sugar
½ cup toasted slivered blanched almonds
¼ cup butter
½ cup sherry or 1 cup orange juice

Peel the grapefruit and oranges, removing all white membrane; section, being careful to avoid connecting tissue. Peel, core, and cut the pears into eighths and slice the bananas. Arrange the fruit in layers in a shallow 2-quart baking dish, sprinkling each layer with sugar. Sprinkle almonds over the fruit. Dot with butter and pour the sherry or orange juice over the fruit. Bake 20–30 minutes in a 350° oven. Serve hot. Serves 8.

COOKTIPS

To peel grapefruit and oranges easily, let them stand in hot water for 8 minutes before using the sharp knife. Before squeezing, dip citrus fruits in hot water.

Rhubarb which has been grown in a hot-house gives off more liquid in cooking than that which has been grown outdoors.

You will find it easier to prepare dates if you cut them with scissors, dipping the scissors in cold water to prevent sticking.

Wash strawberries before hulling so they won't bleed.

HOT FRUIT COMPOTE I

1 (1 lb. 1 oz.) can red plums
1 (1 lb. 1 oz.) can peach halves
1 (1 lb. 1 oz.) can apricot halves
1 (1 lb. 1 oz.) can pitted Bing cherries
2–3 tablespoons butter
¼ cup kirsch (optional)
Brown-Sugar Sauce* (optional)

Drain the plums and pit them carefully. Drain the remaining cans of fruit, putting all of the syrup together. Arrange the fruit in a casserole, beginning at the bottom with peaches, then plums, apricots, and last the cherries. Pour enough mixed fruit syrup over to reach just about the top. Add the butter, and kirsch if you wish. Cover and put aside until dinnertime; then warm, covered, in a 300° oven for about ½ hour. Serve hot, with or without Brown-Sugar Sauce. Serves 8.

HOT FRUIT COMPOTE II

2 seedless oranges
1 (1 lb. 13 oz.) can whole apricots
1 (1 lb. 13 oz.) can greengage plums
1 tablespoon slivered orange rind
½ teaspoon almond flavoring
1 tablespoon lemon juice

Peel the oranges with a sharp knife, removing all white membrane; section, avoiding connecting tissue. Mix with the apricots and plums in a large skillet or chafing dish. Add the orange rind and simmer until fruits are heated through. Flavor with almond flavoring and lemon juice. Serves 8.

HOT FRUIT COMPOTE III

2 seedless oranges
1 (1 lb. 4 oz.) can red plums
1 (1 lb. 13 oz.) can pear halves
1 (1 lb. 4 oz.) can peach halves
¼ cup frozen orange-juice concentrate
½ teaspoon almond flavoring
2 cups cooked fresh or drained canned chestnuts

Peel and slice the oranges, removing all white membrane. Drain the plums. Heat the pears and peaches and their syrup with the plums and the oranges. Add the orange-juice concentrate, almond flavoring, and chestnuts and reheat. Serves 10.

FRUIT CREAM COMPOTE

1 (8 oz.) can apricot halves
1 (8 oz.) can peach slices
1 (8 oz.) can pineapple slices
1 (8 oz.) can pear slices
1 cup sugar
1 tablespoon lemon juice
½ teaspoon grated lemon rind
½ teaspoon vanilla
1 cup strawberries
1 cup fresh or thawed frozen blueberries
*   (packed without sugar)*
1 pint lemon sherbet
1 quart vanilla ice cream

Drain the syrup from the canned fruits into a small saucepan, reserving the fruits. Add the sugar, lemon juice, and rind. Bring to a boil and simmer for 20 minutes. Add the vanilla and cool. Pour over reserved fruits, pack into jars, cover, and refrigerate. They may be prepared as much as a week in advance. To serve, hull and slice the strawberries and add with the blueberries to the other fruit. Spoon alternate mounds or scoops of sherbet and ice cream into a bowl. Ladle some of the fruits with syrup over and pass the rest. Serves 8–10.

MACEDOINE OF BAKED FRESH FRUIT

About 8 cups prepared assorted fruit:
Pineapple	*Pears*
Blueberries	*Apples*
Strawberries	*Peaches*
Raspberries	*Apricots*
Bing cherries	*Mangoes*

⅓ cup honey
⅓ cup orange juice
1 tablespoon grated orange rind
¼ cup crème de cacao, Cointreau,
*   Curaçao, or Grand Marnier (optional)*

Select any combination of 3 or 4 fruits which are available, using berries and cut-up pineapple and other fruit, such as pears, apples, or peaches. These should be peeled, pitted, and cut in half or in quarters. Make your own combinations of fruit. Arrange the fruit attractively in a shallow baking dish. Mix the honey, orange juice, and grated orange rind and pour over the fruit. Add the liqueur if you wish. Bake in a 350° oven for 20–30 minutes. Serve warm. (Failing fresh fruit, use canned, with less honey, and bake only long enough to heat through, 10–15 minutes.) Serves 8.

WHOLE FRUIT COMPOTE   *(Plate 32)*

8 peaches
8 pears
Lemon juice
8 red plums
7–8 cups sugar
3-inch piece vanilla bean
2 teaspoons grated lemon rind
Zabaglione Sauce* or Custard Sauce*
*   (optional)*

Peel the peaches and pears, keeping them whole and leaving pear stems on. Place in a bowl and sprinkle with lemon juice to prevent discoloration. Prick the plums to prevent skins from bursting. Mix the sugar and 6 cups water in a heavy kettle with the vanilla bean and lemon rind. The amount of sugar and the cooking time will depend upon the ripeness of the fruit. Cook to a thin syrup—about 10 minutes. Add pears and peaches and cook gently, turning them often, about 20 minutes, until they start getting glossy. Add the plums and cook all together until fork-tender. Then remove with a slotted spoon. Arrange fruit in a large bowl. Bring syrup to a boil and pour all or part of it over the fruit. Serve hot or cold, plain or with Zabaglione Sauce or Custard Sauce. Serves 8.

BAKED FRUIT COMPOTE

3 seedless oranges
¾ pound seedless white grapes
1 (1 lb. 13 oz.) can peeled whole apricots
2 packages frozen peaches
1½ tablespoons finely slivered crystallized
*   ginger*
2 pears
2 teaspoons cornstarch
Kirsch (optional)

Peel the oranges with a sharp knife, removing all white membrane, and cut into sections, avoiding all connecting tissue. Save the juice. Put the orange sections and grapes into a large bowl. Pit the apricots and add with the thawed peaches and the ginger. Peel, core, and slice the pears and add to the other fruit. Blend the cornstarch with the orange juice and stir into the fruit mixture. Flavor with a little kirsch if you like. Arrange the fruit in a shallow 2-quart casserole and add enough water to cover the fruit. Bake in a 350° oven for about 1 hour. Serve hot, or allow to cool and then chill for about 1 hour. Serves 8.

HOT CURRIED FRUIT COMPOTE
(Low Calorie)

2 (8 oz.) cans artificially sweetened mixed
   fruits
¼ cup dark brown sugar
2¼ teaspoons curry powder
1 cup yoghurt

Put fruit and liquid in a large skillet. Sprinkle with sugar and curry. Heat gently until warm. Do not stir, but baste from time to time. Serve warm with yoghurt on the side. Serves 6 (about 100 calories per serving).

HOT CURRIED FRUIT

2 (1 lb.) cans fruits-for-salad
¼ cup brown sugar
2 tablespoons butter
2 teaspoons curry powder
1 cup yoghurt or sour cream

Drain the fruits and arrange in a shallow 1½-quart baking dish. Sprinkle with the brown sugar, dot with butter, and sprinkle the curry powder on top. Cover and bake in a 350° oven for 20 minutes. Serve hot, topped with yoghurt or sour cream. Serves 4–6.

FRUIT AND CHEESE

Briffault says, "Cheese complements a good meal and supplements a bad one." Cheese, one of the oldest of foods, was made first in Asia, then Europe, and much, much later in America. There are now over 400 kinds that have different names in France alone! Many cheeses bear the name of the place of their origin— Roquefort and Camembert for those cities in France (in the town of Camembert there is a huge monument to Mme. Haul, the creator of Camembert, 1761), Swiss for the Alpine country of Switzerland, and Romano for Rome. However, there are less than a dozen different *types* of cheeses, such as very hard cheese like Parmesan, hard such as Cheddar and Edam, semisoft like Roquefort and Muenster, soft such as Camembert and Brie, and unfermented like cottage and cream, and process cheeses.

Keep cheese refrigerated, preferably in a covered container or wrapped in foil. Be sure to remove from the refrigerator some hours before serving so the cheese will be at room temperature.

Cheese served with fruit or with crackers or French bread or hard rolls makes a satisfying and distinguished ending to a meal.

Apples and pears, polished and arranged on a tray or in a bowl, are the best fruits to serve with cheese. You may top with grapes or cherries if you wish. Put an assortment of cheese on a tray with crisp crackers. Suggested cheeses are: Cheddar or Cheddar-type; Edam or Gouda; Roquefort or blue; cream; Camembert, Brie, or Liederkranz. You may prefer to arrange fruit and cheese on the same platter. Crackers are optional, since fruit and cheese are delicious eaten together.

FRUIT CHEESE PLATTER FOR A BUFFET

2 clusters grapes
1 pint strawberries
1 cantaloupe peeled and cut into wedges
2 apples cut into slices
2 pears cut into slices
3 peaches cut into quarters
12 prunes plumped
2 (3 oz.) packages cream cheese
1 teaspoon grated orange rind
¼–½ pound Cheddar cheese cubed
¼–½ pound Swiss cheese cubed
Paprika

Arrange the chilled fruit around the outside of a large platter, leaving room in the center for cubes of cheese. If any of the fruit is canned, drain it thoroughly. Soften 1 package cream cheese, add orange rind, and beat until fluffy. Cut the prunes halfway through lengthwise with a sharp knife and remove the pits; fill prunes with the cream-cheese mixture. Stick a toothpick in each cube of cheese. Make the other package of cream cheese into balls, dust with paprika, and put a toothpick in each. Put all the cheese in the center. Serves 8.

Plate 32. A WHOLE FRUIT COMPOTE made with fresh plums, peaches, and pears cooked in a syrup flavored with lemon and vanilla. Serve hot or cold with fluffy ZABAGLIONE SAUCE, pictured in the left foreground.

Plate 33.
THREE-FRUIT
GARLAND.

Plate 34. WATERMELON SHERBET garnished with honeydew melon balls and a sprinkling of blueberries.

CHAPTER EIGHT

Special Salads

Fruit salads and aspics are especially refreshing for dessert after a hearty meal. Try a combination of grapefruit and avocado, apple and celery, oranges and pineapple, bananas and nuts, or pears and cream cheese. Choose an appropriate dressing—sweet or tangy—and serve it on the salad, or offer a choice of two dressings so each may select to his taste.

FRUIT SALAD COMBINATIONS *(Serve with or without water cress or other salad greens)*	SUGGESTED DRESSINGS
Orange sections	Chutney Dressing
Bananas with chopped walnuts	Boiled Fruit Dressing
Avocado and apple	Cooked Lemon Dressing
Apple and pear	Sour-Cream Roquefort Dressing
Grapefruit and avocado	Lemon French Dressing
Cantaloupe or other melon with berries	Special Salad Dressing
Peaches and oranges	Sour-Cream Dressing
Berries and cottage cheese	Creamy Mayonnaise
Orange and grapefruit sections	Curry Dressing
Pineapple slices with banana	Cream- or Cottage-Cheese Dressing
Pear halves and pitted prunes	Creamy French Dressing
White grapes and slivered toasted almonds	Sour-Cream Dressing with Honey
Apples, celery, and nuts	Mayonnaise
Raw fruits	Cream-Cheese Dressing
Tropical fruits	Curry Dressing
Strawberries and grapefruit sections	Rum French Dressing
Cooked fruits	Honey Lime Dressing
Pear halves with grated soft Cheddar cheese ⎫ Bing cherries stuffed with cream cheese ⎬ Prunes stuffed with cottage cheese ⎭	Mayonnaise, Mayonnaise Fruit Dressing, or Almond Mayonnaise on the side

FRESH FRUIT SALAD

½ pineapple
1 pint strawberries
1–2 oranges or papayas
1 banana
2–3 peaches or 1 package frozen
1 cup seedless white grapes
Honey Lime Dressing*

Peel the pineapple and cut in wedges; slice the berries; section the oranges or peel and slice the papayas; slice the banana; peel and slice the peaches, or thaw and drain if using frozen. Combine all of the fruit and toss very gently with about half of the Honey Lime Dressing. Pass the remaining dressing. Serves 6–8.

FRUIT SALAD

1 (1 lb. 4 oz.) can Bing cherries
1 (1 lb. 4 oz.) can pears
1 package frozen pineapple chunks
½ cup slivered fresh kumquats or orange sections
½ cup mayonnaise
½ cup sour cream

Drain the cherries. Drain and dice the pears. Cut the pineapple chunks into 2–3 pieces each. Combine all the fruit. Blend the mayonnaise and sour cream together and mix with the fruit. Chill. Serves 6.

WALDORF SALAD

1 cup mayonnaise
1 cup sour cream
2 tablespoons honey
3 cups diced tart apples
2 cups diced celery
1 cup coarsely chopped walnuts
2 cups halved, seeded red grapes (optional)

Mix the mayonnaise, sour cream, and honey together. Add the apples and blend well with the dressing to prevent discoloration. Add the celery and walnuts; mix again and chill. For a change, try this salad with the addition of grapes. Serves 6–8.

BANANA WALDORF SALAD

Mix 2 sliced bananas with the apples and proceed as for Waldorf Salad.* Serves 8.

PEAR WALDORF SALAD

Substitute diced fresh pears for apples and proceed as for Waldorf Salad.* Serves 6–8.

CRANBERRY GRAPEFRUIT SALAD

2 envelopes unflavored gelatin
4 cups cranberry juice
⅔ cup sugar
1½ cups split blanched almonds
3 cups grapefruit sections
Greens (optional)
Almond Mayonnaise* or Boiled Fruit Dressing*

Mix the gelatin with ½ cup cranberry juice. Heat 1 cup of the juice and add to the gelatin. Stir until dissolved. Add the sugar and remaining cranberry juice. Chill until thick and syrupy. Put a portion of the jelly in a 2-quart mold and chill until barely firm. Keep the rest of the jelly warm. Arrange half the almonds and grapefruit sections in a layer over the jelly. Cover with a little more jelly and chill until firm. Repeat with a layer of the remaining almonds, grapefruit, and cranberry jelly. Chill until thoroughly set. Turn out and garnish with greens if you wish. Serve with Almond Mayonnaise or Boiled Fruit Dressing. Serves 8.

SPICED PEACH SALAD

1 (1 lb. 4 oz.) can cling-peach halves
¾ cup cider vinegar
⅓ cup sugar
1 stick cinnamon
1 teaspoon whole allspice
1 head lettuce
Seedless grapes
1 (11 oz.) can mandarin-orange sections
2 tablespoons chopped preserved ginger
¼ cup Lemon French Dressing*
2 tablespoons honey

Drain the peaches and set them aside. Measure ½ cup syrup into a saucepan. Add the vinegar, sugar, cinnamon, and allspice. Mix, bring to a boil, and simmer gently for 10 minutes. Remove from heat, add the peach halves, and cool. Cover and chill overnight. To serve, place peach halves, hollow side up, on the lettuce. Fill each peach half with grapes and mandarin-orange sections. Sprinkle with ginger. Combine the Lemon French Dressing with the honey. Pass with the salad. Serves 6.

APRICOT FRUIT ASPIC

3 envelopes unflavored gelatin
1 (1 lb. 13 oz.) can apricots
1 pint ginger ale
¼ cup lemon juice
1 teaspoon grated lemon rind
Assorted fresh and frozen fruit: grapes
(seeded or seedless), strawberries,
grapefruit sections, orange sections,
pineapple, raspberries, pears, melon balls
Cooked Lemon Dressing*

Mix the gelatin with 1 cup cold water and heat until dissolved. Drain the apricots and reserve the syrup. Pit the apricots and purée them in a blender or rub through a strainer. Mix the purée, syrup, and gelatin. Add the ginger ale and flavor with lemon juice and lemon rind. Stir thoroughly. Chill until thick and syrupy, stirring occasionally until the froth has disappeared. Pour into a 1½-quart ring mold and chill until firm. Unmold on a large round platter. You may fill the center and decorate the sides with an assortment of fresh and/or frozen fruit. Serve with Cooked Lemon Dressing if you wish. Serves 6–8.

MELON ASPIC

2–3 ripe honeydew melons
3 envelopes unflavored gelatin
1½ teaspoons lemon juice
4 peaches or 1 package frozen sliced peaches
Salad greens (optional)
2 cups watermelon balls
About 2 cups fresh or canned pineapple
chunks
Camembert Dressing* or Mayonnaise Fruit
Dressing*

Remove the seeds from the honeydew melons. Scoop out all soft flesh and purée in a blender or food mill, or rub through a medium-fine sieve. Heat the gelatin with ½ cup melon purée until the gelatin is dissolved. Add the gelatin mixture and lemon juice to 3½ cups melon purée. Mix well. Pour into a 1-quart mold and chill until firm. Slice the fresh peaches or thaw the frozen ones. When ready to serve, unmold onto a cold platter. Put water cress, chicory, or other greens around the base of the mold if you wish. Place separate mounds of each fruit on the greens or around the mold. Serve with Camembert Dressing or Mayonnaise Fruit Dressing. Serves 6–8.

MOLDED CRANBERRY SALAD I

1 cup walnut halves
2 sticks cinnamon
24 cloves
4 cups cranberries
1 cup sugar
½ teaspoon salt
2 envelopes unflavored gelatin
⅔ cup diced celery
1 cup drained crushed pineapple
Creamy Mayonnaise* (optional)

Cover the walnuts with water and boil for 3 minutes. Drain and chop. Toast in a 300° oven until dry and slightly golden. Add the cinnamon and cloves, tied in a cheesecloth bag, to the cranberries and cook in 2 cups water until the cranberry skins pop. Purée the cranberries with their liquid. Add the sugar, salt, and gelatin and cook for 5 minutes more. Chill until thick and syrupy. Add the celery, pineapple, and walnuts. Mix well and pour into a 5-cup mold. Chill until firm. Creamy Mayonnaise is suggested. Serves 6–8.

MOLDED CRANBERRY SALAD II

1½ pounds cranberries
1 (1 lb. 4 oz.) can crushed pineapple
3 packages lemon-flavored gelatin
2 envelopes unflavored gelatin
1½ cups sugar
1 teaspoon cinnamon
½ teaspoon nutmeg
1½ cups chopped celery
1½ cups chopped walnuts
Juice 1 lemon
1 orange
Greens (optional)
Sour-Cream Dressing* or other dressing

Cook the cranberries in 3 cups water until the skins pop. Drain the pineapple and add enough water to the syrup to make 1 cup liquid. Add the gelatins to the liquid. Drain the cranberries and add 3 cups boiling juice to the gelatin mixture (if necessary, add a little boiling water to make 3 cups). Purée the cranberries and stir in the sugar, cinnamon, and nutmeg. Add with the celery, nuts, pineapple, lemon juice, and the orange, ground fine, to the gelatin mixture. Mix well and spoon into a 3-quart ring mold. Chill until firm. Unmold, garnish with greens if you wish, and serve with Sour-Cream Dressing or your favorite fruit-salad dressing. Serves 12–15.

APPLE CELERY ASPIC

> 2 packages lemon-flavored gelatin
> 2 cups cider
> ¼ cup lemon juice
> Pinch salt
> 3 cups diced red apples (unpeeled)
> 2 cups diced celery
> Cooked Lemon Dressing* or Sour-Cream
>   Dressing*

Dissolve the gelatin in 1½ cups hot water. Add the cider, lemon juice, and salt. Chill until thick and syrupy. Fold in the apples and celery and spoon into a 2-quart mold or 12 individual molds. Chill until firm. Unmold and serve with Cooked Lemon Dressing or with Sour-Cream Dressing. Serves 12.

SPICED PEACH AND CRANBERRY SALAD

> 1 (1 lb. 14 oz.) can peach halves
> 1 tablespoon mixed pickling spices
> 12 whole cloves
> 2 (2-inch) sticks cinnamon
> ⅓ cup light brown sugar
> 3 tablespoons vinegar
> 2 envelopes unflavored gelatin
> ½ orange
> 1½ cups cranberries
> ½ cup sugar
> 1 tablespoon lemon juice

Drain the peach halves, reserving 1¼ cups syrup. Tie the spices in a cheesecloth bag and add to the peach syrup with the brown sugar and vinegar. Simmer 10 minutes. Add the peaches and simmer 5 minutes. Remove the spice bag and peaches. Drain the peaches on paper toweling. Mix 1 envelope gelatin with ¼ cup cold water, add to the hot peach syrup, and stir until dissolved. Add enough cold water to make 1½ cups. Chill until thick and syrupy. Pour a ¼-inch layer in the bottom of a 1-quart ring mold. Chill until firm. Arrange the peaches hollow side up in the mold and pour the remaining gelatin mixture over them. Chill until firm. Remove the seeds from the orange and put through a food grinder with the cranberries. Add the sugar and let stand an hour or so. Mix the remaining envelope gelatin with 1¼ cups cold water and heat until dissolved. Add to the cranberry mixture with the lemon juice. Chill until thick. Pour over the peach layer and chill until firm. Serve with a dressing of your choice. Serves 8.

LIME AND GINGER SALAD

> 1 (1 lb.) can pear slices
> 1 package lime-flavored gelatin
> 1 teaspoon finely chopped preserved
>   or crystallized ginger
> ¼ teaspoon salt
> 1½ teaspoons vinegar
> 2 (3 oz.) packages cream cheese
> Salad greens and pear halves (garnish)
> Mayonnaise* or Mayonnaise Fruit
>   Dressing*

Drain the pear slices, reserving the syrup. Dissolve the gelatin in 1 cup boiling water. Simmer the ginger in ½ cup pear syrup for 5 minutes. Add, along with ½ cup cold water, to the lime gelatin. Stir in the salt and vinegar and pour a ½-inch layer of the gelatin in a mold. Chill until almost firm. Meanwhile, chill the rest of the gelatin until it is slightly thickened. Beat until it is light and frothy. Mix the cream cheese until smooth with a small amount of the gelatin mixture, then fold it into the rest of the whipped gelatin. Cut the pears into ½-inch cubes and fold in last. (You should have 2 cups cubed pears.) Pour the fruit mixture over the clear layer when it is almost set. Chill until firm. Turn out and garnish if you wish with salad greens and pear halves. Good with Mayonnaise or Mayonnaise Fruit Dressing. Serves 6.

FROSTY CHEESE FRUIT SALAD

> 1 (1 lb. 14 oz.) can apricot halves
> 1 (1 lb. 14 oz.) can cling-peach slices
> 2½ cups creamed cottage cheese
> ½ cup mayonnaise
> 1 tablespoon lemon juice
> 1 package frozen strawberries
> ½ cup chopped walnuts

Drain the apricots and peaches; save the 2 cans. Cut the fruit into bite-size pieces. Whip the cottage cheese, mayonnaise, and lemon juice with an electric mixer or in a blender. Stir in the fruit and walnuts. Pour into the cans, cover with foil, and freeze for several hours until firm. You may keep this salad in the freezer for several weeks. Remove from freezer 20 minutes before serving. Open the other end of the cans and push the salad out. Slice and serve. Dressing is not necessary, but pass Honey Lime Dressing* or Mayonnaise Fruit Dressing* if you wish. Serves 10–12.

PISTACHIO CHEESE SALAD

1 envelope unflavored gelatin
2 (8 oz.) packages cream cheese
½ cup crumbled Roquefort cheese
1 cup coarsely chopped pistachio nuts
½ cup chopped celery
1 cup heavy cream
Lettuce
Mayonnaise Fruit Dressing* or Cooked
    Lemon Dressing* (optional)

Mix the gelatin with ¼ cup water. Dissolve over hot water. Cream the cheeses together until fluffy. Fold in the gelatin, pistachios, celery, and the cream, whipped. Spoon into a 1½-quart mold and chill until set. Unmold on a bed of lettuce. Serve with Mayonnaise Fruit Dressing or Cooked Lemon Dressing if you wish. Serves 6–8.

PLUM ASPIC

2 (1 lb. 14 oz.) cans peeled whole greengage
    plums
2 envelopes unflavored gelatin
2 tablespoons lemon juice
1 cup seedless grapes
2 cups cantaloupe balls
Creamy Mayonnaise* or other dressing

Drain the plums, reserving 1 cup of the syrup. Pit and purée the plums; you should have about 3 cups of purée. Mix the gelatin with ½ cup cold water. Add to the plum purée and the reserved syrup. Heat and stir until the gelatin dissolves. Add the lemon juice. Chill until thick and syrupy. Fold the grapes and cantaloupe balls into the mixture and spoon into a 7-cup mold. Chill until firm. Serve with Creamy Mayonnaise or other dressing. Serves 12.

STRAWBERRY GELATIN SALAD

1 package strawberry-flavored gelatin
2 teaspoons unflavored gelatin
Juice 2 lemons
2 packages frozen whole strawberries
Mayonnaise* (optional)

Add 2 cups hot water to the strawberry gelatin and stir until dissolved. Mix the unflavored gelatin with the lemon juice, add to the hot strawberry-flavored gelatin, and stir until all gelatin is dissolved. Cool. Stir in the thawed strawberries and spoon into 8 individual molds or a 1½-quart mold. Chill until set and unmold. Mayonnaise is recommended. Serves 8.

FRUIT SALAD RING

1 (1 lb. 14 oz.) can apricot halves
Juice 1 lemon
1 (3 oz.) package cream cheese
2 envelopes unflavored gelatin
1 cup diced celery
1½ cups chopped apple
¾ cup Boiled Dressing*
½ cup heavy cream
Greens (garnish)

Drain the syrup from the apricots. Measure 1¼ cups and bring to a boil. Purée the fruit through a sieve or in a blender. Add lemon juice to this with the softened cream cheese. Mix 1 envelope gelatin with ¼ cup water and then dissolve in ¾ cup hot apricot syrup. Stir this into the apricot-cheese mixture. Spoon into a 2-quart ring mold. Chill until just set. Soften the rest of the gelatin in ¼ cup water and add to the rest of the hot syrup (about ½ cup). Heat to dissolve. Cool. Meanwhile, mix the celery, apple, Boiled Dressing, and cream. Stir in the cool gelatin mixture. When the mold is just set, pour this Waldorf salad part over the first layer. Chill until set. Unmold on a large platter and garnish with greens if you wish. Serves 8.

SOUR-CREAM FRUIT MOLD

2 packages lime-flavored gelatin
1 (8 oz.) can crushed pineapple
1 (8 oz.) can pear halves
1 cup sour cream
Melon balls or sweetened fruit (garnish)

Dissolve the gelatin in 1½ cups boiling water; then add 1½ cups cold water and stir well. Drain the syrup from the pineapple and pears, combine the syrups, and add ⅔ cup to the gelatin. Stir well and chill until thick. Dice the pears and add with the pineapple and sour cream to the chilled gelatin mixture. Mix carefully and thoroughly. Pour into a 5½-cup ring mold and chill until firm. Unmold and garnish with melon balls or other sweetened fruit. Serves 6–8.

HAWAIIAN SALAD

1 cup sour cream
½ can frozen limeade concentrate
2 egg whites
3 tablespoons finely grated preserved ginger
3 tablespoons syrup from preserved ginger
Food coloring (optional)
Fresh fruit: melon, bananas, pineapple,
*   mango, grapes, etc.*
6 tablespoons toasted chipped coconut

Combine the sour cream, thawed limeade concentrate, stiffly beaten egg whites, ginger, and ginger syrup. Mix well, tint pale green if you like, and freeze. Cut up enough fresh fruits to make 4 servings. Arrange the fruits in a serving dish and sprinkle with the coconut. Add scoops of the sherbet and serve with the dressing of your choice. Serves 4.

FRUIT SALAD WITH FROZEN CHEESE SQUARES

3 (3 oz.) packages cream cheese
¾ cup mayonnaise
2 tablespoons lemon juice
1 teaspoon salt
1 envelope unflavored gelatin
1 (1 lb. 4 oz.) can crushed pineapple
¼ cup minced green pepper
1 tablespoon grated onion
¾ cup heavy cream
1 quart strawberries
1 quart cantaloupe balls
1 quart grapefruit sections
1 quart orange sections
Assorted greens
Fruit French Dressing*

Let the cheese soften at room temperature, then beat until smooth. Add the mayonnaise, lemon juice, and salt. Beat again. Heat the gelatin in 3 tablespoons water until dissolved. Drain the juice from the pineapple and add to the gelatin. Beat into the cheese mixture. Stir in the pineapple, green pepper, and onion. Fold in the cream, whipped. Pour into freezing trays

to a depth of 1½ inches. Freeze until very firm but not solid. Cut into 16 squares. Arrange on a platter alternately with hulled strawberries and other fruits which have been chilled. Garnish with salad greens and serve with Fruit French Dressing. Serves 12–16.

JELLED FRUIT AND COTTAGE-CHEESE SALAD

FRUIT LAYER

1 envelope plus 1 teaspoon unflavored gelatin
¼ cup lemon juice
½ cup orange juice
1 tablespoon grated lemon rind
3 tablespoons sugar
3 peaches
1 cup watermelon balls
1 cup casaba-melon, cantaloupe, or
*   honeydew-melon balls*
½ cup seedless white grapes

CHEESE LAYER

1 envelope unflavored gelatin
⅓ cup lemon juice
5 tablespoons sugar
2 cups cottage cheese
Frozen melon balls and peaches (garnish)
Mayonnaise Fruit Dressing*

Fruit Layer. Mix the gelatin with 1 cup cold water. Heat and stir until dissolved. Add the lemon and orange juices, lemon rind, and sugar. Chill until slightly thickened. Peel, pit, and slice the peaches and mix with the melon balls and grapes. Fold into the gelatin and pour into a 2-quart mold. Chill until almost set.

Cheese Layer. Mix the gelatin with 1 cup cold water. Heat and stir until dissolved. Add the lemon juice, sugar, and the cottage cheese which has been rubbed through a sieve. Blend thoroughly and pour over the partially set fruit layer. Chill until firm. Unmold to serve. Frozen melon balls and peaches may be used for garnish. Serve with Mayonnaise Fruit Dressing. Serves 8.

SALAD DRESSINGS

BOILED DRESSING

2 tablespoons flour
2 teaspoons sugar
½ teaspoon dry mustard
1 teaspoon salt
Dash cayenne
3 egg yolks
¾ cup milk
2 tablespoons butter
¼ cup vinegar
2 tablespoons light cream

Mix the flour, sugar, mustard, salt, and cayenne together. Beat the egg yolks slightly. Add ¼ cup milk and mix with the dry ingredients to make a smooth paste. Put into a double boiler and add the butter. Stir constantly while adding ½ cup milk alternately with the vinegar. Cook, stirring, until smooth and thick. When cool, thin to the consistency you wish with about 2 tablespoons cream. Yield: about 1¼ cups.

FRUIT FRENCH DRESSING

¼–½ cup grapefruit juice
1 tablespoon lemon juice
1 teaspoon salt
¼ teaspoon pepper
¾ cup salad oil
Sugar

Add the fruit juices to the salt and pepper in a bowl and stir. Then add the oil and mix thoroughly. Add sugar to taste. Yield: about 1 cup.

COOKED LEMON DRESSING

2 eggs
6 tablespoons sugar
½ cup lemon juice
2 teaspoons butter
⅛ teaspoon salt
2 tablespoons light cream

Beat the eggs very well. Add the sugar, lemon juice, butter, and salt. Cook over direct heat, stirring constantly, until sauce is thick and fluffy. Cool. Before serving, add the cream. Yield: about 1 cup.

RUM FRENCH DRESSING

2 tablespoons lemon juice
2 tablespoons rum
Pinch salt
1 tablespoon sugar
⅔ cup salad oil

Stir the lemon juice, rum, salt, and sugar together. Add the oil and mix thoroughly. Yield: about 1 cup.

LEMON FRENCH DRESSING

¼ cup lemon juice
1 teaspoon salt
¼ teaspoon pepper
¾ cup salad oil

Add the lemon juice to the salt and pepper in a bowl or jar and stir. Add the oil and mix thoroughly. Yield: 1 cup.

CREAM FRENCH DRESSING

⅓ cup sugar
2 teaspoons paprika
2 teaspoons salt
1 teaspoon dry mustard (optional)
1 teaspoon dried tarragon
1 cup salad or olive oil
½ cup vinegar
⅓ cup cream

Put the sugar, paprika, salt, mustard, and tarragon into a bowl. Add alternately the oil and vinegar, stirring constantly. Beat with a rotary beater for 2 minutes, add the cream slowly, and continue beating for 1 minute longer. Yield: about 2 cups.

HONEY LIME DRESSING

¾ cup salad oil
⅓ cup honey
¼ cup lime juice
2 tablespoons lemon juice
1 teaspoon grated lime rind
¼ teaspoon dry mustard
½ teaspoon paprika
2 tablespoons toasted sesame seed

Combine all the ingredients and beat with a rotary beater. Yield: about 1½ cups.

CURRY DRESSING

⅔ cup salad oil
1 tablespoon vinegar
1 tablespoon lemon juice
1 tablespoon orange juice
½ teaspoon sugar
½ teaspoon salt
¼–½ teaspoon curry powder
Pinch rosemary (optional)

Mix the oil, vinegar, and lemon and orange juices together in a jar. Season with the sugar, salt, curry, and the rosemary if you wish. Shake vigorously. Yield: about ¾ cup.

CREAM-CHEESE DRESSING

½ pound cream cheese or small-curd
  cottage cheese
½ cup milk
3 tablespoons vinegar
1 teaspoon salt
1½ teaspoons sugar

Mix the cream or cottage cheese and milk together until smooth. Add the vinegar, salt, and sugar. The consistency should be a little thinner than mayonnaise; if too thick, add a little more milk. Yield: about 1½ cups.

CAMEMBERT DRESSING

4 ounces Camembert cheese
1 (8 oz.) package cream cheese
⅓ cup tarragon vinegar
⅓ cup buttermilk
Pinch white pepper
½ teaspoon sugar

Soften the cheeses at room temperature. Beat them together until well blended. Then beat in the vinegar, buttermilk, pepper, and sugar. Strain to remove any Camembert rind. Chill for about an hour and beat again before serving. Yield: about 2 cups.

CHUTNEY DRESSING

1 cup salad oil
⅓ cup vinegar
1 teaspoon salt
½ clove garlic
1 cup chutney

Mix the salad oil, vinegar, and salt together.

Add the garlic, crushed. Cut the larger pieces of chutney into small pieces and add with its syrup to the mixture. Put into a jar and shake well or beat with a rotary beater. For a smoother dressing, buzz in a blender. Yield: 2⅓ cups.

BOILED FRUIT DRESSING

1 tablespoon sugar
1 tablespoon cornstarch
Pinch salt
1 egg
½ cup orange juice
½ cup pineapple juice
2 tablespoons lemon juice
Grated lemon rind
½ cup heavy cream

Mix the sugar, cornstarch, and salt. Stir in the beaten egg. Combine with the fruit juices and a little grated lemon rind. Cook over low heat, stirring constantly, until thickened. Chill. When ready to use, stir in the cream, whipped. Yield: about 2 cups.

MAYONNAISE

2 egg yolks
½ teaspoon salt
¼ teaspoon dry mustard
⅛ teaspoon white pepper (optional)
Few grains cayenne pepper (optional)
1 cup oil (part olive oil)
2 tablespoons lemon juice or vinegar

Have all ingredients and the bowl cool before making mayonnaise. Put the egg yolks, salt, mustard, and pepper and cayenne if you wish into the bowl. Add the oil a few drops at a time, stirring steadily with a wire whisk, fork, or wooden spoon. When the sauce starts to thicken, the oil may be added a little more quickly—a teaspoon at a time or in a slow stream. Mayonnaise is likely to separate if oil is added too quickly at the start. As the mayonnaise gets too thick to handle, thin with a little lemon juice or vinegar. If the mayonnaise should separate, stop at once and start another egg yolk in a bowl; add oil a drop at a time, and after the mayonnaise is thickened you can stir in the separated first mixture very slowly without damaging the whole. Mayonnaise may be made in a blender; start with egg yolks, salt, and mustard and add the oil slowly while running the blender at low or medium speed. An electric mixer at medium or low speed is also satisfactory. This dressing will keep well, especially if you add a tablespoon of hot water before storing. Yield: about 1½ cups.

MAYONNAISE FRUIT DRESSING

½ cup mayonnaise
1 teaspoon grated orange rind
Juice ½ orange
1–2 tablespoons sugar
⅛ teaspoon nutmeg
¼ teaspoon cinnamon
½ cup cream

Combine all the ingredients except the cream. Blend well. Fold in the cream, whipped. Yield: about 1¾ cups.

ALMOND MAYONNAISE

1 cup mayonnaise
¼ cup slivered blanched almonds
¼ teaspoon almond flavoring

Mix the ingredients together and chill overnight. Yield: about 1¼ cups.

CREAMY MAYONNAISE

½ cup mayonnaise
¼ cup heavy cream
½ teaspoon sugar

Mix all of the ingredients together. Yield: ¾ cup.

SPECIAL MAYONNAISE
(Low Calorie)

½ teaspoon unflavored gelatin
1½ cups skim milk
2 egg yolks
2 tablespoons sugar
1 teaspoon dry mustard
1 teaspoon salt
¼ cup vinegar or part vinegar and part
   lemon juice

Add the gelatin to the skim milk and heat until the gelatin is dissolved, stirring constantly. Mix the egg yolks and sugar with the mustard and salt. Add a little of the hot milk to the egg-yolk mixture and mix well. Then add remaining milk and pour into a double boiler. Keep the water in the bottom of the double boiler just simmering during the cooking. Cook, stirring constantly, for 10 minutes, until slightly thickened. Be careful not to overcook. Remove from heat and add vinegar, or vinegar and lemon juice, very slowly while stirring constantly. Chill well. This will thicken as it cools. Yield: 1½ cups.

SOUR-CREAM DRESSING

½ cup sour cream
½ cup salad oil or mayonnaise
1 tablespoon honey or 1 teaspoon sugar
2 tablespoons lemon juice
2 tablespoons grapefruit juice (optional)
Pinch salt

Mix all of the ingredients together thoroughly. Yield: about 1 cup.

SOUR-CREAM ROQUEFORT DRESSING

1¼-ounce wedge Roquefort cheese
½ cup sour cream
2 tablespoons lemon juice
¼ teaspoon salt
Dash pepper

Crumble the Roquefort cheese and mix with the sour cream. Add the lemon juice, salt, and pepper. Mix thoroughly. Yield: about ¾ cup.

COOKTIP

When peeling citrus fruits or pineapple, do so over a bowl to catch the juice.

SPECIAL SALAD DRESSING
(Low Calorie)

1 clove garlic
3 tablespoons lemon juice
2 tablespoons powdered pectin
½ teaspoon salt
Dash pepper
Dash paprika

Slash the clove of garlic in several places. Mix all the ingredients with ½ cup water in a jar. Refrigerate several hours. Shake the dressing well and remove the garlic before using. Yield: about 1 cup.

SWEET-SOUR DRESSING

¾ cup sugar
1 teaspoon salt
1 teaspoon dry mustard
1 teaspoon paprika
½ teaspoon celery seed
⅓ cup vinegar
1 cup salad oil
1 teaspoon grated onion (optional)

Mix the sugar, salt, mustard, paprika, celery seed, and vinegar in a saucepan. Simmer until the sugar is dissolved. Remove from heat. Cool. Add the salad oil, and the onion if you wish. Blend thoroughly. Refrigerate. Whip slightly before using. Yield: about 2 cups.

POPPY-SEED DRESSING

¾ cup salad oil
¼ cup wine vinegar
1 tablespoon lemon juice
½ teaspoon dry mustard
1 teaspoon salt
1 tablespoon sugar
1 cup mayonnaise
2 tablespoons poppy seed

In a bowl put the salad oil, vinegar, lemon juice, mustard, salt, and sugar. Beat with a rotary beater 3 minutes. Add the mayonnaise and beat 3 minutes more. Add the poppy seed and beat until blended. This dressing will not separate. Yield: about 2 cups.

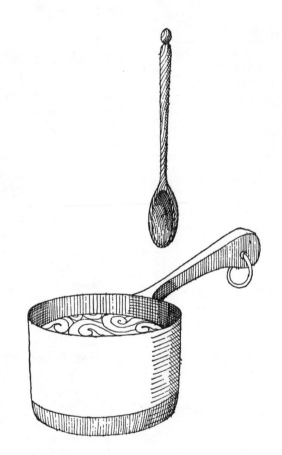

CHAPTER NINE

Heavenly Hot Breads

TEA OR DESSERT BREADS

Nut breads and other sweet breads, coffeecake, and rolls can be served as dessert, especially with coffee or tea. They are also good served with fruit or a pudding or even with ice cream. Loaves should be cooled in the pan for 5 or 10 minutes before turning out onto a rack to cool completely. Loaves of tea or dessert bread are easier to cut the second day; they taste better then too. Nut bread is almost impossible to slice when warm and fresh. Dessert breads are best when sliced thin. Wrap the loaf in foil or waxed paper to store. A loaf will serve 8 as a dessert; however, as a dessert accompaniment it will serve about 12.

DOUGHNUTS

Doughnuts, served hot, appeal to about everyone. They may be iced, dusted with sugar, filled or garnished with jam or jelly, or served plain. Homemade doughnuts with coffee or cider have been justly popular for generations.

PANCAKES

Pancakes—thin or thick, white or tan, milk or buttermilk—can be dessert food when served with syrup, soft maple sugar, jam or jelly, or lemon and sugar. Whip up as much batter as you think you'll need, maybe a little more, and put it in a commodious pitcher. It's fun and convenient to cook your pancakes at the table. Pancakes are fried on a griddle or in a skillet; however, the process is referred to as baking, perhaps because very little or no grease is used. The griddle should be hot enough so that a drop of water bounces. If using equipment with temperature controls, follow the indicator. Pour the batter onto the hot griddle, and when bubbles form on top of the cake turn it with a pancake turner or spatula to brown on the other side. Serve at once, or cover with a towel and keep in a very slow oven.

WAFFLES

Waffles are kissing cousins of pancakes, but their form is dissimilar. They are baked in a waffle iron and should be an even golden brown and, unlike their cousins, they should be crisp. You may test the heat of the iron with a drop of water as you test a griddle. Most electric waffle irons are very intelligent; they have heat controls with a light to tell you when the right temperature is reached; they maintain the proper heat and will not burn your waffles. Have the batter ready in a pitcher. Fill the waffle iron ¾ full and cook 4–6 minutes. Waffles are not turned. They should be served immediately with maple or other syrup, honey, molasses, jelly or jam, ice cream, or with fruit or sauce.

NUT BREAD

3⅓ cups cake flour
4½ teaspoons baking powder
1 teaspoon salt
½ cup sugar
1 cup chopped nuts
2 eggs
1 cup milk
½ cup melted butter

Sift the flour, baking powder, salt, and sugar together. Stir in the nuts. Mix the well-beaten eggs with the milk and butter. Add to flour mixture and stir only until well mixed. Bake in a greased 9×5×2¾-inch loaf pan in a 350° oven for 1 hour. Turn over on rack and let cool a few minutes before removing from the pan. Wrap in foil to store. It is easier to cut the second day. Serves 8.

APRICOT NUT BREAD (Plate 35)

1½ cups dried apricots
¾ cup sugar
5 teaspoons baking powder
½ teaspoon salt
½ teaspoon baking soda
2¾ cups flour
1 egg
1 cup buttermilk
3 tablespoons melted shortening or cooking oil
1 cup chopped walnuts

Soak and drain the apricots and cut into thin strips. Sift the dry ingredients together. (Reserve 1 tablespoon flour to dredge apricots.) Mix the well-beaten egg with the buttermilk and add to dry ingredients with the melted shortening or oil, stirring only until mixed. Fold in the nuts and the apricots which have been dredged with the remaining flour. Pour into a greased 9×5×2¾-inch loaf pan. Bake in a 350° oven for about 1 hour. Turn out and cool on a rack. Wrap in foil. This bread slices better the second day. Serves 8.

CRANBERRY NUT BREAD

1 cup cranberries
1¼ cups sugar
3 cups flour
4½ teaspoons baking powder
1 teaspoon salt
3 tablespoons grated orange rind
1 cup milk
3 tablespoons melted butter
1 egg
½ cup chopped walnuts or pecans

Coarsely grind the cranberries, mix with ¼ cup sugar, and set aside. Sift the remaining cup sugar with the flour, baking powder, and salt. Add the grated orange rind. Blend in the milk, butter, slightly beaten egg, and nuts. Fold in the cranberries and pour into a greased 9×5×2¾-inch loaf pan. Bake in a 350° oven for 1 hour. Turn out and cool on rack. Wrap in foil to store. This bread will slice better the second day. Serves 8.

BANANA BREAD

⅓ cup shortening
¾ cup light brown sugar
1 cup mashed bananas (2–3 bananas)
2 eggs
1½ cups flour
1 teaspoon salt
1 teaspoon baking soda
½ cup milk
½ cup chopped walnuts

Cream the shortening with the sugar. Add the mashed bananas and well-beaten eggs. Sift the flour with the salt and soda and add alternately with the milk. Stir in the nuts. Bake in a greased and floured 9×5×2¾-inch loaf pan in a 350° oven for 1 hour. Turn out and cool on a rack; wrap in foil. Serves 8.

RAISIN WALNUT BREAD

2 cups chopped seeded raisins
2 cups flour
½ teaspoon salt
¼ cup butter
¾ cup brown sugar
1 egg
1 teaspoon baking soda
1 cup broken walnuts

Pour 1 cup boiling water over the raisins and let cool at room temperature. Sift the flour and salt together. Cream the butter and sugar until light and fluffy. Add the slightly beaten egg and beat well. Add the soda to the cooled raisins and stir thoroughly. Add the flour and raisins alternately to the creamed mixture. Fold in the walnuts. Bake in a greased and floured 9×5×2¾-inch loaf pan in a

350° oven for about 1 hour, until the top springs back to the touch. Cool thoroughly and wrap in foil to store. Slice the second day. Serves 8.

RAISIN NUT BREAD

1 cup whole-wheat flour
½ cup flour
⅓ cup sugar
1 teaspoon baking soda
½ teaspoon salt
1 cup whole bran
1 egg
1 cup buttermilk
½ cup dark molasses
½ cup chopped walnuts
½ cup chopped raisins

Sift the flours, sugar, soda, and salt into a large bowl. Add the bran. Beat the egg slightly and mix with the buttermilk. Add to flour mixture with the molasses. Mix well. Stir in the walnuts and raisins. Mix until blended. Pour into a greased and floured 9×5×2¾-inch loaf pan. Bake in a 350° oven for 50–55 minutes. Slice the second day. Serves 8.

DATE NUT LOAF

1 (1 lb.) package pitted dates
2 teaspoons baking soda
½ cup butter
2 cups sugar
2 eggs
4 cups cake flour
½ teaspoon salt
½ teaspoon nutmeg
½ teaspoon cinnamon
1 cup chopped nuts

Cut the dates into pieces with scissors. Dissolve the soda in 2 cups boiling water, pour over the dates, and let stand about 15 minutes, until the water is cool. Cream the butter with the sugar. Add the well-beaten eggs. Sift the flour, salt, nutmeg, and cinnamon together. Take about ¼ cup of the dry ingredients and mix with the nuts. Add the rest to the creamed mixture alternately with water from the dates. Beat smooth. Add the dates and floured nuts last. Mix thoroughly. Bake in 2 greased 9×5×2¾-inch loaf pans in a 350° oven for about 1¼ hours. Cool, wrap in foil, and store overnight. This is also good served warm with whipped cream. Serves 14–16.

ORANGE NUT BREAD

2 tablespoons shortening
1 cup honey
1 egg
1 tablespoon grated orange rind
2½ cups flour
1 tablespoon baking powder
½ teaspoon salt
¼ teaspoon baking soda
¾ cup orange juice
¾ cup chopped nuts

Cream the shortening and add the honey gradually, beating well. Add the well-beaten egg and orange rind. Sift the flour, baking powder, salt, and soda together. Add alternately with the orange juice. Stir in the nuts. Bake in a greased 9×5×2¾-inch loaf pan in 325° oven for 1¼ hours. Cool and wrap in foil to store. This bread slices better the second day. Serves 8.

COOKTIP

To cover yeast doughs for rising, use a clear plastic wrap or foil to retain moisture and to prevent a crust from forming.

CRANBERRY ORANGE BREAD

1 cup cranberries
2 cups flour
½ teaspoon salt
1½ teaspoons baking powder
½ teaspoon baking soda
1 cup sugar
Juice 1 orange
Rind 1 orange
2 tablespoons shortening or cooking oil
1 egg
1 cup chopped nuts

Chop the cranberries. Sift the dry ingredients together twice. To the orange juice and rind add the shortening or oil and enough boiling water to make ¾ cup. Add to the dry ingredients. Then add the beaten egg. Mix just enough to blend ingredients. Add the nuts and cranberries. Mix. Pour into a greased 9×5×2¾-inch loaf pan. Bake in a 325° oven for 1 hour. Remove from pan, cool, and wrap in foil to store. Serves 8.

GLAZED ORANGE ROLLS

1½ cups milk
1 cup plus 2 tablespoons sugar
1 teaspoon salt
⅓ cup shortening
2 packages active dry or compressed yeast
1 egg
5 cups flour

GLAZE

¼ cup grated orange rind
1 cup orange juice and pulp
1 cup butter

Scald the milk and add 2 tablespoons sugar, salt, and shortening. Let cool to 110°–115°. Stir in the yeast which has been softened in ¼ cup warm water. Then stir in the well-beaten egg and add the flour. Knead the dough into a ball and place in a greased bowl. Cover and let rise until doubled in bulk. While the dough is rising, make the syrup.

Glaze. Mix the orange rind with the juice and finely cut pulp. Add remaining 1 cup sugar and the butter. Bring the mixture to a boil, stirring constantly, and cook about 6 minutes, until thick, (228°). Cool. It should be quite thick.

Divide the dough into 4 pieces and roll each into a rectangle about 7×12 inches. Spread generously with syrup to within an inch of the edge all around. Roll up like a jelly roll, pinching the edges to seal firmly. Cut into 1-inch slices. Before arranging the rolls in greased muffin pans, put ½ teaspoon syrup in the bottom of each section. Sprinkle a little extra syrup on top. Let rise until about doubled in bulk. Bake in a 375° oven for about 10 minutes. Turn out on a baking sheet, letting the syrup run down over them. Yield: 4 dozen.

SOUR-CREAM TWISTS

4 cups flour
1 teaspoon salt
1 cup shortening
1 package active dry or compressed yeast
1 egg plus 2 egg yolks
1 cup sour cream
1 teaspoon vanilla
½ teaspoon grated lemon rind
1 cup raisins
⅔ cup sugar
1 teaspoon cinnamon (optional)

Sift the flour and salt into a bowl. Cut in the shortening with a pastry blender or 2 knives. Soften the yeast in ¼ cup warm water (110°–115°). Beat the egg and yolks together until light. Combine with sour cream, yeast, vanilla, lemon rind, and raisins. Stir into the flour mixture and mix thoroughly. Let rise in refrigerator 2 hours. (This dough has more the quality of pastry and it does rise in the refrigerator.) Measure the sugar. You may use it all but should not use more. Sprinkle some sugar lightly over the breadboard; place the dough on the board and sprinkle sugar very lightly over the dough. Roll out into a 12-inch square. Fold the dough from each side to make 3 layers. Roll out again and repeat the folding, using a little more sugar on the board and on the dough to prevent sticking. Cut into strips 1 inch wide and 4 inches long. Twist each 3 or 4 times. Lay them a couple of inches apart on baking sheets. Sprinkle with the remaining sugar, mixed with the cinnamon if you wish. No additional rising is needed. Bake in a 375° oven for 18 minutes, until light brown. Yield: about 3 dozen twists.

BUTTERSCOTCH TEA ROLLS

1¼ cups milk
7 tablespoons butter
1 package active dry or compressed yeast
¼ cup sugar
1 egg
3½ cups flour
1¼ teaspoons salt
Cinnamon

GLAZE

1 cup light brown sugar
¼ cup soft butter
2½ tablespoons light corn syrup

Heat the milk to the simmering point, add ¼ cup butter, and remove from heat, stirring to melt the butter. Combine the yeast and sugar. When the milk mixture is warm (110°–115°), stir in the yeast mixture. Beat the egg until frothy and work in the yeast mixture along with the flour and salt to form a soft dough. Sprinkle with a little flour and shape into a ball. Put into a greased mixing bowl, cover, and let rise until doubled in bulk.

Glaze. Meanwhile, make the glaze by mixing the ingredients together.

Grease muffin pans which have very small cups. Put ½ teaspoon glaze in the bottom of each. Roll out enough dough on a floured board to make a strip 20 inches long by 4 inches wide by ⅛ inch thick. Spread with 3 tablespoons melted butter and sprinkle lightly with cinnamon. Roll the dough up the long way so that the piece is still 20 inches long. Cut the roll of dough into 1-inch slices. Place in muffin pans, cover with cloth, and let rise until doubled in bulk. Bake in a 400° oven for 12–15 minutes, until the rolls are golden brown and the glaze bubbles up. Remove from oven and turn out on a baking sheet, letting the glaze run down over the rolls. Yield: 5 dozen small tea rolls.

BLUEBERRY MUFFINS

¼ cup butter
¼ cup sugar
1 egg
2 cups flour
1½ cups blueberries (fresh or partially thawed frozen)
1 tablespoon baking powder
¼ teaspoon salt
1 cup milk

Cream the butter with the sugar. Add the well-beaten egg. Mix but do not beat. Take 2 tablespoons of the flour and mix with the blueberries. Sift the rest of the flour with the baking powder and salt. Add the milk alternately with the dry ingredients, stirring only enough to mix. The batter will not look smooth. Fold the blueberries into the batter. Fill greased muffin pans ⅔ full and bake in a 400° oven for 25–30 minutes, until light tan. Serve hot. Yield: 12 muffins.

SPICED WALNUT MUFFINS

2 cups biscuit mix
½ cup sugar
½ teaspoon cinnamon
¼ teaspoon nutmeg
1 egg
⅔ cup milk
3 tablespoons melted shortening
⅔ cup chopped walnuts

Mix the biscuit mix with the sugar, cinnamon, and nutmeg. Add the beaten egg, milk, and shortening. Mix well. Fold in the nuts. Fill 12 well-greased muffin pans ⅔ full. Bake in a 400° oven for 15 minutes, until golden. Yield: 12 muffins.

QUICK COFFEECAKE

1½ cups flour
2 teaspoons baking powder
½ teaspoon salt
¼ teaspoon nutmeg
6 tablespoons sugar
2 tablespoons shortening
1 egg
½ cup milk

CRUMB TOPPING

¼ cup sugar
2 tablespoons flour
1 teaspoon cinnamon
1 teaspoon nutmeg
1 tablespoon butter

Sift the flour, baking powder, salt, nutmeg, and sugar together. Cut in the shortening with a pastry blender or 2 knives until the mixture is quite fine. Beat the egg slightly and combine with the milk. Add the liquid all at once to the dry mixture and stir together with a fork. Spread out in a greased 8-inch cake pan.

Crumb Topping. Mix together the sugar, flour, cinnamon, nutmeg, and butter with a fork until crumbly.

Sprinkle the topping on the batter. Bake in a 400° oven for 25 minutes. Serves 6.

SUNBURST COFFEECAKE

1 package hot-roll or coffeecake mix
½ cup confectioners' sugar
1 tablespoon milk
½ teaspoon vanilla
Candied cherries (garnish)
Walnuts (garnish)

Prepare the mix according to package directions. After it rises, punch down and divide dough into 12 parts. Roll each piece into a strip 8 inches long. With 6 strips make U-shaped pieces and place on greased baking sheet with ends toward the center, forming a scalloped circle. Arrange remaining 6 strips on sheet so the ends meet in the center and each oval covers the joining ends of the first U-shaped pieces. Let rise again until doubled in bulk. Bake in a 400° oven for 20–30 minutes, until golden brown. Cool on a rack. Brush with glaze made by mixing the sugar, milk, and vanilla. Garnish with cherries and nuts. Serves 6–8.

SCHNECKEN

1 package active dry or compressed yeast
2 cups plus 2 tablespoons milk
7 cups flour
1½ cups sweet butter
1½ cups sugar
3 eggs plus 1 egg yolk
½ cup chopped toasted almonds
½ cup chopped mixed candied fruits
½ cup raisins
¼ cup currants
2 teaspoons cinnamon

Soften the yeast in ¼ cup warm milk (110°–115°) for about 5 minutes. Combine 2¼ cups flour with 1¾ cups milk to form a smooth batter. Add the yeast and mix well. Cover, set in a warm place, and let rise until doubled in bulk. Melt the butter and add 1 cup to the dough with ½ cup sugar, 3 beaten eggs, and the remaining flour. Mix until smooth. Roll out on a well-floured board into a rectangle ¾ inch thick. Mix the remaining ½ cup melted butter with remaining sugar, the nuts, fruits, raisins, currants, and cinnamon. Spread over the dough, then roll the dough carefully into a long cylinder. Cut into ½-inch slices and place on a greased baking sheet. Cover and let rise in a warm place for about ½ hour. Mix the remaining 2 tablespoons milk with the egg yolk and brush the tops. Bake in a 425° oven for 15–20 minutes, until golden brown. Yield: 2½ dozen.

COFFEECAKE

1½ cups dark brown sugar
2 tablespoons flour
2 tablespoons cinnamon
3 tablespoons melted butter
⅛ teaspoon salt
1 cup chopped nuts

BATTER

1½ cups flour
1½ teaspoons baking powder
¼ teaspoon salt
2 eggs
1 cup sugar
¼ cup melted butter
½ cup milk

Mix the sugar, flour, cinnamon, melted butter, salt, and nuts together and set aside.

Batter. Sift the flour, baking powder, and salt together. Beat the eggs until very light and thick. Add the sugar a spoonful at a time, beating after each addition. Stir in the butter, which should be melted but not hot. Add the sifted dry ingredients alternately with the milk and beat smooth.

Spread half the batter on the bottom of a greased 8×8×2-inch pan. Sprinkle with half of the spiced-sugar mixture. Cover with the rest of the batter and finish with the rest of the sugar on top. Bake in a 350° oven for 50–60 minutes. Serve warm. Serves 6.

BUTTERSCOTCH BUBBLE LOAF

(Plate 10)

1 package active dry yeast
2 cups warm milk
1 teaspoon salt
1¼ cups sugar
1 egg
5½–6 cups flour
1 cup melted butter
1 cup brown sugar
½ cup chopped blanched almonds
½ cup chopped walnuts
½ teaspoon cinnamon
8 candied cherries

Dissolve the yeast in milk along with the salt and ¼ cup sugar. Let stand a few minutes. Add the egg and 3 cups flour. Beat until smooth. Work in ½ cup melted butter and enough of the remaining flour to make the dough easy to handle but not too stiff. The dough should be somewhat sticky. Knead it a few minutes on a lightly floured board. Round up in a greased bowl, bringing the greased side up. Cover and let rise until doubled in bulk. Punch down and let rise again. In separate bowls mix the brown sugar with the almonds, and the remaining 1 cup sugar with the walnuts and cinnamon. Pinch off the dough into balls the size of walnuts and dip in remaining melted butter. Then roll half the balls in the brown-sugar mixture and the others in the cinnamon-sugar mixture. Alternate these balls 2 layers high in a greased 10-inch tube pan. Cut the candied cherries into halves and insert here and there. Let rise again until almost doubled, about 1 hour. Bake in a 375° oven about 40 minutes, until golden. Cool just a few minutes in the pan and invert on a platter. Serve warm. Serves 10.

SWEDISH COFFEECAKE

2 packages active dry or compressed yeast
½ cup milk
2 tablespoons butter
½ cup sugar
2 teaspoons salt
10 cardamom seeds
3 eggs
4–5 cups flour

Soften the yeast in ½ cup warm water (110°–115°). Let stand for 5 minutes; stir well. Scald the milk and pour onto the butter, sugar, and salt. Crush the cardamom seeds and add to the milk mixture. When warm, add 2 beaten eggs and the yeast. Mix in the flour, shape into a ball, and put into a greased bowl. Cover and let rise in a warm place until doubled in bulk. Shape into 3 strips and cut each strip in half. Braid 3 strips and pinch the ends together for each loaf. Place in 2 greased 9× 5×2¾-inch loaf pans and let rise until doubled in bulk. Bake in a 350° oven for 30–40 minutes. Ten minutes before loaves are done, brush with the remaining egg mixed with 3 tablespoons water. Serves 12–16.

STREUSEL-FILLED COFFEECAKE

1½ cups plus 2 tablespoons flour
1 tablespoon baking powder
¼ teaspoon salt
½ cup sugar
1 egg
½ cup milk
6 tablespoons butter
½ cup brown sugar
½ cup chopped nuts
1½ teaspoons cinnamon

Sift 1½ cups flour, baking powder, salt, and sugar together. Beat the egg lightly and add the milk and ¼ cup melted butter. For the streusel mixture, melt the remaining butter in a small saucepan. Remove from heat and stir in the brown sugar, chopped nuts, cinnamon, and remaining flour. Add the egg mixture to the dry ingredients, stirring just enough to mix. Pour half the batter into a greased 9×5× 2¾-inch loaf pan. Sprinkle half the streusel mixture over this. Spread the remaining dough over the top and sprinkle with remaining streusel mixture. Bake in a 375° oven for ½ hour. Serves 8.

DANISH KRINGLE

2 cups flour
1½ tablespoons sugar
½ teaspoon salt
½ cup soft butter
½ cup milk
1 egg yolk
1 package active dry yeast

FILLING
¼ cup butter
½ cup dark brown sugar
1 cup chopped pecans
1 egg white

GLAZE
1 cup confectioners' sugar
1½ teaspoons milk
¼ teaspoon vanilla

Mix the flour, sugar, and salt together. Cut in the butter until the mixture is like coarse meal. Scald the milk, cool slightly, and then stir in the egg yolk. Add to the flour mixture. Add the yeast to ¼ cup warm water (110°–115°) and let stand 5 minutes. Add to batter and mix thoroughly, scraping the dough from the sides of the bowl frequently. The dough will be quite soft. Cover tight and chill at least 2 hours and no more than 48 hours. Prepare the filling before shaping the kringles.

Filling. Cream the butter and brown sugar until fluffy. Stir in the pecans. Beat the egg white slightly.

Divide the dough into 2 parts, returning 1 to the refrigerator. Roll the dough out into a 6 ×18-inch rectangle on a well-floured pastry cloth or board. Brush a 3-inch strip down the center with half the egg white and spread half the pecan mixture on this strip. Fold over one side of the dough and then other, with a 1½-inch lap to cover the filling. Pinch the dough to close the fold. Pick up the kringle carefully and arrange on a baking sheet in a horseshoe shape, pinching the ends to seal. Prepare and shape the second kringle as the first, using the remaining egg white and pecan filling. Cover and let rise in a warm place 30–45 minutes, or until an indentation remains when a finger is pressed gently on the side of the dough. Bake in a 400° oven for 20–30 minutes, until golden brown. Cool slightly.

Glaze. Beat the confectioners' sugar, milk, and vanilla together and spread over the top of the kringles. Serve warm. Serves 12.

SWEDISH NUT RING

> ¾ cup milk
> ¼ cup shortening
> ¼ cup sugar
> ½ teaspoon salt
> 1 package active dry or compressed yeast
> 1 egg
> 3½–4 cups flour
> 2 tablespoons soft butter
> ½ cup finely chopped walnuts
> ¼ cup dark brown sugar
> ½ cup confectioners' sugar
> Maraschino cherries (garnish)

Scald the milk and add the shortening, sugar, and salt. Stir until shortening is melted. Cool to room temperature. Soften the yeast in ¼ cup warm water (110°–115°). Add with the beaten egg and the flour to the milk mixture. Mix until the dough comes away from the sides of the bowl. Turn out onto a floured board and knead for 5 minutes. Place in a greased bowl, set in a warm place, and let rise until doubled in bulk. Punch down and roll into an 18×7-inch rectangle. Spread with soft butter, walnuts, and brown sugar. Roll as for a jelly roll, starting from the long edge; there should be about 3 turns. Place on a baking sheet; shape into a circle with the seal on the bottom. Flatten the roll slightly and make 6 slashes in the top. Set in a warm place to double in bulk. Bake in a 350° oven for 20–25 minutes, until golden brown. Frost with a glaze made of the confectioners' sugar mixed with 1 tablespoon water. Sprinkle with more chopped nuts and decorate with slices of maraschino cherries if you wish. Serves 12.

QUICK BISCUIT COFFEECAKE

> ½ cup brown sugar
> 3 tablespoons butter
> ¼ cup coarsely chopped pecans
> 1 package refrigerated unbaked biscuits

Spread the sugar evenly over the bottom of a 9-inch round pan. Dot with butter and sprinkle with nuts. Open the package of biscuits, separate, and place them on top of the nuts. Bake in a 400° oven for 20 minutes. Cool in the pan for 1 minute, then turn them upside down on a plate and serve hot. Serves 6–8.

SALLY LUNN (Plate 37)

> 1 package active dry or compressed yeast
> ¾ cup milk
> ½ cup butter
> ⅓ cup sugar
> 3 eggs
> 1 teaspoon salt
> 4 cups flour

Soften the yeast in ¼ cup warm water (110°–115°). Heat the milk to warm and combine with the yeast. Cream the butter and sugar together. Add the well-beaten eggs and mix. Add salt to the flour and stir into the butter alternately with the milk mixture. Beat thoroughly with a wooden spoon and turn into a buttered bowl. Let rise in a warm place 1–1½ hours, until doubled in bulk. Beat again and pour into a well-buttered 2-quart ring mold or 10-inch angel-cake pan. Let rise again for about 40 minutes, until doubled in bulk. Bake in a 350° oven for 45 minutes. Unmold and serve warm. Serves 6–8.

DATE SCONES (Plate 35)

> 2 cups flour
> ½ cup sugar
> 2 teaspoons cream of tartar
> 1 teaspoon baking soda
> ¾ teaspoon salt
> ½ cup butter
> ½ cup finely chopped pitted dates
> 3 eggs

Sift the dry ingredients together twice. Using a pastry blender or 2 knives, cut the butter into the flour mixture until it resembles fine bread crumbs. Add the dates and toss to distribute them evenly. Add 2 slightly beaten eggs and mix with a fork until the mixture forms a ball and leaves the sides of the bowl. Roll or pat out ½–⅔ inch thick on a lightly floured board. Cut into rounds with a 2-inch cooky cutter. Flour the cutter each time before using. Place about 2 inches apart on a greased baking sheet. Brush the tops with slightly beaten egg. Bake in a 400° oven for 15 minutes, until golden. Cool slightly on a rack. These are especially good served warm, split in half, and buttered. (They will keep for several days stored in airtight containers; you must warm them before serving.) Yield: about 18 scones.

NEW ENGLAND JOHNNYCAKE

1 cup flour
1 tablespoon baking powder
1 teaspoon salt
1 egg
1 cup yellow corn meal
¼ cup melted butter
2 tablespoons dark molasses
1⅓ cups milk

Sift the flour, baking powder, and salt together. Add the slightly beaten egg and the remaining ingredients and beat until smooth. Pour into a well-greased 8×8×2-inch pan and bake in a 375° oven for ½ hour, until it springs back to the touch. Turn out upside down on a rack, let cool a minute or two, cut into 2-inch squares, and serve immediately. Yield: 16 squares.

STOLLEN *(Plate 36)*

¾ cup milk
½ cup sugar
½ teaspoon salt
2 packages active dry or compressed yeast
6 cups flour
2 eggs
¾ cup very soft butter
¼ teaspoon nutmeg
1½ cups currants
½ cup diced citron
½ cup candied lemon peel
½ cup candied cherries
Grated rind 1 lemon
½ cup coarsely chopped blanched almonds
3 tablespoons melted butter
Confectioners' sugar

Scald the milk, add the sugar and salt, and cool to room temperature. Soften the yeast in ½ cup warm water (110°–115°). Mix with 1 cup flour and the milk mixture. Cover and let rise until doubled in bulk. Add the slightly beaten eggs to the sponge with the butter, remaining 5 cups flour, and nutmeg. Also add the currants, citron, lemon peel, cherries, lemon rind, and almonds. Turn out onto a floured board and knead until very elastic, adding only enough flour to keep the dough from sticking to the board. Put into a buttered bowl and brush the top with melted butter. Cover and let rise in a warm place until doubled in bulk. Punch down and divide into 2 parts. Roll each into a rectangle ½ inch thick, spread with melted butter, and fold the dough over lengthwise. Place on a buttered baking sheet, cover, and again let rise in a warm place until doubled in bulk. Bake in a 350° oven for 50 minutes. Dust with confectioners' sugar. Wrap and store the loaves overnight. Serves 14–16.

DOUBLE FRUIT BRAIDS *(Plate 36)*

2 teaspoons sugar
2 packages active dry yeast
⅔ cup milk
½ cup sugar
¼ teaspoon salt
6 tablespoons shortening
4 eggs
6 cups flour
1 cup candied cherries
1 pound raisins
½ cup chopped mixed candied fruits
Melted butter
Confectioners'-sugar icing

Dissolve the sugar in ⅔ cup warm water in a large mixing bowl. Stir in the yeast and let stand 10 minutes. Scald the milk and add the sugar, salt, and shortening. Mix well and cool to 110°–115°. Add to the yeast mixture along with 3 well-beaten eggs and 3 cups flour. Beat until smooth. Cut the cherries into halves and mix in with the raisins and candied fruits. Work in the remaining flour. Turn the dough out onto a lightly floured board and knead until smooth and elastic. Then place in a greased large bowl, brush the top with a little melted butter, cover, and let rise in a warm place until doubled in bulk. Punch the dough down and divide into 2 equal parts for 2 loaves. Divide each part into 4 equal portions. Shape 3 of the portions into 12-inch strands. Place on a lightly greased baking sheet and braid loosely, tucking the ends under. Divide the remaining portion of dough into 3 parts, shape into strands 10 inches long, and make another braid. Place on top of the first braid on the baking sheet and tuck the ends of top braid into the braid below. Repeat for the other braided loaf and place on baking sheet next to the first one. Cover and let rise again until doubled in bulk, about 1 hour. Brush the top of braids with the remaining egg and bake in a 350° oven for 35–40 minutes, until golden. If you like, glaze with a confectioners'-sugar icing while the bread is still warm. Serves 20.

CHRISTMAS BRAIDS

2 cups milk
½ cup shortening
⅔ cup sugar
2 teaspoons salt
¼ teaspoon crushed cardamom seed
1 teaspoon cinnamon
2 packages active dry or compressed yeast
2 eggs
8 cups flour
1 cup white raisins
1 cup slivered citron
1 cup sliced candied cherries
Melted butter

Scald the milk. Put the shortening, sugar, salt, cardamom seed, and cinnamon into a large bowl. Add the hot milk. Cool to 110°–115° and add the yeast which has been softened in ¼ cup warm water. Next, add the beaten eggs and 4 cups flour. Mix well and add the raisins, citron, and cherries. Beat in the remaining flour. Place the dough in a greased bowl, cover, and let rise until doubled in bulk. Punch down and knead on a lightly floured board. Shape into 2 braids, place on a greased baking sheet, and let rise again. Bake in a 350° oven for 45 minutes. Brush with butter and cool on a rack. Serves 14–16.

Doughnuts

DOUGHNUTS

4 cups flour
1 teaspoon salt
2 tablespoons baking powder
½ teaspoon cinnamon
¼ teaspoon nutmeg
1 cup sugar
2 eggs
1 cup milk
¼ cup melted shortening or cooking oil
Confectioners' sugar (optional)

Sift the flour, salt, baking powder, cinnamon, nutmeg, and sugar together. Beat the eggs with the milk and add to the dry ingredients with shortening or oil. Mix the dough lightly and roll ½ inch thick on a floured board. Cut with a floured doughnut cutter. Fry a few at a time in hot deep fat (370°) until golden brown on both sides. Drain on paper toweling.

The "holes" may be fried too; they cook very quickly. Sprinkle the doughnuts with confectioners' sugar or roll them in the sugar, or use Doughnut Glaze* if you wish. Yield: about 32 doughnuts.

SOUR-MILK DOUGHNUTS

4 cups flour
2 teaspoons cream of tartar
1 teaspoon salt
¾–1 cup sugar
1 teaspoon cinnamon
½ teaspoon nutmeg
1 teaspoon baking soda
1 cup sour milk or half sour milk and half sour cream
1 egg
1½ tablespoons melted shortening
1 cup chopped nuts (optional)

Sift the flour, cream of tartar, salt, sugar, cinnamon, and nutmeg together. Dissolve the soda in sour milk or part sour milk and part sour cream. Beat the egg and add to the milk with the shortening. (If you use any cream, omit the shortening.) Mix with the dry ingredients. Turn out on a floured board, a small amount at a time. Roll to ½-inch thickness, using as little flour as possible. Cut with a floured doughnut cutter. Fry in hot deep fat (370°) and drain on paper toweling. If you wish for a change to use chopped nuts, use about 3¼ cups flour instead of 4. Yield: about 3 dozen doughnuts.

RAISED DOUGHNUTS

1½ cups milk
2 tablespoons sugar
1 teaspoon salt
⅓ cup shortening
1 egg
2 packages active dry or compressed yeast
4–4½ cups flour

Heat the milk and put into a large bowl with the sugar, salt, and shortening. Mix and let cool to 110°–115°. Add the well-beaten egg. Dissolve the yeast in ¼ cup warm water and add to the mixture. Add flour to make a stiff dough. Put the dough in a warm place, cover, and let it rise until doubled in bulk. Place on a lightly floured board and roll to ½-inch thickness. Cut with a floured 3-inch doughnut cutter

Plate 35. An English Afternoon Tea. VICTORIA SPONGE, DUNDEE CAKE, a platter of assorted sandwiches, a plate of DATE SCONES, and a tiered server presenting ENGLISH MATRIMONIALS, LEMON CURD TARTS, BRANDY SNAPS, APRICOT NUT BREAD, and TEACAKES FOR A PARTY.

Plate 37. SALLY LUNN, a Southern sweet bread.

Plate 36. STOLLEN, DOUBLE FRUIT BRAIDS, an iced RAISIN PECAN CAKE, and an apothecary jar filled with hard candies.

Plate 38. CREPES (French pancakes) stacked in a chafing dish.

or mold with your hands into small shapes, rolls, or twists. If you use a doughnut cutter, be sure to use the "holes" too. Cover and let stand for an hour. Fry a few at a time in hot deep fat (370°) until well browned. They will puff in the fat and should be turned once. Raised doughnuts are good served warm, sugared or not. Yield: about 30 doughnuts.

CRULLERS

4 eggs
⅔ cup sugar
1 teaspoon grated lemon rind
⅓ cup milk
⅓ cup melted shortening
3½ cups flour
1 teaspoon salt
1 tablespoon baking powder
½ teaspoon nutmeg
½ cup cinnamon sugar

Beat the eggs until light. Gradually add the sifted sugar. Beat well until thick and lemon-colored and sugar is dissolved. Add the lemon rind, milk, and shortening. Sift the flour, salt, baking powder, and nutmeg together. Stir these dry ingredients into the egg mixture. Roll out part of the dough at a time to ¼-inch thickness on a lightly floured board. Keep the remaining dough chilled while frying each batch. Cut into strips and twist or cut with a doughnut cutter. Fry in hot deep fat (370°) until golden and crisp. Drain on paper toweling. Roll in cinnamon sugar. Yield: about 4 dozen crullers.

DOUGHNUT GLAZE

1½ cups confectioners' sugar
1 teaspoon vanilla

Make a smooth paste by blending the sugar with ¼ cup water. Add the vanilla. Dip one side of each doughnut in this glaze and drain on a rack. Yield: enough glaze for about 4 dozen doughnuts.

FRIED KNOTS

1 package hot-roll mix
Hot maple syrup

Prepare the roll mix according to package directions or make a batch of your own recipe. When the dough has risen, punch it down and shape into strips 8 inches long and ¾ inch wide. Twist these into very loose knots and fry in hot deep fat (370°) until golden on both sides. Serve with hot maple syrup. Yield: about 1 dozen fried knots.

RAISED POTATO DOUGHNUTS

2 cups milk
1 cup sugar
½ cup shortening
1½ teaspoons salt
1 cup freshly mashed potatoes (¾ pound)
1½ packages active dry or compressed yeast
3 eggs
½ teaspoon lemon flavoring
½ teaspoon cinnamon
8 cups flour

Scald the milk. Add the sugar, shortening, salt, and the potatoes. Stir and cool to 110°–115°. Meanwhile, soften the yeast in ¼ cup warm water and let stand 5 minutes. Add the milk and potato mixture with the well-beaten eggs. Flavor with lemon and cinnamon. Add a small amount of the flour at a time, working to a smooth dough with a strong spoon until all flour is added. Turn into a greased bowl, cover, and let rise in a warm place until it holds the impression of your finger when you touch it lightly. Then punch down to release air bubbles. Turn out on a lightly floured board and roll to ¼-inch thickness. Cut with a floured doughnut cutter, place on a floured towel, and cover with another towel. Let rise in a warm place until doubled in bulk. Fry in hot deep fat (370°) until golden, turning once gently with a fork. Drain on paper toweling. Yield: 5–6 dozen doughnuts.

Pancakes

PANCAKES

1¼ cups flour
1½ teaspoons baking powder
¼ teaspoon salt
1¼ cups milk
2 tablespoons melted butter
1 egg

Mix the dry ingredients together. Add the milk and melted butter to the beaten egg. Make a hole in the center of the dry ingredients, pour in the liquids, and stir only until mixed. This should be done in a few seconds without worrying about lumps. Bake on a hot griddle. Yield: 10 (5-inch) pancakes.

GERMAN PANCAKES

1 cup milk
¾ cup flour
Pinch salt
2 teaspoons sugar
3 eggs
¼ cup melted shortening
Butter
Apple Filling for Pancakes,* cooked
  blueberries, or Chocolate Cream Sauce*
  (optional)
Cinnamon sugar (optional)
Lemon juice (optional)
Rum or kirsch (optional)

Beat the milk, flour, salt, and sugar with a whisk until smooth. Add the eggs and blend. To make the pancakes, heat a tablespoon of shortening in a 10-inch skillet until it sizzles. You will need just a skim, so pour out excess. Add ¼–⅓ cup batter to the skillet, tipping it from side to side so the entire bottom is covered with a thin layer. When the batter bubbles and is brown underneath, lift up with a spatula and add a bit of butter, swirl the butter around, and turn the pancake to brown the other side. Lift out onto paper toweling and then put onto a warm platter. Wipe out the skillet with paper toweling and start another pancake. If you wish, spread each pancake with Apple Filling for Pancakes, cooked blueberries, or Chocolate Cream Sauce and fold into a roll. If you don't use a filling, top with cinnamon sugar and a squeeze of lemon juice. You may sprinkle with kirsch or rum and serve flaming. Yield: 6 (10-inch) pancakes.

APPLE PANCAKES

1½ cups flour
½ teaspoon salt
2½ teaspoons baking powder
1 tablespoon sugar
1 egg
1½ cups milk
3 tablespoons melted butter
1 cup peeled, cored, chopped apple

Sift the dry ingredients together. Beat the egg until light and combine with the milk and melted butter. Add to the dry ingredients and mix thoroughly. Add the chopped apple. Bake on a lightly greased hot griddle. Yield: 12 small pancakes.

CORN-MEAL APPLE PANCAKES

1½ cups flour
1 tablespoon baking powder
1 teaspoon salt
¼ teaspoon allspice
½ cup corn meal
1½ cups milk
3 tablespoons melted shortening
1 egg
3 tablespoons molasses
½ cup finely chopped tart apple

Sift the flour with the baking powder, salt, and allspice. Mix in the corn meal. Stir together the milk, shortening, beaten egg, molasses, and apple. Add to dry ingredients. Mix just enough to blend. Drop by spoonfuls onto a hot griddle. Turn only once. Serve with hot or cold syrup. Yield: 14–16 (6-inch) pancakes.

BLUEBERRY PANCAKES

2 eggs
2 cups buttermilk
1½ cups flour
2 tablespoons sugar
½ teaspoon salt
2 teaspoons baking soda
2 cups fresh or frozen unsweetened
  blueberries

Beat the eggs and add the buttermilk. Sift the flour, sugar, salt, and soda together. Combine with the liquids. Fold in the blueberries. Drop the batter by tablespoonfuls onto a hot griddle to bake. Yield: 16 (4-inch) pancakes.

GERMAN APPLE PANCAKES

1 recipe German Pancakes*
3–4 apples

Cook the pancake batter for 1 minute. Cover with thin slices of the pared, cored apples. Add 2–3 tablespoons batter to anchor the apples. Cook until pancake is browned; then turn and brown the other side. Yield: 5–6 (10-inch) pancakes.

COTTAGE-CHEESE PANCAKES

1 cup cottage cheese
1 tablespoon melted butter
Pinch salt
1 tablespoon flour
2 eggs
Jam or jelly
Superfine sugar

Rub the cheese through a sieve or beat until creamy. Add the butter, salt, flour, and the well-beaten eggs. Beat with a rotary beater until smooth. Use about ¼ cup batter for each pancake. Bake on a hot griddle. Serve with jam or jelly, rolled or flat. Sprinkle with sugar. Yield: about 6 pancakes.

SOUFFLE PANCAKES

6 tablespoons buttermilk-pancake mix
½ teaspoon salt
6 eggs
6 tablespoons sour cream

Put the pancake mix and salt in a mixing bowl. Beat the egg yolks until thick and lemon-colored. Add the egg yolks and sour cream to the dry ingredients and mix just enough to blend. Fold in the beaten egg whites. Bake on a hot griddle. Serve with butter and honey or maple syrup, or use Blueberry Sauce* or other pancake sauce. Yield: 8 pancakes.

PUFFY DUTCH PANCAKE

2 eggs
½ teaspoon salt
1 teaspoon sugar
¼ cup flour
½ cup milk
3 tablespoons butter

Put the eggs, salt, sugar, flour, and milk in a bowl. Beat all together with a rotary beater until very light and well blended. Heat 1 tablespoon butter in a 9- or 12-inch skillet with a heatproof handle until very hot, but don't let it burn. Pour in the batter and cook 1 minute to brown the bottom. Transfer the skillet to a 450° oven and bake 5 minutes. Reduce heat to 375° and bake for 10 minutes, until it rises and is nicely browned. Remove to a serving platter and dot with remaining butter. Serve with a mixture of ¼ cup honey and 1 tablespoon lemon juice over the pancake or with fruit or other sauce. Serves 2.

SWEDISH PANCAKES

1 cup flour
¼ teaspoon salt
¼ cup sugar
6 eggs
6 tablespoons melted butter
1 cup milk
1 cup heavy cream
Confectioners' sugar
4 cups lingonberry preserves

Sift the flour, salt, and sugar together. Beat the eggs until light and add the butter, milk, and cream. Add to the flour mixture and beat until smooth. Pour tablespoonfuls of batter onto a hot buttered griddle. The cakes brown almost at once; turn them and let the other side brown. Stack on a platter and keep warm in a warm oven. If you have a Swedish plätar pan, increase the milk to 2 cups. Brush each section of the pan with a little melted butter and proceed as above. Sprinkle with confectioners' sugar and serve with lingonberries. Serves 12.

APPLE FILLING FOR PANCAKES

6–7 apples
1 cup sugar
Cinnamon and/or nutmeg (optional)

Peel, core, and cut the apples in half; then slice very thin. Bring 1 cup water to a boil, add the apples, and cook until almost tender —a very few minutes, depending upon how thin the apple slices are. Stir in the sugar, and the spice if you wish, and cook a few minutes more, until the apples are transparent. Keep warm until ready to use. Yield: filling for 6 (10-inch) pancakes.

SCOTCH PANCAKES

2 cups flour
½ teaspoon salt
2 tablespoons sugar
1 teaspoon cream of tartar
1 teaspoon baking soda
2 tablespoons dark corn syrup
¾ cup milk
1 egg

Sift the flour, salt, sugar, cream of tartar, and soda together. Add the syrup, milk, slightly beaten egg, and ½ cup cold water. Beat until smooth. Use about 1 rounded tablespoon batter for each cake. Bake on a hot griddle. Good with hot Butterscotch Maple Syrup.* Yield: about 40 (2-inch) pancakes.

Crêpes (French Pancakes)

These delicious thin pancakes are served for dessert with sauces or preserves or lemon and sugar, or they may be stuffed with fruit or cheese. The batter is made of eggs, flour, and liquid (usually milk). It should be thin and smooth, the consistency of cream. Crêpe batter should not be beaten too much. If there are any lumps, strain the batter. Let it stand 2 hours before using.

Crêpes are best made in a small frying or omelet pan—5-6 inches in diameter. Brush the hot pan with a little oil or butter and pour in a small amount of batter to cover the bottom of the pan thinly (a scant ¼ cup is usually enough). Lift the pan from the stove and tilt quickly in all directions so that the batter is evenly distributed. Cook each crêpe over medium heat until the underside is delicately browned; then turn with a spatula (or with your fingers) and brown the other side. Repeat until all the batter is used. If you can conveniently have two pans going at the same time, it will speed things up; however, you will be kept very busy. Stack the crêpes with pieces of waxed paper between, or fold in halves, then in quarters, or roll. Cover them with a towel, waxed paper, or a large bowl and keep warm in the lowest possible oven. A serving is usually three or four crêpes.

The most famous sauce for crêpes is Suzette. It is traditional to make Crêpes Suzette in a flat chafing dish at the table, but it is not essential.

CREPES I

3 eggs
½ teaspoon salt
1½ teaspoons sugar
1 scant cup flour
2 cups milk
2 tablespoons butter

Beat the eggs until light, add the salt and sugar, and mix well. Continue beating and alternately add the flour, milk, and melted butter. Proceed as for Crêpes.* Yield: 15–18 crêpes.

CREPES II

¾ cups flour
1 egg plus 1 egg yolk
1 tablespoon cooking oil
1½ cups milk
¼ teaspoon salt

Mix the flour with the egg and yolk, oil, 1 cup milk, and the salt. Beat together until smooth. Add the remaining milk. Beat, strain if necessary, and put the batter in the refrigerator for ½ hour. If the batter is not the consistency of thin cream, add a little more milk. Proceed as for Crêpes.* Yield: about 12 crêpes.

CREPES III

2 cups flour
4 eggs
2½ cups milk
1 tablespoon sugar
1 teaspoon salt
1 teaspoon vanilla

Mix the flour, eggs, 1½ cups milk, sugar, salt, and vanilla. Beat with a rotary beater until smooth. Add the remaining milk, beating steadily. Proceed as for Crêpes.* Yield: about 24 crêpes.

SUZETTE SAUCE I

⅔ cup sugar
½ cup butter
1 piece lemon with rind
2 pieces orange with rind
1 cup strained orange juice
1 tablespoon grated orange rind

2 tablespoons Cointreau or Curaçao
2 tablespoons Benedictine or kirsch
or ¼ cup any one or combination
¼ cup brandy

Light the flame under a pan (a large flat one). Put in the sugar and butter; stir until the color of the butter darkens. Add the lemon and orange pieces, rind side down, and press with a spoon to extract oil from the skin. Add the orange juice and grated rind. When the sauce has bubbled a few minutes, remove the lemon and orange pieces and put in the crêpes one at a time. Unfold until coated with sauce, refold, and push to side of pan. Continue in this manner until all have been unfolded and refolded. Spoon sauce over these. Add the liqueurs, let heat a minute without stirring, add the brandy, and light with a match. Spoon flaming sauce over the crêpes. Serve about 3 to each person with a spoonful of sauce. Yield: sauce for about 24 crêpes, serves 8.

SUZETTE SAUCE II

½ cup butter
¼ cup sugar
¼ cup orange juice
Few drops lemon juice
2 teaspoons grated orange rind
2 tablespoons Curaçao
2 tablespoons Cointreau
or ¼ cup of either liqueur
¼ cup brandy

Cream the butter, sugar, orange juice, lemon juice, and orange rind together. You can make this basic mixture ahead. When ready to serve, put half the mixture in a chafing dish or flat pan and melt it. Add half the Curaçao and Cointreau and 9 crêpes. Turn the pancakes in the sauce, add half the brandy, and light. Serve flaming. Repeat. Yield: enough sauce for 18 crêpes, serves 6.

SUZETTE SAUCE III

5 lumps sugar
1 orange
¼ cup butter
Few drops lemon juice
¼ cup orange liqueur such as Curaçao,
Cointreau, or Grand Marnier, or a
combination
¼ cup brandy

Rub the lumps of sugar on the orange skin until they are covered with oil from the orange skin. Mash them in a flat pan with the butter, juice from the orange, and lemon juice. Add the liqueur. Heat. Put in the crêpes, spooning sauce over them. Fold each crêpe over twice. Add the brandy and ignite. Yield: sauce for 18 crêpes, serves 6.

SPECIAL CREPE SAUCE

1 (11 oz.) can mandarin oranges
2 tablespoons sugar
Rind 1 orange
2 teaspoons cornstarch
¼ cup orange juice
1 tablespoon dark rum

Pour the liquid from the mandarin oranges into a saucepan; add the sugar and orange rind cut into thin strips. Press the rind with a teaspoon to release oils. Cook gently until the liquid thickens and rind is tender. Remove rind. Add the cornstarch to the orange juice and add to saucepan; heat again until mixture is thickened and no taste of cornstarch remains; then add the rum. Cook a minute and add the oranges. Yield: about 1¾ cups.

COOKTIP

Use only good wine, rum, or brandy or other spirits in cooking. The alcohol evaporates and the flavor comes through. If serving wine at dinner, try to save the last inch or two in the bottle for use in cooking a future dish.

COTTAGE-CHEESE BLINTZES

*Crêpes 1 or 11**
1 pound cottage cheese
1 tablespoon butter
2 egg yolks
1 tablespoon sugar
Sugar (garnish)
Jelly or jam
Sour cream

Fry the crêpes on one side only. Mix the cottage cheese, butter, egg yolks, and sugar. Put about 2 tablespoons of this mixture in the center of the browned side of each crêpe. Roll the edges over from both sides and tuck in the ends. Fry, folded side down, in butter until golden; then turn and brown the other side. Blintzes are served with sugar, jelly or jam, and sour cream. Yield: about 16 blintzes.

CREPES AUX POMMES
(Apple Pancakes)

> 2 cups thick applesauce
> ½ cup plus 6 tablespoons pineapple or peach jam
> Grated rind 1 lemon
> ½ cup toasted slivered blanched almonds
> Crêpes I or II*

Heat the applesauce with ½ cup jam, the lemon rind, and 2 tablespoons water. Cook until fairly thick. Spread a layer of this on each crêpe, piling one on top of another. For the sauce, beat remaining jam with ½ cup water, add almonds, and cook to syrup consistency. Pour over the crêpes. Cut like cake into V-shaped pieces. Serves 4–6.

CREPES AUX FRAMBOISES
(Raspberry Pancakes)

> 1 pound cream-style cottage cheese
> 1 (8 oz.) package cream cheese
> Crêpes II*
> 4 packages frozen raspberries
> 3 tablespoons butter
> 2 tablespoons grated orange rind
> 1 tablespoon lemon juice
> Sugar
> 2 tablespoons cornstarch
> ¼ cup brandy (optional)
> Sour cream (garnish)

Blend the cheeses together and spread each crêpe generously with the mixture. Roll and place side by side in an oblong cake pan or baking dish. Do not stack. Thaw the raspberries and buzz in a blender, or crush and then strain through a fine sieve. Add butter, orange rind, lemon juice, and a little sugar to taste. Bring to a boil and stir in the cornstarch which has been blended with a little cold water. Boil 1 minute. Spoon about half the sauce over the rolled crêpes, cover with foil, and put aside. About 20 minutes before serving, heat in a 350° oven. Heat remaining sauce in a double boiler; add brandy if you wish. Serve with the sauce poured over the crêpes and topped if you wish with fluffs of sour cream. Serves 8.

COOKTIP

A bit of sugar in pancake or waffle batter makes them brown more quickly.

BUCKWHEAT CREPES

> 1 tablespoon olive oil
> 3 tablespoons brandy
> Pinch salt
> 1 cup sour milk
> 1¾ cups buckwheat flour
> 4 eggs

Mix the oil, brandy, salt, milk, and flour together. Add the eggs one at a time, working them in to prevent lumping. Thin with a little more milk if you wish. Bake on a hot buttered or oiled griddle. Serves 6.

BUCKWHEAT CAKES

> ½ cup flour
> ½ cup buckwheat flour
> 2 teaspoons baking powder
> 2 tablespoons sugar
> ½ teaspoon salt
> ½ cup milk
> 2 tablespoons melted butter
> 1 egg

Sift the flours, baking powder, sugar, and salt together. Add milk and butter to the beaten egg yolk. Add the flour mixture all at once and stir just enough to dampen the flour. Add a little more milk if necessary to make the batter just thin enough to pour. Fold in the egg white, beaten stiff. Bake on a hot griddle. Yield: 8 (5-inch) cakes.

BLINI

> 1 package active dry yeast
> 3½ cups milk
> 2½ cups flour
> 4 eggs
> Pinch salt
> ½ cup heavy cream

Soften the yeast in 2 cups warm milk (110°–115°). Add ½ cup flour and mix. Let stand in a warm place for 2 hours to rise. Add remaining 2 cups flour, the slightly beaten egg yolks, remaining 1½ cups milk, and the salt. Mix thoroughly with a light touch. The mixture should not be heavy. Beat the egg whites until a soft peak forms and fold into the batter. Add the cream, whipped. Let the batter rise another ½ hour. Make small cakes. Fry in butter in a small pan or on a griddle. The cakes should be 4–5 inches across. Good with jelly and sour cream or with any fruit preserves. Serves 8–10.

APPLE BLINTZES

*Crêpes I or II**
3 apples
4 tablespoons brown sugar
½ teaspoon cinnamon
⅓ cup sugar
Sour cream (optional)

Peel, core, and slice the apples and cook gently for about 12 minutes in a saucepan with the brown sugar and cinnamon. Stir while cooking. Cool. Cook the blintzes on one side only and stack, cooked side up. Put 1 tablespoon of the apple mixture on each cake, turn in ends, and roll up. Bake in a 350° oven until browned, about 20 minutes. Serve sprinkled with sugar and with sour cream if you wish. Serves 6.

Waffles

WAFFLES

2 cups flour
1 tablespoon baking powder
2 tablespoons sugar
½ teaspoon salt
2 eggs
¼ cup butter
1 cup milk

Sift the flour, baking powder, sugar, and salt together. Beat the egg yolks until light and combine with the melted butter and milk. Add to the dry ingredients and mix until smooth. Beat the egg whites until a stiff peak forms. Fold into the batter. Bake in a waffle iron. Yield: 2 (10-inch) waffles.

CRISP WAFFLES

2 cups cake flour
4 teaspoons baking powder
½ teaspoon salt
1 tablespoon sugar

1 cup milk
½ cup light cream
2 eggs
⅔ cup melted butter

Sift the flour, baking powder, salt, and sugar together twice. Stir in the milk, cream, and beaten egg yolks. Beat until smooth. The batter will be quite thick. Add the butter and beat again thoroughly. Beat egg whites until a soft peak forms; fold them into the batter. Bake in a preheated waffle iron until crisp and golden. Yield: 2 (10-inch) waffles.

BUTTERMILK WAFFLES

3 eggs
2 cups buttermilk
2 cups flour
½ teaspoon salt
1 tablespoon baking powder
½ teaspoon baking soda
6 tablespoons shortening or cooking oil

Beat the egg yolks until thick. Add the buttermilk. Sift the flour, salt, baking powder, and soda together. Combine with the yolk mixture. Beat smooth. Stir in the melted shortening or oil. Fold in the stiffly beaten egg whites. Bake in waffle iron. Yield: 3 (10-inch) waffles.

CINNAMON WAFFLES

*1 recipe Waffles**
2 teaspoons cinnamon

Use your favorite waffle recipe or a prepared mix. Add the cinnamon to the dry ingredients and bake as usual. Serve with butter and honey or syrup.

FRENCH-TOAST WAFFLES

6 thick slices white bread
Soft butter
½ cup milk
2 eggs
¼ teaspoon salt

Use day-old bread and spread both sides of each slice with the soft butter. Dip into a mixture of milk, beaten eggs, and salt. Do this quickly so that the bread is only coated, not soaked. Bake in a waffle iron until golden and sizzling. Serves 4–6.

CHOCOLATE WAFFLES

1¾ cups flour
4 teaspoons baking powder
½ teaspoon salt
6 tablespoons sugar
1 cup milk
2 eggs
3 tablespoons shortening
2 ounces chocolate

Sift the flour, baking powder, salt, and sugar together. Add the milk to the well-beaten eggs. Beat gradually into the dry ingredients. Melt the shortening and chocolate over hot water and add to batter. Bake in waffle iron. Try serving à la mode with ice cream and Chocolate Sauce* or with just chocolate sauce. Yield: 2 (10-inch) waffles.

PECAN WAFFLES

2 cups flour
¾ teaspoon salt
1 tablespoon baking powder
2 tablespoons sugar
¼ cup melted butter
2 eggs
1½ cups milk
½ cup coarsely chopped pecans

Sift the flour, salt, and baking powder together twice. Add sugar, butter, and egg yolks beaten with the milk. Mix until smooth. Beat egg whites until stiff but not dry and fold into batter. Mix in chopped pecans. Bake in a hot waffle iron until golden. Serve with butter and hot Butterscotch Sauce* if you wish. Yield: 2 (10-inch) waffles.

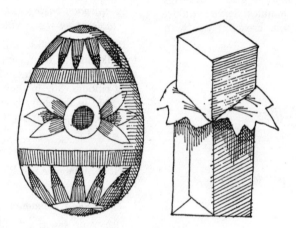

CHAPTER TEN

Seventy-seven Sauces

Complement your puddings with a sauce. Don't use a sauce as a cover-up but rather to augment, enhance, and improve. Make the sauce tempting and almost irresistible.

There are sauces which are part of the dish itself, such as the custard with cottage pudding or the custard for floating island to float on. There are sauces for contrasting flavor and texture, such as fruit sauce for a bread pudding and caramel sauce for a baked custard. There are sauces which transform commercial desserts into homemade ones; and there are sauces which serve as a dessert, such as applesauce.

Devote yourself to your sauce, and your audience will be devoted to you.

Legend:
The aunt of Brillat-Savarin was herself a gourmet. She died at the age of ninety-seven. In her early nineties she was ill and finishing a rich dinner in bed. "I feel the end approaching," she breathed. "Quick, bring me my dessert, coffee, and liqueur."

APRICOT SAUCE I

2 (12 oz.) cans apricot nectar
Grated rind 1 orange
Juice 1 lemon
2 tablespoons butter
Cointreau or apricot liqueur (optional)

Empty the apricot nectar into a saucepan and add the grated orange rind, lemon juice, and butter. Cook for 5 minutes. Add a little liqueur if you wish. Serve with cut-up fresh or frozen fruit or as a pudding sauce. Yield: about 3 cups.

APRICOT SAUCE II

2 cups puréed apricots
2 tablespoons lemon juice
1 teaspoon grated lemon rind
1 tablespoon rum (optional)

Mix all the ingredients. Yield: about 2 cups.

APRICOT-NECTAR SAUCE

¼ cup sugar
1 tablespoon cornstarch
2 cups canned apricot nectar
2 teaspoons lemon juice
1½ cups chopped, peeled very ripe apricots
2 tablespoons apricot brandy or Cointreau (optional)

Mix the sugar with the cornstarch. Combine with the apricot nectar. Cook and stir until smooth and thickened; continue to simmer, stirring, for 5–7 minutes. Add the lemon juice. Cool. Add the apricots, and brandy or Cointreau if you wish. Chill. Good with ice cream or pineapple or lemon sherbet. Yield: about 3 cups.

APRICOT SOUR-CREAM HONEY SAUCE

1 (1 lb. 14 oz.) can apricots
½ cup honey
½ teaspoon salt
1 teaspoon grated lemon rind
1 tablespoon lemon juice
2 cups sour cream

Drain and purée the apricots; you should have about 1¼ cups purée. Add the remaining ingredients and mix well. This sauce keeps several days in the refrigerator. Good served with fruit or on puddings. Yield: about 1 quart.

APPLE LEMON SAUCE

2 cups applesauce
¼ cup light brown sugar
¼ teaspoon cinnamon
½ teaspoon grated lemon rind

Combine the applesauce with the sugar, cinnamon, and lemon rind. Cover and chill. Very good served over lemon sherbet. Yield: about 2¼ cups.

BLUEBERRY SAUCE

1 package frozen sweetened blueberries
1–2 sticks cinnamon
½ cup sugar

Heat the berries, cinnamon sticks, and sugar in a saucepan. Simmer about 20 minutes, until the syrup is reduced and thick. Remove cinnamon. Good served hot with pancakes or waffles or over ice cream. Yield: about 1½ cups.

BING-CHERRY SAUCE

1 (1 lb. 13 oz.) can pitted Bing cherries
1 tablespoon cornstarch
Pinch salt
¼ cup sugar
1 tablespoon butter
2 teaspoons lemon juice
2 tablespoons kirsch (optional)

Drain the cherries and reserve the syrup; you should have 1 cup. Mix the cornstarch, salt, and sugar together in a saucepan. Add the cherry syrup and mix well. Cook and stir over medium heat until mixture comes to a boil; then simmer about 5 minutes. Remove from heat and add the butter and lemon juice. Cool and add the cherries. Add the kirsch if you wish. Particularly good served on strawberry ice cream. Yield: about 3½ cups.

JUBILEE SAUCE

1 (1 lb. 13 oz.) can pitted Bing cherries
1 tablespoon cornstarch
¼ cup brandy or kirsch

Drain the cherries. Mix the cornstarch with 2 tablespoons of cherry juice. Add the remaining juice—about 1 cup. Cook until clear and thickened. Add the cherries and heat for 1–2 minutes. Pour in the heated brandy or kirsch and ignite. Stir to keep the flame burning. This is effective cooked at the table in a chafing dish. Especially good over vanilla ice cream. Yield: about 3 cups.

SPICY BING-CHERRY SAUCE

3 tablespoons cornstarch
2 (1 lb. 13 oz.) cans pitted Bing cherries
Juice 1 orange
4 tablespoons lemon juice
2 tablespoons light brown sugar
3 cloves
2 blades mace
½ stick cinnamon
1 tablespoon orange flavoring
1 tablespoon butter
½ teaspoon almond flavoring
Red food coloring (optional)

Blend the cornstarch with ¼ cup cold water until smooth. Heat together 2 cups syrup from the cherries, orange juice, 3 tablespoons lemon juice, the cornstarch paste, sugar, cloves, mace, and cinnamon. Cook, stirring constantly, until thickened and clear. Remove the whole spices; add the orange flavoring, butter, remaining lemon juice, and almond flavoring. When well blended, stir in the cherries, and a few drops red food coloring if you wish. Heat the sauce 5 minutes more, stirring occasionally. Serve over ice cream or puddings. Yield: 2 quarts.

SPICED CHERRY AND PEACH SAUCE

1 (1 lb.) can pitted Bing cherries
¼ cup sugar
1 small piece stick cinnamon
2 tablespoons lemon juice
¼ teaspoon cloves
¼ teaspoon nutmeg
2 tablespoons cornstarch
2 packages frozen sliced peaches

Drain the juice from the cherries and add the sugar, cinnamon, lemon juice, cloves, and nutmeg. Simmer very slowly for 10 minutes; then remove the stick of cinnamon and add the cornstarch which has been mixed with 2 tablespoons cold water. Stir and cook until thickened and clear. Then add the cherries and the thawed peaches and juice. Heat all together. Especially good served over vanilla ice cream. Yield: about 1 quart.

CHERRY AND STRAWBERRY SAUCE

1 (1 lb. 13 oz.) can pitted Bing cherries
2-inch strip lemon peel
1½ tablespoons lemon juice
1½ tablespoons cornstarch
1 cup sliced strawberries
2–3 tablespoons cherry liqueur or brandy (optional)

Drain the syrup from the cherries. Add the lemon peel and lemon juice to the syrup. Mix the cornstarch with 2 tablespoons water and stir into the syrup. Cook and stir about 20 minutes, until clear and thickened. Add the cherries and chill, stirring occasionally. Just before serving, add the strawberries and flavor with cherry liqueur or brandy if you wish. Yield: about 3 cups.

LEMON RICE CREAM SAUCE

¼ cup sugar
1 teaspoon grated lemon rind
2 tablespoons lemon juice
½ teaspoon vanilla
Dash nutmeg
1½ cups heavy cream
2 cups cooked rice

Add the sugar, lemon rind, lemon juice, vanilla, and nutmeg to the cream, whipped. Fold in the cold rice and chill. This may be used as a sauce for baked apples or other cooked fruit. Yield: about 5 cups.

LEMON CHEESE

3 eggs
1 cup sugar
¼ cup lemon juice
2 tablespoons melted butter
½ teaspoon grated lemon rind

Beat the eggs until thick. Mix the sugar with lemon juice and add very slowly to the eggs, beating continuously. Then add the melted butter and lemon rind. Cook in a double boiler until very thick, stirring constantly. When the spoon leaves a streak in the sauce, it's done. Pour into a jar when cool, cover tight, and refrigerate. This will keep for a week. Serve with spongecake, in tart shells, or as a cake filling. Yield: about 2 cups.

LEMON SAUCE I

1 tablespoon cornstarch
½ cup sugar
Pinch salt
2 tablespoons lemon juice
1 teaspoon grated lemon rind

Mix the cornstarch, sugar, and salt together thoroughly. Stir in 1 cup boiling water. Bring slowly to a boil, stirring constantly; then simmer 5 minutes. Remove from heat and add lemon juice and rind. Serve warm. Yield: about 1 cup.

LEMON SAUCE II

1 cup sugar
3 tablespoons cornstarch
⅛ teaspoon salt
1 egg yolk
¼ cup butter
¼ cup lemon juice
Grated rind 2 lemons
Dash nutmeg

Mix the sugar, cornstarch, and salt together. Then slowly mix in 2 cups boiling water and simmer 5 minutes, stirring constantly. Remove from heat. Stir the hot mixture into the egg yolk a little at a time. Return to heat for 1 minute. Add butter, lemon juice, grated rind, and nutmeg. Serve warm or cold. Yield: 3 cups.

BRANDY CRANBERRY SAUCE

1½ cups whole-cranberry sauce
¼ cup brandy
2 tablespoons cornstarch

Mix the ingredients together. Heat and stir until thick and glossy. Serve warm over puddings or on ice cream. Yield: about 1¾ cups.

HONEY LEMON SAUCE

2 eggs
5 tablespoons sugar
1 tablespoon honey
1 tablespoon grated lemon rind
1 tablespoon lemon juice
Pinch salt
½ cup heavy cream

Beat the egg yolks well, gradually add 1 tablespoon sugar and the honey, and beat until light. Add the lemon rind and the juice. Beat the egg whites until they stand in peaks and gradually beat in the salt and remaining sugar. Fold into the egg-yolk mixture and then fold in the cream, whipped. Chill. Yield: 1 quart.

FLUFFY ORANGE SAUCE

1 egg yolk
¼ cup sugar
2 tablespoons orange juice
1 teaspoon grated lemon rind
2 teaspoons grated orange rind
1 cup heavy cream

Beat the egg yolk and add the sugar, orange juice, and fruit rinds. Cook in a double boiler until thick, stirring constantly. Cool. Fold into the cream, whipped. This sauce is especially recommended for fruit. Yield: about 2 cups.

ORANGE MINT SOUR-CREAM SAUCE

2 teaspoons orange juice
1 teaspoon grated orange rind
1 teaspoon sugar
Pinch salt
2 teaspoons finely chopped mint
1 cup sour cream

Add the orange juice, orange rind, sugar, salt, and mint to the sour cream. Mix well and chill. Serve with fruit compote or a macédoine of fruits. Yield: about 1 cup.

ORANGE STRAWBERRY SAUCE

1½ cups orange juice
2 tablespoons sugar
1 tablespoon cornstarch
½ teaspoon vanilla
¼ teaspoon almond flavoring
1½ cups sliced strawberries
½ cup toasted slivered blanched almonds
  (optional)

Heat the orange juice with the sugar. Add the cornstarch moistened with 2 tablespoons water. Cook until thick and clear, stirring frequently. Cool; add vanilla and almond flavoring. Just before serving, stir in the sliced strawberries, and almonds if you wish. Yield: about 3½ cups.

SOUR-CREAM ORANGE SAUCE

3 tablespoons butter
½ cup confectioners' sugar
⅓ cup sour cream
3 tablespoons orange juice
1 teaspoon grated orange rind

Cream the butter and sugar thoroughly. Beat in the sour cream, orange juice, and rind. Especially good with sponge-, pound-, or white cake. Yield: about 1 cup.

AMBROSIA SAUCE

4 seedless oranges
1 (3½ oz.) can flaked coconut

Cut the peel from the oranges with a sharp knife, being careful to cut away all white membrane. Section the oranges, removing each section from its membrane as you cut. Then cut into bite-size pieces, retaining all juice. Add coconut and stir. Chill. Yield: about 2 cups.

PEACH SAUCE

1 (1 lb.) can cling-peach slices
1 cup heavy cream
1 egg yolk
2 tablespoons honey
¼ teaspoon almond flavoring

Drain the peaches and cut into pieces. Whip the cream until slightly thickened. Beat in the egg yolk. Drizzle in the honey and continue beating until sauce is thick and creamy. Fold in the peaches and almond flavoring. Chill. Stir sauce well before serving. Yield: about 1 quart.

RASPBERRY ORANGE SAUCE

3 packages frozen raspberries
Juice 1 orange
Grated rind ½ orange
3 tablespoons sugar
2 tablespoons cornstarch
1 tablespoon brandy (optional)

Thaw the raspberries and rub through a fine sieve. Put into a saucepan and add the orange juice, rind, and sugar. Stir in the cornstarch blended with a little cold water or brandy and water. Bring to a boil. Reduce heat and simmer until thickened and all taste of cornstarch is gone. Serve cold. Yield: about 3 cups.

STRAWBERRY PUREE

2 packages frozen strawberries
1 teaspoon lemon juice
2 tablespoons liqueur (optional)
Sugar

Thaw the berries and rub through a fine sieve, or buzz in a blender and then strain. Add the lemon juice, the liqueur if you wish, and a little sugar to taste. Try brandy, rum, kirsch, or Cointreau. Yield: about 2 cups.

RASPBERRY PUREE

Substitute 2 packages frozen raspberries for the strawberries and proceed as for Strawberry Purée.* Particularly good served over fresh strawberries.

FRESH STRAWBERRY PUREE

1 pint strawberries
1 cup sugar
2 teaspoons lemon juice
2 tablespoons strawberry jelly (optional)

Hull the berries and sprinkle with sugar. Put into a saucepan, cover, and simmer very slowly for 10 minutes, until berries are tender. Rub through a fine sieve. Add the lemon juice. Add the jelly if you wish; stir and heat until jelly is melted and blended with the purée. Add more lemon juice to taste. Good with ice cream and puddings. Yield: about 1 cup.

TUTTI-FRUTTI SAUCE

¼ pound pitted dates
1 (8 oz.) jar maraschino cherries
1 (8 oz.) can white figs
Pinch salt
¼ pound toasted blanched almonds
½ cup sugar
2 tablespoons rum or sherry

Cut the dates into small pieces. Add the maraschino cherry juice. Cut the cherries and figs into small pieces and add these. Let stand for several hours or overnight. Add the salt and the almonds cut in half. Boil the sugar with ½ cup water for 5 minutes. Add to the fruit and chill. Add the rum or sherry. This will keep several days. Yield: about 3 cups.

STRAWBERRY LIQUEUR SAUCE

*1 quart fresh strawberries or 3 packages
sliced frozen*
Sugar
*3–4 tablespoons Grand Marnier or other
orange liqueur*

Hull the fresh strawberries and cut in half,
or thaw the frozen ones. Put into a small saucepan with sugar to taste (about ½ cup for
fresh, less for frozen). Heat until the berries
are hot, but not mushy. Remove from heat
and stir in the Grand Marnier. Serve warm.
Yield: 3–4 cups.

SPECIAL MELBA SAUCE

1 pint strawberries or 1 package frozen
1 pint raspberries or 1 package frozen
1 (8 oz.) jar Melba sauce
2–3 tablespoons lemon juice
¼ cup orange liqueur (optional)

Hull the fresh strawberries and pick over the
raspberries. Buzz them in a blender or force
through a food mill. If using frozen fruit,
thaw, purée, and put through a sieve to remove seeds. Mix in the Melba sauce, lemon
juice, and a liqueur such as Curaçao, Cointreau, or Grand Marnier if you wish. Yield:
about 3 cups.

FRUIT SAUCE WITH WATER CHESTNUTS

2 tablespoons butter
1 (5 oz.) can water chestnuts
1 (1 lb. 4 oz.) can pineapple juice
1 can frozen tangerine-juice concentrate
2 sticks cinnamon
½ cup sugar
¼ cup cornstarch
¼ teaspoon ginger
⅛ teaspoon salt
2 tablespoons lemon juice
2 teaspoons grated lemon rind

Heat 1 tablespoon butter in a skillet; add
the water chestnuts, sliced, and stir until butter is absorbed and water chestnuts lightly
browned. Remove from heat. In a large saucepan mix the pineapple juice with ½ cup water. Add the tangerine-juice concentrate and
cinnamon. Bring to a boil, reduce heat, and
simmer 5 minutes. Meanwhile, mix the sugar,
cornstarch, ginger, and salt in a bowl. Pour a
little of the fruit juices into the cornstarch mixture and stir until smooth. Return to fruit
juices and cook, stirring, until clear and thickened. Remove from heat. Add the lemon juice,
lemon rind, and remaining butter. Cool at room
temperature. When cool, remove cinnamon
sticks and chill. Just before serving, add the
water chestnuts. This sauce keeps well for
about a week. Serve with a combination of
fresh fruits. Yield: 3 cups.

CARDINAL SAUCE

1 (12 oz.) jar strawberry jelly
*¼ cup grenadine or maraschino cherry
syrup*
¼ cup lemon juice
¼ cup orange juice

Melt the strawberry jelly with grenadine or
maraschino cherry syrup in a saucepan. Remove from heat. Stir in the lemon juice and
orange juice. Cool. Particularly good on stewed
pears. Yield: about 1 quart.

BROWN-SUGAR SAUCE

1 pint sour cream
4 tablespoons dark brown sugar

Put the sour cream in a bowl and stir in 3
tablespoons sugar. Sprinkle the remaining
sugar over the top. Yield: 2 cups.

BURNT-SUGAR SYRUP

¾ cup sugar
¾ cup hot water

Heat the sugar slowly in a skillet, stirring
gently, until melted and dark amber in color.
Remove from heat and stir in the hot water.
This will boil up a great deal. When it has
subsided, return to low heat. Stir gently until
all the caramelized sugar is dissolved. Cool
to room temperature before using. Yield:
about ½ cup.

COFFEE BURNT-SUGAR SYRUP

Substitute very strong coffee for the water
in the above recipe.

THREE-FRUIT RUM SAUCE

2 peaches
1 banana
Lemon juice
1 cup pineapple apricot preserves
½ cup rum
1 cup crushed pineapple
½ cup flaked coconut

Peel and slice the peaches and banana. Sprinkle with lemon juice to prevent darkening. Warm the preserves with the rum in a small saucepan over very low heat. Combine with the peaches, banana, pineapple, and coconut. Good served warm or cool with peach or vanilla ice cream. Yield: about 1 quart sauce.

BUTTERSCOTCH SAUCE I

½ cup butter
2 cups brown sugar
2 teaspoons cornstarch
1 teaspoon vanilla

Boil the butter and sugar. Add the cornstarch dissolved in ½ cup water. Cook to soft-ball stage (234°). Add the vanilla. Serve hot or cold. Particularly good over vanilla or chocolate ice cream. Yield: about 1½ cups.

BUTTERSCOTCH SAUCE II

1½ cups dark brown sugar
⅔ cup light corn syrup
¼ cup butter
¾ cup evaporated milk

Measure all the ingredients except evaporated milk into a heavy 2-quart saucepan. Heat to the soft-ball stage (234°–238°). Remove from heat; mix in the evaporated milk a little at a time. Keep warm over low heat. Stir before using. Yield: 2½ cups.

BUTTERSCOTCH RUM SAUCE

1½ cups sugar
1¼ cups light corn syrup
½ cup butter
2 cups light cream
½ teaspoon vanilla
2–3 tablespoons light rum

Cook the sugar, corn syrup, butter, and 1 cup cream until it reaches the firm-ball stage (246°). Stir in the remaining cream and bring to a boil. Lower heat and cook 15–20 minutes, until thickened, stirring occasionally. Add vanilla and rum. Cool. This sauce keeps well in the refrigerator. Let stand at room temperature about an hour before serving. Good with ice cream. Yield: 3 cups.

BUTTERSCOTCH MAPLE SYRUP

1 cup brown sugar
1 cup maple syrup
¼ cup butter
2 teaspoons vanilla
1 teaspoon salt
1½ cups light cream

Put the sugar and maple syrup in a saucepan. Heat gently until the sugar dissolves; then boil rapidly for 5 minutes. Remove from heat immediately. Add the butter, vanilla, and salt. Do not stir. Allow to cool a little. Add the cream and beat until well blended and creamy. Yield: about 3 cups.

CHOCOLATE SAUCE

2 tablespoons butter
2 ounces unsweetened chocolate
1 cup sugar
Pinch salt
½ teaspoon vanilla

Cook the butter, chocolate, sugar, and salt with ½ cup water, stirring constantly, until the chocolate is melted. Boil until the sauce is as thick as you like it. Remove from heat and add the vanilla. Serve warm. Yield: about 1 cup.

COCOA CHOCOLATE SAUCE

Substitute ¼ cup cocoa for the chocolate and reduce the butter to 1 tablespoon. Proceed as for Chocolate Sauce.*

EASY CHOCOLATE SAUCE

1 (6 oz.) package semisweet chocolate bits
⅔ cup evaporated milk
2 tablespoons butter
⅛ teaspoon salt
1 teaspoon vanilla

Melt the chocolate over hot water. Add the milk gradually, stirring until smooth. Stir in the butter, salt, and vanilla. Yield: about 1⅓ cups.

CHOCOLATE CREAM SAUCE

1⅓ cups milk
3 ounces unsweetened chocolate
Pinch salt
⅓ cup sugar
2 teaspoons cornstarch
1 teaspoon vanilla
⅓ cup light cream

Heat the milk, chocolate, and salt in a double boiler. When blended, add the sugar. Heat until sugar is dissolved. Mix the cornstarch and 2 tablespoons water and add to the sauce. Cook, stirring constantly, until the mixture is smooth and thick. Cool slightly and flavor with vanilla. Add the cream and chill. Yield: about 2 cups.

CHOCOLATE FUDGE SAUCE

3 ounces unsweetened chocolate
¼ cup butter
1½ cups confectioners' sugar
1 (6 oz.) can evaporated milk
Pinch salt
½ teaspoon vanilla

Heat all the ingredients except vanilla in a double boiler. When the chocolate has melted, mix well and cook ½ hour, stirring now and then. Add the vanilla. Good served warm over ice cream. This is a fudgy, rich thick sauce. Yield: 2 cups.

MOCHA FUDGE SAUCE

Proceed as for Chocolate Fudge Sauce,* adding 5 teaspoons instant coffee or 4 teaspoons instant espresso before cooking.

BRANDY CHOCOLATE SAUCE

2 ounces unsweetened chocolate
½ cup strong coffee
2 cups sugar
Pinch salt
¼ cup brandy or sherry, Marsala or port wine

Melt the chocolate in ¼ cup water in a double boiler. Add the coffee, sugar, and salt. Cook for 5 minutes, until sugar dissolves. Remove from heat and add the liquor. Yield: about 1½ cups.

CHOCOLATE CUSTARD SAUCE

2 ounces sweet baking chocolate
1 cup Custard Sauce*

Heat the chocolate with 2–3 tablespoons water until it is melted. Add slowly to the hot custard and mix well. Yield: about 1 cup.

COFFEE CREAM SAUCE

2 teaspoons instant coffee
¾ cup heavy cream
¼ teaspoon vanilla
3 tablespoons sugar

Sprinkle the instant coffee over the cream. When most of the coffee has dissolved, add the vanilla and whip the cream stiff, adding the sugar as you beat. Yield: about 1½ cups.

CARAMEL NUT SAUCE

2 cups light brown sugar
6 tablespoons butter
¾ cup evaporated milk
¾–1 cup chopped walnuts

Put the brown sugar and butter in a heavy saucepan. Cook over moderate heat, stirring constantly, until sugar is melted. Then let it bubble gently several minutes. Meanwhile, heat the evaporated milk with ¾ cup water. Mix with the melted sugar and stir over low heat until sugar is dissolved. Boil 8 minutes, stirring often. Cool. Beat with a rotary beater until much lighter in color. Chill. Before serving, beat a little more and stir in the nuts. Serve cold, or reheat in a double boiler and serve hot. Very good on ice cream or with baked custards. Yield: about 3 cups.

CUSTARD SAUCE

4 egg yolks
¼ cup sugar
⅛ teaspoon salt
½ teaspoon grated lemon rind
2 cups milk
½ teaspoon vanilla

Mix the egg yolks, sugar, salt, and grated lemon rind together in a double boiler. Scald the milk and gradually stir into the egg mixture. Cook over simmering water, stirring constantly, until the mixture thickens and coats a spoon. Remove from heat, cool thoroughly, and add vanilla. Chill. Yield: about 3 cups.

MOCHA CUSTARD SAUCE

2 cups milk
1 package vanilla pudding mix
2 tablespoons instant coffee
½ ounce unsweetened chocolate
1 teaspoon vanilla

Add the milk to the vanilla pudding. Dissolve the instant coffee in 1 cup cold water and add to the pudding mixture. Heat, stirring constantly, until thickened. Add the chocolate and stir until melted. Remove from heat and add vanilla. Cool. If the sauce is too thick, add a few tablespoons of milk and stir well. Yield: about 3 cups.

SATINY MOCHA SAUCE

1 (12 oz.) package semisweet chocolate bits
6 tablespoons hot strong coffee
1 teaspoon vanilla

Buzz the chocolate in a blender with the steaming-hot coffee and the vanilla at low or medium speed until the chocolate is melted and sauce is smooth. Especially good with vanilla ice cream. Yield: about 1¼ cups.

VANILLA CUSTARD SAUCE

1 vanilla bean
2 cups milk
6 tablespoons sugar
4 egg yolks
¼ teaspoon salt

Simmer the vanilla bean, split lengthwise, for 5 minutes with the milk. Mix the sugar with the egg yolks and salt. Pour a little of the hot milk into the egg mixture, blend well, and then stir into the hot milk. Cook and stir in a double boiler until mixture coats a spoon. Remove vanilla bean just before serving. Serve cold or warm over cake, soufflés, or fruit. Yield: about 2½ cups.

EASY RUM CUSTARD SAUCE

1 (3¾ oz.) package instant vanilla
  pudding mix
2 cups milk
1 cup light cream
2 tablespoons rum

Mix the pudding mix with the milk, cream, and rum. Beat with a rotary beater. Chill. Stir before serving. Yield: about 3 cups.

ORANGE CUSTARD SAUCE

2 cups milk
¼ cup sugar
2 teaspoons grated orange rind
½ teaspoon orange flavoring
8 egg yolks

Heat the milk, sugar, orange rind, and flavoring in a double boiler. Add warm milk mixture a little at a time to the slightly beaten egg yolks, beating constantly. Return mixture to double boiler over just-simmering water. Cook and stir just until thickened. Serve warm in a sauce bowl. Especially good with orange soufflé. Yield: about 3½ cups.

GOLDEN CUSTARD SAUCE

3 tablespoons butter
2 tablespoons flour
¾ cup sugar
Pinch salt
2-inch piece vanilla bean or 2 teaspoons
  vanilla
5 egg yolks
1 cup heavy cream
3–4 tablespoons brandy

Melt the butter; add the flour, sugar, and salt and stir until blended. Add 1 cup boiling water slowly, stirring constantly, and then add the vanilla bean. Stir continuously until thick. Remove from heat and take out vanilla bean or add the vanilla. Add the hot mixture slowly to the beaten egg yolks and beat with a rotary beater for a couple of minutes. Chill. Fold in the cream, whipped, and the brandy. This rich sauce is delicious served with cake or puddings. Yield: about 3½ cups.

PORT-WINE CUSTARD SAUCE

8 egg yolks
½ cup sugar
2 tablespoons lemon juice
⅛ teaspoon salt
1 cup port wine
1 cup heavy cream

Beat the egg yolks with the sugar, lemon juice, and salt until light and fluffy. Cook in a double boiler, stirring constantly while slowly adding the port. When the mixture is thick, remove from heat and cool. Fold in the cream, whipped. Yield: about 1 quart.

CUSTARD EGGNOG SAUCE

2 cups light cream
¼ cup sugar
6 eggs
Pinch salt
Pinch nutmeg
¾ teaspoon grated orange rind
2 teaspoons rum

Scald the cream and stir in the sugar. Gradually add the slightly beaten egg yolks. Season with salt, nutmeg, and orange rind. Heat over simmering water until custard is thickened and coats a spoon. Beat the egg whites until they stand in soft peaks. Stir in the hot custard and add the rum. Chill before serving. Yield: about 1 quart.

FOAMY EGGNOG SAUCE

1 egg
½ cup sugar
½ cup heavy cream
1 teaspoon vanilla

Beat the egg white until frothy; then gradually add ¼ cup sugar and beat until mixture is glossy and forms a stiff peak. Whip the cream; add the remaining sugar. When quite thick, gradually add the slightly beaten egg yolk and the vanilla; then fold in the egg-white mixture. Yield: about 1½ cups.

ZABAGLIONE SAUCE   (Plate 32)

6 egg yolks
¾ cup confectioners' sugar
¾ cup Marsala or sweet sherry

Beat the egg yolks until thick; continue to beat while adding the sugar gradually and next the Marsala or sherry. Cook over boiling water while beating until thick and foamy, about 7 minutes. Chill. Particularly good served cold over fresh berries or peaches, or served cold or warm over canned greengage plums, apricots, or white peaches. Orange juice may be substituted for the wine if you prefer. Yield: about 3 cups.

COOKTIP

To soften brown sugar, put it in a warm oven for 10–15 minutes and use immediately.

GINGER SAUCE

1 cup sugar
¼ teaspoon grated lemon rind
3 tablespoons finely chopped crystallized ginger

Boil all of the ingredients for 5 minutes in 1½ cups water. Cool and chill. Especially good on ice cream. Yield: about 1½ cups.

BROWN-SUGAR HONEY SAUCE

1 cup brown sugar
1 cup honey
½ teaspoon salt

Mix the sugar with ½ cup water and boil for 5 minutes. Then add the honey and salt; stir until blended. A good sauce for ice cream or puddings. Yield: about 2 cups.

HONEY FLUFF SAUCE

1 package vanilla pudding mix
¼ cup honey
3 egg whites

Make the pudding according to package directions, and while still hot stir in the honey. Set aside and cool; then fold in the stiffly beaten egg whites. Chill. Good served with fruit or steamed pudding. Yield: about 3 cups.

MAPLE SAUCE

1 cup maple sugar or maple syrup
Pinch salt
2–3 tablespoons heavy cream

Simmer the sugar and ½ cup boiling water for 3–4 minutes. Cool slightly and add the salt and cream. If using maple syrup, omit the water and heat the syrup before adding the cream. Mix well. A good sauce for sundaes. Yield: about 1 cup.

MINCEMEAT SAUCE

1½ cups canned mincemeat
6 tablespoons thawed frozen pineapple-grapefruit-juice concentrate
3 tablespoons dark brown sugar
½ cup chopped walnuts

Mix together the mincemeat, pineapple-grapefruit concentrate, ¼ cup water, and the sugar. Bring to a boil and add the walnuts. Delicious served hot over ice cream. Yield: about 2¼ cups.

FLUFFY MINT SAUCE

¼ cup mint jelly
2 tablespoons light rum (optional)
½ cup heavy cream

Add 2 tablespoons boiling water to the mint jelly. Heat and stir until smooth. Cool slightly. Add, with the rum if you wish, to the cream, whipped. Good served over chocolate ice cream. Yield: about 1 cup.

MARSHMALLOW MINT SAUCE

½ cup sugar
Few sprigs mint
8 large marshmallows
1 egg white
Mint flavoring
Green food coloring

Cook the sugar and mint in ¼ cup water for a few minutes, until you get a thin syrup. Remove mint and stir in the marshmallows cut into pieces. Remove from heat and let stand a minute or two. Beat the egg white until a soft peak forms. Add the syrup, beating all the while. Flavor with a drop or two of mint and color very delicately. Especially good with ice cream. Yield: 1½ cups.

MOUSSELINE SAUCE

2 egg yolks
⅔ cup confectioners' sugar
1 teaspoon vanilla
1 cup heavy cream
½ teaspoon grated lemon rind

Beat the egg yolks, gradually adding the sifted sugar, then vanilla. Beat until mixture is light and fluffy. Fold in the cream, whipped, and lemon rind. Chill. Yield: 3 cups.

WHIPPED-CREAM SAUCE

1 cup heavy cream
1 egg
¼ cup sugar
Pinch salt
⅓ cup melted butter
2 teaspoons rum

After you have whipped the cream until thick and glossy, whip the egg with the same beater. Beat in the sugar, salt, and butter. Fold this into the whipped cream. Chill and add the rum. This is especially good on warm gingerbread. Yield: 2½ cups.

HARD SAUCE

½ cup butter
1½ cups confectioners' sugar
Pinch salt
1 teaspoon vanilla

Cream the butter with the confectioners' sugar, salt, and vanilla. Beat until light and fluffy. You may add rum or rum flavoring to taste instead of the vanilla if you wish. Chill. Yield: about 1½ cups.

BRANDY HARD SAUCE

Proceed as for Hard Sauce.* Omit the vanilla and substitute approximately 2 tablespoons brandy.

ORANGE HARD SAUCE   (Plate 17)

Proceed as for Hard Sauce.* Omit the vanilla and substitute 2 teaspoons grated orange rind and 2 tablespoons orange juice or orange-flavored liqueur.

LEMON HARD SAUCE

Proceed as for Hard Sauce.* Omit the vanilla. Stir in 2 teaspoons grated lemon rind and 1 tablespoon lemon juice after the mixture is fluffy and thick.

BROWN-SUGAR HARD SAUCE

⅓ cup butter
1 cup brown sugar
2 tablespoons rum, sherry, or port
* or 1 teaspoon vanilla*

Cream the butter and sugar together thoroughly. Add the flavoring and beat until fluffy. Chill. Yield: about 1 cup.

CARAMEL HARD SAUCE

½ pound caramels
1 cup butter
1 cup confectioners' sugar

Melt the caramels with 3 tablespoons hot water in a double boiler. Cool to room temperature. Cream the butter and add the sugar a tablespoonful at a time, beating well. Blend in the melted caramels thoroughly. Chill. Yield: about 2 cups.

MACAROON SAUCE

10 dry macaroons
3 tablespoons brown sugar
2 cups sour cream
2 tablespoons rum or 2 teaspoons rum
    flavoring (optional)

Crumble the macaroons into quite small pieces. Add the sugar and cream. Add the rum or rum flavoring if you wish—the sauce is flavorful without it. Mix well and refrigerate for several hours so that the macaroons will soften and flavor the cream. Do not stir again or the macaroons will break into small particles. Serve with ice cream or puddings. Yield: about 2½ cups.

VANILLA WHIPPED-CREAM SAUCE

2 tablespoons butter
3 tablespoons flour
1 cup milk
½ cup sugar
2 teaspoons vanilla
2–3 tablespoons brandy (optional)
1 cup heavy cream

Melt the butter in a saucepan and blend in the flour. Add the milk and sugar and cook over low heat, stirring constantly, until thick and boiling. Stir in the vanilla, and the brandy if you wish. Refrigerate overnight. Whip the cream and fold in just before serving. Yield: about 3 cups.

Candy
Is dandy
But liquor
Is quicker

Ogden Nash,
Many Long Years Ago

Have you ever heard of the Sugar-Plum Tree?
'Tis a marvel of great renown!
It blooms on the shore of the Lollipop sea
In the garden of Shut-Eye Town.

Eugene Field, *The Sugar-Plum Tree*

Plate 39. Confections, starting at the bottom: STUFFED KUMQUATS, GREENGAGE-PLUM PASTE, CANDIED ORANGE AND GRAPEFRUIT PEEL, ROYAL BRITTLE, SUGARPLUMS, and CANDIED CRANBERRIES.

Plate 40. A box of candy: SUGAR MINTS, MARZIPAN STRAWBERRIES, TAFFY NUGGETS, COCONUT FUDGE, and CHOCOLATE NUT FUDGE.

CHAPTER ELEVEN

Sugar and Spice

Do you remember the cotton candy at the fair, the salt-water taffy at the seashore, popcorn at the movies, peanuts at the circus, chocolates at the matinee, the taffy pull at home, fudge in the kitchen?

Anyone for fudge? The best rainy day, or any day, get-together for the whole family is to make some candy. Dad or Junior can be the hero of such a kitchen session; no one would dream of calling candy-making "sissy." These candy bees can be an introduction to the social side of cooking: fun for all with a delicious treat to follow.

Candy is temperamental; its temperature needs to be taken carefully and with a thermometer, not by guess. Measure with care and follow instructions and you will produce delectable sweets.

Most candy is made of sugar, liquid, and flavoring; temperature does the rest. Use a large heavy saucepan for candy-making. Accuracy is more important for fondant and fudge than for taffies. Fudge and other soft candies are cooked to the soft-ball stage, 234°–244° on a candy thermometer. Fudge is cooled at room temperature until the bottom of the pan is comfortably warm to the hand, 110°, before beating. When cooking candy such as brittles and taffies to a very hard stage, over 254°, crystals are likely to form on the sides of the pan; wipe them off with a fork or stick wrapped with a piece of cloth dipped in hot water. Uncooked candy is easy to make, and good too. It's almost foolproof.

Temperature Table for Candy Syrups

Syrup	230°	
Thread	230°–234°	*When dropped from a spoon:* Spins a thread about 3 inches long.
Soft Ball	234°–244°	*When dropped into very cold water:* Can be formed into a very soft ball which flattens slightly.
Firm Ball	244°–248°	Can be formed into a ball which barely holds its shape.
Hard Ball	248°–254°	Can be formed into a firm ball which is hard enough to hold its shape, yet pliable.
Very Hard Ball	254°–265°	Can be formed into a very rigid ball.
Light Crack	270°–284°	Separates into heavy threads which are hard but not brittle and will make a crackling sound when rapped against side of cup.
Hard Crack	290°–300°	Separates into hard brittle threads.
Caramelized Sugar	310°–338°	Sugar liquefies and darkens to a golden or dark brown in the pan.

CHOCOLATE FUDGE   (Plate 10)

2 cups sugar
1 cup confectioners' sugar
1 cup light cream
2 ounces unsweetened chocolate
2 tablespoons butter
1 teaspoon vanilla
¼ cup strong coffee
½ cup heavy cream
4 ounces unsweetened chocolate
1 teaspoon vanilla
1 tablespoon butter
½ cup chopped nuts or 8 large
    marshmallows (optional)

Mix the sugars, cream, and chocolate in a heavy saucepan. Heat until mixture reaches soft-ball stage (234°). Stir just enough to keep fudge from sticking. Remove from heat. Add butter and vanilla. Do not stir again until fudge is lukewarm (110°). Stir until it loses its shine. Spread in a greased 8×8×2-inch pan. Cut into squares when cool. Yield: about 2 pounds.

DARK CHOCOLATE FUDGE

2 cups brown sugar
½ cup sugar
Pinch salt

Mix the sugars thoroughly with the salt, coffee, cream, and chocolate, grated, in a large heavy saucepan. Cover until mixture comes to a boil. Uncover and continue cooking without stirring to the soft-ball stage (238°). Remove from heat; add vanilla and butter. Cool to 110°. Beat until mixture becomes light and creamy. Add the nuts or the marshmallows, cut into small pieces, if you wish. When the candy begins to stiffen, pour into a buttered 8×8×2-inch pan and decorate the top with additional pieces of nuts or marshmallows if you are using them. When fudge is firm, cut into squares. Do not remove from pan until thoroughly cool. Yield: about 2 pounds.

CHOCOLATE NUT FUDGE (*Plate 40*)

2 cups sugar
Pinch salt
1 cup light cream
3 ounces unsweetened chocolate
1 cup confectioners' sugar
1 tablespoon butter
1 teaspoon vanilla
1 cup coarsely chopped Brazil nuts, walnuts,
*   or pecans*

Put the sugar, salt, cream, chocolate, and confectioners' sugar together in a large heavy saucepan. Bring to a boil, stirring occasionally. Lower heat and cook without stirring until mixture reaches the soft-ball stage (234°). Add the butter and vanilla. Cool until fudge is lukewarm (110°). Stir until mixture is thick but still glossy. Add ⅔ cup nuts and continue beating until the mixture loses its shine. Pour into a buttered 8×8×2-inch pan. Top with remaining nuts. Cut into squares when cool. Yield: about 1½ pounds.

PANOCHA

1¼ cups dark brown sugar
Pinch salt
¾ cup light cream
1 tablespoon butter
½ teaspoon vanilla
½ cup broken pecans

Put the sugar, salt, and cream into a heavy saucepan and cook over low heat, stirring constantly, until the sugar dissolves. Boil rapidly until mixture reaches the soft-ball stage (236°). Remove from heat and add the butter and vanilla without stirring. Allow mixture to cool; then beat hard until creamy in color and texture. Fold in the nuts and pour into a well-buttered 8×8×2-inch pan. Cut into squares when cool. Yield: about 1 pound.

RAISIN PEANUT PANOCHA

1½ cups sugar
1½ cups light brown sugar
¾ cup evaporated milk
½ teaspoon cream of tartar
1½ tablespoons light corn syrup
¾ cup white raisins
½ cup crunchy peanut butter

Mix the sugars, evaporated milk, cream of tartar, and corn syrup in a large heavy saucepan. Bring to a boil, stirring constantly. Continue cooking, stirring often, until mixture reaches the soft-ball stage (236°). Remove from heat and cool at room temperature without stirring until the bottom of the pan is comfortably warm to the hand (110°). Add the raisins and peanut butter. Beat until candy holds its shape. Drop from a teaspoon onto waxed paper. Yield: 2 pounds.

COCONUT FUDGE (*Plate 40*)

3 cups sugar
¼ cup light corn syrup
¼ teaspoon salt
1½ cups light cream
1 tablespoon butter
1½ teaspoons vanilla
1 (3½ oz.) can flaked coconut

Mix the sugar, corn syrup, salt, cream, and butter together in a large heavy saucepan. Stir over moderate heat until sugar is dissolved; then continue cooking without stirring until candy reaches soft-ball stage (234°). Remove from heat, add vanilla, and let cool at room temperature until lukewarm (110°). Stir until mixture is thick and loses its gloss. Add 1 cup coconut and turn into a buttered 8×8×2-inch pan. Sprinkle the remaining coconut over the top and press lightly into the candy. When firm, cut into squares. Yield: about 2 pounds.

GINGER NUT FUDGE

3 cups sugar
¼ cup cocoa
3 tablespoons dark corn syrup
1 cup evaporated milk
Pinch salt
2 tablespoons butter
1 teaspoon vanilla
¼ teaspoon baking powder
1 cup chopped walnuts
¼ cup chopped preserved ginger

Mix the sugar, cocoa, syrup, milk, and salt in a heavy saucepan. Cook over low heat without stirring. When boiling, add the butter, stir once or twice, and cook to soft-ball stage (238°). Remove from heat and add the vanilla and baking powder. Cool 15–20 minutes. Beat until candy is thick and has no gloss. Stir in the nuts and ginger and pour quickly into a greased 8×8×2-inch pan. Cut into squares when cool. Yield: 2 pounds.

WHITE FUDGE WITH CHOCOLATE TOPPING

4 cups sugar
¼ teaspoon salt
1½ cups heavy cream
1 cup milk
2 tablespoons light corn syrup
2 teaspoons vanilla
2 ounces unsweetened chocolate
1 teaspoon butter
¼ cup chopped blanched pistachio nuts

Mix the sugar, salt, cream, milk, corn syrup, and vanilla together in a large heavy saucepan. Bring to a boil and continue boiling until the soft-ball stage is reached (236°). Remove from the heat and cool to 110°. Stir until the mixture stiffens and loses its shine. Quickly turn it into a greased 9×9×2-inch pan and spread evenly. Cool. Melt the chocolate with the butter. Spread on top of the candy and sprinkle with the chopped pistachio nuts. Yield: about 2½ pounds.

DIVINITY

2½ cups sugar
½ cup light corn syrup
2 egg whites
1 teaspoon vanilla
½ cup candied cherries (optional)
½ cup chopped toasted blanched almonds (optional)

Mix the sugar, corn syrup, and ½ cup water. Cover and bring to a boil slowly. Uncover and boil without stirring until syrup reaches the soft-ball stage (235°). Remove from heat immediately. Beat the egg whites stiff and add half the syrup gradually while beating continuously with a wire whisk or an electric beater. Let this stand. Cook the rest of the syrup to the hard-ball stage (250°). Pour this syrup in a thin stream over the egg-white mixture, beating all the while. Add the vanilla and beat until mixture loses its shine. The cherries and nuts may be added toward the end of the beating. Drop by teaspoonfuls onto waxed paper and cool. Yield: about 1¾ pounds.

SEA FOAM DIVINITY

2 cups light brown sugar
3 cups sugar
½ cup light corn syrup

½ cup dark corn syrup
Pinch salt
2 egg whites
1½ teaspoons vanilla
1 cup coarsely chopped toasted almonds

Mix the sugars, corn syrups, and 1½ cups water together. Cover and bring slowly to a boil. Uncover and cook over moderate heat to the hard-ball stage (252°). Remove from heat and let stand a few minutes. Add the salt to the egg whites and beat until a stiff peak forms. Pour the syrup into the egg whites in a steady stream, beating vigorously. Continue beating, and flavor with vanilla and add part of the nuts. Continue beating until the mixture thickens and will stand in a peak when dropped from a spoon. Drop by spoonfuls as quickly as possible onto buttered pans or pour into a buttered 9×13-inch pan. Garnish with the remaining nuts. Yield: about 2½ pounds.

COOKTIPS

Grease the pot (double boiler) in which you wish to melt chocolate.

To facilitate measuring molasses, grease the cup in which it is to be measured.

CHOCOLATE CARAMELS

4 ounces unsweetened chocolate
2 cups sugar
1⅓ cups dark corn syrup
2 cups heavy cream
⅛ teaspoon salt
¾ cup evaporated milk
¼ cup butter
1 teaspoon vanilla
2 cups chopped nuts (optional)

Melt the chocolate. Bring the sugar, corn syrup, 1 cup cream, and the salt to a boil, stirring occasionally. Add the remaining cream and the evaporated milk very slowly so the mixture does not stop boiling. Cook to the firm-ball stage (246°). Add the butter and cook, stirring gently, for just a few seconds longer, until blended. Remove from heat. Add the vanilla, chocolate, and the nuts if you wish. Stir until the chocolate blends. Pour into a buttered 9×9×2-inch pan. Cool but do not refrigerate. Turn out onto a board and cut into small squares with a firm-bladed knife, using a sawing motion. Yield: about 2 pounds.

MAPLE HONEY NOUGAT

2 cups sugar
½ cup maple syrup
½ cup honey
2 tablespoons butter
2 egg whites
½ teaspoon vanilla
1 cup nut meats

Put the sugar, syrup, honey, and ¼ cup water in a heavy saucepan. Stir until the sugar dissolves. Cook, without stirring, to the hard-crack stage (290°). Remove pan from heat, stir in the butter, and pour the syrup in a thin stream over the stiffly beaten egg whites, beating constantly. Continue to beat until very stiff. Add the vanilla and nuts. Drop by spoonfuls onto waxed paper, or pour into a well-buttered pan and mark in squares while still warm. Yield: about 1½ pounds.

RUM BALLS

½ pound vanilla wafers
1 cup nut meats
2 tablespoons cocoa or 1 ounce
  unsweetened chocolate
½ cup light corn syrup
¼ cup rum or brandy
Confectioners' sugar

Grind the vanilla wafers and nuts fine, or buzz them in a blender. Blend in the cocoa or melted chocolate, corn syrup, and rum or brandy to form a stiff paste. Dust the palms of your hands with confectioners' sugar and roll small pieces of the mixture into small balls. Set aside to dry for about 1 hour. Roll in confectioners' sugar and store in an airtight container for a few days to mellow. Yield: 4 dozen balls.

CHOCOLATE CHEWS

¼ pound marshmallows
½ cup broken walnuts
8 candied cherries
1 pound semisweet chocolate

Line an 8×8×2-inch pan with an 8×12-inch piece of waxed paper, letting it extend 2 inches up 2 sides. Cut the marshmallows in half and scatter them over the bottom of the pan. Sprinkle the nut meats in between. Cut the cherries in half and add these next. Melt the chocolate in a double boiler, stir until smooth, and pour evenly over the marshmallows, nuts, and cherries. Tap the pan several times on the counter to settle the chocolate. Let stand in a cool place to harden. Lift out of pan, pull off paper, and cut candy into squares. Yield: 1½ pounds.

MAPLE CREAMS

1½ cups maple syrup
½ cup heavy cream
¼ teaspoon salt
About ¼ pound pecan halves or blanched
  almonds

Put the syrup, cream, and salt in a heavy saucepan and stir until blended. Cook slowly, without stirring, to the soft-ball stage (236°). Pour onto a platter and let stand until lukewarm. Beat with a spoon until mixture lightens in color and begins to set. Taking a teaspoonful at a time, roll into balls in the palms of your hands. Place on waxed paper and press a pecan half or almond into each patty, flattening it slightly. Yield: about ¾ pound.

BUTTERMINTS

¼ cup butter
2 cups sugar
8 drops oil of peppermint
Food coloring (optional)

Put 1 cup water and the butter in a heavy saucepan and cook over high heat until the butter melts. Add the sugar and stir until dissolved. Then, without stirring, boil rapidly until syrup reaches the very-hard-ball stage (260°). Remove from heat and pour syrup on a buttered marble slab or metal tray. Do not scrape the pan. The syrup should cover a surface measuring about 12×16 inches. Sprinkle with oil of peppermint and with 3–4 drops food coloring if you want colored mints. Let the syrup cool slightly; then fold edges over peppermint and coloring. Butter your hands and pull the candy as soon as cool enough to handle, keeping the grain in one direction. When it loses its gloss and becomes stiff, stretch into a long rope about ½ inch thick and cut with scissors into 5-inch pieces. Let the mints stand 8–12 hours. Yield: 1 pound.

SUGAR MINTS   (Plate 40)

5 cups sugar
Pinch cream of tartar
4 cups confectioners' sugar
1 teaspoon peppermint flavoring

Combine the sugar with 2 cups water and the cream of tartar. Bring to a boil and cook to the thread stage (230°). While boiling, brush the sides of the kettle with a pastry brush dipped in water to wipe away any sugar crystals. Remove immediately from heat. Add the confectioners' sugar and flavoring. Stir with a hand whip until creamy, about 2–3 minutes. Drop from the tip of a teaspoon onto waxed paper, or use a 1-pint plastic funnel and the handle of a wooden spoon. Insert the spoon handle into the opening of the funnel. Pour in the hot candy syrup and then, by raising and lowering the wooden spoon, drop the candy onto the waxed paper to any desired size. Keep the unused syrup quite hot, but do not boil. The total time for making this candy is 10 minutes. One caution: be sure that all tools are ready where you want them before you start. Store the candy in an airtight container for 2 days. You may decorate if you wish with Royal Ornamental Frosting.* Yield: about 2¼ pounds.

NUT CARAMELS

3 cups sugar
3 cups light cream
¾ cup light corn syrup
½ teaspoon salt
⅓ cup butter
1 teaspoon vanilla
¾ cup broken walnuts

In a heavy saucepan combine the sugar, 2 cups cream, the corn syrup, and salt. Cook slowly over medium heat to the soft-ball stage (236°), about 20 minutes. Add the butter and remaining cream alternately in 5 additions, beginning and ending with butter. Stir constantly and do not allow the mixture to stop boiling. Continue to cook slowly to the hard-ball stage (252°), about 25 minutes. Remove from heat and stir in the vanilla and nuts. Pour into a lightly buttered 9×9×2-inch pan. Cool completely, turn out onto a board, and cut into 1-inch squares with a sharp knife, using a sawing motion. Wrap each square in foil or Saran to keep fresh. Yield: 2½ pounds.

CHOCOLATE NUT TRUFFLES

2 ounces unsweetened chocolate
1 (15 oz.) can sweetened condensed milk
1 cup chopped nuts

Melt the chocolate in the milk in a double boiler. Stir and cook until thick. Cool and drop by teaspoonfuls into the nuts and then form into small balls. Chill. Yield: 3 dozen truffles.

PEANUT BRITTLE I

1 cup dark corn syrup
⅛ teaspoon salt
1 cup sugar
2 tablespoons butter
1½ cups shelled peanuts
1 teaspoon baking soda

Mix the corn syrup, salt, sugar, butter, and ¼ cup water in a large heavy saucepan. Cook to the light-crack stage (280°). Stir in the peanuts gradually so that the mixture will continue to boil. Cook, stirring frequently, to the hard-crack stage (300°). The color of the mixture will darken slightly. Remove from the heat. Stir 2 teaspoons hot water into the baking soda and beat thoroughly into the brittle. Turn out onto a heavily buttered baking sheet and spread out as thin as possible. Let cool slightly, about 5 minutes; then turn the warm brittle upside down. Stretch to desired thickness, let cool, and break into irregular-shaped pieces. Yield: about 1¼ pounds.

PEANUT BRITTLE II

2 cups sugar
¼ teaspoon cream of tartar
2 tablespoons molasses
2 tablespoons butter
½ teaspoon salt
2 cups salted peanuts
1½ teaspoons baking soda

Cook the sugar, ½ cup water, and cream of tartar in a large heavy saucepan without stirring until it reaches the light-crack stage (280°). Add the molasses, butter, and salt and cook, stirring constantly, to the hard-crack stage (300°). Add the peanuts and baking soda at once and mix quickly. Pour onto a well-greased platter or baking sheet and quickly spread thin with a spatula. When cool, break into pieces. Yield: 1½ pounds.

ROYAL BRITTLE   *(Plates 10 and 39)*

½ cup walnut halves
½ cup pecan halves
½ cup almonds
½ cup pistachio nuts
½ cup filberts
1 cup candied cherry halves
1 cup candied pineapple chunks
2 cups sugar
¾ cup light corn syrup
2 tablespoons butter
½ teaspoon vanilla or orange flavoring

Mix the nuts and fruit. Spread in an oiled 15½ ×10½ ×1-inch pan or in a layer about ½ inch deep on a marble slab. Mix the sugar, corn syrup, and 1 cup water in a large heavy saucepan and cook slowly, without stirring, to the hard-crack stage (300°). Remove from heat and add the butter and flavoring. Pour evenly over the fruits and nuts. Do not scrape the pan. Cool until almost firm, break into bite-size pieces, and cool completely. Store in a tightly covered container. Yield: about 3 pounds.

MOLASSES TAFFY

2 cups sugar
1½ cups molasses
½ cup melted butter

Mix the sugar, molasses, and 1½ cups water in a heavy saucepan. Add the butter. Cook, stirring at first, to the very-hard-ball stage (258°). Pour onto a greased platter or 2 or 3 greased pie plates. As the edges cool, turn toward the center with a spatula. When the taffy is cool enough to handle, butter your hands slightly and pull until it loses its gloss and is quite firm. Make into rolls, braids, or ropes and cut at once with scissors. Yield: about 1½ pounds.

TAFFY NUGGETS   *(Plate 40)*

½ cup butter
2 cups sugar
1¼ cups light molasses

Melt the butter in a large heavy kettle and then add the sugar, molasses, and 1½ cups water. Stir well and heat slowly until the sugar is dissolved. Cook rapidly at first, lowering the heat to prevent burning as the mixture thick-

ens. When the syrup reaches the very-hard-ball stage (258°), pour the mixture into 3 buttered pie plates. As the edges cool, turn the taffy toward the center with a spatula, or the edges will be hard before the center is cool enough to pull. When cool enough to handle, butter your hands slightly and pull the candy with the tips of the fingers until it is light in color and very stiff. Stretch and twist into a rope about ¾ inch thick. Cut with scissors into desired lengths and wrap each piece in Saran. Yield: about 1½ pounds.

SALT-WATER TAFFY

2 cups sugar
1 cup light corn syrup
1 teaspoon glycerine
½ teaspoon salt
1 tablespoon butter
2 teaspoons vanilla

Mix the sugar, syrup, 1¼ cups water, glycerine, and salt in a large heavy saucepan. Stir until the sugar dissolves. Cook, without stirring, to the very-hard-ball stage (265°). If sugar crystals form on the sides of the pan, remove with a piece of damp cheesecloth wrapped around a fork. Remove pan from the heat. Stir in the butter and vanilla. Pour into a greased pan and cool just until it can be handled. Butter your hands and pull until taffy loses its gloss and is quite firm. Make into rolls, braids, or ropes and break into pieces or cut with scissors. Yield: about 1 pound.

PEANUT-BUTTER TAFFY

2 cups sugar
2 cups light corn syrup
1 teaspoon vanilla
¼ teaspoon salt
5 tablespoons peanut butter

Mix the sugar, syrup, and ¾ cup water in a heavy saucepan. Cover until it comes to a boil. Cook until it reaches the very-hard-ball stage (258°). Remove from heat and add vanilla and salt. Then add the peanut butter. Pour onto a buttered plate. Cool enough to handle. Butter your hands and pull the candy, keeping the grain in one direction. When it loses its gloss and becomes firm, stretch into a long rope about ½ inch thick and cut with scissors into 1-inch pieces. Yield: about 2 pounds.

BUTTERSCOTCH DROPS

2 cups sugar
½ cup light corn syrup
½ cup butter
1½ teaspoons vanilla

Put the sugar, syrup, and ⅔ cup water in a heavy saucepan. Stir until the sugar dissolves. Cook, without stirring, to the hard-crack stage (290°). Remove pan from heat and stir in the butter and vanilla. Drop by teaspoonfuls onto waxed paper, or pour into a buttered pan and mark off in squares while the mixture is still warm. Yield: about 1 pound.

GUMDROPS

3 envelopes unflavored gelatin
2 cups sugar
⅛ teaspoon salt
1 teaspoon grated lemon or orange rind
1 tablespoon lemon or orange juice
Food coloring

Mix the gelatin, sugar, salt, and 1 cup water in a heavy saucepan. Bring to a boil and simmer, without stirring, for 10 minutes. Remove the pan from the heat and stir in the remaining ingredients. Add a few drops of the food coloring of your choice. Taste for flavor; add more juice if you wish. Pour into a square pan which has been rinsed with cold water. Chill overnight. Cut into squares and roll in additional sugar or in colored sugar. Yield: about 1¾ pounds.

GREENGAGE-PLUM PASTE   (*Plate 39*)

2 (1 lb. 1 oz.) cans greengage plums
1 cup sugar
1 teaspoon unflavored gelatin

Pit and purée the plums. Put into a heavy saucepan with the sugar and the plum syrup. Cook over medium heat, stirring occasionally, until mixture begins to thicken; lower heat and stir constantly until the mixture drops like jelly from the spoon. Soften the gelatin in 1 tablespoon water, add, and stir until dissolved. Pour into a lightly greased 8×8×2-inch pan. Chill. Turn onto a heavily sugared surface, cut into small pieces, and roll in sugar. Let dry. Store between layers of waxed paper in an airtight container. Yield: about 1 pound.

TURKISH PASTE   (*Plate 10*)

Proceed as for Gumdrops,* but roll the squares of candy in confectioners' sugar.

STRAWBERRY PASTE

2 (12 oz.) jars strawberry jelly
2 (8 oz.) jars apple jelly
6 envelopes unflavored gelatin

Melt the jellies in a saucepan over low heat. Mix the gelatin with 2 tablespoons water and add. Continue heating and stirring until the gelatin dissolves. Strain into an 8×8×2-inch pan. Let stand, loosely covered, at room temperature overnight. Cut into squares and roll in granulated or confectioners' sugar before serving. Yield: about 2½ pounds.

COCONUT CANDY

3 cups grated or flaked coconut
3 cups sugar
¾ cup evaporated milk
1 tablespoon butter
Pinch salt
1 teaspoon vanilla

Mix all the ingredients except the vanilla. Stir and cook in a heavy saucepan until the sugar is dissolved and mixture comes to a boil. Keep stirring and cook until thick. Stir in the vanilla and turn out on a buttered platter. Spread with a wooden spoon but do not smooth (surface should be rough). When slightly cooled, cut into pieces; don't separate until cold and hard. Yield: about 1½ pounds.

CHOCOLATE COCONUT CANDY

Add 3 tablespoons of cocoa to Coconut Candy* when the mixture is cooking.

ALMOND PASTE

1 cup (4 oz.) chopped blanched almonds
½ cup superfine sugar
1 egg white

Grind or pound the almonds very fine in a mortar and pestle or buzz them, a few at a time, in a blender. Mix in the sugar and slightly beaten egg white and work into a smooth paste. Use your hands to do this if you wish. Yield: about 1 cup.

CREAMY PRALINES

2 cups sugar
1 cup dark brown sugar
½ cup milk
½ cup condensed milk
¼ cup butter
¼ teaspoon salt
3 cups broken pecans

Combine all the ingredients except the nuts in a heavy saucepan. Bring slowly to a full rolling boil over medium heat. Add the nuts and continue boiling until candy reaches the soft-ball stage (234°). Remove from heat and stir only enough to give a creamy look. Drop by tablespoonfuls onto buttered baking sheets. Cool. Yield: about 6 dozen pralines, about 2 pounds.

MOLASSES PRALINE CREAMS

2 cups sugar
½ cup dark molasses
1 cup heavy cream
Pinch salt
1 teaspoon vanilla
1 tablespoon butter
2 cups pecans or walnuts

Mix the sugar, molasses, cream, and salt together in a heavy saucepan. Cover tight and cook over low heat, gradually increasing the heat until mixture comes to a full boil. Uncover and cook without stirring until it reaches the soft-ball stage (235°). Set candy pan in a pan of cold water. Add vanilla and butter. Don't stir. When the candy is cool enough to touch with your fingers (about 120°), stir until thick. Add the nuts and continue to stir. When it begins to lose its shine and the color lightens, pour into a well-buttered 8×8×2-inch pan. Cut into squares when set. Yield: 1½ pounds.

PISTACHIO PRALINES

1 cup dark brown sugar
1 cup sugar
1 cup coarsely chopped blanched pistachio nuts

Mix the sugars with ¾ cup warm water in a heavy saucepan. Cook over medium heat. Stir only until dissolved; then continue to boil until syrup reaches the soft-ball stage (234°). Remove from heat and cool for a minute. Add the nuts and heat again for 1 minute. Stir un-til mixture begins to form crystals; drop at once by spoonfuls onto oiled paper or a buttered baking sheet. Make the pralines about 2 inches in diameter. Let stand about ½ hour, until hard. If the candy thickens before you have finished pouring, set the saucepan over boiling water for a moment to soften. Yield: about 1 pound.

CREOLE CREAM CANDY

1 egg white
3 cups confectioners' sugar
1 teaspoon vanilla
Food coloring (optional)
Nuts (optional)

Beat the egg white with 2 tablespoons water until a stiff peak forms. Gradually add the sugar until a very stiff mixture is formed. You may need to use more or less sugar, depending upon the humidity. When it is the consistency that will mold well, add the vanilla; divide into batches and color as you like. This can be shaped in the hands, cut with a small cutter, or made into balls around a nut. Yield: about 1 pound.

SPICED CANDY ROLL   (Plate 10)

½ pound (1–1½ cups) whole shelled Brazil nuts
½ pound pitted dates
3 cups graham-cracker crumbs
1 (8 oz.) jar maraschino cherries
½ pound marshmallows
1 tablespoon grated orange rind
⅓ cup orange juice
⅛ teaspoon cinnamon
⅛ teaspoon nutmeg
⅛ teaspoon cloves
⅛ teaspoon allspice
⅛ teaspoon ginger

Put the nuts in a bowl, saving ¼ cup for later use. Add the dates, graham-cracker crumbs, and cherries, drained. Melt the marshmallows with the orange rind, orange juice, and spices in a double boiler. Stir occasionally. When the marshmallows are melted, stir into the nut mixture. Blend thoroughly and shape with your hands into 2 rolls about 9 inches long. Wrap each roll in waxed paper and chill for 6–8 hours. Unwrap, roll in chopped remaining Brazil nuts, and cut into ¼-inch slices for serving. This candy slices best when chilled. Yield: 2¼ pounds.

MARZIPAN STRAWBERRIES   (Plate 40)

Red food coloring
1 (8 oz.) can almond paste
½ cup sugar
1 egg white
1 cup confectioners' sugar
1 teaspoon butter
Green food coloring

Knead the red food coloring a few drops at a time into the almond paste to make an even strawberry color. Blend a few drops red food coloring into the sugar to obtain the same shade of red. Pinch off pieces of almond paste and form each into a strawberry shape. Roll in red sugar. Beat the egg white until frothy. Add confectioners' sugar and continue beating until the mixture holds very firm peaks. Add the softened butter and a few drops green food coloring and mix well. Put the green frosting through a pastry tube to make a leaf or two on top of each strawberry. Yield: about 20 strawberries, about ½ pound.

FONDANT

2 cups sugar
3 tablespoons light corn syrup
Flavoring (optional)
Food coloring (optional)

Put the sugar, syrup, and 1⅓ cups water in a saucepan. Heat and stir until the sugar is dissolved; then boil rapidly, without stirring, to the soft-ball stage (238°). Remove crystals from the sides of the pan with damp cheese-cloth wrapped around a fork. Pour out onto a moistened slab or platter and cool to room temperature. Work the fondant back and forth with a spatula or spoon until it begins to turn cloudy. Scrape up quickly into a ball and knead until smooth and pliable. Form into shapes and place on waxed paper, or cover and store in the refrigerator for a day or two before using. Add coloring and flavoring at the soft-ball stage; however, if you wish to divide one batch for several flavors or colors, work the color into the fondant as you knead it. Yield: about 1¼ pounds.

SUGARPLUM FONDANT

3 cups sugar
2 teaspoons vinegar
⅛ teaspoon cream of tartar

½ teaspoon cinnamon
½ cup coarsely chopped citron
½ cup coarsely chopped candied cherries
½ cup raisins
½ cup coarsely chopped walnuts or pecans

Mix the sugar, vinegar, cream of tartar, cinnamon, and ½ cup water in a heavy sauce-pan. Place over medium heat and bring to a boil. Continue boiling until the firm-ball stage is reached (244°). Wipe the sides of the kettle occasionally with a wet cloth. Do not stir. Pour immediately into a greased platter or pan. Do not scrape out the kettle. As the edges of the syrup cool, quickly turn them into the center. Continue turning until the mixture just begins to turn white. Add the fruits and nuts. Knead and shape into 2 rolls, wrap with foil, and al-low to season overnight. Slice ¼ inch thick. Yield: 2 pounds.

TAFFY APPLES

6–8 apples
1 cup sugar
1 cup light corn syrup
Red food coloring
Cinnamon or peppermint flavoring

Wash and dry the apples, remove stems, and stick the pointed end of a lollypop stick into the stem end of each apple. Combine the sugar, corn syrup, ½ cup cold water, and a few drops red food coloring in a heavy saucepan. Cook over medium heat, stirring constantly, until mixture boils. Then cook, without stir-ring, until it reaches the light-crack stage (280°). Remove from heat and add a little cinnamon or a few drops of peppermint flavor-ing. Dip the apples in the syrup, twirling to cover the entire surface. Place on a rack to cool. Yield: 6–8 apples.

APRICOT BALLS

¾ cup dried apricots
¾ cup flaked coconut
½ cup chopped nuts
1 tablespoon lemon juice
½ teaspoon grated lemon rind
½ teaspoon grated orange rind
Additional coconut or chopped nuts
  (optional)

Wash and drain the apricots. Add the coco-nut and nuts. Put through a food grinder. Add lemon juice and lemon and orange rinds. Knead with your hands until well blended. Roll into small balls. The balls may be rolled in chopped nuts or coconut. Yield: 3 dozen balls.

STUFFED DATES   (*Plate 10*)

3 pounds pitted dates
½ cup butter
⅛ teaspoon salt
1½ cups confectioners' sugar
1 teaspoon grated orange rind
¾ cup finely chopped walnuts
1–2 tablespoons brandy (optional)
Sugar

Split the dates with a sharp knife without cutting clear through. Spread the dates open and lay them on trays. Cream the butter, salt, and confectioners' sugar together until very light and fluffy. Add the orange rind, walnuts, and the brandy if you wish. If you use brandy, you may need a little more confectioners' sugar. Stuff the dates generously, using 2 whole dates to make one. Roll in sugar and let stand 4–5 hours. Yield: 7–8 dozen.

FIG AND NUT CANDY

¾ cup sugar
1½ cups molasses
Pinch salt
¾ cup butter
Pinch baking soda
1 teaspoon vanilla
½ teaspoon almond flavoring
1 cup finely cut dried figs
3 cups chopped mixed nuts

Mix the sugar, molasses, and salt in a deep heavy saucepan. Cover and bring to a boil slowly. Uncover and continue cooking, stirring occasionally with a wooden spoon, until it reaches the very-hard-ball stage (265°). Add the butter and continue cooking to the light-crack stage (280°). Remove from heat and add the soda, vanilla, almond flavoring, and the prepared figs and nuts. Mix just enough to blend. Pour into a well-buttered 8×8×2-inch pan. Let stand at room temperature until cold. Loosen the block of candy around the edges and turn out in one piece onto a breadboard. Cut into small squares with a firm-bladed knife. Mark the line of cutting and use a sawing motion. Keep stored at room temperature. Yield: 2½ pounds.

CANDIED CRANBERRIES   (*Plate 39*)

1 cup cranberries
1¼ cups sugar

Select firm red berries; wash, dry, and prick each with a needle 2 or 3 times. Mix 1 cup sugar and 1 cup water in an 8-inch skillet. Heat until the sugar is dissolved. Then cook until syrup spins a thread (234°). Add the cranberries and cook very, very gently until the berries are glazed and translucent. Remove berries one at a time to waxed paper and let stand about 24 hours, until dried. Roll in remaining sugar. Yield: 1 cup.

CANDIED GINGER GRAPEFRUIT PEEL

Peel 2 grapefruit
2 cups sugar
1 teaspoon ginger
⅛ teaspoon salt
1½ teaspoons unflavored gelatin

If the outer skin of the grapefruit seems hard, grate the surface gently before peeling. Cut the peel into narrow strips. Cover with water and boil 15–20 minutes. Drain and repeat with fresh water twice. Drain the peel (there should be about 2 cups). Add the sugar, ginger, salt, and 1½ cups water. Cook slowly in an open kettle until the syrup is quite heavy. Do not allow to overcook or caramelize. Remove from heat, cool slightly, and add the gelatin which has been softened in 2 tablespoons cold water. Stir well to dissolve the gelatin. Let rind stand in the syrup until thoroughly cool, then drain and roll pieces in additional sugar. The gelatin keeps the peel soft inside. Yield: about 100 small strips.

STUFFED KUMQUATS   (*Plate 39*)

1 (12½ oz.) jar preserved kumquats
Sugar
¼ cup chopped crystallized ginger
¼ cup chopped glacéed cherries

Drain the kumquats, cut each in half, and scoop out the pulp, being careful not to break the shells. Arrange on sugar in a small pan and sprinkle sugar very thickly over them. Allow to dry for 24–36 hours. Shake off excess sugar and fill each half with a mixture of the chopped ginger and cherries. Yield: about 4 dozen filled kumquat halves.

CANDIED ORANGE AND GRAPE-FRUIT PEEL   (*Plate 39*)

6 seedless oranges
3 thick-skinned grapefruit
2 tablespoons salt
Sugar

Wash the fruit well and then remove peel in quarter sections. Soak the peel overnight in 2 quarts cold water to which the salt has been added. Drain, put into a saucepan, cover with cold water, and bring to a boil. Repeat this 3 times, then cook until peel is soft. Drain and cut with scissors into petal-shaped pieces, diamond shapes, or strips. Weigh the peel and put an equal amount of sugar into a saucepan. Add 1 cup water, bring the syrup to a boil, add the peel, and cook gently until it is transparent and tender. Remove each piece separately and put on a rack to drain. When cool, roll pieces in sugar and put out on trays to dry, one layer deep. Store in an airtight container. Yield: about 8 dozen pieces.

CANDIED VIOLETS

Violets
2 egg whites
Confectioners' sugar

Use violets of any shade and take the flowers only—no stems. If you can pick them in the fields in the sun, so much the better. Beat the egg whites lightly, just so they are broken up. Sift the confectioners' sugar into a saucer. Dip each violet in the egg whites, then in the sugar; shake off excess sugar and dry on a baking sheet in a warm place or in the oven at the lowest possible temperature. These are decorative and good to eat too. Two egg whites will coat quite a few violets.

POPCORN BALLS   (*Plate 10*)

3 quarts freshly popped corn
½ teaspoon salt
1 cup dark molasses
1 cup light corn syrup
1 tablespoon vinegar
3 tablespoons butter

Put the popped corn with salt in a large bowl. Mix the molasses, syrup, and vinegar in a large heavy saucepan. Boil until syrup reaches the light-crack stage (270°). Remove from heat, add the butter, and stir only enough to mix. Pour the syrup over the popcorn and stir constantly to coat it evenly. Butter your hands and form into 2-inch balls. Yield: about 30 small balls.

CHERRY POPCORN BALLS

¾ cup light corn syrup
1 cup sugar
¼ teaspoon salt
2 tablespoons butter
1 cup candied whole cherries
5 quarts freshly popped corn

Mix the corn syrup, ½ cup water, the sugar, and salt together. Bring to a boil. Wipe off the crystals from the sides of the pan as you go. Cook to the hard-ball stage (250°). Add the butter and cook to very-hard-ball stage (260°). Mix the cherries through the popcorn in a large pan and pour the syrup over in a stream while stirring to coat it all evenly. While still hot, shape into balls with your hands. If the popcorn balls are to be kept for a few days, wrap each separately in waxed paper or Saran to prevent them from becoming sticky. Yield: 20 large balls.

HONEY POPCORN BALLS   (*Plate 11*)

⅓ cup honey
1 cup light molasses
¼ cup light corn syrup
½ cup butter
⅔ cup sugar
1 quart popped white corn
1 cup coarsely chopped roasted cashew nuts

Cook the honey, molasses, corn syrup, butter, and sugar together slowly, stirring occasionally, until the mixture reaches the very-hard-ball stage (260°). Do not overcook. Remove from heat and pour over popped corn and cashews. Allow to cool a little. Butter your fingers lightly and mold into balls. Cool on a buttered dish or tray. Yield: about 12 small balls.

CHOCOLATE NUT CLUSTERS

1 (6 oz.) package semisweet chocolate bits
3 tablespoons dark corn syrup
1 cup nut meats

Melt the chocolate over hot water. Add the corn syrup and 1 tablespoon hot water. Remove from heat and stir in the nuts—peanuts, cashews, almonds, walnuts, or pecans. Drop by teaspoonfuls onto waxed paper. Chill. Yield: about 1½ dozen.

SUGARPLUMS (*Plate 39*)

1½ pounds large dried prunes

FILLING

1 egg white
1 teaspoon vanilla
1 teaspoon cream of tartar
1¾ pounds confectioners' sugar
¼ cup softened butter
¼ cup chopped candied cherries
½ cup chopped candied pineapple
½ cup flaked coconut

Filling. Beat the egg white, ¼ cup cold water, vanilla, and cream of tartar until frothy. Add the sugar gradually while beating. When the mixture is thick and smooth, work in the butter with your hands or a wooden spoon, and then the fruits, drained if necessary, and the coconut. Cover and store in a cool place for several days.

Steam the prunes in a little water for a few minutes; they should be softened but not soft. Cut each prune open just enough to remove the pit. Place a generous spoonful of filling in each, fold the prune halves tight around the filling, and garnish the top with a sliver of candied cherry if you wish. Store in an airtight container. Dates, apricots, or figs may be used in place of prunes. If you use figs, make a slit large enough to hold the filling. If dates or apricots, proceed as for prunes. Yield: 5½–6 dozen candies.

CHOCOLATE COCONUT KISSES

2 egg whites
¼ teaspoon cream of tartar
½ cup sugar
¼ teaspoon salt
½ teaspoon vanilla
1 (6 oz.) package semisweet chocolate bits
1 (3½ oz.) can flaked coconut

Beat the egg whites. Add the cream of tartar and then the sugar gradually while beating. When stiff, add the salt and vanilla. Fold in the melted chocolate bits and the coconut. Drop onto brown paper on a baking sheet. Bake in a 325° oven for about 20 minutes. Yield: about 2½ dozen.

ORANGE-SUGARED WALNUTS

2 cups walnut halves
2 cups sugar
10 tablespoons orange juice
Grated rind 1 orange
¼ teaspoon salt

Boil the nuts in water for 3 minutes. Toast lightly in a 300° oven for 15–20 minutes. Mix the sugar, orange juice and rind, and salt. Cook this syrup to the soft-ball stage (238°). Remove from heat. Add the nuts and stir slowly; try not to break the nuts. When the syrup begins to whiten and get sugary, lift out the walnuts in their sugar coating with a fork, a piece at a time. Dry on waxed paper. Store in a tightly covered container. Yield: about 1½ pounds.

CARAMEL PECANS

¾ cup sugar
1 (3½ oz.) can pecan halves

Caramelize the sugar in a skillet over low heat. When all the sugar has liquefied, turn off the heat and stir in the pecan halves. Drop in clusters onto a greased baking sheet. Store in a tightly covered container as soon as they are cooled. Yield: 10–12 clusters.

SPICED NUTS

¼ pound walnut or pecan halves or almonds
1 cup sugar
1 teaspoon salt
1 teaspoon ginger
½ teaspoon nutmeg
¼ teaspoon cloves
1 egg white

Freshen the nuts by heating in a 350° oven for a few minutes. Sift the sugar, salt, and spices together 3 times. Add 1 tablespoon cold water to the egg white and beat until frothy but not too stiff. Dip the nuts in the egg white and then roll in the sugar mixture. Cover the bottom of a baking sheet with some of the leftover sugar mixture. Arrange the nuts in this so they do not touch. Sift the remaining spiced sugar over the top. Bake in a 275° oven for about 1 hour. Remove nuts from the baking sheet immediately and shake off excess sugar. Yield: about ½ pound.

EASY CHOCOLATE NUT CANDY

1 (6 oz.) package semisweet chocolate bits
3 tablespoons evaporated milk or heavy
  cream
6 tablespoons confectioners' sugar
1 cup broken walnuts
½ teaspoon vanilla
Pinch salt

Melt the chocolate with the evaporated milk or cream in a double boiler. Remove from heat. Stir in the sugar, nuts, vanilla, and salt. Drop by teaspoonfuls onto waxed paper or a greased baking sheet. Yield: about ¾ pound.

HONEY-COATED FILBERTS

1 cup filberts
½ cup sugar
1 tablespoon honey

Toast the filberts in a 350° oven for 10–15 minutes. Rub off as much skin as possible beforehand. Heat the sugar in a skillet slowly until it melts and begins to caramelize. Add the honey and blend in. Stir in the whole filberts. Drop in clusters onto a greased baking sheet. When cool, store in a tightly covered container. Yield: about ½ pound.

COOKTIPS

To blanch almonds, boil them in water for 1–2 minutes, drain, and the skins will pop off if you squeeze them one at a time between your fingers while still wet and warm.

To toast almonds, spread them whole, slivered, or ground on a baking sheet and put in a 350° oven for a few minutes. Stir and watch, as they get too brown very quickly.

To pulverize macaroons easily, break them into pieces and put them in a 200° oven for ½ hour to dry out. When cool, roll, grind, buzz in a blender, or pound in a mortar.

To peel dried fruits more easily, wash in warm water, cover with boiling water, and let stand until cool.

As the last taste of sweets, is sweetest last . . .
Shakespeare, *King Richard II,* Act I

COOKING AT HIGH ALTITUDE

The boiling point of liquid drops about 2° every 1000 feet above sea level—since liquid boils at a lower temperature the cooking time must be increased.

The conversion of any recipe for use at high altitudes depends on many factors. Rules or tables for adapting recipes can only be a guide, and personal experimenting may be necessary to obtain successful results.

When baking cakes at an altitude of 4000 to 6000 feet, we recommend the following ingredient changes:

2–3 teaspoons less shortening per cup
2–3 tablespoons less sugar per cup
¼–½ teaspoon less baking powder, or ¼ less than total amount
2–3 tablespoons more liquid per cup
2 tablespoons more flour per cup

Also increase the baking temperature 10°–15°; the baking time usually stays the same.

Above 5000 feet test confections by the old-fashioned descriptions—soft-ball, hard-ball, etc.—instead of using a candy thermometer.

Pies and cookies are not affected appreciably.

GLOSSARY

A LA MODE: A term used for pie or cake with ice cream served on top.

BAKE: To cook by dry heat, usually in an oven.

BASTE: To moisten with liquid while cooking or cooling.

BATTER: A mixture of flour, liquid, and other ingredients.

BEAT: To mix vigorously with a mixer, spoon, or fork, over and over or with a rapid rotary motion, to form a smooth mixture.

BLANCH: To plunge into boiling water to whiten or facilitate peeling.

BLEND: To combine several ingredients thoroughly together.

BOIL: To cook in a liquid which is hot enough to bubble constantly.

BOMBE: A molded frozen dessert.

BROIL: To cook by an open source of heat.

BRUSH: To paint with a liquid, such as melted butter, egg, or cream.

CALORIE: A unit of heat; energy-producing value.

CARAMELIZE: To heat sugar until melted and brown.

CASSEROLE: An ovenproof dish, usually with a lid, in which food is cooked and served.

CHILL: To refrigerate until very cold.

COMPOTE: Stewed fruit, usually a combination of fruits.

CONFECTIONERS' SUGAR: Fine powdered sugar, usually designated 4x or 10x, used chiefly in frostings.

COTTAGE PUDDING: Plain cake cut in pieces and covered with crushed or stewed fruit, cream, custard, or other sauce.

CREAM: To rub with a spoon or other utensil to make smooth and creamy.

CREPES: Thin pancakes.

CUT IN: Term usually used for combining shortening and flour with two knives or a pastry blender.

DEEP-FRY (FRY): To cook, immersed, in deep very hot fat or oil.

DEMITASSE: A small cup, usually for after-dinner coffee.

DICE: To cut into very small cubes.

DOT: To put small pieces, usually butter, on the top of food.

DREDGE: To cover or coat, usually with flour or sugar.

DUST: To sprinkle with a light coating, usually either flour or sugar.

FLAKE: To break up into small pieces.

FLAMBE: To cover with spirits, such as brandy, and ignite.

FOLD: To combine gently two or more ingredients or mixtures while avoiding loss of air.

GLAZE: To cover with a glossy finish, such as a thin sugar syrup.

GREASE: To cover lightly with butter, margarine, oil, or fat.

KNEAD: To work or press dough into a smooth mass, using the hands.

MACEDOINE: A mixture of cut-up fruits.

MARINATE: To soak in a marinade or other liquid, such as fruit juice, usually to add flavor.

MARZIPAN: Almond paste.

MASK: To cover with sauce, such as jelly, mayonnaise, or aspic.

MINCE: To chop very fine.

MOUSSE: A frothy, smooth mixture, usually with whipped cream or egg white, often frozen.

PARE: To peel; to cut or shave the skin off.

PARFAIT: A frozen dessert, with whipped cream, usually served in glasses.

PETITS FOURS: Small cakes, frosted and usually decorated.

POACH: To cook in simmering liquid.

PUREE: To rub food through a sieve or food mill or buzz in a blender.

REDUCE: To lessen a quantity of liquid by boiling it away rapidly in an uncovered pan.

RICE: To put through a ricer or sieve.

SAUTE: To cook in a little butter or other fat in a skillet on top of the range.

SCALD: To heat a liquid to just below boiling point; to immerse in a boiling liquid for a few minutes only.

SHORTENING: A fat (including butter) suitable to use in baking.

SHRED: To pull apart or grate into small pieces.

SIFT: To shake through a fine strainer.

SIMMER: To cook in liquid just below boiling point on top of the range.

SKEWER: A long thin metal, wooden, or bamboo stick used for holding fruit or other foods together.

SKIM MILK: Milk from which the fat has been removed.

SLIVER: To cut into thin long pieces.

STEAM: To cook in steam over boiling water or in a very small amount of water in a tightly covered pot or pressure cooker.

STIR: To rotate a spoon or fork through a mixture, often to combine ingredients.

SUPERFINE SUGAR: Finer than granulated but not so fine as confectioners' sugar; formerly called "powdered."

INDEX

ALL MEASUREMENTS ARE LEVEL

Pinch or dash means less than ⅛ teaspoon
3 teaspoons=1 tablespoon
4 tablespoons=¼ cup
5 ⅓ tablespoons=⅓ cup
16 tablespoons=1 cup=8 ounces
2 tablespoons=1 ounce
2 cups=1 pint=1 pound (liquid measure)
2 pints=1 quart

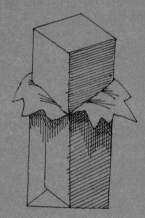

EGGS

5 eggs=about 1 cup
8–10 egg whites=1 cup
12–15 egg yolks=1 cup

BUTTER OR MARGARINE

2 tablespoons=1 ounce
½ cup=¼ pound=1 stick
2 cups=1 pound

DAIRY

Sour cream and buttermilk are the commercial variety
1 cup milk=½ cup evaporated milk+½ cup water
1 cup milk=¼ cup powdered whole milk+1 cup water
1 cup cream=2 cups whipped cream
1 cup cottage cheese=½ pound

FLOUR

Flour is sifted before measuring
4 cups all-purpose flour=1 pound
1 cup cake flour=1 cup all-purpose flour less 2 tablespoons
2 tablespoons flour=1 tablespoon cornstarch for thickening
5 teaspoons flour=2 teaspoons arrowroot for thickening

SUGAR

Confectioners' sugar is measured before sifting
Brown sugar is measured firmly packed
2 cups sugar=1 pound
3 ¼-4 cups confectioners' sugar=1 pound
2 ¼ cups brown sugar=1 pound